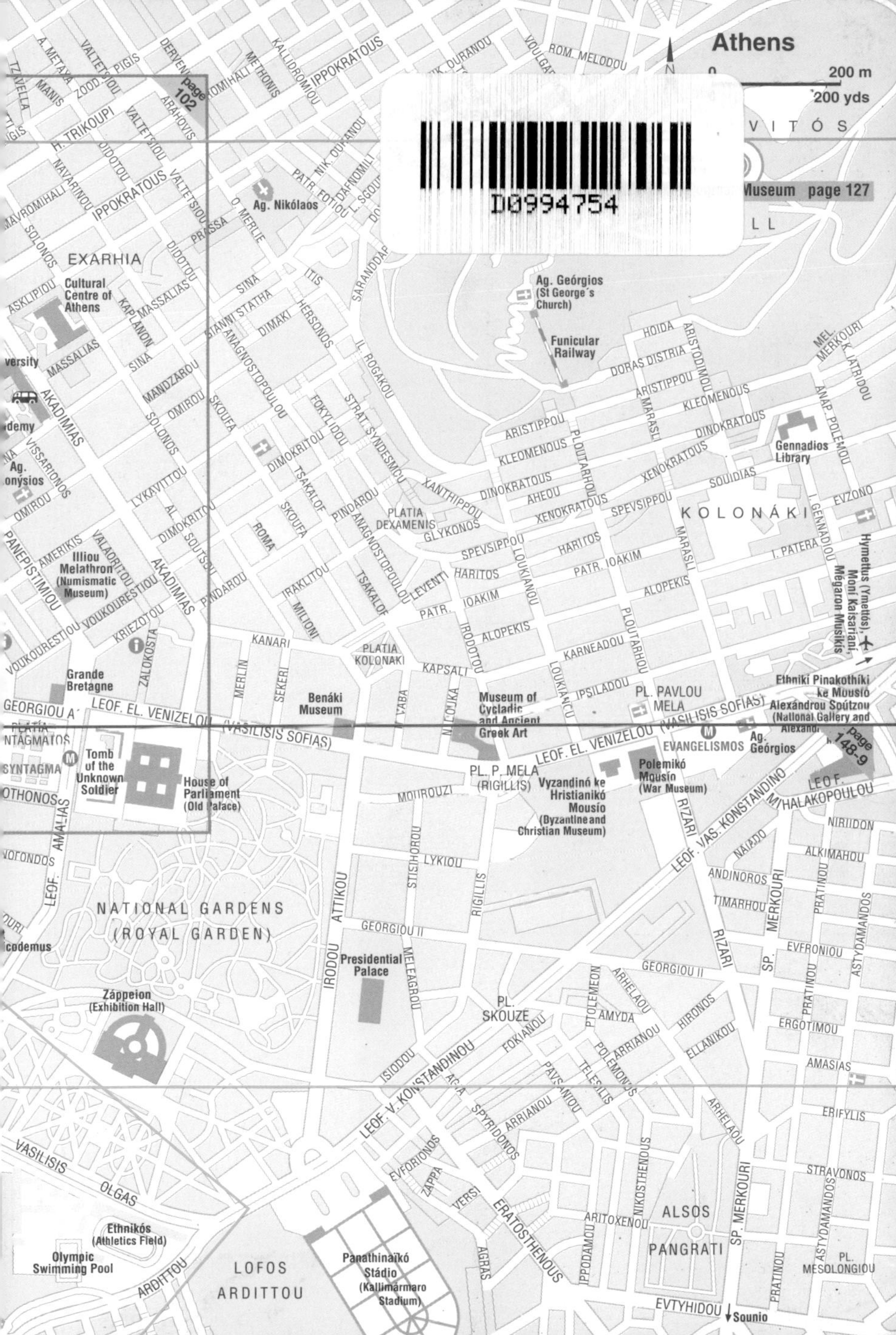
Athens
0
200 m
200 yds
D0994754
Museum page 127
page 102
page 148-9
EXARHIA
Cultural Centre of Athens
Ag. Nikólaos
Ag. Geórgios (St George's Church)
Funicular Railway
Gennadios Library
KOLONÁKI
PLATIA DEXAMENIS
PLATIA KOLONAKI
Illiou Melathron (Numismatic Museum)
Grande Bretagne
Benáki Museum
Museum of Cycladic and Ancient Greek Art
PL. PAVLOU MELA
Ethniki Pinakothíki ke Mousío Alexándrou Soútzou (National Gallery and
EVANGELISMOS
Ag. Geórgios
Tomb of the Unknown Soldier
SYNTAGMA
House of Parliament (Old Palace)
PL. P. MELA (RIGILLIS)
Vyzandinó ke Hristianikó Mousío (Byzantine and Christian Museum)
Polemikó Mousío (War Museum)
Hymettus (Ymettós), Moní Kaisarianí, Mégaron Musikis
NATIONAL GARDENS (ROYAL GARDEN)
Presidential Palace
Záppeion (Exhibition Hall)
PL. SKOUZE
LEOF. VAS. KONSTANDINOU
LEOF. V. KONSTANDINOU
LEOF. EL. VENIZELOU (VASILISIS SOFIAS)
VASILISIS OLGAS
Ethnikós (Athletics Field)
Olympic Swimming Pool
LOFOS ARDITTOU
Panathinaïkó Stádio (Kallimármaro Stadium)
ALSOS PANGRATI
PL. MESOLONGIOU
EVTYHIDOU
Sounio
IPPOKRATOUS
AKADIMIAS
PANEPISTIMIOU
SOLONOS
SKOUFA
HERODOU ATTIKOU
SP. MERKOURI
RIZARI
ARDITTOU

Other Insight Guides available:

Alaska
Amazon Wildlife
American Southwest
Amsterdam
Argentina
Arizona & Grand Canyon
Asia, East
Asia, Southeast
Asia's Best Hotels and Resorts
Australia
Austria
Bahamas
Bali & Lombok
Baltic States
Bangkok
Barbados
Belgium
Belize
Berlin
Bermuda
Brazil
Brittany
Buenos Aires
Bulgaria
Burgundy
Burma (Myanmar)
Cairo
California
California, Southern
Canada
Caribbean
Caribbean Cruises
Channel Islands
Chicago
Chile
China
Colorado
Continental Europe
Corsica
Costa Rica
Crete
Cuba
Cyprus
Czech & Slovak Republic
Delhi, Jaipur & Agra
Denmark
Dominican Rep. & Haiti
Dublin
East African Wildlife
Eastern Europe
Ecuador
Edinburgh
Egypt
England
Finland
Florida
France
France, Southwest
French Riviera
Gambia & Senegal
Germany
Glasgow
Gran Canaria
Great Britain
Great Railway Journeys of Europe
Great River Cruises of Europe
Greece
Greek Islands
Guatemala, Belize & Yucatán
Hawaii
Hungary
Iceland
India
India, South
Indian Wildlife
Indonesia
Ireland
Israel
Istanbul
Italy
Italy, Northern
Italy, Southern
Jamaica
Japan
Jerusalem
Jordan
Kenya
Korea
Laos & Cambodia
Lisbon
Madeira
Malaysia
Mallorca & Ibiza
Malta
Mauritius Réunion & Seychelles
Melbourne
Mexico
Miami
Morocco
Namibia
Nepal
Netherlands
New England
New Mexico
New Orleans
New York State
New Zealand
Nile
Normandy
North American and Alaskan Cruises
Norway
Oman & The UAE
Oxford
Pacific Northwest
Pakistan
Peru
Philippines
Poland
Portugal
Provence
Puerto Rico
Rajasthan
Rio de Janeiro
Romania
Russia
Sardinia
Scandinavia
Scotland
Sicily
South Africa
South America
Spain
Spain, Northern
Spain, Southern
Sri Lanka
Sweden
Switzerland
Syria & Lebanon
Taiwan
Tenerife
Texas
Thailand
Trinidad & Tobago
Tunisia
Turkey
Tuscany
Umbria
USA: On The Road
USA: Western States
US National Parks: West
Utah
Venezuela
Vienna
Vietnam
Wales

INSIGHT CITY GUIDES
(with free restaurant map)

Athens
Barcelona
Beijing
Boston
Bruges, Ghent & Antwerp
Brussels
Cape Town
Florence
Hong Kong
Kuala Lumpur
Las Vegas
London
Los Angeles
Madrid
Montreal
Moscow
New York
Oxford
Paris
Perth & Surroundings
Philadelphia
Prague
Rome
St Petersburg
San Francisco
Seattle
Singapore
Sydney
Taipei
Tokyo
Toronto
Vancouver
Venice
Walt Disney World/Orlando
Washington, DC

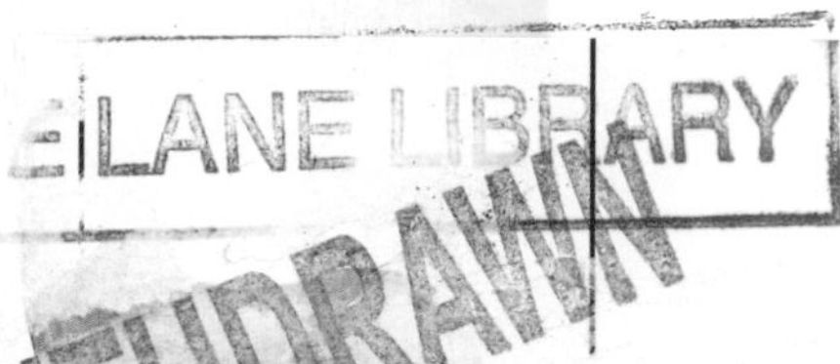

INSIGHT CITY GUIDE

athens

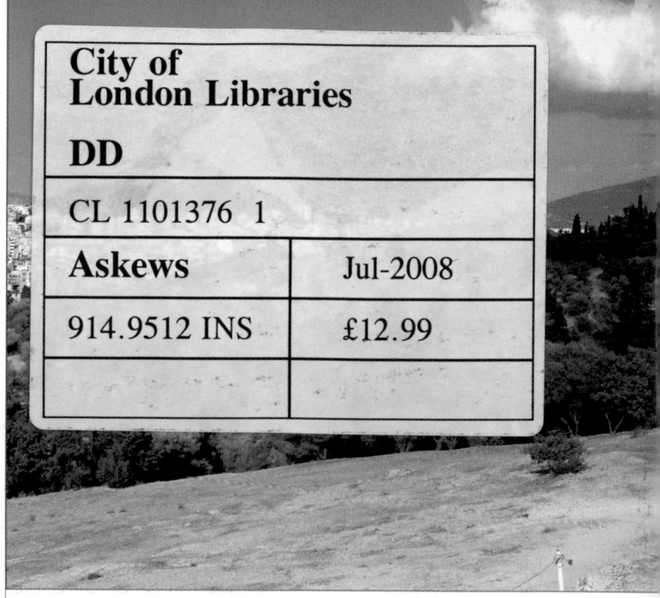

INSIGHT GUIDE
ATHENS

Managing Editor
Maria Lord
Copy Editors
Alexia Georgiou
Jeffery Pike
Art Director
Ian Spick
Picture Editor
Hilary Genin
Cartography Editor
Zoë Goodwin
Production
Kenneth Chan
Editorial Director
Brian Bell

Distribution

UK & Ireland
GeoCenter International Ltd
Meridian House, Churchill Way,
West Basingstoke, Hants RG21 6YR
Fax: (44) 1256 817988

United States
Langenscheidt Publishers, Inc.
36–36 33rd Street 4th Floor
Long Island City, NY 11106
Fax: (1) 718 784-0640

Australia
Universal Publishers
1 Waterloo Road
Macquarie Park, NSW 2113
Fax: (61) 2 9888 9074

New Zealand
Hema Maps New Zealand Ltd (HNZ)
Unit D, 24 Ra ORA Drive
East Tamaki, Auckland
Fax: (64) 9 273 6479

Worldwide
Apa Publications GmbH & Co.
Verlag KG (Singapore branch)
38 Joo Koon Road, Singapore 628990
Tel: (65) 6865-1600. Fax: (65) 6861-6438

Printing

Insight Print Services (Pte) Ltd
38 Joo Koon Road, Singapore 628990
Tel: (65) 6865-1600. Fax: (65) 6861-6438

First Edition 1991
Third Edition 2007

ABOUT THIS BOOK

The first Insight Guide pioneered the use of creative full-colour photography in guidebooks in 1970. Since then, we have expanded our range to cater for our readers' need not only for reliable information about their chosen destination but also for a real understanding of that destination. Now, when the internet can supply inexhaustible (but not always reliable) facts, our books marry text and pictures to provide that much more elusive quality: knowledge. To achieve this, they rely heavily on the authority of locally based writers and photographers.

How to use this book

The book is carefully structured both to convey an understanding of the city and its culture and to guide readers through its sights and activities:

◆ To understand Athens today, you need to know something of its past. The first section covers the city's history and culture in lively, authoritative essays written by specialists.

◆ The main Places section provides a full run-down of all the attractions worth seeing, as well as places to eat. The main places of interest are coordinated by number with full-colour maps.

◆ The Travel Tips listings section provides a point of reference for information on travel, hotels, shops and festivals. Information may be located quickly by using the index printed on the back cover flap – and the flaps are designed to serve as bookmarks.

◆ Photographs are chosen not only to illustrate geography and buildings but also to convey the moods of the city and the life of its people.

The contributors

This new edition of *Athens* was commissioned and edited by **Maria Lord**, **Alexia Georgiou** and **Jeffery Pike** and builds on the success of earlier editions. The Features and Places sections and Travel Tips have been restructured and almost completely rewritten for this new version.

The revised Places chapters and the extensive Travel Tips are the work of **Marc Dubin**, a part-time resident of Greece, traveller and author, who worked on the very first edition of this book. He has put his considerable knowledge of the city to excellent use in the lively accounts of the city's districts, and excursions from Athens, as well the comprehensive listings sections. He also wrote the Features chapter on Food and Drink.

The history chapters were completely revised by editor and writer **Jeffery Pike**, who also did much of the copy editing for the book.

The new chapter on The Athenians was written by author and Athens resident **Sofka Zinovieff**. Her book *Eurydice Street* is a keen-eyed dissection of the city's mores, charms and culture.

The wide-ranging chapter on Athens' cultural life is by **Gall Holst-Warhaft**, an expert on *rebétika* and professor in the department of Classics and Comparative Literature at Cornell University.

The current edition builds on the excellent foundations created by writers of previous editions of the book, most notably **Rowlinson Carter**, who wrote the original history chapters, and **J.A. Lawrence**, who, along with **Elizabeth Boleman Herring**, contributed many of the orignal Places sections. Piraeus was covered by **B. Samantha Stenzel**, while the sections on Dafní, Kessarianí and the excursions were initially written by **Martha Ellen Zenfell**, who was also the original editor of the guide.

Two new photographic shoots were commissioned for this book. The photographers, **Richard Nowitz** and **Glyn Genin**, are both APA regulars and did a remarkable job of covering the city, its outlying areas and the excursions.

Thanks go to **Roger Williams**, who helped get the text into shape and also worked on the picture edit.

CONTACTING THE EDITORS

We would appreciate it if readers would alert us to errors or outdated information by writing to:

Insight Guides, P.O. Box 7910, London SE1 1WE, England. Fax: (44) 20 7403-0290. insight@apaguide.co.uk

www.insightguides.com

In North America:

www.insighttravelguides.com

Contents

Introduction

History

Features

Places

Photo Features

Information Panels

Travel Tips

Maps

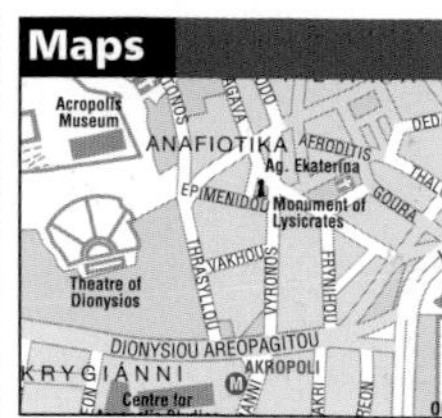

THE BEST OF ATHENS

Art, culture, food, the sites where democracy took shape... Here, at a glance, are our recommendations for your visit

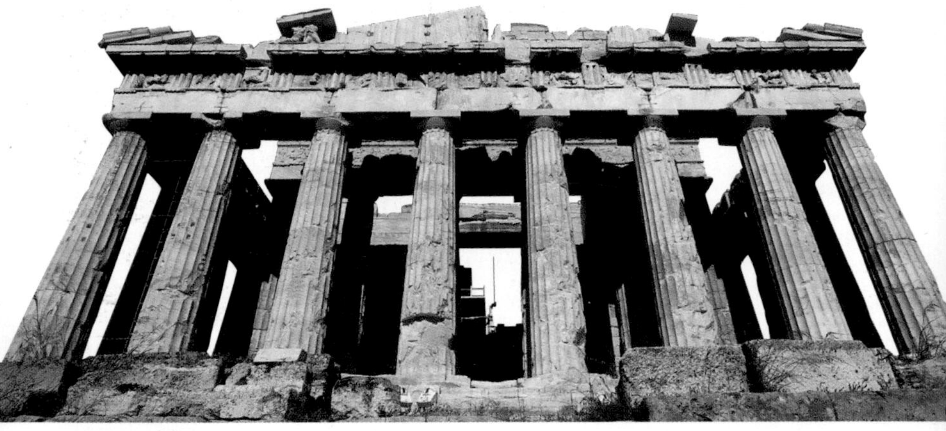

ANCIENT SITES

- **The Acropolis** Crowning the city, this ancient site of sacred temples and iconic structures – such as the Parthenon and the Erechtheion, with its graceful porch of the Caryatids – has come to embody the essence of Classical Greek architecture. *See page 80*
- **Theatre of Dionysios** The sprawling remains of this amphitheatre, scooped from the southeastern flank of the Acropolis, witnessed the birth of tragedy and comedy. *See page 78*
- **Temple of Olympian Zeus** Most impressive of Athens' Roman relics, with 15 of its original Corinthian columns still standing. *See page 77*
- **Ancient Agora** Once the centre of the city's religious, commercial and public life, it's where you'll find the remarkably preserved Hephaisteion – a precious clue to how the Parthenon must have once appeared. *See page 87*
- **Tower of the Winds** Weather vane, sundial and water clock rolled into one, this eight-sided marble structure is carved with representations of each of the winds. *See page 89*
- **Keramikos** The most important cemetery of Ancient Athens, with tombs pre-dating 1000 BC. *See page 90*

BEST VIEWS OF THE CITY

- **Lykavitós** Climb the stair-streets or ride the funicular up the slopes of Athens' most popular hill. At the summit is the chapel of Ágios Geórgios along with some magnificent vistas. *See page 119*
- **Filopáppou** Cypress, pine, shrubs and flowers line the paths to unbeatable views of the Acropolis, at dusk especially. *See page 147*
- **The Pnyx** This ancient assembly place has excellent views of the city. *See page 87*
- **Rooftop bars** Drink in some gorgeous cityscapes along with your apéritif by heading for the terraces of the city's most stylish hotels. Try the Grande Bretagne, the Hilton, the St George and the Hera. *See page 231*

ABOVE The Parthenon is weighty with symbolism.
BELOW: From Lykavitós Hill, the world's spread at your feet.

CHURCHES

- **Athens Cathedral (Mitrópoli)** A mish-mash of architectural styles it may be, but this is the seat of the Greek Orthodox archbishop and regularly packed. *See pages 101–102*
- **Mikrí Mitrópoli** Right next door to the cathedral is its tiny 12th-century predecessor and saving grace, with sculpted reliefs of Roman, Hellenistic and Byzantine origin. *See page 102*
- **Kapnikaréa** Inside, this 11th-century gem is a mix of medieval mosaics and neo-Byzantine frescoes created in the 1950s by Fotis Kondoglou. *See page 101*
- **Ágios Dimítrios Lombardiáris** A scenic location at the foot of the wooded hill of the Muses makes this barrel-vaulted basilica a favourite for weddings. *See page 147*
- **St Nicodemus (Russian Church)** The largest medieval structure in Athens harbours some fascinating wall paintings. *See page 108*
- **Agía Marina** With its red-and-white striped façade and outcrop of small domes, this popular church honours the protectress of pregnant mothers and infants. *See page 137*

BEST SHOPPING

- **Monastiráki flea market** Jumble of antiques, junk, and second-hand books, records and clothing. *See pages 103–104*
- **Ermoú, Eólou, Stadíou** High-street clothing and stores. Shops in the smaller surrounding roads are still grouped by trade. *See pages 103–104.*
- **Kolonáki** Boutiques, homewares and luxury labels European-style, plus the Attika department store on its fringes. A mecca for the jet-set and the well-heeled. *See page 119*
- **Centre of Hellenic Tradition** Good quality Greek crafts: embroidery, pottery and more. *See page 253*

CENTRAL ATHENS

- **Sýntagma Square** The modern-day hub of Athens. It's dominated by the Parliament building, in front of which an honour guard of 'kilt'-clad *évzones* keep watch over the Tomb of the Unknown Soldier. *See page 113.*
- **Pláka** Huddled at the foot of the Acropolis, the old quarter is a maze of narrow shady streets, lined with restaurants and immaculately restored Neoclassical houses. *See pages 93–99*
- **Royal Garden** Green avenues and little paths meander among flowerbeds, ancient stone seats and 500 different varieties of plants. *See page 117*
- **Panathinaïkó Stadium** Originally built in 330 BC, this stunning marble stadium was rebuilt for the first modern Olympics of 1896 then renovated for the 2004 Games. *See page 152*
- **University, Academy, National Library** Standout trio of grand Neoclassical design, built in the years after Independence by the Danish Hansen brothers. *See page 161*

ABOVE Athens' Byzantine churches hold many fine mosaics **LEFT:** Sweet treats. **BELOW:** *Droméas* (The Runner), made from shards of glass, is opposite the Hilton.

Best Museums and Galleries

- **Benáki Museum** Arguably Athens' best museum has an eclectic collection spanning all of Greek history; see the two fully reconstructed mansion rooms. Separate Islamic art collection in Keramikós district. *See pages 122–125*
- **National Archaeological Museum** World's most comprehensive collection of treasures from Greek antiquity, including the bronze Young Jockey and Horse and the gold mask of Agamemnon. *See pages 132–135.*
- **Museum of Greek Folk Art** Outstanding display of regional Greek costumes, with Carnivalwear for the 12 Days of Christmas and more. *See page 97*
- **Museum of Cycladic Art** The wonderful early-Cycladic sculptures – stylised but moving works which were to influence Picasso – steal the show. *See pages 117–118*
- **Bath-house of the Winds** Explore a warren of rooms at this restored 16th-century *hamam* (Turkish bath). *See page 97*
- **Tekhnópolis** Former gasworks transformed into avant-garde arts and performance space. Incorporates the Maria Callas Museum. *See page 142*
- **National Gallery** Lively gallop through Greek painting and sculpture that doesn't neglect the social context. *See page 153*
- **Children's Museum** An emphasis on play gives young children plenty to build, paint and deconstruct. *See page 97*
- **Byzantine and Christian Museum** Another top-ranker since its 2004 revamp. Early Christian and Byzantine art treasures, liturgical objects, frescoes and icons. *See page 155*

Above: Group of Aphrodite and Pan at the National Archaeological Museum.
Below Left: *Horiátiki* salad.
Below: Cycladic figurine circa 3rd millennium BC.

Food and Eating Out

- **Central Market** Elegant, Neoclassical Varvákio, at the heart of the market district, holds the fish and meat bazaar while fruit and vegetables occupy the square across Athínas, redeveloped to include an elevated café. *See page 105*

Mezedopolía These serve up small dishes, *mezédes*, originally designed to accompany a shot of ouzo. The district of Psyrrí packs in the trendiest exponents. *See pages 60 and 138*

- **Greek wine** Following a renaissance, Athens remains one of the best places to enjoy little-known Greek labels. *See page 61*
- **Petrálona**. Those in the know head for this residential area's unpretentious, good-value tavernas. *See pages 146 and 157*
- **Mastiha Shop** Chewing gum, biscuits, soaps, all made from mastic (the sticky resin of the mastic bush, cultivated only on Híos). *See page 253*

BEACHES

- **Aktí Astéros, Glyfáda** Upscale, pricey beach, but you get what you pay for in terms of amenities: ball courts, pool and the like. *See page 175*
- **Voúla Próti & Voúla Déftera** Low admission fees, beach volleyball and slightly more manageable crowds *See page 176*
- **Várkiza** Broad V-shaped bay divided into private (with watersports and lifeguards) and public sections. Fairly easy to park. *See page 177*
- **Ágios Kosmás Ellinikó** Small, privately run beach with clean water and low-key activities. *See page 179*
- **Áttika Vouliagméni** Longest beach around whose western end is free and unamenitied, attracting a young crowd. *See page 176*
- **Vouliagméni Rock Lido** Curious swimming hole cum spa. *See page 177*

EXCURSIONS

- **Delphi** Set on the slopes of Mt Parnassós in the midst of olive groves, this idyllic ancient site was also regarded as the spiritual centre of the classical world by the ancients. *See pages 221–225.*
- **Kessarianí Monastery** Walled, 11th-century monastic complex nestled in a fold of Mt Ymittós. The interior of the main church is emblazoned with vivid frescoes, mostly from 1682. *See page 195*
- **Saronic Islands** Among them Égina, with plenty to occupy weekending Athenians; and Ýdra, its chic horseshoe harbour ringed by the stone-built mansions of its former sea captains. *See pages 201–209*
- **Theatre of Epidávros** Gloriously preserved, this amphitheatre from the late 3rd century BC is renowned for its startling acoustics. *See page 216*
- **Návplio** With no less than three castles set on its towering, fortified crag, and an old quarter that has preserved much of its Venetian and Ottoman heritage, this port town has bags of atmosphere. *See page 217*
- **Sounion** At the windswept tip of Southern Attica, the Temple of Poseidon occupies a dramatic site overlooking the Aegean. Come for the spectacular sunsets. *See page 184*
- **Mycenae** Among the remains of the Bronze Age royal citadel are some extraordinary beehive-shaped tombs. Acess is through the famous Lion Gate with its sculpted lintel. *See page 214*

ABOVE: Temple of Poseidon.
BELOW: Insignia of the Athens Metro.

MONEY SAVING TIPS

Athens Metro A one-week pass is outstanding value at 10 euros and is good for 168 hours, from the minute of validation, on all forms of transport – buses, trams and metro.

From the airport Express buses prefixed 'X' provide links to Sýntagma Square, Kifissiá and the port of Piraeus, a cheaper alternative to the metro. At peak traffic times and with only light luggage, you might consider using the X94 bus up to Ethnikí Ámyna metro station and continuing your journey into town from there by metro: usually, this actually works out cheaper and quicker than using solely the infrequent light-rail/metro combination which has its own inconspicuous airport station next to the Hotel Sofitel.

Taxis Numerous and affordable. A taxi into town from the airport will take about the same time as the express bus and will cost roughly 26 euros to Sýntagma Square. Prices are posted by the taxi rank at the airport.

Admission Enquire whether there is an advantageously priced joint ticket available with other nearby museums and sites (as is the case with the Acropolis). Admission is generally free on Sundays and public holidays from November to March. Those aged 60 and over, certified teachers and university instructors often get one third off, while students pay about half.

A City of Many Parts

Beyond the wonderful ancient monuments of the Parthenon and Agora lies a city of many competing and conflicting histories, peoples and ideas; a melting pot on the cusp of Europe and Asia, tradition and modernity

The visitor's perception of Athens constantly jumps between conflicting and contrasting images and ideas. For many, the city symbolises a whole body of thought and artistic endeavour that has, since the Renaissance, influenced much in later European philosophy, art, architecture and political ideology. Others see a modern, sprawling city that seems to exist between Europe and West Asia, in parts anarchic, run-down and riven by national and cultural faultlines, elsewhere traditional, quiet and safe in its Greek identity. Overlying this is a place apparently in thrall to fevered consumption, the flow of western European and North American capital (both cultural and monetary), and a modernity that gains its credibility from originating outside of the country.

Athens is all these things and more, existing simultaneously and intersecting in fascinating and unlooked-for ways: the scientist who is proud of his or her membership of the Orthodox Church as a badge of Greek identity; the special accord given to the family and its traditional values in a city where it can sometimes seem as though hedonism has been elevated to a fine art; or as a place that presents itself as the cradle of a purely Greek civilisation or embodiment of the national project but which is built on wave upon wave of immigrants; be they Dorians, Romans, Ottomans, and Greek-speakers from Smyrna, or the more recent arrivals from Albania, West Africa or Pakistan.

By now it should be clear that Athens is a place whose history is not only encapsulated by the symbols of the Parthenon or the city's Byzantine monasteries (themselves part of conflicting ideologies, on the one hand a classicizing view of the Greek nation promoted chiefly by foreign philhellenes, and on the other one rooted in the traditions of the Orthodox Church that looks, ultimately, back to the age of Constantine), but a whole concatenation of peoples, ideas and histories. It is this diversity that makes Athens such a worthwhile destination, and the Athenians themselves such a fascinating, disparate, and, at times disputative, group of people. ❑

Preceding pages: the Erechtheion on the Acropolis at night; the "Mask of Agamemnon". **Left:** the city viewed from Lykavitós hill, looking past the Acropolis to the sea.

Decisive Dates

c.3000 BC Evidence of first settlement around the Acropolis.
c.1400 Acropolis becomes royal fortress.
c.1200 According to legend, King Theseus unites the province of Attica, with Athens as its capital.
12th century Dorians occupy much of the Greek mainland, but not Attica.
c.1000 Athens expands beyond the Acropolis to the northwest, first Agora is built.
7th century Homer's *Iliad* and *Odyssey* mention Athens only in passing.

620 Draco drafts strict new law code.
594–3 Democratisation under the constitution of Solon.
566 First Panathenaic Games.
560 Peisistratus seizes power in popular coup, becomes "tyrant" of Athens.
555 Peisistratus driven into exile.
546 Peisisitratus returns, becomes sole ruler for 20 years.
c.530 New temple of Athene built on the Acropolis.
527 Peisistratus dies, succeeded by his sons Hippias and Hipparchus.
514 Hipparchus assassinated, Hippias establishes dictatorship.
510 Hippias overthrown with help from Sparta. Cleisthenes takes charge. Sweeping democratic reforms.
499 Athens sends fleet to support Ionians of Asia Minor in their revolt against Persia. King Darius vows vengeance against Athens.
490 Darius invades mainland Greece, but is defeated by Athenians at Marathon.
490–480 Profits from Laurion silver mine used to enlarge Athens' navy.
480 Persia invades under Xerxes. Held up by Spartans at Thermopylae but capture Athens and burn the city. Greek fleet (mostly Athenian) defeats Persian navy.
479 Persians retreat defeat at Plataea by Greek troops. Rebuilding of Athens begins, including Long Walls joining the city to the port of Piraeus.
461 Pericles replaces Cimon as ruler of Athens.
461–429 The "Golden Age" under Pericles. Construction of the Parthenon and other Classical buildings.
431 Start of the Peloponnesian War against Sparta.
430–428 Plague wipes out a quarter of Athens' population, including Pericles.
404 Peloponnesian War against Sparta ends in defeat. Athens in decline.
338 Philip II of Macedon conquers Athens and other Greek states.
336 Murder of Philip and succession of his son, Alexander the Great.
336–323 Expansion of Alexander's empire through the Mediterranean and Middle East as far as India.
146 Romans subjugate Macedonia, destroy Corinth and occupy Greece.
86 After Athens supports Pontus against Rome, Sulla attacks the city, Piraeus is destroyed. Athens loses all political influence, Corinth becomes capital of the Roman province.
AD 54 Paul the Apostle visits Athens.
117 Emperor Hadrian resumes construction of the Temple of Olympian Zeus.
150 Herod Atticus becomes patron of the city, builds the theatre that bears his name.
267 Athens attacked by Goths.
330 Constantinople becomes capital of

the Byzantine Empire, many of its treasures having been removed from Athens.
529 Schools of Neo-Platonic philosophy closed by Justinian I, temples reconsecrated as Christian churches.
1204 The Franks and Venetians capture Constantinople, and proceed to divide Greece between them.
1456–1821 Athens under Ottoman rule from Istanbul (Constantinople).
1687 Venetians besiege the Acropolis: the Parthenon, used as a Turkish gunpowder store, partially destroyed.
1801 Lord Elgin removes the Parthenon marbles to London.
1821 Rebellion against Turkish rule.
1821–29 Greek War of Independence.
1832 Prince Otto of Bavaria selected by Western powers as king of Greece.
1834 Capital of Greece transfers from Návplio in the Peloponnese to Athens.
1838 The Royal Palace (now the Parliament) completed on Sýntagma Square.
1863 After Otto's deposition, a Danish prince becomes King George I of Greece.
1896 The first modern Olympic Games held in Athens.
1910 Eleftherios Venizelos becomes Prime Minister.
1912–13 The Balkan Wars.
1913 George I assassinated, succeeded by Constantine and his wife Sofia.
1914 World War I causes a "National Schism" between Constantine (for neutrality) and Venizelos (for the Allies).
1916 Venizelos forms provisional government in Thessaloníki.
1917 Allies drive out Constantine; Venizelos reinstated in Athens, brings Greece into the war.
1920–23 Greece at war with Turkey.
1922 Constantine deposed, succeeded by his son George II.
1923 End of Greek–Turkish war sees massive influx of Greek refugees from Asia Minor to Athens and Piraeus. George II deposed, a republic declared.
1935 Monarchy is restored, George II reinstated.

LEFT: a red-figure Classical vase.
RIGHT: the first modern Olympic Games, 1896.

1936 George supports dictatorship of General Mataxas.
1940 Mataxas refuses Mussolini's forces access to Greece – *Óhi* (No).
1941 40,000 Athenians die in severe food shortages caused by the German and Italian occupation.
1944 Liberation of Greece.
1944–49 Greek Civil War.
1967 Military coup: King Constantine II exiled. Military junta led by Colonel Papadopoulos rules Greece.
1973 Popular protest at Athens Polytechnic crushed with bullets and tanks.

1974 Overthrow of the military junta.
1975 Republican constitution is inaugurated.
1981 Greece joins European Community.
1985 Athens becomes Europe's first Cultural Capital.
1998 Devaluation of the *drachma* to prepare for European monetary union.
1999 Earthquake in Athens kills 138, makes 100,000 homeless.
2002 Greece adopts the euro in place of the *drachma*.
2004 Athens hosts the Olympic Games.
2005 Károlos Papoúlias is elected Greece's first socialist president. ❑

ANCIENT ATHENS

For two thousand years it was alternately invaded by foreigners, attacked by other Greek states, ruled by tyrants and condemned to centuries of relative obscurity. Yet no city has contributed more to European civilisation than Athens

The legacy of ancient Greece – hugely influential in the development of European culture, philosophy and politics – is so closely associated with Athens and notable Athenians that it is easy to assume that the city has always held centre-stage, that for centuries Athens was the capital of the Greek world. Not so. In the first place, Athens was not the capital of ancient Greece: there was no such country, only hundreds of independent Greek-speaking cities and towns on the mainland, on the islands and in Asia Minor (modern Turkey). An independent, united Greek nation did not exist until AD 1830; Athens became its capital four years later.

An outburst of innovation

Even within the long history of ancient Greek city-states, Athens was not always predominant. For centuries it was just one of many lesser towns, an insignificant player compared with major forces such as Mycenae, Corinth, Thebes and Sparta. The Athenians hardly get a mention in Homer's epic account of the Trojan War. By the time the Romans swallowed up Greece as part of their empire, Athens was once again a minor provincial town.

And yet, somewhere in between, something remarkable happened in Athens. There was an astonishing outburst of artistic, literary, philosophical and political innovation that has been compared to the Italian Renaissance, the Reformation and the Age of Enlightenment.

LEFT: Kyre in peplos, c. 530BC, found in the Acropolis.
RIGHT: the Doric order Hephaisteion in the Agora.

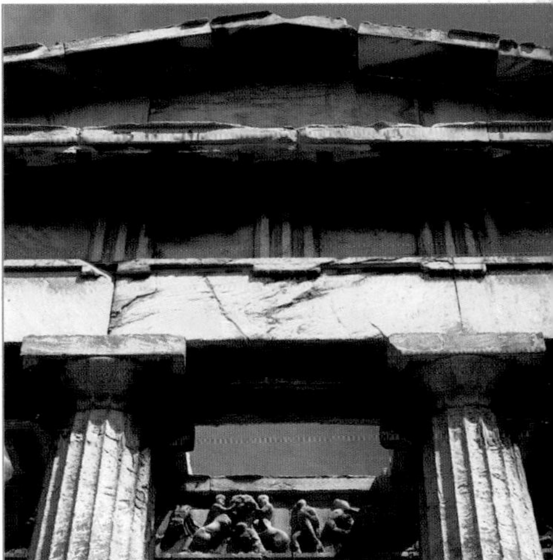

A TEMPLATE FOR CIVILISATION

Athens had a rudimentary form of democracy, being the first state in which every citizen, a highly proscribed category, could vote on matters such as declaring war and raising taxes. Athens laid some of the foundations of European theatre, and was home, to prose writers such as Herodotus (the "Father of History") and Thucydides (arguably the first historian in the modern sense of the word). Athenians created temples and other public buildings that still impress and inspire architects, and sculptures that influenced artists from the Romans to Michelangelo. And Athens was the milieu in which philosophers such as Socrates and Plato flourished.

BARBARIAN SPEAKERS

A favourite name for "foreigner" among the ancient Greeks was *barbaros* – an onomatopoeic word referring to the sound of a language they couldn't understand.

The city's pioneering achievements in democracy, philosophy and architecture secured it a place in the history of European civilisation. Yet this phenomenal flowering took place within little more than a century, in a town with a population of a few hundred thousand, whose only natural resources were a silver mine and some olive trees.

The first Athenians

Long before this explosion of creativity, people were living on the site of modern Athens, taking advantage of the defensive potential of the hill we know as the Acropolis. Archaeological finds of burnished pottery indicate a settled population in the Neolithic period (before 3000 BC) but the first evidence of buildings dates from the Late Bronze Age, particularly the 13th century BC. It may have been around this time that the 12 towns of Attica (villages in reality) were united under the leadership of Athens, an event ascribed by later generations to King Theseus, whose other legendary pastimes included killing the minotaur in its labyrinth in Knossos.

The minotaur story was invented centuries later by Athenians wishing to associate their ancestors with the downfall of the Minoan civilisation of Crete. But the Minoans' demise had nothing to do with Athens. It occurred around 1450 BC, for reasons that are not fully understood. What is certain is that, following the sudden collapse of Minoan culture, the Greek-speaking Mycenaeans took over their role in Crete and the Aegean, just as they had established dominance in mainland Greece.

From the 15th century BC, Athens was part of the Mycenaean world – but a relatively unimportant one. The main centre was Mycenae itself, the city of the legendary Agamemnon, but Thebes, Tiryns and Pylos were scarcely less important. From the abundance of gold and jewellery recovered from tombs, the Greeks seem to have been enormously prosperous between 1400 and 1250 BC.

THE TRUTH ABOUT THE TROJAN WAR

The most vivid source of knowledge about Mycenaean Greece is Homer's *Iliad.* Homer was probably born about 400 years after the Trojan War – thought to have been waged from 1194 to 1184 BC – and he worked only from oral tradition, so much of the historical detail is suspect.

According to legend, the war was over the abduction of Helen, the wife of King Menelaus of Sparta, by Paris of Troy. It was her beautiful face that inspired the Greeks to launch a thousand ships. It was also the war of the wooden horse, which taught the lesson about not trusting Greeks who bear gifts.

The truth about the Trojan War is rather more prosaic. The Mycenaean Greeks' extravagant tastes could not be satisfied locally. There was hardly any copper in Greece, no tin, and therefore no bronze for their prized weapons. And the growing city-states were barely self-sufficient in food.

Troy stood at the entrance to the Dardanelles, commanding the trade route between Europe and Asia. It also controlled access to the Black Sea, which the Greeks decided was an ocean of unlimited potential. Troy stood in the way of Greek commercial expansion, and the real Trojan War seems to have been fought for economic reasons.

It was during this period that a palace was built on the north side of the Acropolis in Athens, near the site of the later Erechtheon, and the citadel was surrounded by thick stone walls. In Mycenaean cities, the fortified citadel was reserved for the king and trusted nobles; the workers lived in villages outside.

Although the Greeks won the Trojan War *(see box on opposite page)*, the victory did not bring the anticipated return. On the contrary, Mycenaean power never recovered from the war effort, and it was too weak to resist an invasion building up on its northern frontiers.

Athens seems to have played an insignificant part in the Trojan War and therefore suffered less than other parts of Greece. But the Athenians in their walled Acropolis were aware of the danger of invasion, and a flight of stairs was hastily cut into the rock to reach the additional sources of water that would be needed during a long siege.

In the event, Athens was neither besieged nor conquered by the invaders, but the other Mycenaean cities were. The administrative system the Mycenaeans inherited from the Minoans had been changed into what would now be recognised as a government and civil service, but it now collapsed. Greece was dominated by the new, Dorian, arrivals for the next 400 years, until the invaders were assimilated with the earlier inhabitants to produce a more robust, hybrid "Greek" identity.

LEFT: the owl, symbol of Athens, on a drachma.
ABOVE: a Mycenaean *tholos* tomb.

Dorian conquest

The Dorians who replaced the society established by the Mycenaeans came from the northwest, from Macedonia and Epirus, but spoke a dialect of Greek. They were efficient troops who went to war in chariots, wore a panoply of bronze armour and carried long swords, iron-tipped spears and round shields.

The Dorians moved southward into central Greece and then into the southern Aegean area in successive migrations beginning about 1100 BC. They swept away the last of the declining Mycenaean civilisation – except in the well-fortified city of Athens and regions to the northeast, where perhaps the mountainous terrain made the Dorians' cavalry and chariots less effective. (In the 5th-century BC the historian Thucydides unkindly suggested that Attica was overlooked because it contained nothing worth conquering.)

Of the original Greek tribal groups, the Aeolians took refuge from the Dorians on the northwest coast of Asia Minor, while many Ionians fled to the central coast and the islands of Lesbos, Samos and Chios. In time, assimilation drew Ionians and Dorians closer together, and the old divisions tended to crumble when faced by a common, non-Greek enemy like the Persians. But Athens always identified itself as Ionian, and the age-old animosity between Ionians and Dorians was to assert itself centuries later in the Peloponnesian War.

The stirrings of democracy

Not much is known about Athens between the 11th and 7th centuries BC. At some point, hereditary kingship gave way to an aristocratic oligarchy, in which power resided in the hands of nine officers *(archons)* elected annually from the great families. The principal civil and judicial officer, the "eponymous *archon*", gave his name to his year of office. One *archon* called *basileus* (king) was a throwback to the days of monarchy, but this "king" was an elected officer whose role was limited to religious affairs and presiding over the Council of Elders called the Areopagus, after the hill near the Acropolis where the proceedings were held.

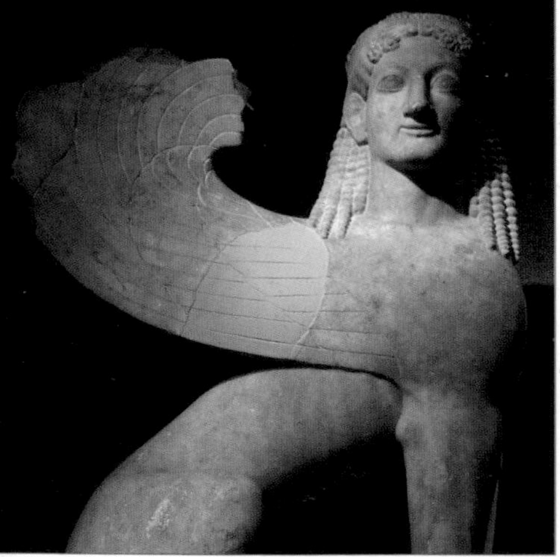

The only Athenians eligible to serve as archons were the *eupatridai* – nobles by birth. Originally it was a job for life. The term of office was later reduced to 10 years, then to a single year, after which, since they could not be re-elected, ex-*archons* became life members of the Areopagus. In some of the city-states during this period, the concentration of power in aristocratic hands led to popular unrest. Occasionally, an ambitious man would harness this discontent and seize sole power for himself. The Greek word for this style of self-appointed leader was *tyrannos*, but his rule was not necessarily tyrannical. The word simply described one who grabbed power rather than inheriting it or being appointed by his peers.

Athens' first would-be tyrant was a noble called Cylon, who attempted to seize control around 632 BC. Lacking a popular powerbase, his coup was unsuccessful, but fear of a similar uprising was probably responsible for the decision, around 621, to have the laws of Athens written down for the first time.

A dynasty of tyrants

Solon's reforms *(see box below)* loosened the stranglehold of the wealthy aristocratic clans,

THE WISDOM OF SOLON

The penalties for wrong-doing were dictated by custom and could be severe – enslavement for debt, for example, and death for stealing a cabbage. Draco, who was given the job of tidying up the legal process, has rather unfairly been saddled with the reputation of setting these penalties (hence the word "draconian").

In 594 BC, a remarkable man called Solon became *archon*. He had the vision to see that the old aristocratic order was the object of such resentment that it was only a matter of time before another would-be tyrant such as Cylon came along. Solon's wide-ranging constitutional reforms were designed to improve the condition of debt-ridden farmers and the middle classes who were excluded from government, while not alienating the increasingly wealthy landowners and aristocracy.

Solon cancelled all debts, and freed those who had become enslaved to their creditors. However, his reforms went far beyond the economic sphere. Declaring that all free Athenians were equal under the law, he abolished inherited privileges and restructured political power into four social classes, defined by wealth. Now members of the first two classes were eligible to hold office, and members of all four could elect *archons*, sit on juries and vote on legislation in the general assembly, the *ecclesia*.

but perhaps Athens was not yet ready for fully-fledged democracy. When Solon stepped down from office at the end of his archonship, the city was divided into factions. One party, the men of the coast (consisting mainly of the middle classes and peasants, and led by Megacles) supported his reforms. The other side, the men of the plain (mainly land-owning *eupatridai*, led by Lycurgus), were understandably keen on the restoration of an aristocratic government. The hostility between them meant that the city was ripe to be taken over by a single leader who could unite it – a "tyrant". And one was waiting in the wings.

Peisistratus was a nobleman who had gained military fame during a brief war between Athens and Megara. To further his political ambitions he portrayed himself as the champion of the rural proletariat, and organised his own faction, the hill party. However, it took him several attempts to become the ruler of Athens. In 561 BC he briefly seized the Acropolis, until most of the citizens united to drive him out. His next attempt, five years later, was a theatrical affair. He entered the city dressed in shining armour, with a tall beautiful woman at his side. He claimed she was the goddess Athena and he was a hero destined to rule. This time the people were more welcoming. Even after "Athena" was exposed as a girl from a nearby village, he still was acclaimed ruler by many, until Lycurgus and Megacles made common cause to drive out the tyrant.

The legacy of Peisistratus

Peisistratus spent a decade away from Athens, exploiting a silver mine in Thrace and using the funds it supplied to raise a private army of non-Athenians. Finally in 546 he returned at the head of his troops, launched a surprise

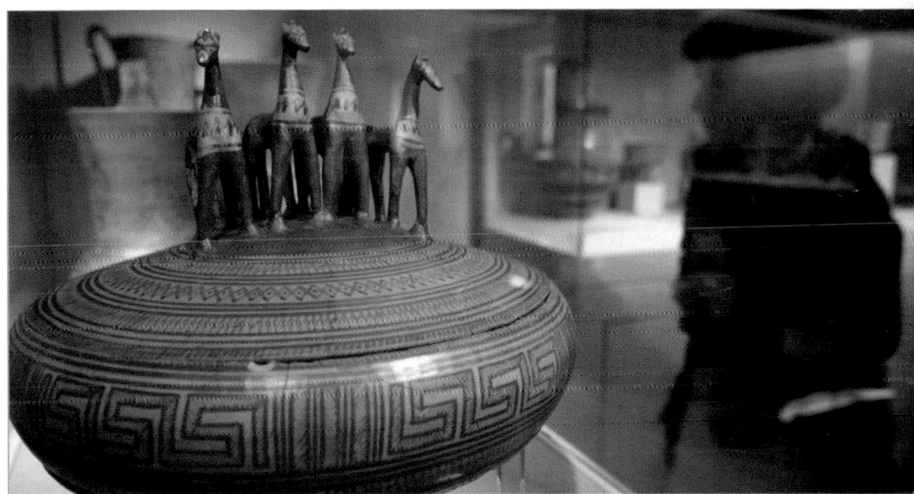

LEFT: the "Sphynx of the Acropolis", from around 530 BC. **ABOVE:** a Geometric-era bowl from the Goulandris museum in Kolonáki.

THE BIRTH OF GREEK THEATRE

Peisistratus encouraged the worship of Dionysus. The main feature of the annual Dionysian festival, besides drinking and merry-making, was a musical contest between choirs dressed as goats. As the themes presented in song and dance became more wide-ranging, the goatskins were replaced by more appropriate costumes. In a remarkably short time, the pagan goat ceremonies became tragedies created by dramatists such as Aeschylus. This was the birth of Greek theatre. Peisistratus was probably also responsible for having the epic poems of Homer, so long an oral tradition, written down for the first time.

attack on Athens and seized power for good.

With popular support from all classes, Peisistratus embarked on a programme of social reform and public works that laid the groundwork for Athens' rise to eminence. He promoted the Panathenaea, the festival which culminated in a procession up to the Acropolis to present the goddess Athena with a new robe. (This was the subject of Phidias's frieze on the Parthenon a century later.) The tyrant was so ambitious that his greatest undertaking, a new temple to Zeus near the Acropolis, was not completed for another 600 years, and only then by a philhellenic Roman emperor, Hadrian.

In the military sphere, Athens under Peisistratus established hegemony in the Dardanelles. Trade flourished and Athens first coined its famous silver coins with Athena's head on one side and an owl on the other.

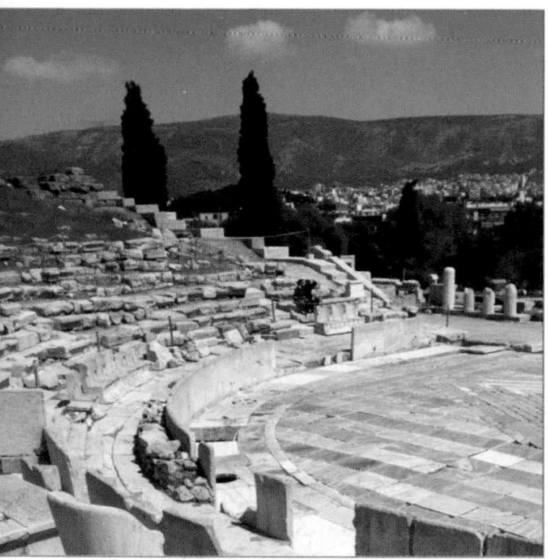

When he died in 527 BC, Peisistratus left behind an Athens that was economically more stable, militarily stronger and culturally richer than he had found it. He had laid the foundation for Athens' rise to glory.

He was succeeded by his sons, Hippias and Hipparchus. Not everyone was happy with what seemed to be a developing dynasty of tyrants, and an assassination attempt in 514 succeeded in killing Hipparchus. Hippias survived and grew increasingly suspicious and repressive.

The noble Alcmaeonid family, many of whom had been exiled for their part in Cylon's attempt at tyranny a century earlier, still took an active interest in Athenian affairs. They were appalled at Hippias' increasingly cruel and irrational behaviour, and enlisted Sparta's help to replace the tyrant with one of their own, Cleisthenes.

In 510 a Spartan force entered Athens and drove out Hippias, no doubt expecting him to be replaced by a regime less hostile to Sparta than Peisistratus and his sons had been. But Cleisthenes surprised everyone by inventing, in effect, the world's first basic democracy *(see panel below)*.

Invaded by Persia

In 498 BC, as a token of solidarity, Athens sent 20 ships across the Aegean to help the Ionian Greeks in their seemingly hopeless rebellion against the Persians, who were intent on con-

THE BIRTH OF DEMOCRACY

When Sparta invaded in 510, the Alcmaeonids and other nobles hoped for a return to the sort of oligarchy that assured their ascendancy. But the new ruler, Cleisthenes, had very different ideas about the political system.

Although his new position owed everything to well-lubricated nepotism, he declared that there would never be political stability in Athens as long as noble families competed to advance their own interests. He put the affairs of state into the hands of a representative government elected on a regional basis which cut right across established family lines.

He abolished the traditional tribes based on families, and organised citizens into 10 tribes based on geographical location. Each tribe contained communities from three different regions, the city, the coast and the plain. Cleisthenes then reorganised the 400-seat Council *(boule)* set up by Solon into a new body of 500, with 50 members from each of the new tribes. Thus each village, however small and remote, had some input into the process of government. But the Council of 500 did not have absolute power in Athens' affairs. It could not, for instance, declare war. Decisions like that, and the power of veto over the Council, lay with the Assembly (ecclesia), at which every single male citizen could now vote.

MARATHON RUNNER

A legend sprang up after the battle of Marathon that a messenger called Pheidippides, sent to request help from Sparta, ran non-stop from Athens, covering the 240 km (150 miles) in two days, delivered his message and promptly died of exhaustion. Sadly, although the name of Marathon persists in the modern athletic event, there is no truth in the tale. A messenger was undoubtedly sent, but on horseback for the sake of speed.

solidating the Ionian settlements in Asia Minor into their burgeoning empire. The Athenian contribution was minimal, and their troops were retiring from an unsuccessful attack on Sardis when, by accident, a fire started and the town burned to the ground. The Athenians decided they had better go home.

That might have been the end of the story, but King Darius of Persia heard about the fire and asked who was responsible. One of his aides mentioned the Athenians. "The Athenians?" Darius was puzzled. "Who are they?" He was prepared to be reasonable with these obscure upstarts. He sent ambassadors to ask for an apology and a token of submission – but the Athenians threw the visitors into the pit where they usually deposited the bodies of executed criminals. This disrespect to the Persian Empire could not be tolerated. Now Darius desired not just an apology but vengeance.

The battle of Marathon

The punitive expedition he sent to Greece in 490 BC numbered 25,000 men, who landed unopposed near the plain of Marathon, about 40 km (25 miles) from Athens. The Athenians could muster only 10,000, augmented by a further 1,000 from neighbouring Plataea. They had sent word to Sparta requesting reinforcements but, according to the historian Herodotus, the Spartans were celebrating a religious festival which forbade them from leaving home before the full moon.

Inspired tactics by the Athenian commander Miltiades literally outflanked the Persians, surrounding their foot-soldiers while the cavalry were absent from the field (possibly the horses were being watered). According to Herodotus, the Greeks won a decisive victory, losing only 192 men to the Persians' 6,400.

Marathon was a humiliating defeat for Darius and a startling boost to Athens' prestige within the Greek world. The Persians withdrew to lick their wounds, but left little doubt that they would return. Fortunately for Athens, a leader had emerged who had the strategic insight to prepare the city to defend itself.

As *archon* in 493 BC, Themistocles had overseen the development of Piraeus as a port for the first time, and throughout his career he continued to champion the Athenian navy as its most formidable weapon. When substantial

silver deposits were discovered in the state-owned mine near Laurion, Themistocles persuaded the Assembly to devote the proceeds into building more *triremes* (newly-developed warships with three banks of oars). In the decade following the first Persian invasion, the Athenian navy grew from around 70 to more than 200 ships.

Meanwhile, Darius died and was succeeded by his son Xerxes, who assembled a massive army and fleet to finish what his father had started. The unprecedented size of his forces made their progress quite slow, which gave the Greeks plenty of time to prepare their defence. This time, several cities banded together in a

LEFT: Theatre of Dionysios. **RIGHT:** stone models of theatre masks at the National Museum.

league against Persia. Sparta commanded the allied army and Athens the navy, which numbered about 350 ships – about one-third the size of the huge Persian fleet. According to Herodotus, Xerxes' army was so big that when they stopped after a thirsty day's marching they were capable of drinking a river dry.

Like any invasion of the Greek mainland from the north, the Persian army had to funnel its way through the narrow pass at Thermopylae where formidable mountains reached to the sea. In 480, when Xerxes' troops arrived, the pass was barely wider than a chariot, though today the sea has receded to widen the gap to more than a mile.

A mere 300 Spartans under Leonidas were deployed to defend the pass, and they were so confident about their chances against the Persians that they passed their time "bathing and combing their hair". The Persians discovered that a track through the mountains bypassed the bottleneck at Thermopylae, so the spirited defence put up by well-groomed Spartans was to no avail. The Persians moved southwards and the civilian population of Athens was sent to the island of Salamis before the invaders reached the city.

With the citizens absent, the Persian army destroyed many Athenian buildings. Meanwhile, the navy, battered by storms on the voy-

The Birth of the Athenian Empire

Attica was not rich, and the naval construction programme that Themistocles had pushed through was paid for with revenue from the Laurion silver mine, where the underground working conditions were appalling. The measures taken to replenish the state coffers after the victory over Persia also show a less palatable side of Athenian history.

Athens established the Delian League as a common defence against future foreign threats. It began as a voluntary confederation of cities including most of Ionia and nearly all the Aegean islands. Athens, taking advantage of its current prestige, took charge of the money which members subscribed to the fund. The treasury was on the sacred island of Delos and was supposed to pay for the construction and maintenance of a fleet, but it was soon apparent that the Athenians were dipping in to it to pay for the restoration of their ruined city.

The contributors protested that their money was being squandered on the aggrandisement of a single member. Athens responded by closing down the treasury on Delos and transferring the money to Athens "for safekeeping". When member states expressed a wish to leave the league, they were whipped into line by Athens. The Delian League had become, in effect, the Athenian Empire.

age south, had reached the coast near Athens but was tricked into rowing all night in the narrow strait between Salamis and the mainland and were exhausted when they met the Greek fleet. The citizens of Athens watched the battle from the island, Xerxes from a marble throne on a hill on the other side. The Greeks were outnumbered, but their ships were stronger and their tactics more astute. The Persians were outmanoeuvred and badly beaten. Many of their ships were sunk, the remainder fled back to Asia.

Xerxes too returned to Persia that winter, but his army remained in Greece. It was finally driven home after the battle of Plataea in 479 BC, where it was defeated by a combined force of Spartans, Tegeans and Athenians.

Greek forces, with Athens in the vanguard, had vanquished the largest invading force Europe had ever seen. Athens had provided more than half the ships for the decisive victory at Salamis and took most of the credit, to add to the glory already earned at Marathon. Athenian supremacy among the Greek states was for the moment unassailable.

The Golden Age

The middle of the 5th century BC was a golden age for the city. Leadership of the Delian League *(see box on opposite page)* brought prosperity, security and confidence. Poetry, drama and philosophy flourished, and Athens celebrated its success with magnificent new buildings, including the Parthenon, the Propylaea, the Erechtheion and the Temple of Athena Niké. The way Athens handled the league's money may have been unscrupulous, but 2,500 years later it is something for which visitors to Athens may feel grateful. The Acropolis would have looked very different without it.

War between Greeks

Although they excluded women, men with a foreign parent, immigrants and slaves – groups which amounted to at least four-fifths of the population – the mildly democratic institutions being fostered in Athens *(see box below)* were viewed with great suspicion by

LEFT: the Parthenon's Panathenaic frieze.
RIGHT: a vase found during the metro excavations.

HOW PERICLES CHANGED THE RULES

The outstanding political figure of the time was Pericles, a statesman, orator and general described by Thucydides, his greatest supporter, as "the first citzen of Athens". He was a charismatic leader, immensely popular with a majority of citizens, a patron of the arts, a dynamic soldier and, like his great-uncle Cleisthenes, a political reformer.

Under Pericles, the government of Athens took a more revolutionary turn. Whereas members of the Council of 500 had previously been drawn by lot from a list of approved (but not representative) candidates, it was decreed that in future the names of all citizens would go into the hat as contenders for office. Because poor citizens who might be chosen by this means would not be able to afford to give up their time to the state, state officials would receive salaries.

The concessions applied only to adult male citizens – a minority group made even smaller by a change to the citizenship qualifications enacted by Pericles. No man was now a citizen unless both his mother and father had been citizens and legally married. Under this rule, some of the city's most effective leaders – Themistocles and Cleisthenes, for example – would not have qualified because their mothers were not from the city.

other city-states, whose kings, despots and oligarchies saw no merit in sharing their powers. Many Greek cities, and Sparta in particular, were as uneasy about this flowering of rudimentary democracy as they were about the growth of Athens' empire. It was perhaps inevitable that sooner or later hostilities would break out between Athens, with its Ionian allies, and the descendants of the Dorians in the Peloponnese.

The Peloponnesian War, chronicled in Thucydides' detailed and absorbing history – the first of its kind – dragged on from 431 to 404 BC largely because Athenian strength lay in its navy and Sparta's in its army, which made it practically impossible for the two to get to grips with each another. It was brought to an end when Athens committed its fleet to a pointless attack on Sicily and Sparta acquired a navy of its own, from Persia.

Exile by Referendum

One odd innovation in 5th-century Athens was the practice of ostracism; banishing an individual to 10 years' exile on the basis of popular opinion. First, a vote was taken as to whether there should be an ostracism in principle. If the voters wanted one, a second vote was held in which citizens could write the name of any Athenian onto a piece of broken pottery (a potsherd or *ostrakon*). The person whose name appeared on most *ostraka* was exiled from the city for a decade. It was probably introduced as a defence against over-ambitious demagogues. The first ostracism, in 487 BC, expelled Hipparchos, a relative of the tyrant Peisistratus.

The Thirty Tyrants

Pericles died two years after the outbreak of the war, and the peace terms imposed on the defeated Athenians dismantled many of his achievements. Athens was effectively stripped of the empire it had built up, and the democratic institutions were replaced by an oligarchical "Government of the 400". Assassination – surprisingly rare in what was generally a bloodthirsty climate – brought that government down after four months.

The Athenians wanted to revert to democracy, but Lysander, the Spartan victor, insisted they stick to an oligarchy. Accordingly, the "Thirty Tyrants" came into being, but they also were not successful. Lysander must have decided to let the Athenians pursue their democratic instincts, and Eucleides, the new *archon*, devised a scheme which put practically every man in the city on the state payroll.

Alexander the Great

But the political debate was made inconsequential by the threat of yet another invasion. The Macedonians, who thought of themselves as thoroughly Greek but were regarded by their southern brethren as barbarians, had imperial ambitions. King Philip of Macedon pounced on the northern areas and then went on to defeat all of the south except Sparta. Macedonia had rich resources in cereals, gold and timber, whereas the city-states to the south had worn themselves out through warfare. Following Philip's assassination, his son Alexander, soon to become "the Great", took over.

Alexander had studied philosophy under Aristotle, but it was in war that he excelled. His all-conquering march to Egypt, across Persia, through Afghanistan and into India has passed into legend. Even the southern Greek states were impressed. When Alexander asked their permission to call himself the son of a god, they responded that he could be the son of anyone he liked.

Alexander was probably unstable in some ways, but he alone was capable of holding his prodigious empire together. When he died in Babylon in 323 BC, his generals struggled for a generation to make it work. For a while, the whole of the eastern Mediterranean and West Asia had been "Greek". Thereafter it was divided into three kingdoms, all of which remained nominally Greek: Macedonia, under various dynasties; Asia, under the Seleucids; and Egypt, under a long line of Ptolemies.

The rise of Alexandria in Egypt had the most direct bearing on Athens because it took away the city's intellectual pre-eminence. The schools of philosophy in Athens continued, but scholars and scientists were attracted to the great library which Alexander had founded in Egypt. Politically, Athens was allowed to pursue its idiosyncratic democratic inclinations, but it had lost its place in the limelight.

The Romans made their first significant contact with the Greeks when Philip V of Macedonia threw in his lot with Carthage during the Second Punic War between Carthage and Rome. The most familiar story from the Punic Wars is Hannibal's crossing of the Alps with his elephants, but far to the east the war meant that anyone who opposed Macedonia was therefore on the side of Rome. Athens and the other Greek cities had never stopped sniping at Macedonia, so shortly after Rome's defeat of Philip in 197 BC, the Roman consul Flamininus turned up at the Isthmian Games to meet Rome's new-found Greek allies. He grandly pronounced the freedom of Greece, and in 194 BC Rome oversaw the removal of all Macedonian garrisons from Greek territories. For the moment, the Greek world was free and independent again.

LEFT: the prow of a replica *trireme*.
ABOVE: Alexander the Great defeats Darius and the Persian army in Anatolia in 333 BC.

The Romans march in

But Rome was expanding in all directions. Continuing squabbles between Greek city-states, and between Greeks and Macedonians, made them easy pickings for the ambitious city on the Tiber. First Macedonia was annexed as a Roman province. Then it was the turn of the Greeks.

In 146 BC, Rome stepped into a dispute between Sparta and Corinth and took the opportunity to subdue them both, razing Corinth to the ground for good measure. *Pax Romana* ("Roman peace") was imposed on the Greeks, who were to be administered by the Roman governor of Macedonia. Although Athens had played no part in the recent hostilities, like the rest of Greece the city was now under the jurisdiction of Rome. ❑

ROMAN AND BYZANTINE ATHENS

Beloved by a succession of emperors, Athens remained a cultural centre during the period of Roman rule. But when the seat of power moved to Constantinople, the city dropped out of view

Athens enjoyed unprecedented peace and special privileges as part of the Roman state, but at times the city seemed to be its own worst enemy. In 88 BC the Athenians made the mistake of supporting Mithridates, king of Pontus in Asia Minor, in one of his military misadventures. Rome was displeased, and in reprisal the Roman general Sulla sacked Athens and levelled the walls of the Piraeus in 86 BC.

Nevertheless, Rome seems to have been remarkably tolerant of its troublesome charge. When the Republic of Rome became the Roman Empire in 27 BC, Greece was already a province (called Achaea) separate from Macedonia. The capital was not Athens, however, but Corinth. This was a sharp blow to Athenian pride because, while Corinth had once been an imposing rival, it too had been destroyed by the Romans for an unrelated misdemeanour and was still in the process of being put together again.

Philhellenic emperors

The early Roman emperors enjoyed demonstrating how cultured they were, and how well educated in the traditions of Classical Greece (to be fair, some of them genuinely were). As a result, although Athens had little significance economically or strategically within the empire, it preserved its reputation as a cultural centre, reflecting its former glory on its new rulers.

Benefits that the Romans bestowed on the city included a large new market for the sale of oil and other commodities, built under emperor Augustus to the east of the old Agora. In the middle of the Agora itself, a new Odeon, or concert hall, was built by Marcus Agrippa, the emperor's son-in-law and one of his chief lieutenants. Another large building, perhaps a law court, was erected at the north-east corner of the square. On the Acropolis a small round temple was built to the goddess Roma and the emperor Augustus.

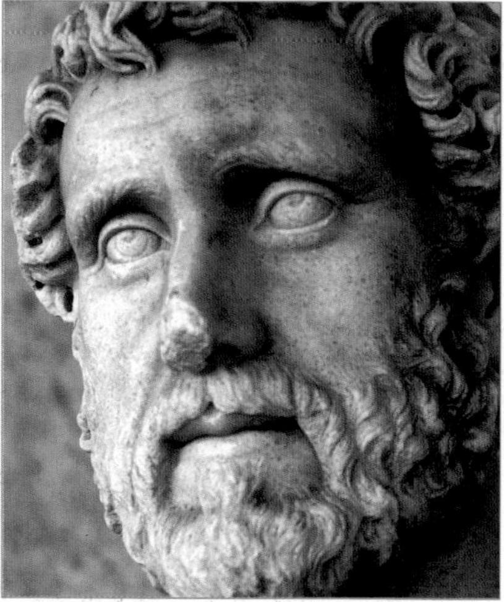

Nero (emperor from 54 to 68 AD), was a patron of the arts and a philhellene. In 67 AD, he demonstrated his love of Greek culture by performing at four major festivals, dancing, singing and carrying away all the prizes. The four great festivals at Olympia, Delphi, Nemea and the Isthmus were all crowded into one year to accommodate the emperor's triumphal tour. "The Greeks are the only people who understand how to be an audience", he said.

Hadrian the builder

Around AD 100, a handsome library decorated with marble sculpture was erected at the south-eastern corner of the Areopagus, the gift of one T. Flavius Pantainus and his family. However, even greater building enterprises were in store. The emperor Hadrian (AD 117–138) looked at the plans for the great temple of the Olympian Zeus, started more than 600 years earlier by Peisistratus. It had been left unfinished since the overthrow of the tyrants, but it was finally completed when Hadrian made the necessary resources available. This temple was the chief ornament of the new eastern suburb of Athens, and Hadrian gave the area a monumental entrance through an arch which bears his name.

The emperor was consciously trying to put himself in the same league as the original creators of the city, as revealed by his inscriptions on either side of the arch. One reads "This is Athens, city of Theseus"; the other "This is the city of Hadrian and not of Theseus". Hadrian also built a huge library, a gymnasium and a pantheon (a sanctuary of all the gods).

As if to compensate for the large number of Greeks who had earlier decamped to Alexandria for their intellectual pursuits, Romans now flocked to Athens. Emperor Marcus Aurelius (AD 161–80) encouraged the trend by establishing a new university.

WATER CARRIER

Hadrian had an aqueduct built, bringing water to Athens from the mountains to the north. It has been reconditioned and still serves the modern city.

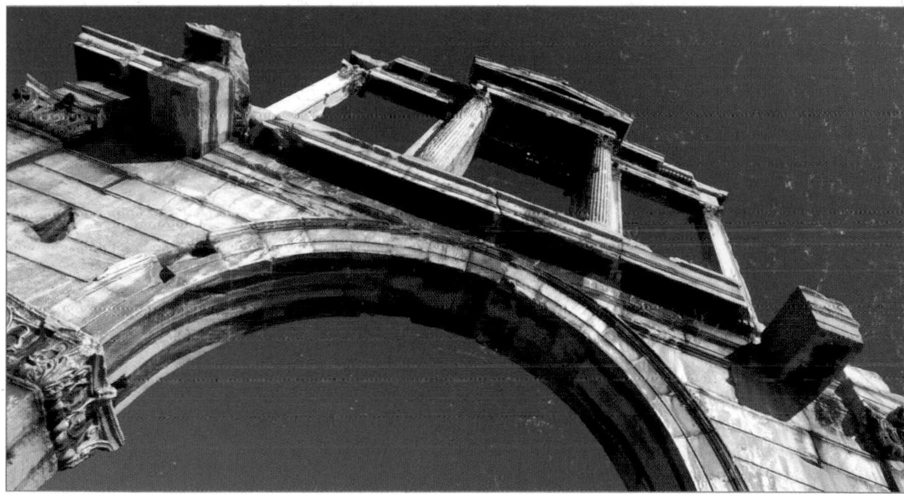

LEFT: bust of Roman emperor Antonius Pius (AD138–161) from the Agora of Atallus.
ABOVE: Hadrian's Arch.

Barbarian hordes

By the 3rd century AD, the northern boundaries of the Roman Empire were under threat from various invaders. Athens had been left unfortified since Sulla captured the city in 86 but during the reign of Valerian (253–60 AD), the city walls were rebuilt to enclose a larger area than ever before, including the new suburb northeast of the Olympieion.

The anticipated barbarian invasion wasn't long in coming, but in the event, the walls were of no avail. The Heruli, a tribe of Goths from northern Europe, stormed into Athens in 267. The historian P. Herennius Dexippus rallied 2,000 men on the city outskirts, but their guerrilla tactics were futile. The lower town was sacked, and all the fine buildings of the Agora were burned and destroyed. However, it seems that the Acropolis held out; at least there is no evidence of extensive damage at this time.

After the destruction

This sack of Athens was as traumatic as the destruction wrought by Xerxes' Persian troops in 480 BC. On that occasion, having defeated the Persians at sea, the Athenians rebuilt their city on a grander scale than ever. This time, however, when the barbarians were driven out by the Romans, the reconstruction was more modest. The Athenians abandoned the outer defences that had been so ineffective and built a new wall with stone taken from ruined buildings in the lower town. The new perimeter, built in the reign of Probus (276–282), was much smaller, and left even the Agora area outside the walls.

For several generations, Athens remained confined within this narrow fortification. But during the 4th and 5th centuries the city experienced a revival. The old outer circuit of walls was restored, and many new buildings were erected. Athens remained the cultural capital of the Greek world and a stronghold of paganism.

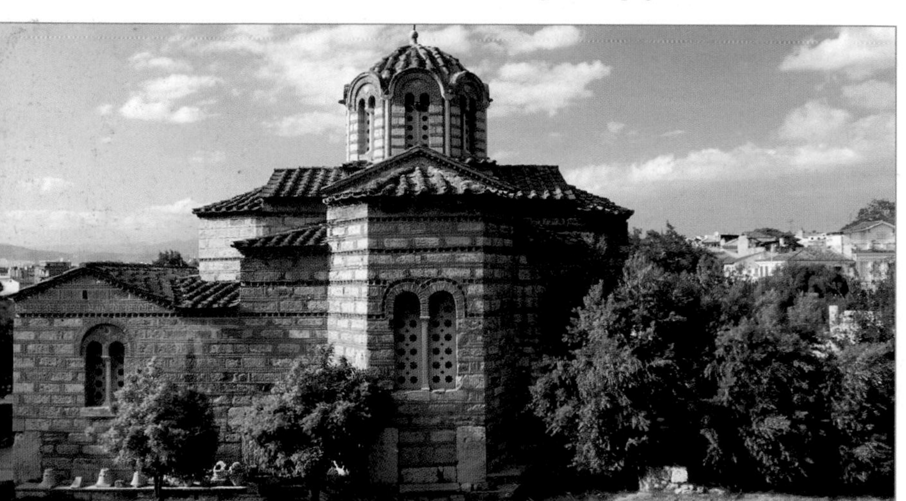

THE ECLIPSE OF LEARNING

The schools of philosophy, where Plato and Aristotle had debated, continued to flourish in the 4th and 5th centuries, and attracted students from all parts of the empire, including Emperor Julian the Apostate and two men who were to become eminent Christian teachers, Basil and Gregory of Nazianzus.

But the empire's conversion to Christianity ended the city's role as a seat of pagan learning: the Emperor Justinian closed the schools of philosophy in 529, whereupon Athens became an almost forgotten provincial town. Power and wealth had long since moved to Constantinople, the new centre of the Greek world.

Athens becomes Christian

St Paul had visited Athens briefly in AD 54, although the time he spent in Corinth (where he established a Christian comunity) was more profitable. In Athens, one former *archon*, Dionysius the Areopagite, was impressed enough to convert to Christianity, but most Athenians were content to remain loyal to the Olympian gods.

In the 5th and 6th centuries, however, after Christianity became the official religion of the empire and pagan worship was abolished by law, churches began to spring up. Sometimes these were ancient temples converted to Christian worship; the temple of Hephaestus (the

Hephaisteion), for example, and the Erechtheon and even the Parthenon itself. There were new churches, too, usually built in a basilica plan with a wooden roof. To judge from the remaining foundations, around 20 of them were built during this period.

Although the Byzantines had control of the Aegean and its islands, in the 7th and 8th centuries their direct command did not extend far beyond the coast. The history of the Greek mainland in this period is of one invasion after another: Huns, Ostrogoths, Vlachs, Slavs, Bulgars, Avars and Cumans.

Not for the first time, Athens and its Acropolis seem to have remained immune. But it was now a small and unimportant town in a backwater of the empire. With the shift of political emphasis to Constantinople, Athens entered a period of decline. The city is hardly ever mentioned in the history of the 7th to 10th centuries, and archaeological remains are few.

Medieval prosperity

Athens was unaffected by the Turkish attacks on the Byzantine Empire after the battle of Manzikert in 1071 and the ensuing civil wars. When the Empire was rescued by the dynamic leadership of the three Comnenus emperors, Alexius I, John II and Manuel Comnenus, Greece benefited from the improved security and a measure of prosperity returned.

The Agora, which had been deserted for centuries, began to be built over, and soon the town became an important centre for the production of soaps and dyes. Venetians and various other traders who frequented the ports of the Aegean were attracted to Athens, and this interest in trade appears to have further increased the economic prosperity of the town. A number of stone and brick Byzantine churches survive from this time, such as Kapnikaréa, and the churches of St Theodore and the Holy Apostles.

But this medieval prosperity was not to last. Throughout the 13th and 14th centuries, Athens was fought over by the Byzantines and the French and Italian knights of the Latin Empire.

The process began with the Fourth Crusade, which set out at the start of the 13th century to capture Jerusalem from the Muslims but ended up attacking Christian Constantinople instead. Constantinople duly fell in 1204, leaving the Crusaders to share out the spoils of the Byzantine Empire. Athens, which most of the Crusaders had never heard of, was allocated to a Burgundian noble named Othon de la Roche, who passed it on after a few years to his nephew, Guy.

Athens managed quite well under its young knight until he made the mistake of hiring some Catalan mercenaries to settle a local dispute. The local dispute was resolved but led to a worse dispute about payment for the Catalans, and the mercenaries found themselves the owners of Athens. They gave it to one of their previous employers, Frederick II of Sicily, but continued to live there. Their Athenian-born offspring did not inherit their fighting qualities, and in 1388 a Florentine banker named Acciajuoli took over the city.

The threat from the Turks

The Florentines were able to hang on for 50 years and demonstrated a certain flair for solving the labour shortage in a depopulated city by bringing in Albanian workers.

In 1453, Constantinople fell to the Turks. Three years later they were hammering at the gates of Athens and could not be denied. ❑

LEFT: a Byzantine church in the Ancient Agora.
RIGHT: an icon in the Byzantine Museum.

THE OTTOMAN ERA

The city – like most of the rest of Greece – was under Islamic rule for nearly four centuries. Athens was an insignificant outpost of the Ottoman Empire, but there remain a few elegant mosques and Turkish baths from the period

The fractious and corrupt Florentine duchy was driven out of Athens by the Ottoman Sultan Mehmet II in 1456. The *turkokratía*, or the period of Ottoman rule of Attica that lasted until 1832, is generally, and erroneously, dismissed as a species of "dark ages" in which nothing of any lasting value was contributed to society in general or to Athens in particular by nearly four centuries of Turkish rule.

The current habit of referrring to "Turkish rule" is in fact a lazy shorthand, as religion, not ethnicity, was the critical divider in Ottoman society. The local Muslim population and members of the Ottoman ruling class were a mix of Albanians and Anatolians, with a small leavening of civil servants from Istanbul of decidedly mixed backgrounds. These included a civil governor, a *mufti* (religious leader) and a military governor in charge of the Acropolis citadel. This motley collection would have been mortified to be called "Turks" – until the 1922–3 establishment of the Turkish republic, it was an insult equivalent to "bumpkin" or "yokel".

Life under Ottoman rule

During the Ottoman period, the population of Athens varied between 10,000 and 17,000, and included gypsies and Africans (descendants of freed Ottoman slaves) as well as Orthodox Christians, both Greek- and Albanian-speaking, who made up between half and two-thirds of the total. Then, as now, Kifissiá was a favourite summer resort for the privileged, and was the only outlying village of Attica that had a mosque; two in fact, as well as a *hamam*, a *kervanserai* and a *medresse* (Koranic academy), all long since vanished.

Athens itself had already become a provincial backwater by late Byzantine times, and Ottoman rule did nothing to change this status, although the city enjoyed various administrative privileges, dating back to Mehmet II's esteem for this ancient seat of learning.

As was usual in conquered towns, a few churches were converted to Islamic use (including the Parthenon, which had been the Byzantine Cathedral of the Virgin), and a few pagan shrines were used in novel ways. The

LEFT: the *medresse* gateway near the Roman Agora.
RIGHT: Iznik tiles from the Benáki Ottoman Museum.

Muslims prayed for rain at the Temple of Olympian Zeus, perhaps mindful of his ancient soubriquet The Thunderer, and gathered there at their major *bayram* or festival.

Notable mosques

A few new mosques were also built. The first of these was the Féthiye Tzamí (Victory Mosque), erected at the edge of the Roman Forum at the behest of Sultan Mehmet II. Still in excellent condition, it is today an archaeological storehouse and not open to the public. Nearby stands the gateway of a *medresse* or Koranic academy, built in 1721 by one Mehmet Fakri; exactly a century later a local *cadi* or judge delivered an oration from this entrance to dissuade the population from massacring the entire male Orthodox population of the city at the outbreak of the Greek Revolution. After independence, the theological students' cells were pressed into service as a prison, and their formerly peaceful courtyard used for hangings from its giant plane tree, until the place was abandoned in the early 1900s. Besides the portal with its inscription, only part of an internal dome survives.

Directly opposite, the Tower of the Winds, while not originally an Islamic monument, was taken over in the 17th century by an order of dervishes as their lodge, where they performed various whirling and chanting exercises, terrifying their superstitious Orthodox neighbours.

The other intact mosque, the Tzisdarákis Tzamí, stands on the north slope of the Acropolis where the Byzantine and Ottoman town clustered. It dominates Monastiráki square but (like the Féthiye Tzami) is missing its minaret. It was erected in 1759 by an Ottoman governor who was promptly disgraced and sacked for removing a column from the Temple of Olympian Zeus with the intent of incorporating it into his new mosque. Today it houses part of the Greek Folk Art Museum. The interior, more interesting than the exhibits themselves, still retains its colourfully striped *mihrab* (a

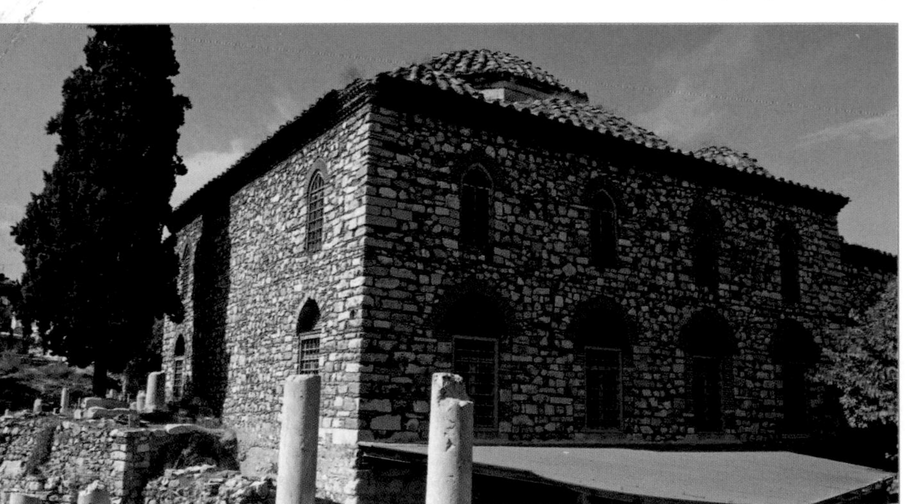

The Abdi Efendi Hamam

The entrance to the baths is inconspicuous but the domes are visible from the outside, as is the typical rust-magenta pigment (continued inside as well).

Because of their recent abandonment and an impeccable restoration, the baths are in fine condition, with the hypocausts (under-floor heating elements) exposed in the caldarium (hot chamber), and the sumptuous apodytíria or changing rooms, added in the 19th century, often used for special events or exhibits. The Abdi Efendi may have begun life with alternating men's and women's shifts for just one facility, but by the 17th century there were two separate bathing areas.

niche that shows the direction of Mecca) and a calligraphic inscription over the entrance.

The Ottomans also built three central *hamams* (baths) near the mosques. The only survivor is the Abdi Efendi Hamam, built in phases from the 15th to the 17th centuries and in use until 1965 *(see box on opposite page)*.

Revolt against the Ottomans

In 1814 three Greek merchants in Odessa formed a secret organisation called "The Friendly Society" (*Filikí Etería*) devoted to "the betterment of the nation", which rapidly acquired a network of sympathisers throughout the Ottoman lands. A number of vain attempts to secure themselves powerful backing were finally rewarded when their members organised an uprising against Ottoman rule in 1821.

Scattered violent incidents merged into a major revolt in the Peloponnese. The Turks found themselves outnumbered and were forced to retreat to their coastal fortresses. Further destruction came in the wake of the uprising. Greeks slaughtered Turks in Trípoli; Turks slaughtered the Greek inhabitants of Híos.

But the struggle for Greek independence, which lasted through to 1832, was not a straightforward affair. Opposing the Ottomans was a motley crew of brigands, militias, merchants, landowners and aristocrats, all as keen to further their own interests as to advance the cause of Greek nationalism. When they were not fighting the Turks they turned on each other.

Soon after the 1821 uprising, no fewer than three provisional Greek governments proclaimed themselves, each poised to take control of the liberated territories. A democratic constitution was drawn up in 1822, then revised in 1823, by which time the three local governments were unified in a central authority. But the following year feuding between rival groups culminated in outright civil war, prompting one chieftain, Makrygiannis, to protest that he had not taken up arms against the Turks to end up fighting Greeks.

Ironically, those who believed most strongly that this was a national struggle were the foreign philhellenes who came to help the Greeks. They were influential in getting Western public opinion behind Greece. Thus Britain, France and Russia, all initially unsympathetic to the Hellenic dream, came to put military and diplomatic pressure on the Turks to acknowledge Greek independence, a policy of "peaceful interference", as the British Prime Minister Lord Canning described it. ❑

LEFT the Féthiye Tzamí. **ABOVE :** Turkish baths, or *hammam,* at the House of the Four Winds.

MODERN ATHENS

The struggle for Greek liberation was a disorderly affair – and since independence, Athens has had an even more unsettled history, involving rule by foreign kings, military dictatorships, occupation by the Nazis and traumatic civil wars

On the morning of 5 January 1824, an exotic party disembarked from two ships at anchor off Mesolóngi at the entrance to the Gulf of Corinth and were rowed ashore. Their baggage included five horses, a Newfoundland dog and a bulldog. They received a welcome of artillery and musket fire from an assortment of Greek independence fighters, among them a very small, fat man dressed in tails and a flat cap.

Somewhat optimistically, given that the rebellion against Turkey was not going at all well, he called himself the president of the Greek senate. A pair of extraordinary, pebbled glasses gave him the appearance of a myopic mouse. Prince Alexander Mavrocordato was about as princely as he was presidential, but he was a survivor and nearly a decade later he became the legitimate prime minister.

Byron meets his destiny

The first of the visitors to step ashore, resplendent in a brand new scarlet uniform, was Lord Byron, the famous poet. But his literary reputation meant less to the reception committee than the fact that he was both rich and committed to Greek independence.

While Napoleon was on the rampage in Europe, Byron as an Englishman had been denied the normal grand tour of Europe and had gone instead to a neglected and generally forgotten part of the world: Greece. His poems, especially *Childe Harold*, about ancient Greek glory enslaved by Turkish barbarity, were acclaimed in England and read like an incitement to revolution. So when the Greeks did indeed rise, Byron felt obliged to join them. He arrived dressed for the part of a general, but he was a military ignoramus.

His devotion to ancient Greece was undiminished, but he was appalled by what he saw as riff-raff who squabbled and, if necessary, murdered one another to get hold of the money he was doling out. Four months after his arrival, Byron was soaked by a downpour while riding, complained of pains in his back, and a few days later died a less than heroic death. Apart from the money and an interven-

LEFT: Andreas Papandreou addressing a 1977 rally.
RIGHT: Lord Byron arrives at Mesolóngi.

tion which saved some Muslim prisoners whom the Greeks would routinely have killed, he had achieved nothing.

It was quite late in the war that Athens in general, and the Acropolis in particular, acquired symbolic status. Previously, according to a Greek account, "almost every [Greek] political or military chief was engaged in a plot to supplant or massacre some rival." A Turkish garrison sat out the turmoil on the Acropolis. They could not leave, but they were under no obvious threat until, during the unusually dry winter of 1821, their water ran out. The terms of their capitulation were safe passage to foreign ships in Piraeus in exchange for their weapons and half of the money they still possessed.

THE FORGOTTEN VOLUNTEERS

The extent to which Byron is venerated in Greece to this day clouds the more important, though often eccentric, contribution by other foreigners on both sides. The Greek cause was taken up in fashionable circles in a manner not unlike the crusading flavour of the International Brigade in the Spanish civil war a century later. Thousands of volunteers rallied to the cause, especially Danes, Germans, Swiss and British followers of the philosopher Jeremy Bentham. Most knew as little about soldiering as Byron did. But they included some volunteers and mercenaries whose participation has been as devalued as Byron's has been exaggerated.

Around 1,150 Turks gave themselves up and were taken to to the Stoa of Hadrian, where they were to wait. But an Athenian mob chased them through the streets, and 400 were killed before finding sanctuary in foreign consulates. A brigand, Odysseus, thereafter occupied the Acropolis. But the Turks were not yet spent, and in 1826, assisted by forces of the Egyptian ruler, Mehemet Ali, they took back most of the mainland. The Acropolis was under siege again, this time with Greeks holed up inside.

The long siege

The Parthenon should not have survived the six-month siege. Despite an undertaking by the sultan, the Turkish soldiers shelled it repeatedly. Unlike Schwarz, the Venetian gunner in 1687, they repeatedly missed. The attempt to relieve the siege in 1827 involved a full cast of eccentric philhellenes, including a French colonel, Charles Fabvier, with his private army; his English arch-enemy, General Sir Richard Church, who to Fabvier's disgust was appointed Commander-in-Chief of the troops; and another Briton, Captain Lord Cochrane, whom the Greeks had appointed Admiral of the Fleet, in exchange for a fat fee.

In their attempt to liberate Athens, Church and Cochrane, who supervised most of the action from their respective yachts, contrived to turn what ought to have been a fairly simple advance from Piraeus into a disaster. Against the local commanders' advice, they chose to make a new landing at the other end of Phaleron Bay. Instead of approaching under the cover of olive groves, the men found themselves exposed to a Turkish howitzer.

Church and Cochrane, coming ashore from their yachts for what they imagined would be a victory celebration, found the remnants of their force tearing towards them with the Turkish cavalry in pursuit. The British commanders did an about-turn and waded into the sea up to their necks to reach their boats. The plan to relieve the siege was abandoned.

The Battle of Navarino

In the end, permanent possession of the Acropolis was decided by the 1827 Anglo-Russian-French Treaty of London. The Greeks agreed to an armistice at once; the Turkish and Egyptian fleets only provisionally so.

Confusion reigned, and on 20 October the flagships at the head of the combined British, French and Russian fleet sailed into Navarino harbour, in western Greece, and dropped anchor within a ship's length of the Turkish and Egyptian admirals and their fleet of 89 warships and about 50 transports. A British frigate sent a boat to ask a fireship to move. Someone let off a musket shot at the boat and hit an officer. An Egyptian ship fired a single cannon round at the French flagship; the French ship fired one back. That was enough to spark off the Battle of Navarino.

"Unabated fury for four hours", the British Admiral Sir Edward Codrington wrote in his dispatch, "and the scene of wreck and devastation which presented itself at its termination was such as has been seldom before witnessed." Codrington himself ended the day with two bullet-holes in his coat and one in his hat. The British, French and Russian navies did not lose a ship, but most were damaged.

Even this "wreck and devastation" did not end the war, which dragged on for another five years while the sultan bickered about the terms of the formal concession of Greek independence. But without a fleet to maintain his armies in Greece, all he could do was postpone the inevitable.

LEFT: a 19th-century watercolour of Athens.
ABOVE: *War Scene*, Theodoros Vryzakis, 1849.

An independent Greece

Under the watchful eye of the "Great Powers" (Britain, Russia and France), the Greeks set up a National Assembly, whose first major project was to negotiate the precise borders of the newly independent country. The process was overseen by Count Ioannis Kapodistrias, a Corfu-born nobleman who had served the Russian emperor Alexander I in the diplomatic service, but resigned when Alexander refused to support the Greeks' struggle for independence. In 1827 the new Assembly, rightly discerning that Kapodístrias was the most eminent Greek-born politician in Europe, elected him *Kyvernítis* (Governor) of the state; in effect, the first president of Greece.

In 1828, Kapodístrias landed at Návplio, the provisional capital (he had never set foot on the Greek mainland before), and set about organising affairs. Besides negotiating the new state's frontiers, he also strove to rebuild the infrastructure of a country that had been ravaged by a destructive war. He reorganised the military, introduced the first modern Greek currency, set up quarantine measures to curb epidemics of typhoid and cholera, and introduced the potato to a skeptical Greek population.

But Kapodistrias's authoritarian style of government offended a number of powerful members of the embryonic Greek state. Growing unrest culminated in his assassination outside a church in Návplio in October 1831.

The "Great Powers" decided that the new country should be ruled by a king. A king, moreover, whom they – not the Greeks – would appoint. They first offered the throne to Prince Leopold of Saxe-Coburg, who accepted, then changed his mind. King Louis I of Bavaria did not want it either, but thought it suitable for his son, the young Otho.

The Great Powers were also instrumental in choosing a permanent capital for Greece. Just as soon as the Ottomans had finally been persuaded to leave the Acropolis, the capital moved to Athens from Návplio in 1834. Young King Otho, or perhaps his regents, had the grace to turn down the idea of a new palace on the Acropolis. Instead, the architects commissioned to build a neoclassical city, were steered away from the historical sites.

Otho's uneasy reign

The yellow building along one side of today's Sýntagma (Constitution) Square, the present Parliament building, was the original palace. A second palace in Herod Atticus Street was later occupied by the king, or president. Not without reason, the Greeks tended to view their monarchs as rather ordinary politicians whom they could take or leave as circumstances and prevailing opinion required.

ATHENS IN 1834

Cleanthes and Schaubert, the architects designing the new palace in 1834 appraised the new capital thus: "The greater number of houses are in ruins, and the rebuilt houses are mostly huts… There are 115 small churches, of which only 28 to 30 are in use, and four mosques, two in use, and two converted into baths."

In pinpointing a suitable location for a palace, the opportunities available to the architects were mostly insect-infected swamps, and it is said that the choice was narrowed down by hanging out pieces of meat and seeing how many maggots each accumulated. The fewer the maggots, the better the place.

Otho made the Greeks wonder whether the institution of a monarchy was what they really wanted. All three of his regents were Bavarians, and every department of administration and education was occupied by Germans. The Greeks thought that by then they ought to have some local voices in government, but Otho refused to grant the constitution which would have given them that right. He was deposed bloodlessly in 1843 after a demonstration in Sýntagma Square but was allowed back into office on the promise of adopting a more accommodating policy in future. In 1862 the Greeks decided he had not kept his promise and he was forced to abdicate.

The country cast an eye over the available royals kicking about Europe for another palace tenant and decided that the choice would be made by referendum. An overwhelming 230,000 out of 240,000 votes cast were for someone who was not available for the post, Prince Alfred of Great Britain, the second son of Queen Victoria. The only Greek candidate got six votes. The British government could not allow Alfred to accept, so it found an alternative in Prince William George of Denmark, like Otho, a teenager.

Divided loyalties

The arbitrary distribution of lesser European kingdoms around members of an extended family inevitably led to some testing divisions of loyalty. The problem manifested itself in Athens during the extraordinary events of December 1916. At that time, King Constantine of Greece, educated at the Kriegsakademie in Berlin and brother-in-law of the German Kaiser, understandably supported Germany in World War I. Eleftherios Venizelos, the Greek prime minister, took the opposing view. Venizelos found himself running a pro-Allied breakaway government from Thessaloníki, while in Athens the king was supporting Germany. Both sides had armies and the Allies, who appreciated Venizélos's support but could not bring themselves to deal too sternly with Constantine, tried to keep the king and the prime minister apart.

When it appeared that Greece was threatened by a civil war, an Allied force of 2,000 French and British troops, supported by ships, was sent to Athens to act as a buffer. The king's forces took up positions just in front of the Acropolis, knowing that the Allied ships would hardly dare to bombard them at the risk of damaging it. Clashes between the ground forces on 1 December 1916 led to a couple of hundred casualties on either side. The Allied troops withdrew the following day, but not before the French ships had bombarded the palace for three hours, sending Queen Sophia into the cellars for safety. The royalist troops then began a systematic hunt for Venizelist sympathisers and killed all they found in cold blood. The Allies promptly recognised the

LEFT: Ioannis Kapodístrias, independent Greece's first prime minister, is assassinated in Návplio, the country's first capital. **ABOVE:** Athens as a village.

Venizelist government and a few months later sent word that they required the king's abdication. "Solicitous as ever of the interests of Greece", he went.

After the departure of King Constantine, Greece entered World War I on the Allied side and therefore shared the spoils at the Peace Conference. Greece made substantial territorial gains, including eastern Macedonia, parts of the coast of Asia Minor and many of the Aegean islands. The population of a greatly expanded Greece exploded from fewer than 3 million to nearly 7 million.

The sense of a homeland recovered stirred foreign as well as Greek emotions, but the country had little chance of meeting the economic expectations of the population, many of whom were homeless. Conditions were especially dire in the countryside and villages, so all roads led to Athens, where they were hardly any better.

The "Great Idea"

The wretched state of the country contributed to the *Megáli Idéa* ("Great Idea"), the extraordinary notion that all would be well if only the old Byzantine empire could be re-established, but this time with Greeks in charge. Turkey might have appeared powerless when the Great Powers dismantled the vestiges of the Ottoman empire as war reparations, but it was not going to countenance Greeks helping themselves to whatever pieces of Turkey they felt they needed to realise their Great Idea, presumably including Constantinople, now Istanbul.

In the event, the Greek army came within 100 km (60 miles) of Ankara, but thereafter the tables turned spectacularly. In February 1922, the Turks took Smyrna, an area on the Turkish coast first settled by Ionians escaping the Dorian invasions and more or less given back to Greece at the post-war peace conference.

The political repercussions of the disastrous adventure might have reminded Greeks that they had a tradition of despotism as well as

THE AFTERMATH OF SMYRNA

After taking Smyrna in 1922, the Turks burnt it to the ground amid the ensuing chaos of escaping Greek soldiers and civilians. A clause slipped into the peace treaty had provided for "the reciprocal and voluntary emigration of persons belonging to racial minorities" – in other words, the repatriation of ethnic Greeks stranded in Turkish territory after the re-drawing of the map, and vice versa.

The principle was brought into play to clear the human debris of the war of the "Great Idea". More than a million Greeks were repatriated, and a large proportion of them found their way to Athens.

democracy. In 1922 Colonel Nikolaos Plastiras led a coup that resulted in the prime minister, the commander-in-chief and other senior government members being court-martialled and shot. Political confusion split the country into republican and royalist factions.

Another soldier, General Theodoros Pangalos, took over in 1925 with the intention of running the country personally. He postponed elections, suspended the constitution, imposed press censorship and threatened to sack the civil service. He did not last long. Inviting comparison with the plotting that went on at the time of Hippias and Cleisthenes *(see page 24)*, he was replaced by General Georgios Kondilis whom Pangolos had previously exiled.

What Metaxas told Mussolini

General Ioannis Metaxas was chosen by King George to head a new government in 1936. A dictator who had modelled himself on Mussolini, he turned against fascism and his mentor in particular with the most famous retort in Greek history. Mussolini, envious of German *Blitzkrieg* successes, sought glory for himself by capturing Greece. The Italian forces began an advance from positions they had already occupied in Albania. Metaxas was given an ultimatum which, in effect, required him to give up Greece without a struggle.

On paper, it was a grotesque mismatch, but Metaxas allegedly responded with one word: *Óhi!* ("No!"). The anniversary of this famous rebuttal is celebrated on 28 October with a national holiday called Óhi Day.

The ferocity of the Greek defence drove the Italian army back into Albania where it had to be rescued by the intervention of Germany. The Germans occupied Greece but not as easily as might have been expected; in fact, the Greek resistance, led by crack British and Commonwealth troops, caused Hitler's invasion of Russia to be postponed for a critical six weeks, which in turn caused the German troops to be trapped by the relentless Russian winter.

It was small bands of Greek guerrillas who helped to delay the invasion of Russia. But divisions between these guerrilla forces during the German occupation were the genesis of the civil war. The resistance, mainly hit-and-run attacks launched from the mountains, eventually hardened into two bitterly hostile groups, one Communist and the other loyal to the Greek government which, with the king, was in exile in England.

Sensing – wrongly – that the fall of Italy and the Allied landings in southern Europe would soon bring about the liberation of Greece, the Communists became less interested in the German occupation than in the swift elimination of potential future rivals. Athens was liberated almost bloodlessly when the Germans withdrew northwards in October 1944, and the British commander ordered the guerrilla forces to disperse and surrender their arms.

LEFT: Constantine I and the royal family at home.
RIGHT: German officers on the Acropolis, 1944.

Disastrous civil war

The Communists responded with a national uprising which at one point left the central district of Athens as one of the few parts of the country not under their control. The uprising was put down, not without difficulty, by British troops diverted from the fighting that was still going on in Italy.

The Communists were split over what to try next. Some wanted to concentrate on infiltrating the political system; others took to the hills again, particularly in the north where they had cross-border support from the communists in Albania and, for a while, in Yugoslavia.

The "third round" of the civil war lasted three years. It was an atrocious business by any standards, and one which today the normally voluble Greeks are loath to discuss. When the Communists looked like losing, tens of thousands of children were taken from their homes and spirited to camps behind the Iron Curtain where it was intended that they would be imbued with the ideology that would equip them one day for the "fourth round". This sorry chapter in Greek affairs was brought to an end largely by the split between Stalin and Tito of Yugoslavia. The latter closed the border to the Communist guerrillas, and without this vital route their revolution was doomed.

In spite of difficulties over Cyprus, Greece made reasonable progress on many fronts after the civil war, and as early as 1951 the Communists were recognised as a parliamentary party. February 1964 was a subtle landmark: Georgios Papandreou won with a clear majority of 53 percent of the votes cast, and it looked as if Greece might at last have torn itself away from the fragile coalitions on which previous governments had depended. But Papandreou 's effort to advance the interests of his son, Andreas, especially after the latter had been identified with a group of allegedly revolutionary left-wing army officers in Cyprus, returned Greek politics to its customary disjointed tension.

The Colonels take over

One crisis led to another until a group of unknown army officers took it upon themselves to rescue Greece from chaos and Communism. Their leader, Colonel Georgios Papadopoulos, described Greece as "a patient strapped to the operating table" on whom he and his colleagues proposed to carry out some surgery. The treatment required the arrest of 7,000 political opponents almost immediately and included, for example, a ban on miniskirts and an order to the civil service to answer all letters within three days. When the king tried to intervene with a feeble counter-coup, he was swiftly swept aside.

Public opinion abroad was outraged by the colonels, who were condemned as an affront to the birthplace of democracy. Ironically, it was in one of the cradles of democracy that, once again, modern democracy was ailing.

The junta collapsed in July 1974 after taking the country to the brink of war with

Above: the actress Melina Mercouri returns to Athens in 1974 after her exile during the Colonels' rule.
Right: an Athenian votes in 2004's general election.

Turkey. Other army officers, perhaps mindful of the "Great Idea" fiasco, forced them out and asked unconditionally for a civilian government. Konstantinos Karamanlis, who had run the country for eight years before Papandreou, returned from exile in Paris for another six years in office.

By the end of his second premiership, in 1980, he had achieved his main objective – membership of the European Community, which Greece joined in January 1981. But in the same year, Karamanlis lost a general election by a landslide to Andreas Papandreou and his new radical party, the Panhellenic Socialist Movement (PASOK).

Papandreou was succeeded by Konstantínos Simítis, who introduced a tight fiscal policy to try to halt Greece's galloping inflation and to conform to EU requirements for adopting the euro. Simitis announced he would not be standing in the 2004 election, which became a showdown between the scions of two political dynasties; Georgios Papandreou, whose father and grandfather had both been prime minister, and Konstantinos Karamanlis, nephew of the former president.

Relations with Turkey

The centre-right New Democracy party soundly defeated the socialist PASOK and Karamanlis became prime minister. He promptly appointed himself Minister of Culture, too, taking on the responsibility for overseeing the preparations for the 2004 Olympic Games, regarded by most as a huge success.

The new government, supported by Papandreou as leader of the opposition, has worked hard to defuse the age-old tensions between Greece and Turkey. Relations between the two nations are perhaps more stable now than they have been for decades. On the economic front, inflation has been dropping steadily from the alarming high rates of the 1980s and '90s, unemployment is falling and Greece is experiencing steady growth within the EU. ❑

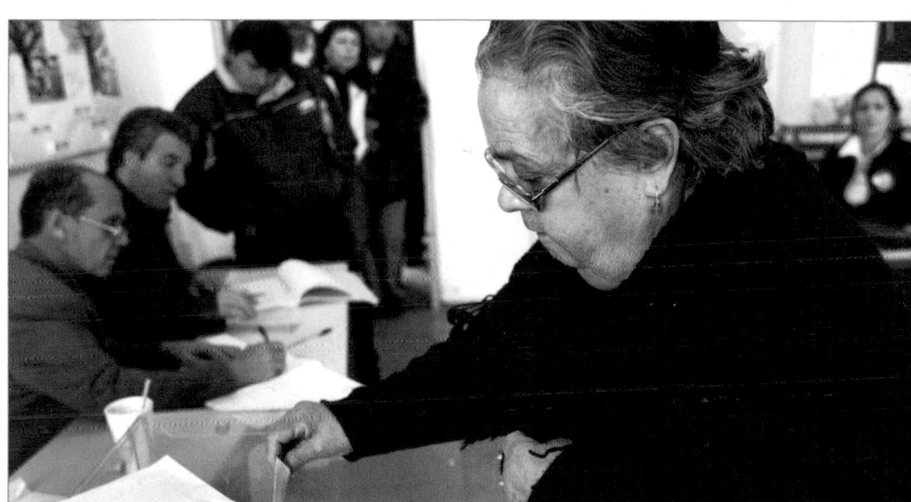

ANDREAS PAPANDREOU

Papandreou was a colourful character. In 1989, aged 70, having nearly died from a heart condition, he made public his affair with a air stewardess, narrowly lost an election to the conservative New Democracy Party, divorced his wife and married the air stewardess, and was implicated in a financial scandal. Cleared of all charges in 1992, he won the election the following year. However, failing health prevented him from exercising firm leadership. He was unable to resolve the problems of the debt-ridden economy or to ease the strains in relations with Greece's Balkan neighbours. Papandreou retired in January 1996 and died in June.

THE ATHENIANS

The citizens of Athens are noisy, spontaneous, unpredictable and passionate about politics and sport. They cherish the traditional values of friendship, family, patriotism and the Orthodox Church, but have also been swift to embrace modern consumerism

Athens is notoriously hard to pin down; a modern-ancient, European-Balkan city, balanced on the cusp of east and west. Its citizens too, defy easy characterisation. Pulled between their traditions and their undying enthusiasm for modernity and consumerism, they are full of contradictions; whatever you find to define them, the opposite may well also be true.

Athenians are often humorously cynical, but they are also seriously patriotic. They are unquestioning about their religious affiliation but they don't take it too seriously and are not above taking measures to avoid attracting the "evil eye". They still perform their traditional dances at parties and celebrations, but few will hesitate to break off in the middle to answer a mobile phone.

In fact, as a cornerstone of contemporary Greek society, mobiles are ever-present, never switched off, used for countless text messages and eminently compatible with the Greek love of spontaneity, lateness, change of plans and conversation.

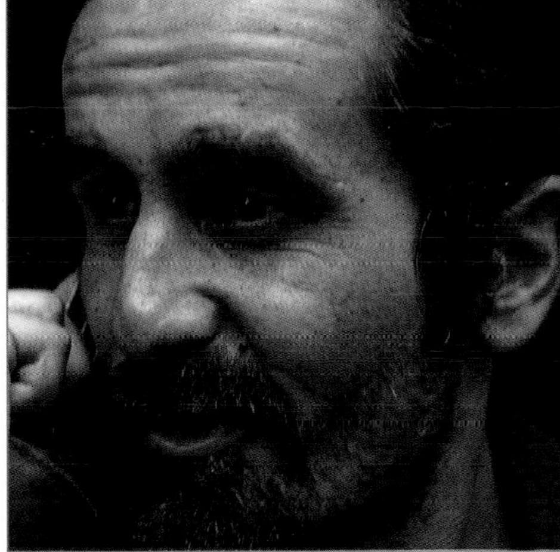

Traditional and modern

Athenians number around 4 million – more than a third of Greece's population of 11 million – if you count the overspill from the capital, which is spreading over surrounding Attica. Anyone walking around the city can easily observe how Athenians loves their traditions, but loves something new and imported even more. The driver of a smart foreign jeep, which is blaring out Greek pop music, puts down his *frappé* (the ubiquitous iced Nescafé) to cross himself when passing a church. He then double-parks outside McDonald's, and clutching his keys, mobile and cigarettes, the vital trinity of an Athenian's existence, he plays with his worry-beads (or their substitute, a key ring) while waiting in line, and buys special Greek Mc-fasting food if it is Lent.

This driver does not use a seat-belt and is far more likely to be killed in his car than his northern European counterpart, but he is nevertheless statistically destined to live to a

LEFT: meeting up in Sýntagma.
RIGHT: a mobile is an essential part of Greek life.

greater age. And that's despite the fact that he smokes, eats too much meat and prefers café life to the gym.

City neighbourhoods

Younger Athenians are the first generation to be born and bred city-dwellers. Their parents and grandparents nearly all came from somewhere else; home was a village or an island, to which they returned for holidays, to vote, to be married, to baptise their children, to pick the olives and to be buried. But each wave of incomers made its mark on Athens. If you take "the electric" train (built in 1869 for a steam engine), you start off in Kifisiá, the northern suburb where high society continues to prefer the cooler climate for its spacious villas. You end up south of the city in Piraeus, the port, which is still proud of its working traditions, its football team (Olympiakós) and its musical waterside dives.

In between these two extremes are countless neighbourhoods, all with different characters: the former industrial area of Gázi ("Gaslands"), undergoing a metamorphosis into a fashionable, arty cultural centre, and now filled with theatres, galleries, restaurants and clubs; the old refugees' districts, where Greeks from Turkey camped after the 1922 "Catastrophe", where you can still identify

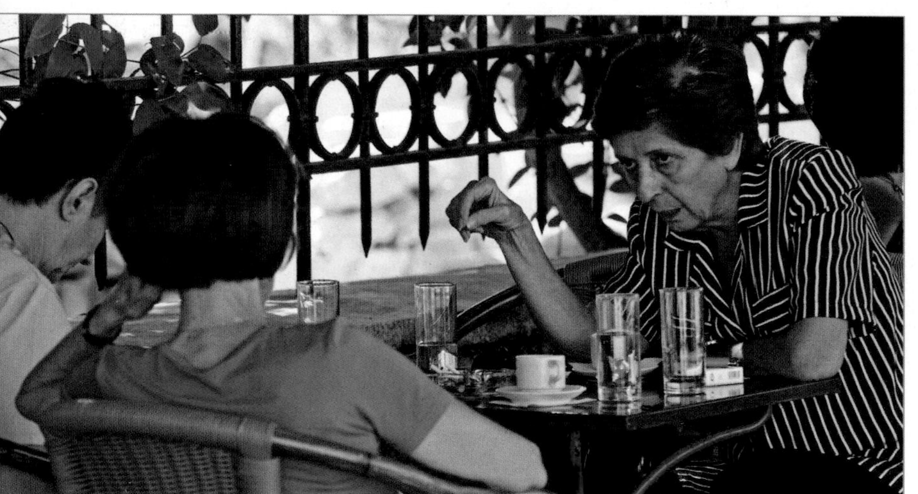

The Weight of History

The bewildered visitor who faces the architectural confusion and chaotic ways of Athens would perhaps empathise more with its ebullient though stressed citizens if offered some explanation. When, in 1834, Athens was selected as capital of the newly independent Greece, it was a scruffy village with some goat-infested ruins. A charming little neo-classical city was established during the 19th century, but there is not much trace of that nowadays. The 20th century made sure of that, with its wars, refugees, dictatorships, Nazi occupation, civil war and migration.

By the 1950s, Greece was shattered, villagers were pouring into the capital, and something had to be done. Using a system known as *antiparohí* ("exchange"), Athenians gave up their attractive family houses with gardens in part-exchange for a couple of apartments in the five-storey concrete block that was quickly thrown up in its place. War-weary and poverty-stricken, most people had little time or inclination for niceties such as planning, prettiness or parks.

By the time the tragically anaesthetic Colonels' tyranny ended in 1974, Athens was an over-built urban jungle, with a dark cloud of pollution hovering above it. However, if Athens' character is founded on past suffering, the good news is that these days it is re-inventing itself

some of the tiny dwellings they built to replace the tents; and the chic, café-society streets of Kolonáki, which are a magnet to anyone with political or social ambitions. Despite their varied and shifting identities, each neighbourhood has a strong sense of community, held in place by its own school, church, weekly street market and a *platía* (square) where children play, adults buy cigarettes or newspapers from the *períptero* (kiosk) and sip coffee in a café.

The legacy of the Olympics

Recent years have seen many dramatic changes in Athens, and none more evident than those associated with the 2004 Olympics. In the run-up to the games, a huge amount of money was poured into building roads, railways, stadiums and a new airport. Gleaming metro and tram systems were inaugurated, interesting modern buildings erected, thousands of trees planted and a beautiful pedestrian walkway replaced the traffic-choked road which previously encircled the Acropolis. The infamous old *néfos* (pollution cloud) appeared to have retreated somewhat, and while the hideous 1960s apartment blocks were not demolished, many were given a facelift and painted.

True, Athens' hugely successful Olympics left the city with daunting debts, some underused sports facilities and a feeling of the morning-after, but it is hard to keep an Athenian down. The economy may be less bullish than it was, but Greeks are still incomparably more wealthy than they were a decade or two ago. Luxury apartment blocks and expensive cars are increasingly prevalent in the capital, and Athenians' growing tendency to run up credit card debt is only a reflection of their newfound dedication to shopping; of all Europeans, Greeks spend the highest percentage of their income on clothes and shoes.

Immigrant workers

Quite apart from architecture and infrastructure, Athens has also changed, yet again, in terms of population. Since the 1990s, more than a million foreign migrants have joined a population of 10 million Greeks, with large numbers in the capital.

Suddenly, all the construction workers were foreigners (many of whom had climbed over dangerous mountains or braved unseaworthy boats to start this new life), and it was hard to find a taverna kitchen without an Albanian chopping vegetables and washing up. Poles, Ukrainians, Serbs, Kurds, Pakistanis, Africans and Chinese all came, occupying the less desirable neighbourhoods and basement flats and taking the jobs Greeks didn't want.

Athenians were initially taken aback by the dramatic influx and a degree of racism flared up (though not to the degree found in the USA and northern Europe). Albanians, who make up around half the total immigrants, were particularly demonised and unfairly blamed for increases in crime. However, as a second generation of migrants grows up attending Greek schools, the tension is gradually decreasing and Greeks are realising that these newest Athenians are contributing in many ways to the life of their city.

Nonetheless, the fact that Athens is the only European capital with no mosque for its Muslim population – although one is now in the planning stage – is a shaming reflection on the prejudices of certain Greek clerics and their supporters. That these sentiments can be

LEFT: an intense discussion over coffee.
RIGHT: browsing in the city centre.

traced back to the Greek perspective on "400 years of slavery" under the Muslim Ottomans, and that minarets symbolised the oppression of the conqueror, should no longer be an excuse.

Everyday religion

Many Greeks feel both blessed and burdened by the glories of their ancient past. History may have given them their language and some beautiful monuments, but its legacy has been manipulated and plundered by outsiders and its images used to prop up dubious political ambitions and a sense of insecurity. If the shining example of Pericles' Athens was one column on which modern Greek identity was founded in the 19th century, the other was the Greek Orthodox Church. And though the ancient ideals were largely theoretical, popular attachment to the living religion was thoroughly hands-on.

Even today, more than 90 percent of Greeks declare themselves Orthodox Christians (the remainder consist of a few Catholics and Jews and a minority Muslim population, mostly in the North).

The Church forms the backdrop to most of life's major events and only a tiny minority avoids being baptised, married and buried under its auspices. Most Greeks are named

FAMILY VALUES

There is little doubt about the central position of the family in Greece. Greeks have the lowest divorce rates in Europe, the fewest babies born outside marriage, extended families that live close together and support each other and children who are placed at the centre of affectionate attention. Shops still shut for several hours in the middle of the day, a timetable created to accommodate the small family business and the traditional midday family meal plus siesta (the period between 2 and 5pm is known as the "public quiet hours", when one should avoid making phone calls and noise).

However, within the sanctuary of the family, there is a darker side and things are changing rapidly. The lack of unmarried mothers corresponds to a high rate of abortions. The continued presence of the older generation brings pressure to conform and conservative values regarding homosexuality and child-rearing, and grandmothers who baby-sit sometimes just reflect the increasing number of badly-paid working women who can't afford to employ a child-minder.

Shops may close for a long lunch-break, but few families gather for a communal midday meal on weekdays, let alone a nap: children have too many lessons, workers have too far to commute, and everyone is just too busy.

after their grandparents with saints' names, which they celebrate on the appropriate name day (even popular ancient Greek names have been allotted their "saint's day"), and there are very few who don't attend midnight Mass at Easter, the greatest religious celebration of the year.

Priests are routinely called in to bless schools, new houses and businesses, for exorcism and for various memorials following a death. And while there are growing calls to separate the Church from the state due to corruption and lack of transparency, it is unquestionably an integral element of Greek existence.

Patronage and corruption

Linking families and sanctioned by the Church is the institution of the *koumbáros* (female, *koumbára*), who acts as best man or woman at weddings, or as a godparent. A *koumbáros* is usually a close friend, but the bond is also a spiritual one, and he or she is treated as an honoured relative. Politicians use this relationship to create political loyalty: many are godparents to dozens if not hundreds of babies, whose extended families are then assumed to be guaranteed voters. Naturally, those families will assume that having a *koumbáros* in Parliament or in the Ministry may well help at some point with smoothing over some paperwork, or with providing a desirable job for life in the public sector.

Patronage and political favours are such an integral part of public life that it is generally accepted that you can't get much done without "knowing someone". Ministers have a special office just for dealing with political favours, known by the originally Turkish word, *rousfetiá*, and despite claims that corruption is being tackled, there is evidence of it at all levels, from big business down to the lowliest public servant. Few Athenians man-

LEFT: An Orthodox baptism in Agía Ekateríni, Pláka.
ABOVE: a sociable drink.

EDUCATION AT ALL COSTS

Every parent believes that education is the key to his or her offspring's advancement in life and is prepared to make huge sacrifices to fund this cause. Unfortunately, despite the state's premise of free education for all, few believe that school alone can provide an adequate quality of teaching.

The parallel system of private crammers known as frontistíria is almost unavoidable if a student wishes to enter university, and while many younger pupils take extra lessons in foreign languages, three-quarters of teenagers in the last three years of school attend these crammers, often until late into the evening.

age to avoid the bureaucrat who expects extra payment to provide some insignificant document, no building goes up without "oiling" those who control the tangle of red tape, and most people assume that you won't get good treatment in a state hospital if you don't give "an envelope" with money to the doctor (who may actually name his or her price).

Political passions

Politics, like sport, is a matter of passionate fanaticism and chauvinism. Loyalty to the Left or Right often goes back generations, and the enmity and prejudices stemming from the horrific Civil War (1944–49, in two phases) and the Colonels' dictatorship (1967–74) are only gradually fading. Nowadays, the two large political parties, the conservative New Democracy and the socialist PASOK, are edging towards the middle ground, and among signs of the diminishing tension is the successful dismantling by police of the notorious home-grown terrorist group, 17 November.

Students, however, are still strongly politicised, with party organisations instigating numerous protests and sit-ins. Athenian politics is never calm. A small but powerful elite forms the centre of the capital's political maelstrom, dominated by owners of TV channels (who often own sports teams and construction businesses as well), influential journalists, powerful lawyers and politicians. Less visible but just as influential are the super-rich ship-owning families, whose dynasties frequently live in Geneva and London as well as Athens, but who retain a firm foothold in their home country.

What freedom means

Ask an Athenian what is the most important quality in life and he or she may well answer *eleftheria* – "freedom". Ever since Greeks used the slogan "Freedom or Death" in their revolution against the Ottomans in 1821, it has been a tenet of what it means to be Greek. These days, it means freedom from the kind of oppressors and bullies who tormented ordinary Greeks for so much of the 20th century, but it also applies at a more personal level. Freedom may just as well mean driving your car as if you were racing on a PlayStation, smoking where it's forbidden or making a noise because it's fun (turning up the TV or the radio, honking the horn or shouting conversations which could be spoken).

Freedom is finding the time to sit down for a lengthy coffee with a friend when you have two jobs, you're late and you've parked the car in the middle of the road. It is also having the spirit to drink, dance and sing. The enduring popularity of this ideal (whose patron saint has to be Kazantzakis' Zorba) is reflected in central Athens' 1am traffic jams, which rival Monday morning gridlock. These are largely due to people arriving at night clubs, with "the *bouzoúkia*" being just as popular as discos.

Fostering friendship

If your family represents security, going out with your *paréa* (a loyal company of friends) represents liberty. Certainly, there is nowhere more representative of Athens' contradictory character than a *bouzoúki* club. It is here that eastern and western music merge, that luxuriously modern laser-lit environments host traditional dances, and that people forget about their frantic, burdensome city lives as they drink whisky, sing familiar songs and dance until dawn, even when they know that they're soon going to be late for work. ❑

LEFT: an anti-war demonstration in Athens.

Olympic Fallout

The wildly successful staging of the 2004 Olympics – arguably eclipsing the 2000 Sydney Games – was a tremendous boost to Greece's (self-) image. Many foreign and domestic journalists had long made a living by slagging off the city's initially disorganised preparations, but on the night they were compelled to eat large portions of humble pie. Despite heavy security, attendees had a great time, and the televised opening and closing ceremonies – even the cheesier bits – were worth several seasons of tourist-board publicity.

In the wake of the Games, Athens undeniably works and looks better. Many infrastructure projects were completed that would not otherwise have been, as the inflexible deadline of August 2004 concentrated minds. Both the new airport and gleaming metro were already operational in 2001, the vital Attikí Odós ring-road by 2002 and the tram by July 2004. Much of the ancient centre *(see page 77)* was pedestrianised and landscaped, with pollution-spewing tour coaches banished from the immediate environs of the Parthenon.

Counting the cost

Spanish architect Santiago Calatrava's daring, wing-like, arc-suspended roof for the main stadium at the Olympic Complex in Maroússi provided an unforgettable logo, visible from afar, in a city not known for strikingly original modern architecture. Calatrava also contributed the pedestrian suspension bridge at Katehåki metro station, the cables held aloft by a steel "tooth" said to be modelled on the prow of an ancient sailing vessel.

But all these goodies didn't come cheap. Even discounting the public transport projects which were part-funded by EU money, the Games cost Greece about €11 billion – nearly three times the original estimate – which included €1bn for security alone. Judging from the experience of Montreal and Munich, this sum will take taxpayers around 25 years to pay off.

The construction of the sporting venues got off to a slow start, and by 2003 the need to complete them on time meant hiring huge numbers of foreign workers at overtime rates (a substantial portion of the cost overrun). Hasty building and corner-cutting frequently resulted in poor-quality workmanship, plus 13 fatal accidents. Since the Games, some of this workforce, rather than go home, found a way to disappear into the burgeoning ranks of illegal immigrants.

The venues themselves – more than 20 of them, some pre-existing – threaten to

become white elephants partly because of their remoteness: they are scattered all across Attikí, as well as in Maroússi. Two local football teams rent out the main stadium, the Ministry of Public Works now occupies the press centre, and the atheletes' village is being converted to affordable housing for essential public workers.

But the fate of the rest is uncertain, other than ongoing maintenance bills and repairs for flaws occasioned by slapdash construction. This probably isn't quite what Games boosters had in mind when they claimed that hosting the Olympics would create thousands of permanent new jobs. ❑

RIGHT: traditional dancers perform at the opening ceremony of the 2004 Olympics.

FOOD AND DRINK

The cuisine of Greece – and Athens in particular – has seen a welcome renaissance in recent years. Side by side with the arrival of international cooking styles, regional and traditional recipes have been refined to produce an authentic and distinctive Greek cuisine. The wines are worth investigating, too

Until the mid-1980s, the Athenian culinary scene was monochrome and, frankly, provincial – and the province in question was contiguous Attikí (Attica), with its typical courtyard-set taverns surrounded by ranks of barrels containing the (in)famous regional wine, *retsína*, apparently the universal solvent for lukewarm portions of oily, orange-and-green-tinted stews.

There were, to be sure, outposts of kebabs and other more elaborate examples of Asia Minor cooking (especially sweets) in the refugee neighbourhoods, a few "continental cuisine" restaurants dotted around the wealthier districts, and a handful of well-hidden *stékia* (hangouts) catering to internally migrated islanders with *oúzo* and functionally presented seafood titbits.

But the casual visitor was unlikely to appreciate these nuances, and apt to come away with an impression of Greek food – "Greese", some cynics opined – as libellous and distorted as "Greek Nights" are to real Greek music, or as Periclean Athens is to the whole spectrum of its history.

At last, an oil shortage

What changed this for ever was the coincidence of increased prosperity and the ability of the younger generation to travel)a few training as chefs overseas, but the majority merely acquiring more sophisticated tastes), and the emergence of a quality wine industry *(see page 57)*, whose products cried out for worthy food to accompany them.

Most importantly, there occurred a rediscovery of – and resurgent pride taken in – the regional specialties of Greece which had been elbowed aside by an infatuation with American-style fast food, for which an earlier generation of returned emigrants was largely to blame.

The traditional styles that re-emerged involved fresh raw ingredients, simple (but not necessarily stark) presentation and minimalist preparation evoking the rudimentary equipment to be found in an olive-grove cottage, alpine shepherd's colony or the deck of a

LEFT: tripe for sale in the central market.
RIGHT: *kouloúria*, traditional street food.

pitching fishing-boat. Traditionally, nothing of any utilitarian value had gone to waste, not even the insipid *koúmaro* (arbutus) fruit, which is fermented into moonshine.

Snails emerging after the first rains, *vólvi* (the onion-like bulbs of a meadow flower), wild asparagus, semi-toxic *ovriés* (bryony) and *hórta* (radicchio, vlyte or chicory) plucked from a hillside, purslane sprigs weeded from the garden; all were fair game for the resourceful, hard-pressed country-dweller, and a world away from the fare trotted out for the holiday-makers who descended on Greece when mass tourism took hold during the 1960s.

Restaurants and specialities

But for "daily use" at a reasonable cost, both Athenians and visitors are likely to repair to one of the following types of establishment. The *inomagerío*, literally "wine-and-cook-house", has seen a revival from near-extinction; its fare overlaps with the nearly-as-endangered *estiatório* ("restaurant"), enthroning the casserole and steam-tray dishes known as *magireftá* ("cooked") or *ladherá* ("oiled" – though nowadays in more moderate quantities).

These include vegetarian dishes – until the 1960s most Greeks only ate meat a few times a month – such as *anginháres ala políta* (artichoke hearts, carrots, dill and potatoes), and *briám* or *tourloú* (the Greek ratatouille), based on courgettes, aubergine (eggplant), tomatoes, garlic and onion. Lentils and chickpeas turn up as hearty soups, *hórta* is boiled to limpness and drizzled with oil and lemon, while mincemeat creeps into *lahanodolmádes* (stuffed cabbage leaves), *giouvarlákia* (rice-and-mince-balls in egg-lemon sauce) and *soutzoukákia* (meat rissoles in a red sauce).

Taverna food

Moving along the spectrum from *estiatória* and *inomagiría* there are *tavérnes* – which tend to have more cold *orektiká* (appetisers), more salads, and some grilled meat dishes – and *psistariés* (grill specialists), which retain salads and appetisers on the menu but dispense entirely with *magireftá*. Pulses are much favoured as *orektiká: fáva* is that bean puréed, then served with chopped onions, lemon

HOW COUNTRY COOKING WAS GIVEN A MAKEOVER

Nostalgia has been a powerful force in rehabilitating Greek country cuisine, now that its associations with peasant poverty have receded; there are celebrity TV chefs, and a growing shelf of cookbooks featuring the most obscure recipes from every corner of the Hellenic world, in particular Crete, which has contributed a disproportionate share to "updated" Greek cuisine.

And, concerning "Greese", there was no longer any need to douse almost everything in ladles of olive oil to create a sensation of fullness and quell hunger-pangs in impecunious eaters of protein-poor dishes. The intrinsic flavour of other ingredients could finally emerge, and for contemporary and/or foreign palates the platters became that much more appetising.

What this means for diners is an elevation of eateries to a new level – both in more attention to the cooking and to the dining environment – plus the resurrection of some types of restaurant that were on the verge of dying out.

There has been a simultaneous arrival in the city of almost every imaginable cuisine, with Italian, Japanese, French and Middle Eastern the most common. Listings magazines arbitrarily subdivide the available options ("modern cuisine", "creative cuisine", "fun restaurants", "lounge restaurants" and so on). Prices can be high.

wedges, a solitary olive and oil – a heavy but much-esteemed comfort food – while *mavromátika* (black-eyed peas) are soaked, boiled and then served chilled garnished with onion and parsley.

Taramosaláta, *tzatzíki* and *melitsanosaláta* will be familiar from the menus of a thousand overseas kebab houses, but in Athens no taverna with an eye to its reputation will avoid making these in-house to a notably chunky consistency; pre-purchased catering packs are for tourist tavernas or "snack bars" only. Similarly, no taverna worth its salt will demur from the task of preparing hand-cut chips, fresh, daily, with a rage lately for round slices, fried and drained to perfection.

Tomatoes, cucumbers, peppers, olives and *féta* cheese are the legendary components of the so-called *horiátiki* or peasant's salad, a summer mainstay. But between October and April when most foreigners are absent, Athenians revel in other raw vegetables: cabbage with grated carrot in early winter, later on various medleys of lettuces, rocket, radishes, spring onions and dill.

Meat dishes

The term *psistariá* covers many categories. A *gyrádiko* specialises in *gýros* (slices of pork cut from a dense-packed cylinder, packed into pitta bread, the Greek equivalent of the Turkish *doner kebab*). A *souvlatzídiko* concentrates on *souvláki*, with perhaps a sideline in "kebab" and *loukániko* (thick, coarse-ground sausage). Traditionally *souvláki* is pork-based between November and April, but made of lamb the rest of the year.

Meanwhile, a *brizoládiko* concentrates on chops, pork chops at that, with perhaps *pantsétta* (spare ribs, not belly-bacon as elsewhere) thrown in. Athenians used not to be big beef-eaters, but recent years have seen a veritable craze for prime cuts – New Zealand Black Angus, Macedonian charolais or water buffalo, Argentine churrasco – and high-end steakhouses serving them up.

The diametric opposite, status-wise, of those are the handful of late-night-to-small-hours *patsatzídika*, most famously in Athens' central meat market, which specialise in *patsás* (tripe soup), the traditional hangover preventative. The game you're most likely to encounter is rabbit, either hunted or farmed, which finds its way on to menus as *kounéli stifádo* (stewed with small onions).

Seafood – at a price

Seafood (including the stereotypical *kalamári* and chips) is seen as such an integral part of a visit to the Athens coast that it may come as a shock to realise just how expensive it is locally, especially wild scaly fresh fish. You're usually better off setting your sights on humble, seasonally available fish than on the gilt-

LEFT: pepper stuffed with mushroom and ewe's milk cheese. **RIGHT:** appetizer with ouzo.

HARD CHEESE

Féta – for which Greece has secured European court rules protecting its "registered trademark" status, akin to France's protective jealousy for the word "Champagne" – is the most famous of numerous Greek cheeses, which come in a wide range, both soft and hard, creamy and sharp. Perhaps suprisingly, Greeks are Europe's top per-capita annual cheese-eaters. Cow, goat and sheep milk, are the raw materials, alone or in unpredictable combinations. Hard cheeses are for grating or grilling, soft or crumbly for spreading and stuffing. *Saganáki* is the term for any suitable cheese, fried, or any cheese-based sauce.

head bream and sea bass familiar from northern European supermarket counters, which are likely to be farmed, or be inferior products imported from Morocco or Egypt. There are *psarotavérnes* (fish specialists) along both the western and eastern Attic coasts, but prices are a good 15 percent higher on average than in the rest of the country.

Seasonally restricted species include shrimp and sole in the spring, swordfish starting in early summer and anchovies, picarel, sardines and sand smelt at the cusp of summer and autumn. For the adventurous, there are unusual molluscs such as *petalídes* (limpets), *gialisterés* (smooth Venus), *kydónia* (cockles), *kténia* (scallops) and *petrosolínes* (razor clams) which must be eaten alive to avoid poisoning; their twitching when dribbled with lemon juice is the defining test.

Even more specialist shellfish include sea-urchin roe, pitched as a natural Viagra; native oysters *(strídia)*, small, round but tasty; and *avgotáraho* (pressed grey-mullet roe from Mesolóngi), used as a flavour-accent in some of the more nouvelle eateries. Year-round staples – and thus often frozen – include cuttlefish *(soupiá)*, grilled or stewed in wine; octopus, *(ktapódi)* treated the same way; and farmed mussels *(mýdia)*, either steamed or served in red piquant *saganáki* sauce.

MORE THAN JUST *OÚZO*

All of the shellfish and other fishy items mentioned above, plus a few meaty titbits and *oúzo* – see opposite – form the stock in trade of the *ouzerí* (plural *ouzeríes*). These were originally simple places in which to down shots of *oúzo*, accompanied by small snacks. But since the early 1990s *ouzeríes* have evolved into more sophisticated eateries, Athens' trendy equivalents of Spanish tapas bars. They are best patronised in a group, where you make your choice from the *dískos* or tray on which the waiter will display the cold platters or *mezedákia*, dipping into these while your hot entrées are cooked to order.

And to finish...

Western-style desserts are recent arrivals in Athens, although some high-end tavernas have become formidably competent at Italian sweets such as *tiramisu* or *pannacotta*. The traditional Greek *epidórpio* (dessert) is generally limited to the usual West Asian sweetmeats such as *bakalavás* and *kataïfi*, milk-based dishes such as *ryzógalo* (rice pudding) or *kréma* (custard), *simigdalísios halvás* (semolina *halvá*) or – increasingly rare these days – *kydóni sto foúrno* (baked quince), available only in the autumn. ❑

ABOVE: Le 48 restaurant and bar.

What to drink

The renaissance in quality Greek **wine** making began some two decades ago, finally taking full advantage of nearly 300 indigenous grape varieties. But the small production capacity of the best vintners means that little of the decent stuff goes abroad to acquire a reputation, so Athens remains one of the best places to enjoy top Greek labels. Names and domaines to look out for include the rival Lazaridis brothers from Drama, Papaïoannnou from Neméa on the Peloponnese, Athanasiadi from central Greece, Tsantali from Rapsáni on the Thessaly-Macedonian border, Spyropoulos and Tselepos from Mandinía in the Peloponnese, Gentilini Robola from Kefalloniá, and almost anything from Límnos. As a general but not infallible rule, the mainland produces better reds, the islands superior whites. Some excellent fortified dessert wines hail from Sámos and Santoríni.

The Greek culinary revolution also rescued bulk or house wine from near-disappearance in the early 1990s, and it's now back in fashion, the magic words are *varelísio* (barrelled) or *hýma* (in bulk). Bulk wine was traditionally kept in barrels – nowadays apt to be merely decorative – but still sold by the quarter-, half- or full litre, served either in glass flagons or the brightly coloured tin "monkey-cups" called *kantária*. Quality is highly variable, so initially sample an unknown vintage in small measures; at any rate it won't break the bank. Bulk *retsína*, pine-resinated wine, is still very much part of the landscape, though a somewhat acquired taste; bottled brands are usually more consistent in quality.

Beer has historically been foreign-label made under licence at just three mainland breweries, Amstel, Heineken and Kaiser being the main brands. However, as part of the re-assertion of Greek pride, several genuinely local lagers have appeared since the late 1990s, capturing a respectable market share. In descending order of consistency and easy availability, they are Mythos, Alpha, Zorbas, Vergina and Pils Hellas. Perhaps best of all, Athens has its very own microbrewery. Craft, out on Alexándras Avenue, make a tasty pilsner and an amber lager.

Oúzo is 40–48 percent alcohol, distilled from grape-mash residue left over from winemaking, and then flavoured with aniseed or fennel. There are nearly 30 name brands of *oúzo*, with the best reckoned to be from Lésvos and Sámos, or Zítsa and Týrnavos on the mainland. Variants of *oúzo* are *tsípouro* (unflavoured, from the north mainland, Thássos and the Sporades) and terebinth-flavoured *tsikoudiá* (from Crete).

RIGHT: the local brew.

You will be served a glass with a few fingers' worth of *oúzo* or *tsípouro*, plus water (in a separate glass) to be tipped into your *oúzo* until it turns a milky white. It is common to add ice cubes *(pagáki)*, a bowl of which will be supplied. The next measure up from a glass is a *karafáki* – a deceptively small 200-ml vial, which will quickly render you legless if you don't alternate tippling with *mezedákia*.

Greek **brandy** (Metaxa) is double-distilled from wines made from three varieties of grape, then married with aged muscat. It comes in three starred grades: the finest, seven-star, has matured in oak barrels for at least seven years. ❑

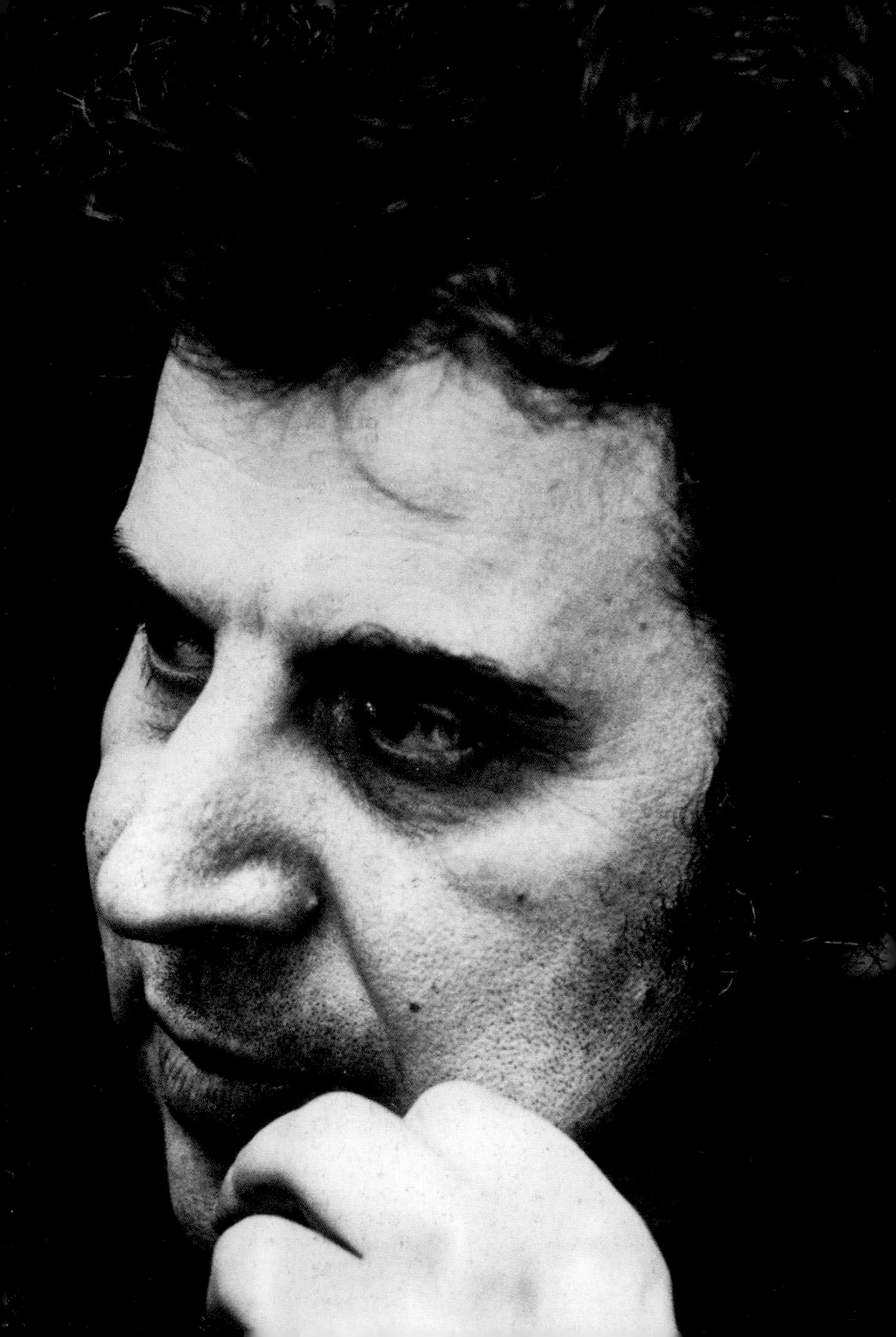

WORDS AND MUSIC

Greek literature flourished in the 20th century, but Athens' primary cultural passion is music, in concert halls, open-air theatres and countless clubs and cafés throughout the city

Like most Mediterranean cities, Athens has a split personality. In summer, the streets fill with tourists. The Athenians who are free to leave head for their summer houses by the sea, but tourists must be entertained and fed, and the so city is alive with talk and the sounds of Greek music until the small hours.

Athens on a summer's night is perhaps the noisiest city in Europe, and the the locals seem to need very little sleep. In trellised courtyards, on rooftops, in the open-air theatre of Dionysíou Areopagítou, at improvised venues among the ruins of antiquity, in suburban parks, or closed-off streets, there are performances of ancient drama, classical music, and every imaginable type of modern Greek music.

All-night sessions

But these performances are only the prelude to an evening's entertainment. After they attend a performance, Greeks get down to the serious business of eating, drinking, and talking, a pastime they never seem to tire of. Serious night-owls may end an evening at a *bouzoúki* club that only really gets going around 1am and continues until the sun rises.

When summer ends and the stream of tourists thins to a trickle, music and drama move inside to the hundreds of small theatres and nightclubs that offer the Athenians a distinctly Greek style of entertainment. This is the season for new theatrical productions and fresh musical offerings. It is the time when publishers release their new titles, and the cultural life of the city thrives. Poets, composers, novelists, film-directors and playwrights meet one another after the long summer holidays and exchange notes on the summer and their new projects. Athens in winter is the testing-ground for artists, above all for singers and musicians, who present their work at the musical clubs of central Athens. A successful season in Athens means a new recording in the spring, and despite the many provincial venues that thrive in winter, Athens is still the capital where the record companies have their headquarters and where reputations are made.

Although more poetry is published in Athens than any other city of Europe, music

LEFT: composer Mikos Theodorakis mixed music with politics. **RIGHT:** Savina Yiannatou.

is probably the most popular and well-patronised art of the city.

For classical music, some of it by contemporary Greek composers, the modern Mégaron Mousikís is the main venue. It is a fine new concert hall offering a steady stream of art music, and it houses an excellent archival music library. In summer, the open-air theatre on Dionysíou Areopagítou offers an alternative and spectacular venue for anything from the Bolshoi Ballet to jazz. What is unique about Athenian musical life are not these international arenas but the hundreds of small venues where distinctively Greek music is performed.

The music of Athens

At the end of the 19th century Athens was still a small provincial capital, embroiled in external and internal struggles that would continue with little respite until the mid-1970s. Despite, and perhaps partly because of the endless years of war, occupation and political strife that beset their country, Greeks continued to patronise the many venues where music was played. In the first decades of the 20th century the Athenians had a passion for musical reviews that featured romantic, European-style songs. Operetta was also popular with the middle classes, and songs from both these forms soon found their way into the tavernas where Athenians still spend a great deal of their time. Two types of musical café also became popular in the period before World War I. One was the *café chantant*, where you could hear European, Greek and Turkish-style music. Another was the *café aman*, where the music resembled that you would have heard in Istanbul or Smyrna.

In 1922, following the disastrous Asia Minor campaign and the compulsory exchange of populations between Greece and Turkey, the population of the new nation swelled by almost a quarter. The refugees from Asia Minor, many of them musicians, brought their music with them, a style familiar to the patrons of the Athenian *cafés aman*. The port of Piraeus, crowded with destitute refugees, became the centre of a fusion between Asia Minor music and local songs accompanied by the *bouzoúki*.

The style that crystalised in the back streets of Piraeus was called *rebétika* (also *rembét-*

HOW THE *REBÉTIKA* HAS CHANGED

Visitors to Athens may be surprised to find that there are still dozens of small clubs where the *rebétika* songs are played. Despite the inevitable amplification, the music sounds much as it did in its heyday. Songs by Markos Vamvakaris, the "father of *rebétika*", by Vassilis Tsitsanis, the most prolific songwriter of the genre, and by many other *rebétika* songwriters still form the core of the repertoire. These days the music tends to be played as something to listen to rather than dance to.

This is a pity because dancing was at the centre of the tradition, especially the solo male dance called the *zeïbékiko*. This dramatic, introspective dance, with its improvised spiralling steps, was where a man both revealed his sorrows and cast them aside. It was customary to order the music you wished to dance to from the *bouzoúki*-player, and to pay for the privilege of dancing alone. The space where a man danced was inviolable, and an intrusion on to the dance-floor could mean a knife fight.

The heyday of the *rebétika* lasted from the 1920s to the 1950s. Moving out of Piraeus and into the nightclubs of Athens, it attracted both working-class Greeks and wealthy Athenians. Conspicuous spending was a feature of the post-war clubs, and thousands of drachmas were thrown on the floor or at the musicians each evening

ika). It was characterised by the use of the *bouzoúki* and its smaller cousin, the *bagláma*, and by songs of the underworld that talked of hashish-smoking tough-guys or *mánges*. Like the tango, a form that had taken Europe by storm, *rebétika* were passionate songs that spoke to the new underclass of urban Greeks who had appeared almost overnight in the capital. The newly-established recording industry and the radio helped spread the music beyond Athens to other urban centres, including the cities of North America, where many Greeks had emigrated. The *rebétika* songs and the dances that went with them became so popular that they are still the basis of most of Greece's popular music.

During the 1960s a new style of music became popular in Athens, one still partly based on the rhythms and modes of the *rebétika*, but mingling these elements with the verse of Greece's most distinguished poets. What took place in Athens in the 1960s was a unique experiment that created some of the most unusual and brilliant popular music in Europe.

The era of Theodorakis

Following the brutal German occupation of 1941–44, and the equally vicious Civil War that followed, Greece slowly began to recover during the 1950s. Among those who had fought in the Resistance against the Germans, and on the Leftist side during the Civil War, were many of Greece's leading intellectuals, writers and composers. A large number of them still languished in prison camps or in exile, but by the end of the decade they began to play an active role in re-establishing Greece's shattered cultural life.

The early 1960s was a heady period of optimism, when Greece's two best known composers worked, sometimes together, sometimes in competition, to create a form of popular music based on the combination of Greek popular music with poetry. One of them was Mikis Theodorakis, the other was Manos Hadzidakis. Hadzidakis had been the first intellectual to champion the working class

LEFT: a club in Pláka in 1960.
RIGHT: *rebétes* in Pireaus in 1928.

ROCK MUSIC MAKES ITS MARK

The extraordinary flourishing of music that took place in the 1960s came to a sudden halt in 1967 with the military coup d'état, whose leaders placed a ban on any performance of music by the communist Theodorakis. For a short time, the whole cultural life of Greece stagnated, but soon new musical voices began to appear.

The most significant was that of the songwriter Dionysios Savvopoulos. Witty, urbane and strongly influenced by popular western musicians like Bob Dylan, Savvopoulos painted a depressing picture of modern Athens, but his blend of rock, folk and Greek music appealed to young Greeks of the 1970s, many of whom listened as much to rock and roll as they did to Greek music. Some of today's leading Greek performers and composers owe their beginnings to working with Savvopoulos, including Nikos Xydakis, Nikos Papazoglou and Eleftheria Arvanitakis.

Despite the restoration of democracy in the mid 1970s, the popularity of the sort of music created by Theodorakis and Hadzidakis waned. In the 1980s the trend toward western music increased, and it looked as if Greek music might lose its strong local character. But in the decade that followed there was a return to local forms, still with rebétika as a strong element, although with borrowings from other Mediterranean styles.

rebétika music and persuade Greek intellectuals that it was a valid musical form. A classically-trained musician, he adapted elements of the music in his settings of several Greek poets, especially Nikos Gatsos.

Theodorakis, who had fought on the communist side in the Civil War, and suffered torture and imprisonment, left Greece in the 1950s to study classical composition under Olivier Messiaen in Paris. When he returned to Greece in 1960, he used the *bouzoúki* and a *rebétika* singer to perform his settings of poems by Yiannis Ritsos. For the following seven years, he poured out an incredible volume of popular music, always using some elements of traditional Greek music, particularly *rebétika*, as a basis, and setting almost all of Greece's leading poets to music.

The Athenian musical scene is no longer dominated by one or two composers, and it is no longer centred close to the Acropolis, in Pláka and adjacent areas. Some performers popular in Athens play crossover music with a jazz-Balkan sound, such as Flóros Florídis, Mode Plagal, Pýros Aíthir and the singer Savina Yiannatou, who performs a wide variety of Mediterranean songs. Other composers, like Stamatis Kraounakis have experimented in a variety of styles, his music complemented by the brilliant lyrics of Lina Nikolakopoulou.

The rise of the novel

The poetry and music that were so intimately connected in Greece still have strong ties, but poetry is no longer the dominant form of Greek literature. The novel has flourished in Greece since the dictatorship of 1967–74, with many of its leading exponents being women.

The high point of modern Greek literature is often taken to be the 1950s and '60s. Poets dominated, but there was also the singular voice of Nikos Kazantzakis, poet, novelist, essayist and playwright, a towering figure whose work became popular in the west through the film adaptations of *Zorba the Greek* and *Christ Recrucified*. His great poetic achievement, *The Odyssey: a Modern Sequel*, also benefited from the splendid English translation by Kimon Friar.

The Greek novel, slow to come of age, is now flourishing, with some excellent English translations available for the non-Greek reader. Vasilis Vasilikos, Margarita Liberaki, Maro Douka, Alki Zeï, Rea Galanaki, Evgenia Fakinou, Kostas Taktsis, Kostas Mourselas and Dido Sotiriou are names to look out for.

Poetry today

Foreign recognition contributed to the success of the four Greek poets best known to English readers: Konstantinos Kavafis (Constantine Cavafy), Yiannis Ritsos, George Seferis and Odysseas Elytis. To be a writer in a language read by only10 million or so people is to be dependent on translation for success.

Cavafy, whose place in the pantheon of modern poetry was firmly established by E.M. Forster and W.H. Auden, never lived in Athens, but had a considerable influence on other Greek poets. Seferis and Elytis both won the Nobel Prize for Literature, assuring modern Greek poetry a prominent place in the western world. Ritsos, who won the Lenin Prize for Literature, has also achieved world status.

Greece's women poets, most of whom grew up in the shadow of these giants, deserve to be better known. One of the most widely translated is Katerina Angelaki-Rooke. Other remarkable modern Greek women poets whose works can now be found in English, are Kiki Dimoula, Jenny Mastoraki and Rea Galanaki. ❑

LEFT: Odysseas Elytis.

Movies in the Open Air

Along with eating out of doors, the summer movie-theatre or *therinó sinemá* has to rank as one of Greece's most enduring and endearing lifestyle contributions, though skyrocketing property values and an increase in the number of air-conditioned indoor multiplexes mean that there aren't as many as there used to be. The *theriná* (in the plural) are essentially open, sturdily-walled areas strewn with gravel and with a concrete screen-wall at the far end. They operate – depending on nighttime temperatures – from about mid-May to mid-September.

They are a great way to catch up on films you missed over the past year, as the programme tends to be quality but not exactly first-run movies. To remain competitive, the formerly wonky, scratchy sound systems have mostly been upgraded. There are usually two screenings, at 8.30pm – later in the summer – and 11pm, with promptness in starting time not always a conspicuous feature. Tickets cost the same as at indoor venues: 7–8 euros.

Public transport being what it is, expect to walk home or take a taxi from the conclusion of a later screening. If you don't read Greek fluently, you might want to gravitate towards the early screening *(provolí)* for another reason; the sound of the 11pm show is often turned down to avoid complaints from neighbours, leaving viewers dependent on the subtitles. (Films in Greece are always shown in the original language with subtitles, never dubbed.)

Generally small round tables are provided between the rows of loose chairs to rest the drinks, crisps, nuts, pizza, sandwiches and other snacks which the management peddles assiduously, especially at the *diálemma* or intermission. There can't be more than 20 or so *theriná* remaining in the greater Athens area.

Among the more beloved – and the most likely to survive – are:

Athinaia, Haritós 50, Kolonáki. A garden with tables, showing mostly arthouse titles; classed as *sinefíl* in Greek listings.
Cine Paris, Kydathinéon 22, Pláka. Rooftop venue with an Acropolis view; mostly comedies and action flicks.
Filothei, Platía Drosopoúlou, Paleá Filothéi. A bit remoter than the others but generally worth the trip out; favours arthouse titles.
Riviera, Valtetsíou 46, Exárhia. Arthouse and thrillers aimed at a student audience.
Thiseion, Apostólou Pávlou 7, Thissío. Hits from the previous year or so.
Zefyros, Tróön 36, Áno Petrálona. A mix of black-and-white classics and arthouse pics.

RIGHT: Melina Mercouri starred in Jules Dassin's 1960 classic *Never on Sunday.*

For current programmes, consult the weekly listings sources such as *Athinormá* (in Greek) and *The Athens News*.

The world became aware of Greek cinema in the 1960s with Jules Dassin's *Never on Sunday* and Michael Cacoyannis' *Zorba the Greek,* both more Hollywood than Greece. From the 1970s, a string oflyrical, contemplative films by Athens-born Theo Angelopoulos helped define a modern Greek style. In the last decade, the most popular home-grown films at the box-office have been witty and sometimes raunchy sex comedies with titles like *The Cow's Orgasm*, *The Mating Game* and *Safe Sex.* ❑

PLACES

A detailed guide to the city with the principal sites clearly cross-referenced by number to the maps

Navigating Athens, particularly in the centre, is relatively straightforward. From just about anywherein the city you can get a view of one of the the two main hills, the Acropolis and Likavitós. The thrill of suddenly catching a glimpse of the iconic ruin of the Parthenon between two buildings is one of Athens' great experiences. Huddled below the eastern face of the Acropolis is Pláka, probably the city's most attractive district. Here is a warren of small streets, some lined with elegant neoclassical mansions that have now been restored to their former glory.

Beyond Pláka is the market district, or Monastiráki. Colourful, hectic and, at times, chaotic, the lanes with their small shops – still zoned as in traditional Asian bazaars – are fascinating, and the whole area reaches its apotheosis with the grand central market (not a place for those with sensitive stomachs).

If the Acropolis and Likavitós form an east–west axis to the centre, north to south the city is traversed by wide boulevards that link Athens' two main squares, Sýntagma and Omónia. Around Sýntagma, or "Constitution" Square, are the former royal palace (now the parliament building), the peaceful retreat of the National Gardens, and the upmarket district of Kolonáki. Stretched out along Vasilísis Sofías, the boulevard that heads east, are some of the city's best museums. North of the rather seedy area around Omónia is the National Archaeological Museum with its huge collection of finds from Classical antiquity.

Further afield are the suburbs, some now up-and-coming after years of industrial decline, others long the retreat of the middle and upper classes. Down to the coast is the vibrant port of Piraeus, a city in its own right. Beyond the city boundaries, either by land or sea are the easily reached islands of the Saronic Gulf, the wonderfully atmospheric site of Delphi, and the Argolid, with some of most important and impressive archaeological sites of the ancient world. ❑

PREVIOUS PAGES: meeting up on Filopáppou hill; where it all began, the Erechtheion on the Acropolis. **LEFT:** Santiago Calatrava's Olympic arches at Maroússi.

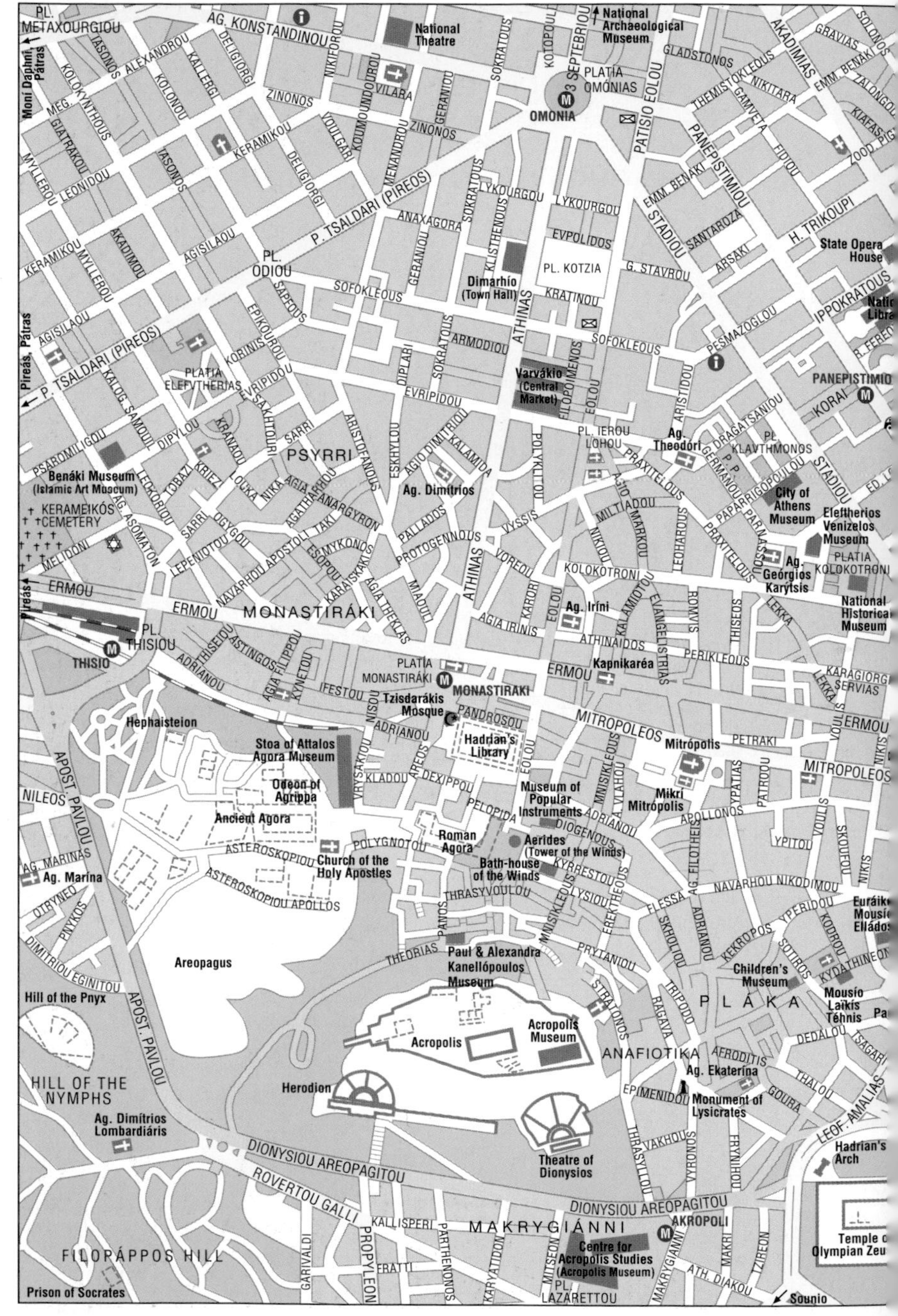
National Theatre
National Archaeological Museum
PLATÍA OMÓNIAS
OMONIA
Dimarhío (Town Hall)
PL. KOTZIA
State Opera House
Varvákio (Central Market)
PSYRRI
Benáki Museum (Islamic Art Museum)
KERAMEIKÓS CEMETERY
Ag. Dimítrios
Ag. Theodóri
City of Athens Museum
Eleftherios Venizelos Museum
Ag. Georgios Karýtsis
National Historical Museum
MONASTIRÁKI
Ag. Iríni
Kapnikaréa
THISIO
Tzisdarákis Mosque
Hadrian's Library
Hephaisteion
Stoa of Attalos Agora Museum
Odeon of Agrippa
Ancient Agora
Mitrópolis
Mikrí Mitrópolis
Museum of Popular Instruments
Roman Agora
Aerides (Tower of the Winds)
Bath-house of the Winds
Church of the Holy Apostles
Ag. Marína
Areopagus
Paul & Alexandra Kanellópoulos Museum
Hill of the Pnyx
Children's Museum
PLÁKA
Mousío Laïkís Téhnis
Acropolis
Acropolis Museum
ANAFIOTIKA
Ag. Ekaterína
Herodion
Monument of Lysicrates
HILL OF THE NYMPHS
Ag. Dimítrios Lombardiáris
Theatre of Dionysios
Hadrian's Arch
MAKRYGIÁNNI
AKROPOLI
Centre for Acropolis Studies (Acropolis Museum)
FILOPÁPPOS HILL
Prison of Socrates
Sounio

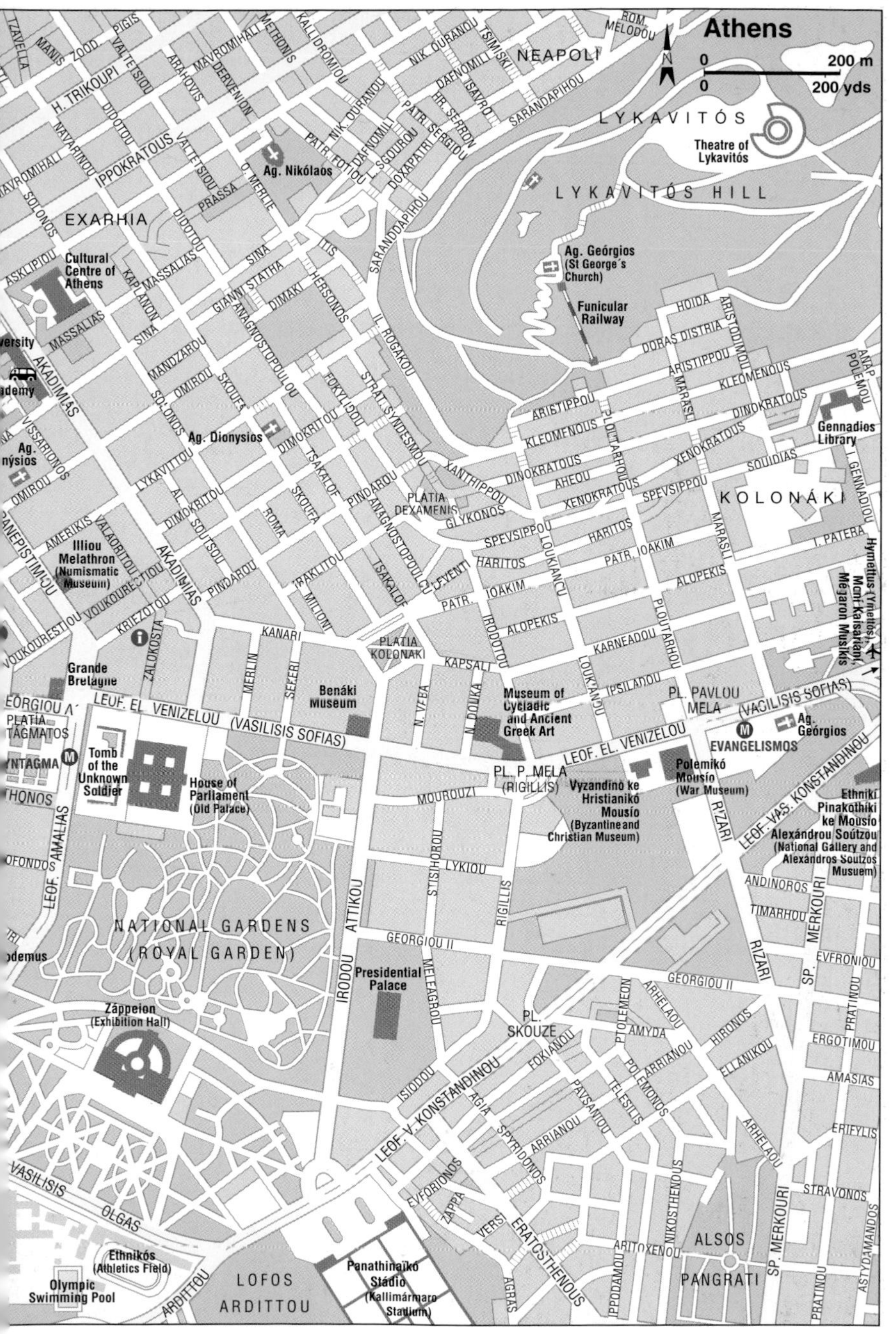
Athens
0 200 m
0 200 yds
NEAPOLI
LYKAVITÓS
Theatre of Lykavitós
LYKAVITÓS HILL
Ag. Nikólaos
EXARHIA
Cultural Centre of Athens
Ag. Geórgios (St George's Church)
Funicular Railway
Ag. Dionysios
Gennadios Library
KOLONÁKI
PLATIA DEXAMENIS
Iliou Melathron (Numismatic Museum)
Hymettus (Ymettós), Moni Kaisarianí, Mégaron Musikis
PLATIA KOLONAKI
Grande Bretagne
Benáki Museum
Museum of Cycladic and Ancient Greek Art
PL. PAVLOU MELA
EVANGELISMOS
Ag. Geórgios
Tomb of the Unknown Soldier
House of Parliament (Old Palace)
PL. P. MELA (RIGILLIS)
Vyzandinó ke Hristianikó Mousío (Byzantine and Christian Museum)
Polemikó Mousío (War Museum)
Ethnikí Pinakothíki ke Mousío Alexándrou Soútzou (National Gallery and Alexándros Soutzos Museum)
NATIONAL GARDENS (ROYAL GARDEN)
Presidential Palace
Záppeion (Exhibition Hall)
PL. SKOUZE
LEOF. V. KONSTANDINOU
LEOF. VAS. KONSTANDINOU
LEOF. EL. VENIZELOU (VASILISIS SOFIAS)
LEOF. AMALIAS
VASILISIS OLGAS
Ethnikós (Athletics Field)
Olympic Swimming Pool
LOFOS ARDITTOU
Panathinaïkó Stádio (Kallimármaro Stadium)
ALSOS
PANGRATI

THE ANCIENT CENTRE

Athens is home to some of the greatest monuments and archaeological sites of the ancient world, from the Temple of the Olympian Zeus, to the Acropolis, to the cemetery at Keramikós, all testify to the vital role the city has played in the development of European thought and culture

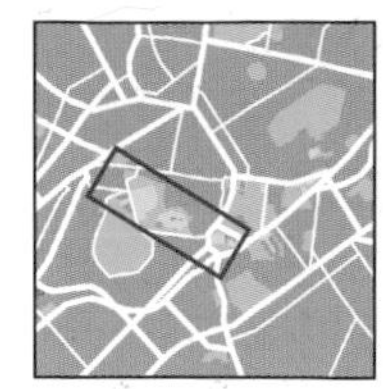

The most famous sights in Athens, evidence of its glorious ancient past, run in a long line from the Temple of Olympian Zeus, past the bulk of the Acropolis and the sprawling site of the ancient Agora, to the cemetery at Keramikós. The best place to start the long journey around the sites, which will take at least a couple of days to explore, are with the Roman monuments on the eastern side of Leofóros Amalías. Almost all of the route has now been pedestrianised and is well signposted.

Hadrian's Arch

Hadrian's Arch ❶, the gateway that today presides over the chaotic main road, was a gift to the city from the Roman emperor Hadrian, who endowed post-Hellenistic Athens with numerous monuments and foundations during his reign in the 2nd century *(see page 31)*.

This arch was intended to separate the classical town from imperial city. Accordingly, the northeast side of the arch is inscribed (in Greek): "This is Athens, city of Theseus", while the opposite side reads "This is the city of Hadrian, not of Theseus." As such, it's not strictly reliable, since there are plenty of Roman-era structures in the Pláka.

However, without doubt the most impressive Roman relic in Athens lies just beyond the arch, the **Temple of Olympian Zeus ❷**. Dedicated by Hadrian in AD 131 seven centuries after its foundations had been laid, it was the largest temple in ancient Greece; today only 15 of the original 104 Corinthian columns remain (Archaeological Site of the Olympieion and Illisos Shrines; open summer daily 8am–7.45pm; admission charge). Whatever the temple's condition, its precincts

LEFT: the Erechtheon on the Acropolis.
BELOW: Hadrian's Arch marks the boundary of the ancient city.

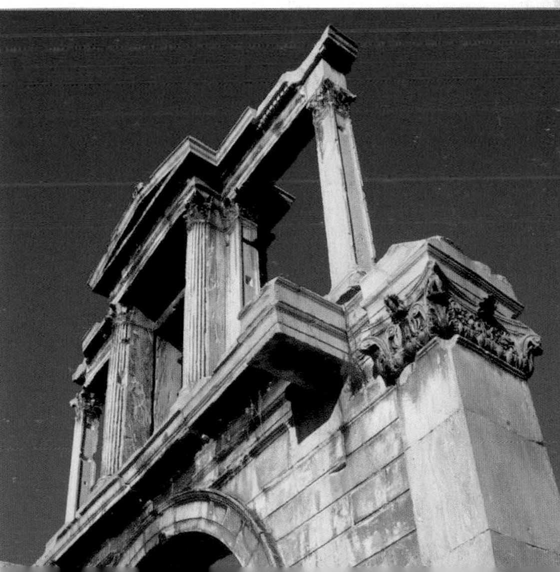

have always been publicly esteemed, if not quite as initially intended. In Byzantine times a stylite perched on one of the surviving architraves; during Ottoman rule Muslims would pray for rain to Allah, whom they somehow syncretised with Zeus Ombrios in his role of thunder god; and until the early 1960s the milkmen of Athens held their annual festival here.

The Herodion looms behind a pine tree.

Bordering the archaeological site to the east is a walkway leading down and south to the only remaining section of the river Ilissós that is not covered or filled in, though its normally dry bed soon disappears into a tunnel beneath Kalirróis. It's hard to believe that this was the burbling river, fed by still-active springs at Kaisarianí, that so delighted Socrates and his entourage.

One fork of the path ends by the church of **Agía Fótini** (1872), just below Arditoú Street. With a fountain and benches in a sunken courtyard, it's a surprisingly quiet refuge only a few metres from the traffic overhead.

Around the Acropolis

From the Arch of Hadrian, cross the busy street and take the newly pedestrianised Dionysíou Areopagítou along to the entrance of the **Theatre of Dionysios** ❸ (open daily summer 8am–7.30pm; admission fee; a single ticket, valid for four days, covers the Acropolis and its museum, the ancient Agora and museum, the north and south slopes of the Acropolis, the Theatre of Dionysios, the Roman Agora, Keramikós and the Temple of the Olympian Zeus). This is the first of the sites on the Acropolis itself, which are now all linked by a footpath running along part of the original encircling road.

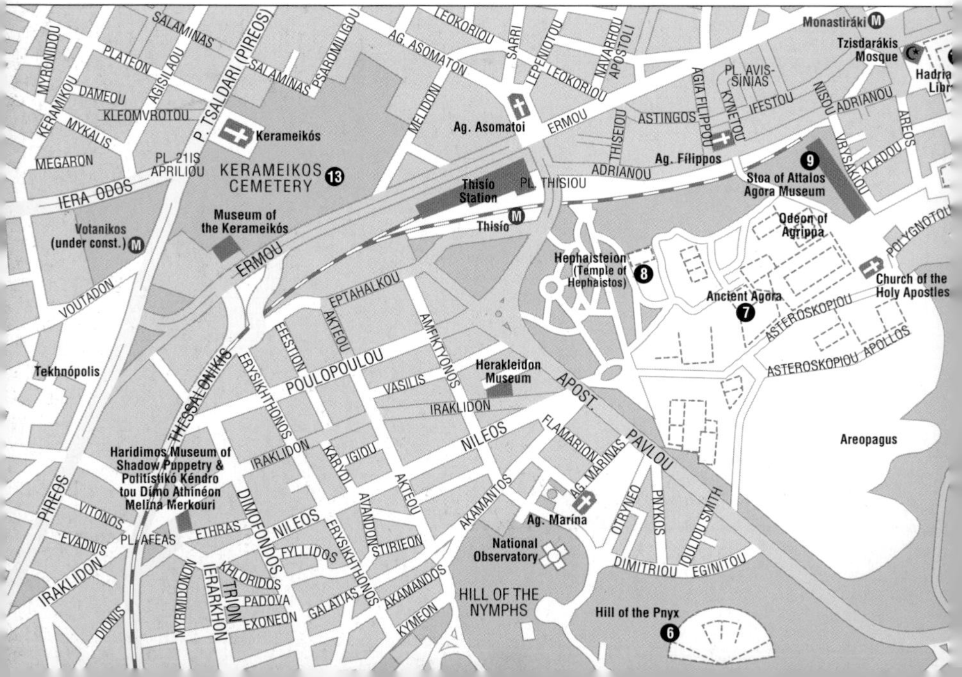

The theatre's origins date back to the 6th century BC, when it was initially a simple, possibly rectangular, structure of wooden stands. Then in 500–470 BC, an amphitheatre was dug out of the hillside. It was in this new space the dramas of Aeschylus, Sophocles and Euripides were first performed. The present structures and shape of the theatre – now being extensively reconstructed – date from the reign of Lykourgos (338–324 BC), and the theatre fell into disuse after the fall of Rome in the 5th century AD. To the right of the ticket booth is a display of mostly Roman sculpture found at the site.

The south and east slopes

On the path between the Theatre of Dionysios and the Herodion you pass the partially reconstructed **Asklepeion** (Temple of Asklepios), founded in 420–419 BC by an Athenian named Telemachos. From here a path heads right to the East Slope. This leads to just below the site of the **Choregic Monument of Thrasyllos** (320– 319 BC), now being reconstructed. The tripod that Thrasyllos installed had later been replaced by a statue of Dionysios, subsequently pinched by Lord Elgin and now to be found in the British Museum. The cave the monument stands in front of is where Pausanias reports that there was a representation of Apollo and Artemis slaughtering the children of Niobe. The cave continued to be used into the Christian era when it was turned into a chapel.

Returning to the Asklepeion and carrying on along the path, by the remains of a Byzantine cistern are what may have been the foundations of a sanctuary to Themis. Close by to the remains is a collection of stele and herms with honorary inscriptions from the 4th–1st centuries BC. Those on the right are decorated only by carvings of male genitals.

The path now passes above, and gives a good vantage point into, the

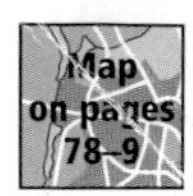

The church of Agía Fótini was built next to an ancient shrine to Pan, evident today only as two flat cuttings in the nearby rock a few steps up the stone path past the church and through the low hedge. An image of Pan was cut on this surface, but is now so worn that it can be seen, if at all, only in the late afternoon when the shadows bring it into relief.

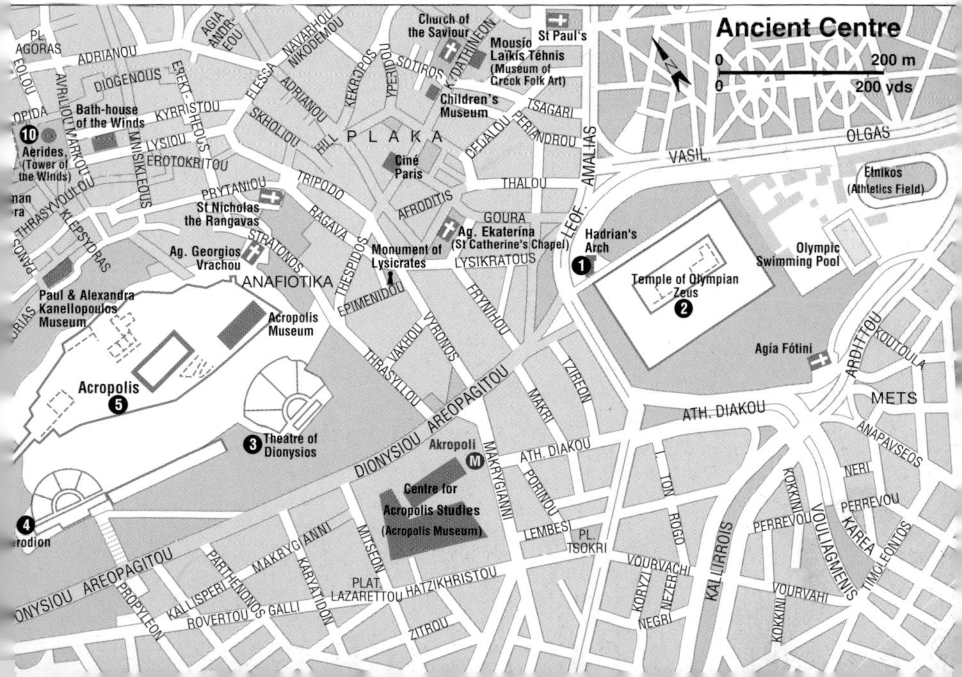

Although it's hard to believe now, at one time the south slope of the Acropolis was a hive of industrial activity and was the site of a 5th century BC metal foundry. Beyond the remains of the sanctuary to Themis, a number of the manufacturing pits have been excavated.

Herodion ❹, or Odeon of Herodes Atticus, a large Roman theatre seating some 5–6,000 spectators. It was built in 160 AD to commemorate Herodes' wife Regilla. The seating behind its impressive facade has now been restored and it serves as a venue for the Athens Festival.

The Acropolis

Beside the Herodion the way climbs steeply and brings you to the entrance of the **Acropolis ❺** (open daily 8am–7.30pm; admission charge), the splendid Propylaia. The Athenian Acropolis, a term which simply means the highest part of the city and hence, usually, a natural fortress, had been graced by fortifications and temples for longer than anyone could remember or imagine. Not even Homer, who is believed to have lived in the 8th century BC and whose *Iliad* describes the war between Mycenae and Troy about 400 years earlier *(see page 20)* knew much about the Athens of Mycenaean times, or at any rate he made very few references to it. What he did mention was a Mycenaean palace on the Acropolis, "the Strong House of Erechtheus".

The much earlier Mycenaean traces on the Acropolis are no more than remnants of a wall, not much to show for the origins of the first truly Greek civilisation (the even earlier Minoans are believed to have arrived from Egypt and Asia Minor). Most of what modern visitors see on the Acropolis is a long way down the road of Greek history and is in any case only a small segment of it, a stripped archaeological carcase.

Before and during the Archaic period, which covers roughly 200 years of erratic rehearsal for the glorious 5th century (BC, of course), the Acropolis was a complex of pagan sanctuaries. It went on to flourish as a triumph of Hel-

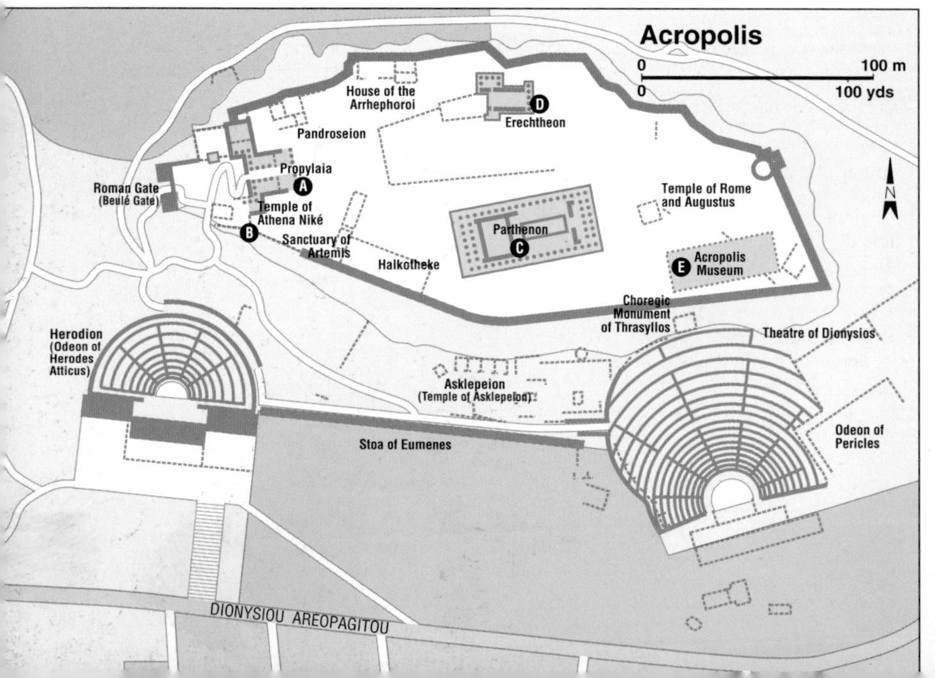

lenistic and then Roman art, degenerated into a miserable walled town which a 13th-century archbishop said was comparable to living in hell, improved slightly as the headquarters of a string of mediaeval dukes and ended up, by the time of Greek independence, as a run-down Turkish castle.

The Propylaia

The **Propylaia** Ⓐ replaced an older gateway built in the time of the tyrant Cimon and, even in its truncated form, it is probably the most impressive of the buildings erected by the Greeks for secular purposes. It incorporated a picture gallery with frescoed walls and a famous ceiling. The building was usually commandeered as the residence of whoever ruled Athens, and as such it was forever being modified to serve particular needs.

In the 3rd century AD, the Romans added a gate which modern visitors pass through on their approach. It was filled in and forgotten when the Acropolis reverted to a military role and, of course, the defenders wanted to make entry as difficult as possible. During the Byzantine period, when the Parthenon was converted into the Church of Our Lady of Athens, the Propylaia was home to Archbishop Michael Acominatos.

By the early 15th century, the Venetian Duke of Athens, Antonio Acciajuoli, was in residence. He added a second storey, battlements and, opposite the Temple of Athena Niké, a square tower 27 metres (89 ft) high. The tower survived until 1874 and would still be there but for the policy of purging the Acropolis of post-Periclean alterations.

The Turkish occupants of the Propylaia made the fatal mistake of storing gunpowder in one of the rooms. When was struck by lightning, two columns collapsed and the pasha and his family were killed, although the walls withstood the explosion remarkably well. Funnelled skywards, the blast made a fiery rocket out of the contents of the building including, one imagines, the pasha and his family. The successor to the unfortunate pasha installed his harem in the Erechtheon.

The War of Independence (1821–32) revived European interest in classical Greece. Athens was an unlovely mess when the Turks finally withdrew, a town with a population of little more than 4,000. Volunteers assumed the responsibility of restoring the Acropolis to its pristine, Periclean condition. Pieces of the Temple of Athena Niké, displaced by the Turkish artillery, were found and reassembled. The forgotten **Roman gate** below the Propylaia was uncovered in 1852 by the French archaeologist Beulé, by whose name it has since been known. The Beulé gate was one of the exceptions to the general rule that any structure not belonging to the Classical Age had to go.

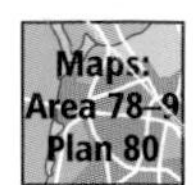

In the 13th century, the pious Michael Acominatos "was moved to tears at the sight of the destroyed walls, the empty streets, and the ragged, badly-fed people". It was he who compared the 30 years he spent in Athens to life in hell and regretted what his term as archbishop had done to him. "I too have fallen into barbarism", he moaned.

BELOW: on the steps of the Propylaia.

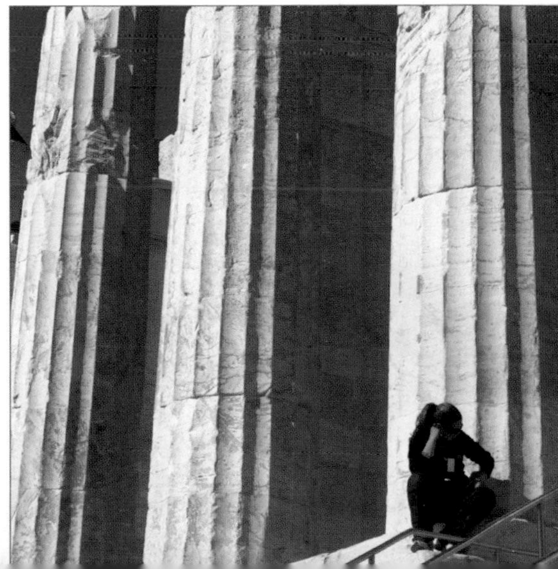

According to legend, Aegeus, the father of Theseus, waited anxiously on the Acropolis for his son's return from confronting the Minotaur in Crete. When he saw the black sails which Theseus had forgotten to exchange for white ones, Aegeus assumed the worst and threw himself off, thereby drowning in (and giving his name to) the Aegean Sea. The story ignores the awkward fact that the distressed king would have crashed on to dry land.

The Temple of Athena Niké

At the beginning of the 5th century BC, Athens was still recovering from two Persian invasions in quick succession *(see pages 25–6)*. The population had fled and Athens was razed in their absence. Rebuilding the houses in and around the Agora was obviously the first priority when the residents returned, and some consideration was given to leaving the wreckage on the Acropolis just where it was as a war memorial.

In spite of the almost total destruction, Athens, capital of Attica, recovered quickly and indeed prospered because of the leading role it had taken in the eventual defeat of the Persians. Attica, unexceptional among hundreds of independent Greek city-states before the Persian invasion, was unexpectedly catapulted to the forefront. The state finances, previously dependent on olive oil exports and a silver mine, were flush with money which the lesser states had agreed to contribute to a common defence fund *(see page 27)*. Athens had no qualms about diverting the money for self-aggrandisement, although some of the contributors were heard to grumble about high-handedness.

Among the ruins left on the Acropolis after the Persian withdrawal were the foundations and a few battered columns of what had been planned as a new temple to Athena. As divine intervention had clearly saved the city from the barbarian onslaught, the people felt obliged to repay their debt to the gods on the grandest possible scale. The existing plans were scrapped and new ones drawn up.

The design and construction of the Parthenon was going to be a big job, so the more modest **Temple of Athena Niké** Ⓑ (or "Athena Victory") was planned as a stopgap. As matters turned out, the design by Callicrates, who also worked on the Parthenon, ran into difficulties and the little temple took longer to complete than its bigger neighbour.

The victory theme involved giving Athena's statue in the temple a pair of wings. According to Pausanius, who visited Athens in the 2nd century AD, the Athenians were worried

BELOW: a pillar from the Olympeion.

about these wings and removed them in case she flew away.

The spot chosen for the Temple of Athena Niké, a promontory on the southwest corner of the Acropolis, was a natural vantage point. It was especially appropriate because it overlooked the island of Salámis, where the Athenian fleet had successfully trapped the Persians, and it also had popular connections with another famous occasion, albeit one with an unhappy ending *(see margin, left)*. The charming small temple is now being reconstructed and with any luck it will soon be possible to see it without its scaffolding.

The Parthenon

Fifteen years under construction, a new temple to the goddess Athena, later to become known as the **Parthenon** **C**, was opened to the public during the Panathenaic festival of 438 BC. The spectacle it presented then hardly matches the familiar ruin we know today.

There was colour everywhere, so much so that some observers found the overall effect offensive. "We are gilding and adorning our city like a wanton woman", Plutarch complained, "decking her with costly statues and offerings and thousand-talent temples."

The Egyptian pyramids impress because of the sheer size of the task undertaken with the tools available. The Parthenon is altogether more subtle, although the fact that such a daunting façade contained just two rooms may be considered slightly extravagant. The first, entered from the east (the opposite side after climbing the hill by the normal route), was the temple proper, containing a celebrated statue of Athena, her skin tones rendered in a layer of ivory and her raiment in gold. The statue was thoughtfully provided with a marble sofa in case it wanted to lie down.

The goddess Athena was worshipped in several guises. The Parthenon was officially the temple of Athena Polias, which acknowledged her role as patroness of the state. Elsewhere she was the distinguished goddess of virginity, as well as of foresight, of horses, of the

The Parthenon seems to have been undergoing interminable restoration work (replacing the steel bonds that were previously used with titanium). Work is now complete on the north-facing Opisthonaos but continues elsewhere.

BELOW: the Acropolis viewed from the west.

trumpet, of the workwoman and of the girdle (armour).

Another statue outside the Parthenon was of Athena Promachos, "The Champion". Made out of bronze, it stood helmet, shoulders and spear above the buildings and was visible from ships at sea, especially when it reflected the sun. Like many of the Acropolis statues, this one was later carted off to Constantinople where in 1203 it met an ignominious end at the hands of a drunken mob.

The Parthenon's mighty columns.

The second chamber in the Parthenon had a separate entrance on the western side. It may have been intended as accommodation for the goddess's handmaidens, but as the handmaidens existed neither as humans nor as statues the somewhat superfluous living-quarters were put to more practical use as a treasury strongroom.

It is the attention to detail by the architect, Ictinus, that is astonishing. The floor, long since butchered, rose towards the centre in the imperceptible gradient of 1 in 450. Paradoxically, it was in order to preserve the illusion of straight lines that there is hardly a straight line or right-angle anywhere. The two rows of columns which form the colonnade slope inwards a fraction, but in the interest of harmony the inner row slightly less so. The difference in the angle is less than 1 percent.

The taper of the columns would have been distorted by strong backlight, so they were given a faint swelling in the middle to counter that effect. Corner columns were made slightly thicker than their neighbours because they caught more light. The back of figures carved in high relief were invisible in normal circumstances, yet they were finished to much the same meticulous standard as front and sides. Was it all absolutely necessary? Would anyone notice or, for that matter, care? The answer, perhaps, was that people might not be able to appreciate the finesse, but the gods would.

BELOW: the east façade of the Parthenon.

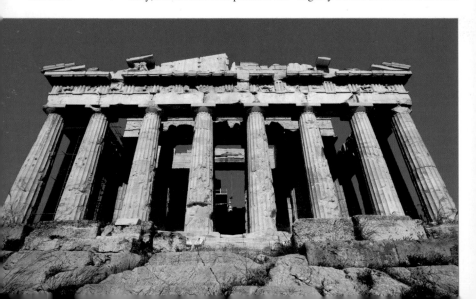

The frieze

One of the great attractions on opening day would have been the frieze which ran high and uninterrupted around 160 metres (524 ft) of the inner wall of the colonnade. Sculpture was normally about gods, prancing horses, heroes slaying monsters and so on, and while there was plenty of that on the pediments and metopes of the Parthenon, the inner frieze broke new ground in depicting common citizens.

One of the conspicuous features of classical Greek architecture was the result of the seemingly mundane invention of the roofing tile. Tiles made sloping roofs possible, and sculptors made the most of the triangle (or pediment) created at either end where the sloping roofs met.

The theme of the frieze was the highlight of the same Panathenaic festival which the critical visitors were themselves engaged in. Every fourth year, the population formed a procession which made its way up and along the Acropolis to present Athena with one of her badges of office, a saffron robe. She and her divine companions were included in the frieze too. Instead of the usual godlike mannerisms, they were lounging about in casual disarray, chatting among themselves while waiting for the procession to arrive.

Further plans

The Periclean plans for the Acropolis included two more buildings. The new **Erechtheon** Ⓓ, replacing one destroyed by the Persians which was the original focus of the Acropolis, was a kind of museum, and it presented special problems for the architect because it had to include a number of immovable sacred objects, such as a snake-pit, a rock which Poseidon once struck with his trident, an olive tree and a saltwater well.

The olive tree enclosed in the Erechtheon was supposedly Athena's gift, the origin of Attica's olive-oil industry. Like crude oil today, olive oil was the principal fuel (not only a food item). The saltwater well puzzled Pausanius because it emitted the sound of waves when the wind blew south. Work on the Erechtheon ceased during the Peloponnesian War and was only resumed afterwards to provide work for the unemployed. Its most famous feature is the Caryatid porch supported on the heads of six women.

The bear cult

The largest building project on the Acropolis, designed by Mnesicles in the same period, would have occupied the whole west side of the Acropolis had it not run into difficulties with priests in charge of the precinct of Artemis Brauronia on the Acropolis. Their cult required young girls to imitate a bear walking on its hind legs and do a lot of running about and dancing in the nude. Pausanias was mystified and not a little cynical about the cult, though it had official status and no Athenian girl was supposed to

Map on page 80

The pedestrianised road that runs from the Theatre of Dionysus to the site at Keramikós largely follows the processional route of the ancient Panathenaic Way.

BELOW: a horse from the pediment of the Parthenon, now in the Acropolis Museum.

marry unless she had participated. Pericles hoped to overcome the religious objections, but in the end the Propylaia was limited to what had once been intended as the central section alone.

Vandalism

Whether as a result of the Propylaia explosion or not, the Turks then stored powder in the Parthenon, and there was a similar combustible outcome. In 1687 a Venetian military force under General Francesco Morosini was trying to wrest the Acropolis from the Turks, who dismantled the Athena Niké temple to make space for a gun battery. The Venetians mounted their guns on Filopáppou hill (the place where Socrates swallowed the hemlock) and pounded what was left of the Propylaia after its recent tragedy.

The gunnery officer, Count de San Felice, was described as "a fool with absolutely no idea of the art of artillery". One of his men with the unlikely Venetian name of Schwarz scored a direct hit on the Parthenon powder room. Three hundred Turks were killed and the houses which had been erected among the historic buildings burned for 48 hours.

As soon as the Turks withdrew from the Acropolis, the Venetians moved in to collect some souvenirs. They attempted to prise the sculpture off the western pediment, and dropped it.

As an act of vandalism, Morosini's pounding of the Propylaia still pales in Greek eyes next to the effort mounted by the British ambassador to Istanbul, Lord Elgin. At the turn of the 19th century, he carried off a treasure trove of Greek antiquity, including half of the frieze depicting the Panathenaic procession. Elgin believed he was saving the marbles for posterity, but the Greeks put a different interpretation on the operation and have campaigned hard to secure their return. The arguments have been acrimonious and new museum has been built on the site of the old Makrygiánni Barracks just below the Acropolis to house them when/if they eventually return.

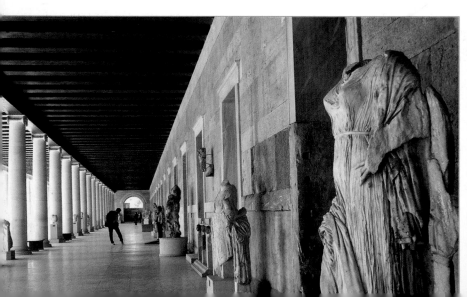

The new Acropolis Museum is designed to hold all the finds from the site plus the Elgin Marbles, currently residing in London.

BELOW: the Stoa of Attalos in the Agora.

The Acropolis Museum

Many of the finds from the Acropolis site are currently on display in a museum on the site itself, in the southeast corner. The **museum** Ⓔ (open Tues–Sun 8am–7pm, Mon 11am–7pm) has some wonderful exhibits, beginning with a fantastic lioness savaging a bull, a carving from the earliest Parthenon (*circa* 570 BC). Other pieces from the original Parthenon include the pediment sculptures, many still preserving their original pigment. Look for the impressive carving of Herakles entwined in the coils of the Triton.

Also here is the "Moschotoros", a famous Archaic statue of a young man carrying a ram across his shoulders (570 BC). Other Archaic treasures include a wonderful carving of a greyhound and some splendid *koure* (figures of young women). Look out for the statue of Athena brandishing a snake, which was originally on the pediment of the Archaic Parthenon.

The museum has a few of the bits and pieces from the Classical pediment of the Parthenon that Elgin didn't manage to get his hands on, as well as a goodly portion of the Panathenaic frieze. Surely the prize exhibits are four of the Caryatids from the Erechtheon (the others are in the British Museum), housed in a specially maintained environment.

The Ancient Agora

Leaving the Acropolis site and taking the pedestrianised way that curves around the northern side of the hill takes you past the **Pnyx** ❻, the ancient assembly place of the city that heard orators such as Pericles and Demosthenes hold forth. Now there is little to see but the view over the city is excellent (be careful on the now very polished steps leading to the top). Beyond the Pnyx and down the hill, is the entrance to the **Ancient Agora** ❼ (open daily 8am– 7.30pm).

The large sprawling site of the Agora, now rather hard to interpret, was the centre of Athenian life. This was where much of the city's trade and administration was carried out. Perhaps the most important building still standing here is the **Hephais-**

The curvaceous, elaborately draped Caryatids – sculpted female figures serving as supportive columns – possibly take their name from the women of Caryae, near Sparta. Known for their beauty, they fulfilled the function of Athenian slaves.

BELOW: the Tower of the Winds in the Roman Agora.

teion ❽ (Temple of Hephaistos, also incorrectly known as the Theseion). This is most complete remaining example of a Doric order temple, dating back to 449 BC. Remarkably preserved, it still retains most if its frieze (in the Ionian style) and ceiling. Although it has been altered over the centuries, particularly when it was turned into a church, this remains our best clue (albeit on a much smaller scale) of how the Parthenon must have appeared.

The Hephaisteion is the best-preserved Doric temple in all Greece.

The other easily identifiable building is the **Odeon of Agrippa** (*circa* 15 BC), a large theatre which later (around 400 AD) became the site of a huge gymnasium. It is chiefly recognisable from the monumental sculptures of Tritons that sit in front of it.

On the far (eastern) side of the Panathenaic Way, the main road through the site, is the obvious **Stoa of Attalos** ❾, reconstructed in its original form in the 1953–6 with money from the United States and now home to the small but fascinating **Agora Museum** (open Tues–Sun 8am–7.30pm, Mon 11am–7.30pm). The museum has been rearranged and ordered chronologically and the exhibits are beautifully displayed.

BELOW: the stoa of Hadrian's Library.

Among the Archaic pieces is a perfume bottle in the shape of a kneeling athelete, and from the Classical era a splendid bronze head of Niké (420–415 BC). However, perhaps the most interesting pieces are the *ostraka*, shards of pot on which citizens wrote the names of those who were to be ostracised (exiled) from the city *(see page 27)*. The ones here are from the ostracism of Themistocles, 482 BC, all scratched with his name.

Also of interest is the *kleoterian*, a device for determining who sat on jury service. Each citizen carried an allotment plate *(pinakia)*, a bronze disc inscribed with his name, father's name and *deme* (which of the four sectors of the city he came from). These discs were used in a kind of complicated lottery to choose jurors at random.

Aerides

Directly below the north face of the Acropolis and to the east of the

Ancient Agora is **Aerides**, a colourful quarter named after the **Tower of the Winds** ⑩, which ends Aiólou Street. The Tower of the Winds is also known as the Horológio (Clock) of Andronicus of Kyrrhos. It is a marble octagonal building on three steps, and served as a weather vane, sundial and water clock. Each face marks a compass point and has a carving of the appropriate wind.

This structure is more complex than it looks. A reservoir of water dropped measured doses into a semicircular cistern outside the wall; there was a sundial on the sides facing the sun. The water probably came from the Klepsydra Spring on the Acropolis. The sides are perfectly aligned as to direction, and could serve as a compass. The weather vane on the peak was shaped like a sea god. Rumour has it that Julius Caesar gave the tower to Athens as a planetarium. During Ottoman rule, the odd little building was used as a *tekke* (dance hall) by Dervishes. Old pictures show an astonishing amount of interior space being used for the ceremonies.

The Roman Agora

Between the Tower of the Winds and Monastiráki Square are the Roman ruins. Just beside Aerides is the **Roman Agora** ⑪ (open daily 8am–7pm). This was a covered market with a colonnade and a double porch over the gate. It was probably built between 17 BC and AD 2. Occasionally in summer it is furnished with chairs and a stage, and used for concerts or plays.

The architrave of the colonnade is inscribed with a dedication to Athena Archegetis and explains that it was funded by Julius and Augustus Caesar. On the north side of the doorway is an edict of Hadrian regarding taxes on oil sales. Inside the wall were rows of shops, some of which have been excavated, and inscriptions giving the names of the shopkeepers were found on the floors and columns. In a corner are the remains of the Féthiye Tzamí (Victory Mosque, *see page 36*). Just inside the Gate are the remains of a giant public toilet dating from the 1st century AD.

A small street called Aréos runs

A kouros *from Kerameikos cemetery.*

BELOW: relaxing in Keramikós.

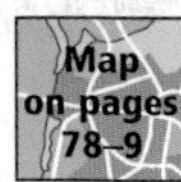

During the excavations for the (old) metro it was found that the Kerameikos cemetery continued to the southwest. Many of the dead here were in a mass grave, placed there after a plague, known from a description by Thucydides, in 430–427 BC.

from Monastiráki Square past the mosque and the adjacent wall of the Stoa or forecourt of **Hadrian's Library** ⓬ (open daily), and into Adrianoú at the south side of the site. The wall of the Stoa is well preserved. A small church was once built on to it but only a bit of mosaic remains.

The library must have been a charming place to visit, laid out with a cloistered arcade around a pool and garden. Three sides of this large building survive. In the east wall were five rooms: the central one housed the books on shelves in the large niche and the four smaller ones which flank it. In AD 410 Governor Herculius built what was probably a lecture hall over the end of the pool – 3 metres (9 ft) of wall still stand. This was converted into a church of the Virgin in Byzantine times.

Kerameikos

At the end of the complex of pedestrianised roads (just beyond Thisío metro station) is the quiet and little-visited site of **Kerameikos** ⓭ (open 8am–7.30pm). The site itself is lovely and you may see tortoises rustling about in the undergrowth. This was once the area where potters *(kerameis)* worked producing Attic vases, from which it derives its name. It is also the site of the most important cemetery of ancient Athens. The earliest tombs date back to the Mycenaean Bronze Age (before 1000 BC) and it continued to be used until the 6th century AD.

There is a small but excellent **museum** on the site (by the entrance) containing much of what has been excavated here, including some fine funerary monuments from the 6th century BC. We can be sure that these all date from before 508 because Cleisthenes banned elaborate funerary monuments from then on. They came back into favour after the Peloponnesian War (late 5th century) before being outlawed again by Demetrius Phalereas around 317–307 BC. One of the very finest pieces is the bull from the tomb of Dionysios of Kollytos (*c.* 340 BC). In addition there is an excellent collection of Geometric and early Archaic pottery.

The Street of the Tombs is where the most luxurious and imposing funerary monuments were placed during the 5th–4th centuries BC. To the east is the "Road to Plato's Academy", where in Classical times the most famous figures, including Pericles, were buried in the public tombs.

Beyond here are remains of the imposing walls built in 478 BC by Themistocles. The two great entrances constructed at the same time are the **Dipylon Gate**, the most important gateway to the city and the beginning of the Panathenaic Way, and the **Sacred Gate**, which marked the beginning of the processional way to the sacred city of Eleusis (modern Elefsína). ❑

BELOW: funerary sculptures in the Kerameikos Museum.

Excavating the Metro

The new Athens Metro Project launched its impressive first phase in January 2000, revolutionising transport in the capital with a fast, modern service and gleaming, marble-clad stations. It retains at its core an older, single line which has bisected Athens north to south since the 1860s. Connecting the capital to its port of Piraeus, and later to the leafy suburb of Kifissia, it was the ISAP (otherwise known as Line 1, now the green M1 on maps) that steam-powered visitors to the first modern Olympic Games when they took place in the city in 1896. In 1904, electrification and the construction of a tunnel from Thisío to Omónia saw the ISAP join the burgeoning ranks of Europe's first metropolitan railways. This was a major innovation greeted with not a little trepidation by Athenian society, some patrons reputedly drawing up their wills prior to a trip through the crackling, subterranean darkness.

However, the realisation of one of the largest public works in Europe has created a fresh buzz for other reasons. Excavations have churned up a past stretching back to antiquity, bringing to light a wealth of archaeological finds such as those from the late Mycenaean to late Roman periods (1100 BC–300 AD) found at Sýntagma Square. Moreover, a sample of those finds are displayed in situ, an inspirational move reinforced by the installation of contemporary Greek artworks in or around most of the metro stations.

Prior to the commencement of works, investigations had been carried out to ascertain which plots were "high risk" in archaeological terms. Conclusions were drawn on the basis of, for example, past finds unearthed while excavating building foundations; ancient records, such as the travel journals of Pausanias; exploration trenches; and ground-penetrating radar.

Major archaeological excavations were performed before construction began at these locations. To safeguard antiquities still further, metro tunnels were then bored at a depth of 20 metres, at times through solid rock, a level lower than most deposits from antiquity. The use of ventilation shafts ensures that archaeological investigations can continue to be performed where important finds are suspected.

Findings have ranged from the neolithic to the modern era; from metal-working shops, aqueducts and cisterns to the shady mysteries of a room whose numerous oil lamps are decorated with erotic scenes. Even those sites some distance from the city centre have thrown up a surprise or two: a sarcophagus at Ethnikí Ámyna, a Roman bath at Amalías.

To date, the Athens Metro archaeological excavations are the largest ever in the Greek capital. A selection of finds are exhibited at the following stations:

Panepistímio: showcases of finds.

Sýntagma: a stratigraphy (geological cross-section); showcase of finds; Roman floor mosaic.

Akrópoli: showcases of finds; stratigraphy; photo of a shaft containing finds; also, replicas of the Parthenon east pediment and of the Parthenon frieze.

Dáfni: stratigraphy; maquette of excavations.

Evangelismós: showcases of finds; small stratigraphy. ❑

RIGHT: the metro station at Akrópoli.

zap51.com

PLÁKA

The old quarter clustering at the foot of the Acropolis has been refurbished and restored, and once again has the feel of a 19th-century village. It has become a delightful, sheltered place to meander in, with Byzantine churches, a fascinating Turkish bath-house and fragments of ancient arches

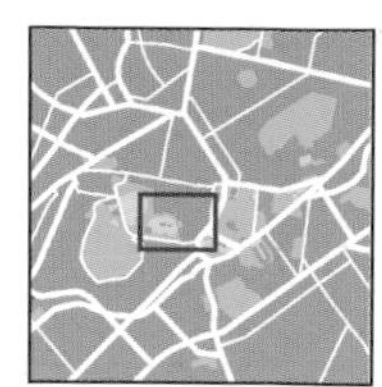

Map on page 94

Pláka has always been the heart of Athens. It is divided into three parts, running from the Anafiótika, the whitewashed 19th-century village clinging to the side of the Acropolis's northeastern slope just beneath the Long Rocks, to Áno (Upper) Pláka, which stretches down to Adrianoú (Hadrian's Street), to Káto Pláka, where the quarter levels off into the city, with Filellínon and the Acropolis on the west.

Now protected by the Greek government, Pláka has been restored to much of its original colour and elegance. And although in many cases the restoration work seems to conform more to a 21st-century notion of what the 18th and 19th centuries were all about, Pláka is a much more pleasant place to be today than it was during the 20th. Pedestrianised streets have replaced formerly frantic thoroughfares like Adrianoú and Kydathinaíon streets.

Pláka's thousand or so buildings date mostly from the 19th century. Very few older buildings survived the era of Ottoman occupation, though there are some ancient houses left standing which are being renovated and are under government protection.

The origin of the area's name is disputed. Popularly, the district is known as the area surrounding the Church of the Transformation on Kydathinaíon Street. (This church – the primary place of worship in Pláka – is just off Níkis street and was erected by Turkish converts to Christianity, and restored by the Russian community in 1834.) Of recent origin, it is believed that the name Pláka was derived from *plákas*, an ancient word for a joke being played, or from a large stone slab found in the area of the Church of St George of Alexandria near Théspidos Street. But

LEFT: 19th-century Anafiótika.
BELOW: Pláka's crowded streets are filled with restaurants.

Shuttered against the midday sun.

another school of thought supports Pláka's being a bastardisation of the Albanian *pliaka*, meaning "old". Albanian residents called this quarter "Pliaka Athena".

No. 96 Adrianoú street, purportedly built by members of the Venizelos family, was erected during the Ottoman era and is one of Pláka's oldest extant buildings. Most pre-revolutionary houses have been lost, but the Venizelos house survived with its courtyard, graceful arches, well and olive-press. It was once divided precisely in half by two heirs: even the well of the house was split. Water was a major problem in Athens then as now, and this is especially so in arid Pláka.

The house, at 5 Sholíou is also an 18th-century survivor. It was once used by the Turks as a their police precinct headquarters. Church, who was at one point Commander-in-Chief of the Greek Revolutionary Forces *(see page 40)*, lived here, as did the Scottish historian George Finlay, who restored this distinctive dwelling with its walls made of small stones, its tiny windows and a single tall chimney.

Greeks, Turks, Franks, Albanians and Ethiopian slaves have populated Pláka in centuries past. In 1841, Hans Christian Andersen met some of the descendants of Ethiopian residents, the precursors of today's Anaphiotes.

Various segments of the quarter still carry their old names which reflect the character of former inhabitants. One area hugging the foot of the Acropolis – or Kástro, as locals have termed it – is called Yerlada. This name, meaningless in Greek, derives from the word *guirlande*, or garland, an appropriate epithet for the Acropolis's slightly fallen halo.

When Athens became the Greek capital in 1834, the city expanded according to a calculated plan

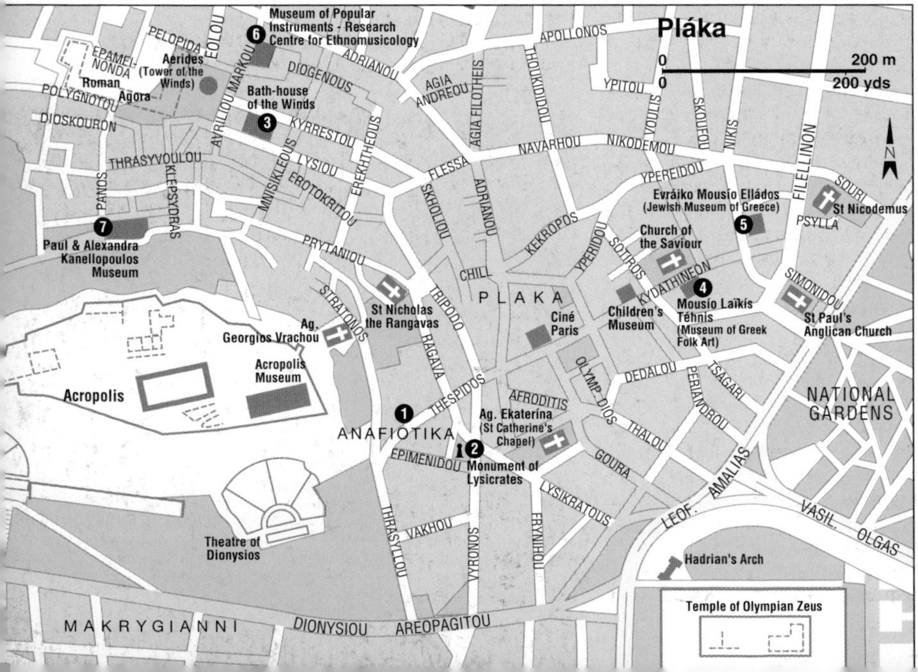

Pláka

0 200 m
0 200 yds

N

Museum of Popular Instruments - Research Centre for Ethnomusicology
Aerides (Tower of the Winds)
Roman Agora
Bath-house of the Winds
Paul & Alexandra Kanellopoulos Museum
St Nicholas the Rangavas
Ag. Georgios Vrachou
Acropolis Museum
Acropolis
Theatre of Dionysios
ANAFIOTIKA
Ag. Ekaterína (St Catherine's Chapel)
Monument of Lysicrates
PLAKA
Ciné Paris
Children's Museum
Mousío Laïkís Téhnis (Museum of Greek Folk Art)
Church of the Saviour
Evráiko Mousío Elládos (Jewish Museum of Greece)
St Nicodemus
St Paul's Anglican Church
NATIONAL GARDENS
Hadrian's Arch
Temple of Olympian Zeus
MAKRYGIANNI
PELOPIDA
EOLOU
EPAMEINONDA
POLYGNOTOU
DIOSKOURON
THRASYVOULOU
PANOS
KLEPSYDRAS
AVRILIOU MARKOU
ADRIANOU
DIOGENOUS
KYRRESTOU
LYSIOU
EROTOKRITOU
MNISIKLEOUS
EREKHTHEOUS
PRYTANIOU
STRATONOS
TRIPODO
RAGAVA
THESPIDOS
EPIMENIDOU
THRASYLLOU
VAKHOU
VYRONOS
FRYNIHOU
DIONYSIOU AREOPAGITOU
AGIA ANDREOU
AGIA FILOTHEIS
THOUKIDIDOU
APOLLONOS
YPITOU
VOULIS
SKOUFOU
NIKIS
FILELLINON
NAVARHOU NIKODEMOU
YPEREIDOU
FLESSA
SKHOLIOU
CHILL
KEKROPOS
YPERIDOU
SOTIROS
KYDATHINEON
SOURI
PSYLLA
SIMONIDOU
DEDALOU
PERIANDROU
TSAGARI
OLYMP DIOS
THALOU
AFRODITIS
GOURA
LYSIKRATOUS
LEOF. AMALIAS
VASIL. OLGAS

towards Sýntagma and Omónia. Large public buildings were erected in the deserted area and drew the population away from "The Rock", yet Pláka stubbornly remained the focus of activity.

Home to many of the young capital's leading families, whose mansions still grace the area in various hues of pastel plaster, Pláka had many firsts. The first High School of Athens was located on Adrianoú street. In 1837, Athens's first university opened at No. 5 Thólos street. The city's first police precinct has always been located in the quarter.

As the city grew and the rich moved to greener pastures, Pláka's decline began. Preserved in its present state due to building restrictions, and thus spared the apartment-block syndrome that hit Athens like a plague of concrete after World War II, Pláka retained its character in spite of the sleazy 1960s and 70s. Now with a government policy fostering renovation and money moving back in, Pláka has once again an exciting neoclassical future.

This is a nice area for visitors interested in unusual small museums and people-watching. Take a walk with a map. The street plan becomes scrambled here and there, a labyrinth which Pláka always has been. Two rules apply to those in doubt: uphill is the Acropolis: downhill are Monastiráki, the Cathedral and Sýntagma Square.

Byzantine church

On the corner of Prytaníou, moving around the curve of the Acropolis, you will find the 11th- or 12th-century Byzantine church of St Nicholas the Rangavas. This basilica, built on an earlier Christian site, is a lovely gingerbread edifice of stone and brick. Its walls include fragments of ancient columns and capitals. The saint's epithet, "Rangavas", can mean either "prodigal, dishevelled, rowdy young man" or "Leviathan".

Whitewashed village

Walking clockwise round the path which circles the Acropolis will bring you to the highest part of Pláka. The Anafiótika, the whitewashed 19th-century jumble of houses tenaciously anchored on the slope, is a village of its own with an interesting history.

Occupied in Neolithic times, the area of the **Anafiótika** ❶ (which means "village of the people from Anafi") was abandoned in classical times when the Delphic oracle proclaimed the site holy ground. During the Peloponnesian War, however, when Attica was beseiged, refugees flooded into Athens and sought refuge in the sheltering caves under the Long Rocks. Later, Ethiopian slaves sealed off the caves with walls.

A law dating from 1834 prohibited building in the area but impoverished Greeks, faced with public building restrictions, have always

Map on page 94

Upper Pláka, later called Rizókastro (Place-built-at-the-foot-of-the-castle), is immortalised in a popular street song: "You Nereid of Rizókastro, I haven't seen eyes like yours before. Going up and down the stairs, I've lost a lot of weight."

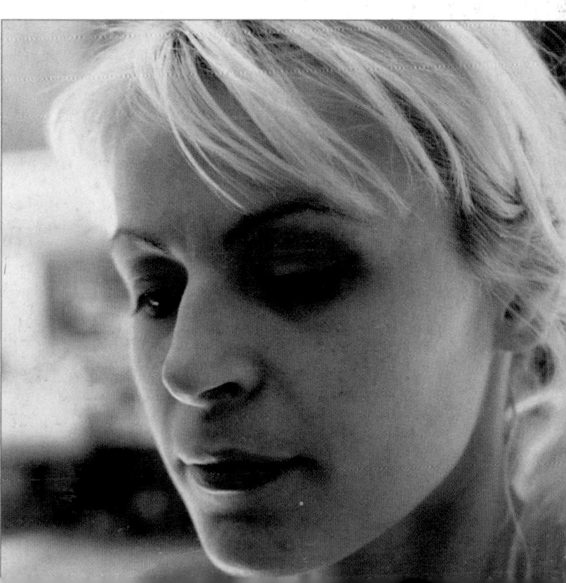

BELOW: a young Athenian.

It was inside the Monument of Lysicrates, when it was part of the Capuchin Monastery, that Lord Byron purportedly composed segments of Childe Harold in 1810–11.

reacted with ingenuity. In the 1830s, stonemasons and master craftsmen from all over the Aegean islands flocked to Athens because of the building boom, and though these skilled islanders erected beautiful mansions for wealthy Athenians, they found buying land, let alone a house, impossible on their wages. The makeshift village they threw up near Káningos Square was soon overrun by the burgeoning city.

Finally, two enterprising craftsmen from Anáfi, a Cycladic island near Santoríni, turned to the steep eastern slope of the Acropolis. Under the pretence of building a church, overnight they put together two houses for their respective families.

Notified of the deed by the inhabitants of Rizókastro, the police came up to inspect but were faced with a fait accompli. After that the Anafiótika grew like a honeycomb. At first it was only Anafiot emigrants, then others drifted in. It was and is a clannish area, as picturesque as a Cycladic island.

The residents restored the half-ruined Church of St George of the Rocks and St Simeon and brought to the latter a miracle-working icon of Our Lady of the Reeds.

Downhill is a landmark square at the junction of Lysikrátous, Epimenídou and Výronos Streets. Here is the graceful **Choregic** (musical competition) **Monument of Lysicrates** ❷ (334 BC), justly famous for its Corinthian capitals and its almost capricious delicacy of design. This "ivory tower" bears the inscription: "Lysicrates of Kikyna, son of Lysitheides, was *choregos*, the tribe of Akamantis won the victory with a chorus of boys: Theon played the flute; Lysiades of Athens trained the chorus; Evainetos was *archon*." The area around the monument has now been tidied up with the Byzantine excavations covered up and the path of old Odos ton Tripodon (Road of the Tripods, 5th–4th century BC) clearly marked.

In the same square is all that remains of the Capuchin Monastery founded in 1658 by French friars of that order, one of whom, Father Francis, first introduced tomatoes to

BELOW: the 4th-century Monument of Lysicrates.

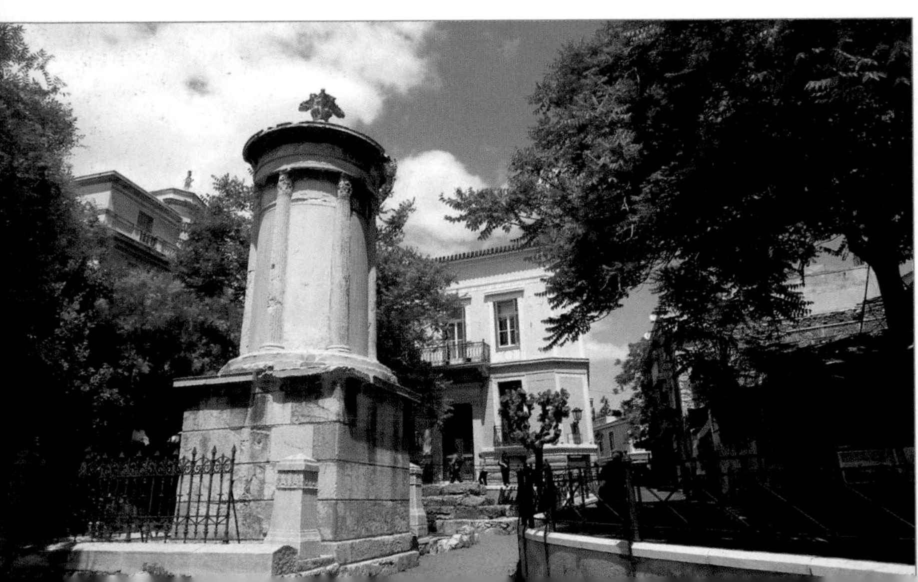

Athens. Father Simon, the superior, bought the Lysicrates Monument in 1669 and the monastery stood till 1821, with the monument itself serving as a friar's cell.

Still in Áno Pláka, in the square just down Lysikrátous toward Hadrian's Gate with a little garden and fronted by two ancient columns, stands **Agía Ekaterína** (St Catherine's Chapel), granted to the Monastery of Mt Sinai during the time of the Patriach Bartholomew, between 1765 and 1782.

Pláka's museums

Pláka is home to a number of small and fascinating museums. One of the most interesting preserves a remnant of Turkish life, the 16th-century **Bath-house of the Winds** ❸ on Kyrrestoú (open Wed–Mon, 9am–2.30pm; admission charge). This *hamam* (Turkish bath) has been beautifully restored and its warren of rooms are very atmospheric to explore *(see page 36)*. A well-produced guide gives background on the building and the place of bathing in Greek and Turkish culture.

Chief among the other museums is the excellent **Museum of Greek Folk Art** ❹ on Kydathinéon (Mousío Laïkís Téhnis; open Tues–Sun 9am–2pm; admission charge). Among the many exhibits is an excellent collection of regional Greek costume, including carnival costumes from the *dodekímero* (12 days of Christmas) and the faintly disturbing *géros* disguise from Skyros. Among the silverwork look for the *támata* (votive offerings) still seen attached to icons in Orthodox churches.

Opposite is the **Children's Museum** (open Tues–Fri 10am–2pm, Sat–Sun 10am–3pm; entrance fee; www.hcm.gr). Geared towards play, this is a good place to visit for people with young children. There is plenty to build, paint and deconstruct; in an inspired piece of foresight, overalls are provided.

At the end of Kydathinéon, on Níkis (No. 39), is the **Jewish Museum of Greece** ❺ (Evráiko Mousío Elládos; open Mon–Fri 9am– 2.30pm, Sun 10am–2pm; admission charge; www.jewishmuseum.gr). After you have rung the doorbell to be admitted you find yourself in a cool, modern interior (based on a spiral) full of exemplary displays. Founded in 1977 to collect, preserve and publicise the surviving heritage of Greece's Jews, it includes religious and ceremonial artefacts, costumes and embroideries, old photos and documents. The museum is particularly effective in demonstrating the long history of Jewish settlement, and tolerance towards it, in this part of the world.

Also in Pláka and housed in a neoclassical mansion, is the excellent **Museum of Popular Instruments–Research Centre for Ethnomusicology** ❻ (open Tues, Thu Sun 10am–2pm, Wed noon–6pm; free), based around the collection of Fívos Anoyanákis. The

Map on page 94

The Jewish museum: Jews have lived in Athens from the 3rd century BC. There are now around 7,000 living in the city.

BELOW: traditional costumes at the Museum of Greek Folk Art.

museum divides the exhibits into aerophones (blown instruments, such as the *flogéra* reed flute), chordophones (stringed instruments, like the *bouzoúki*), idiophones (instruments where the sound is produced by its body, like cymbals) and membranophones ("drums"); each can be heard at the adjacent listening posts. There is also a good shop where you can find rare recordings of Greek traditional music.

The **Paul and Alexandra Kanellopoulos Museum** ❼ (due to reopen soon after restoration: Tues–Sun 8.30am–3pm, Wed until 11pm; admission fee) is uphill from the Tower of the Winds, on the corner of Theorías and Pános streets in two neoclassical mansions with *acroteria*, those familiar scrolled ceramic roof ornaments which echo the classical marble prototypes. The Kanellopoulos is noted for its fine icons, but its collection is eclectic.

An attractive Pláka bar.

The first and second floors house pre-Christian antiquities – Prehistoric, Neolithic, early Cycladic, Minoan, Mycenean etc. Not all the objects are Greek: some are from Egypt and Mesopotamia.

Hellenistic jewellery, 6th-century BC helmets, an exquisite black-figure drinking cup of the "little master" class (also from the 6th century BC) and the matchless icons from both the School of Constantinople and the Macedonian Painting School, together with Coptic textiles, and a variety of statuettes round out this remarkable family collection. A 2nd-century painted portrait of a Woman from Fayoum is also worth seeking out.

First Gothic building

At the corner of Filellínon and Amalías avenue stands St Paul's Anglican Church, founded on Easter Monday 1838 and now resored. This church is still active. Designed by Henry Wadsworth Acland, this was the first Gothic style building in Athens, and it originally stood in a large and ornate garden.

A slab just inside the entrance commemorates the death of one George Stubbs and two merchant navy officers who died in 1685. This is the oldest British monument in Athens. The simple interior of the church is highlighted by stained glass windows depicting St Paul, St Andrew, St Stephen and St Lawrence, together with Joshua and Caleb, and the Life of David.

In the next block is the so-called Russian Church of St Nicodemus. Probably built between 1000 and 1025, it was part of a monastery within Athens's ancient walls. The monastery was destroyed in the 1701 earthquake. Ceded to the Russian Orthodox Community in 1852, the church was eventually restored and is today the largest medieval structure in the city. The belfry and bell were gifts of Czar Alexander II in the 17th century. The fascinating interior wall paintings are the work of the German artist Thiersch. ❑

BELOW: evening in Pláka and the lights come on.

RESTAURANTS & BARS

Restaurants

Ta Bakaliarakia (Tou Damigou)
Kydathinéon Street 41
(metro Akrópoli)
Tel: 210 32 25 084
Open: Mon–Sat D, Sun L and D; closed summer.
Cash only. €€
The last surviving basement outfit in the area, whose décor (except for a photo of Josephine Baker eating here in the 1930s) seemingly hasn't changed since the place was founded in 1865 – thus it has been used as a retro location for some Greek films. The barrels here contain good *retsína*, and of course the cod-with-garlic-sauce (the *bakalarákia* of the name) is the big attraction, though there are other typical dishes such as hand-cut potatoes, okra and *hórta*.

(Palea Taverna tou) Psarra
Erekthéos 16, corner Erotokrítou
(metro Monastiráki)
Tel: 210 32 18 733
Open: L and D daily.
Major credit cards. €€
Founded in 1898, this famous taverna works out of two restored old premises opposite each other on a nicely landscaped, flagstoned square by a small Byzantine chapel. Standard but well-presented Greek starters like mushrooms, *taramosaláta* and *bourekákia* are more accomplished than main dishes (which always include fish). Celebrity patronage over the years – which the management doesn't let you forget – means prices are bumped up relative to portion size.

Klimataria
Klepsýdras 5
Tel: 210 32 11 215
(metro Monastiráki)
Open: daily, D only. €
Tucked away up this stair-street is one of the less touristy tavernas in the area. The food does not rise much above the mundane, but you're here for the slightly eccentric owner and the equally odd interior, often taken over for private functions. Seating on the steps outside in summer.

Kostas
Adrianoú 116
no phone
Open: Mon–Sat 10am–11pm. Cash only. €
There's always a queue leading to the counter of this hole-in-the-wall, take-away *souvláki* booth with no tables or chairs – invariably a good sign. The original Kostas retired, and then died, a few years ago; his daughter and son-in-law ably carry on the tradition.

O Platanos
Diogénous 4
(metro Monastiráki)
Tel: 210 32 20 666
Open: L and D daily except Sun D and Aug.
Cash only. €€
Facing a square near the Tower of the Winds shaded by a namesake *plátanos* (plane tree), this small taverna founded in 1932 stresses meaty stews and *laderá* on its menu. The barrelled *retsína* is exceptionally good, and has been featured in Greek wine guides as an example of what *hýma* wine should be like.

Skholarhio (O Kouklis)
Tripódon 14
(metro Akrópoli)
Tel: 210 32 47 605
www.sholarhio.gr
Open: 11am–2am daily.
Cash only. €
Founded in 1935, this *ouzerí* with its ever-popular sheltered terrace has managed to maintain low prices without sacrificing overly much on quality. Waiters bring nearly 20 different platters – including notorious flaming sausages – to choose from on the *dískos* or giant tray; inexpensive house wine or a carafe of *oúzo* to tipple.

PRICE CATEGORIES

Prices are based on an average meal per person, including house wine:
€ = under €15
€€ = €15–25
€€€ = €25–40
€€€€ = over €40
Key: B = breakfast, L = lunch, D = dinner

Cafés/Bars

Amalthea
Tripódon 16, Pláka.
Crêpes, sweets and non-alcoholic drinks at this slightly pricey but pleasant patisserie-café

Dioskouri
Dioskoúron 13
Location, location, location is the byword of this outdoor spot with an unbeatable view over the Ancient Agora. Light snacks to go with the inevitable *frappés* and hot coffees.

To Tristrato
Dedálou 34, corner Angélou Gerónda
Open: 9am–midnight daily. €
Excellent, versatile café/patisserie which specialises in more recherché desserts like sour-cherry fruit pudding, mastic custard, *ypovrýhio* (mastic "submarine") and pannacotta. Drinks include *eráni* (diluted yogurt), *rakómelo*, home-made liqueurs and a wide range of herbal teas.

zap51.com
xavos

MONASTIRÁKI TO OMÓNIA

The area north of Pláka is Athens' bazaar. It may be named after a Little Monastery, but for thousands of years Monastiráki has been a retail centre. Today it's the place to buy anything from high fashion to high kitsch, from power tools to fresh fish

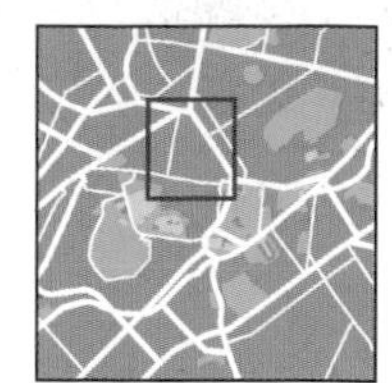

Heading more or less west from Sýntagma Square, Mitropóleos and Ermoú streets mark the transition from Pláka on the south to Athens' main commercial district on the north. Ermoú (dedicated appropriately enough to Hermes, god of commerce) was pedestrianised before the 2004 Olympics and is now a favourite strolling venue; while the clothing shops here can't compare to the boutiques of Kolonáki, they are definitely at the higher end of mid-range, with a host of outlets familiar from elsewhere in Europe.

About 500m along from Sýntagma a little *platía* opens out to accommodate the 11th-century Byzantine church of Kapnikaréa, whose strange name is partly derived from *kápnos* (smoke). Possibly it was endowed by an official responsible for collecting the hearth-tax in Byzantine times. It's erratically open, but if you do gain admission there are excellent frescoes by neo-Byzantine painter Fotis Kondoglou (he's also on view in the Ethnikí Pinakothíki, *page 153*). On the south side of the plaza here is the central branch of Hytíroglou, Greece's most renowned chain of shops selling furniture and fabric by the metre.

Mitropóleos, partly open to traffic, begins amid a handful of fur-coat vendors on the Sýntagma end, passing the tiny, medieval chapel of Agía Dynamís (Holy Strength), a monastic dependency huddling bizarrely among pillars supporting an overhang of the Ministry of Religion and Education building. Apparently, during the Greek Revolution the place was a gunpowder workshop, with the catridges being smuggled out in laundry baskets.

The monstrously ungainly **Mitrópoli** ❶ or Orthodox Cathedral, three blocks downhill on Platía

Map on page 102

LEFT: a corner of Monastiráki Square.
BELOW: a Byzantine mosaic on Kapnikaréa.

The Mitrópoli entrance.

Mitropóleos, is by contrast a good example of too many cooks spoiling the broth, in this case the original design by Danish architect Theophil Hansen for a novel Gothic-Romanesque/Byzantine/Renaissance hybrid. Beginning in the late 1830s, three more architects tackled the project before it was consecrated in May 1862, having absorbed masonry from dozens of older churches. The Cathredral is today the seat of Hristodoúlos, Archbiship of Athens and All Greece (excepting most of the New Territories added after 1913, which are still subject to the patriarch in Istanbul). Inside, on the left, is the sarcophagus of Patriarch Gregory V, whose remains were repatriated here some decades after he was hanged in Constantinople at the outset of the Greek Revolution, for failure to guarantee the non-seditious behaviour or his flock.

Also a masonry cannibal – but a far more graceful one – is the **Mikrí Mitrópoli** or Old Cathedral immediately adjacent, constructed during the 12th century on the site of a still older church, and before that a temple to the goddess of childbirth. Exterior

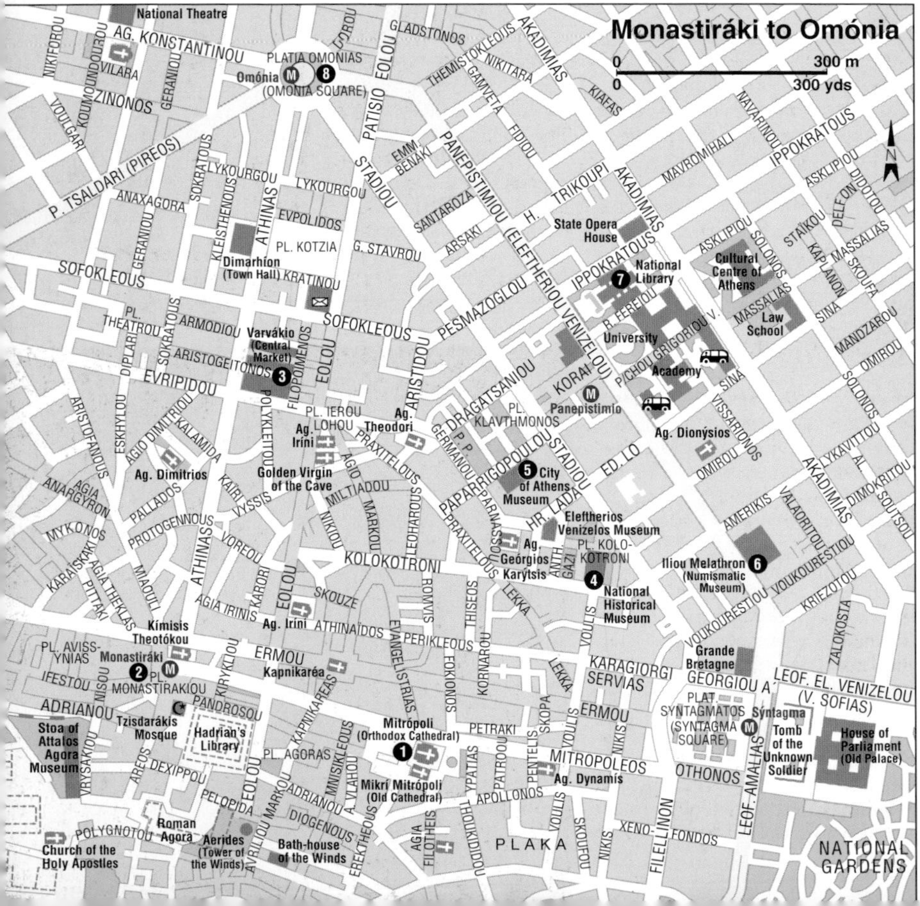

Monastiráki to Omónia

0 300 m
0 300 yds

reliefs, recycled from Roman, Hellenistic and Byzantine sources, include heraldic animal themes, and a frieze setting out the ancient festival calendar, the months denoted by the signs of the zodiac. This plinth was probably removed from a ruined temple of Serapis and Isis which stood nearby. The dedication is double: to the Panagía Gorgeopikóös (The Virgin Swift to Hear) and Ágios Elefthérios, interestingly, the patron saint of mothers in labour.

Within a few blocks below Platía Mitropóleos, traffic is again diverted to Ermoú, and beyond Platía Dimopratiríou – the former municipal auction square – is the pedestrianised approach to Monastiráki, lined with three hotly competing *souvláki/ gýros*-based restaurants. Be careful where you sit, as annexes are ambiguously labelled and table turf-wars prevail.

Monastiráki

Ermoú and Mitropóleos converge at **Platía Monastirakíou** ❷, which takes its name from the little 10th-century monastic church of **Kímisis Theotókou** (Assumption of the Virgin) to one side of the square, all that remains of a once far vaster convent whose grounds extended across the entire area and some way up towards Omónia. Meticulously refurbished externally through the 1990s, it is usually closed; though following many insensitive alterations there is little of note to see inside. The only notes of elegance are provided by the 1920s façade of the metro station, with coconut- and fruit-sellers tending their carts out front, and the **Tzisdarákis Mosque** *(see page 36)* built above the shops whose revenues used to support it in Ottoman times.

Otherwise the square is disappointing: its assorted bank façades, barriers and idling unemployed immigrants offer scant inducement to linger. It is in fact a botched result of an ambitious makeover plan that ran out of steam.

The *platía* is, however, the hub of the historic Athenian bazaar and both tourists and Athenians make a point of calling in at the so-called "flea-market" in two of the six streets which converge here. Pedestrianised Pandrósou, heading east-southeast, was until the 1960s dubbed "Tsarouhádika Lane" after the local trade in *tsaroúhia*, the pom-pommed shoes worn as part of traditional Greek mountain costume. Now the close-packed little stalls stock very ordinary tourist tat such as erotic painted vases, reproduction statues and anti-orthotic sandals.

Iféstou, heading west and also car-free, is more appealing and venerable, following the line of the Byzantine and Ottoman bazaar. These days a mélange of beads, logo T-shirts, military surplus gear, copperware, used CDs, fake designer jeans, musical instruments, a basement at No. 24 full of not terribly covetable, dog-eared paperback books and backgammon sets are on sale. Towards its far end

Busking gypsy musicians, mostly from Romania or Russia and often very accomplished on clarinet, guitar or accordion, wend their way through the crowds or rehearse on Platía Dimopratiríou.

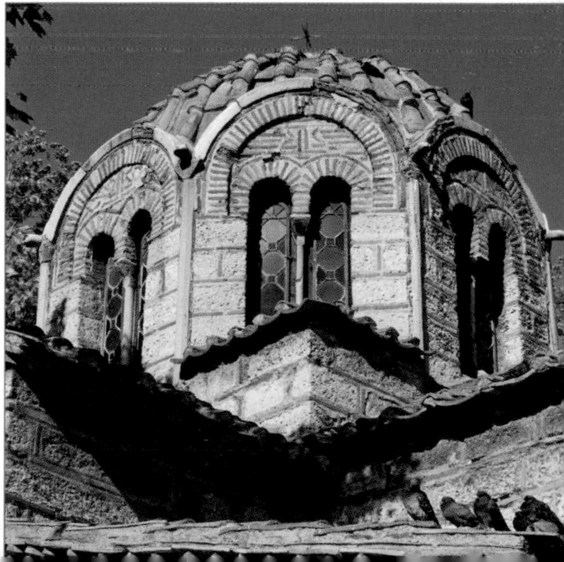

BELOW: Kapnikaréa church on Ermoú street.

TIP

Amazingly, there is a lively commerce in used OTE phone-cards in Greece – some of their "colour" sides are indeed attractive – and you'll often find dealers for these just beyond the church of Ágios Fílippos.

Iféstou opens out into Platía Avissynías, locus of the "real" flea-market and at its liveliest on Sundays. The restored furniture here is exorbitantly priced, most of the kitsch items on display stay there week after week, and those in the know claim that the real deals (relatively speaking) are to be found in the much more chaotic Piraeus flea-market. But especially during low season on a weekday, hard bargaining can secure fair prices for small, intriguing objects such as copper Ottoman-era coffee-grinders and ingenious wooden guards to protect grain-reapers' fingers.

There are a few more indoor antique shops on the farther reaches of parallel Adrianoú just before it meets the 19th-century church of Ágios Fílippos, around which a contingent of hawkers attempt to flog hopeless stock like East German-manufactured alarm clocks and unbranded battery-operated radios from the 1980s, their wares spread on the ground. Savvy Athenians show up mostly to drink and nibble at the various cafés and restaurants which have sprung up since the millennium along Adrianoú, or make an afternoon of it at musical Café Avissynia just off the eponymous square.

The Central Market

The serious *agorá* (marketplace) lies beyond Ermoú; with Athinás and Eólou as its main south-to-north axes, it extends all the way to Omónia Square and Stadíou Street, filling a triangle laid out by the Bavarian town-planners. There are some superb iron-and-glass Belle Époque marquees sheltering shops, especially on Athinaïdos, Evripídou and Athinás streets.

Once upon a time, each patch of street, whether major thoroughfare or one-block, crooked lane jinking along in defiance of the orderly Bavarian vision, would have been the exclusive province of a particular trade, a tradition going back at least to the guilds of the Byzantine era and possibly even Roman times. This homogenity has been much diluted by interlopers – outlets for bolts of cloth, thread, rope, yarn, socks and knickers, ties, cheap watches and clocks, costume jewellery – and the effects of immigration, but you can still see vestiges of this specialisation.

For example, the streets behind Platía Klavthmónos are given over to lighting and electrical appliance shops; wood stoves and barbeques are found only on Ermoú west of Athinás; Athinás itself, at least near Monastiráki, is largely the province of power tools; men's and women's caps are confined to a handful of shops on Vorréou; Praxitélous is full of bead stalls; while the upper reaches of Kolokotróni have a remarkable concentration of ink-cartridge refill franchises.

Eólou has benefited from pedestrianisation like Ermoú, and while it will probably never be as prestigious as Ermoú, already some bars and

BELOW: salted sardines and anchovies.

clubs are moving in to take advantage of the after-dark calm. Serenity of another sort is dispensed right next to the flower market (busiest on Sundays) at **Agía Iríni** church, where the best Greek Orthodox sacred chanting outside of Mount Áthos can be heard most Sundays starting at about 9.30, courtesy of the internationally renowned Byzantine choir led by Lykourgos Angelopoulos.

The only other church of note in the district is the 11th-century, externally relief-carved **Ágii Theodóri** at the east end of Evripídou, generally open all day though there is little to appreciate inside other than smoke-blackened frescoes and the feel of a much-loved, much-resorted-to little shrine. As is the case with all Athens' Byzantine churches, the surrounding ground level has risen in the intervening centuries so the church now looks sunken.

The heart of the market district in all senses is the covered, elegantly neoclassical **Varvákio** ❸ dating from 1879, and bracketed by Athinás and Éolou, and Sofokléous and Evripídou on the north and south respectively. Never mind that growing numbers of Athenians prefer to shop at suburban supermarkets like Alfa Vita, Champion Marinopoulos or Carrefour, or make regular pilgrimages to the IKEA by the airport, the Varvákio still hums with activity from dawn until 3pm every workday.

The interior – with entrances from each of the streets cited above – is taken up entirely by the central fish and meat bazaar, and the latter in particular is not for the sensitive or squeamish: cuts and guts are literally in your face. The fish section encompasses all manner of sea creatures, laid out more enticingly on marble slabs or boxes of ice, their provenance (if Greek and not Moroccan or Egyptian) proudly touted on little signs hand-lettered with indelible marker.

Near the centre are a trio of 24-hour restaurants specialising in *patsás* (tripe and trotter soup), which is especially popular in the small hours when those in search of this traditional hangover cure come to indulge. Up another aisle towards Sofokléous is the incon-

A neo-Byzantine church door handle.

BELOW: fresh fish in the Central Market.

spicuous entrance to one of Athens' last surviving, and most worthwhile, *rebétika* music clubs, Stoa Athanaton.

The chamber of the Old Parliament, which now houses the National Historical Museum.

The fruit and vegetable market occupies the *platía* across Athinás, which was redeveloped during the 1990s to incorporate pedestrianisation, an elevated café and an underground car park. Beyond this, across Sokrátous, lies Platía Theátrou, named for the first theatre in post-1832 Greece. The imposing building is now a primary school.

Evripídou Street has traditionally been home to herbs, spices, nuts and dried fruits, though there's an entire shop selling nothing but cheese, and no shortage of olives, beans and petrified salted cod bursting out of gunny sacks. Flavours and aromas get distinctly more Asiatic as you head west, reflecting the tastes of the new Bengali and Chinese immigrant communities, though sadly the Chinese storefronts, as elsewhere in Greece, seem more interested in flogging cheap and nasty clothing than exotic foodstuffs.

BELOW: one of the many small specialist shops in the area.

Flesh of a different sort from the Varvákio's has long been peddled on Sofokléous, which begins life decorously enough at the Hrimatistírio or Stock Exchange (founded 1876; a new annexe has been built a block away) and then promenades through what remains of Athens' traditional red-light district; the arresting designer Hotel Fresh at No. 26 has been the main engine of a mild gentrification here. Most of the prostitutes have decamped to Keramikós, though a few transvestite practitioners remain.

The Historic Centre

As you tend towards the hypoteneuse of the central triangle, demarcated by Stadíou and Panepistimíou, you enter what is called with some justice the "Historic Centre", the history in question being the years after modern Greek independence. Platía Kolokotróni, at the start of the eponymous street, contains an equestrian statue of the revolutionary war hero Theodoros Kolokotronis, "O Géros tis Moreás" (Old Man of the Morea), rearing up just in front of the **National Historical Museum** ❹ (Tues–Sun 9am–2pm; admission charge). This is housed in the Paleá Voulí (Old Parliament), in which capacity it served from 1871 to 1935; the chamber is maintained as it was then. Three-times premier Theodoros Deligiannis was assassinated on the front steps in 1905, by a gambler infuriated by his campaign against card-and-dice dens. Exhibits cover all eras from the fall of Constantinople to the court of Otho, with special emphasis on the War of Independence, in particular engravings of the key battles, plus plenty of embroidered uniforms and decorated weaponry.

Behind Platía Kolokotróni is the much-rebuilt church of Ágios Geórgios Karýtsis and its little square, on the north side of which is the venerable premises of the Filologikós Sýllogos "Parnassos" (The Parnassos Literary Society), which hosts uplifting talks and chamber-music concerts. A few steps up Hrístou Láda towards Stadíou, at no. 2, is **Eleftherios Venizelos Museum** (Mon–Fri 9.30am–1.30pm; free), containing personal effects and photographic archives pertaining to the early 20th-century statesman who served 12 years as prime minister, between 1910 and 1933; some of the stormiest decades of Greek history.

Just around the corner looms Platía Klavthmónos, which takes its name from the ancient Greek *klavthmón*, or weeping and wailing. The lamentation in question was that of civil servants from nearby ministries, who would be summarily dismissed with each change of government from the mid-1870s to the mid-1890s, when Deligiannis alternated in power with his arch-rival Harilaos Trikoupis. More recent polarisation – in particular the civil war and its aftermath – prompted the erection, in the early 1990s, of the unlabelled statue of three stylised, embracing figures on the Stadíou side of the square, known as Ethnikí Symfilíosi (National Reconciliation).

On the southeast side of Platía Klavthmónos, at Paparrigopoúlou 7, is a relatively modest building which in 1834 was the grandest mansion infant Athens had to offer to the young royal couple Otho and Amelie while a proper palace was being built at what is now Sýntagma. Today it shelters the **City of Athens Museum** ❺ (Mon, Wed–Fri 9am–4pm, Sat–Sun 10am–3pm; admission charge), with several rooms of period furnishings recreating the couple's domestic *milieu* – including a throne room – and a new wing featuring paintings of the town through the 19th century, and a model of Athens as it was in 1842, with just a few hundred buildings.

Continuing northwest, the last square encountered before Omónia is Platía Kotziá, named after a former mayor of Athens. He should probably be execrated rather than honoured for tearing down the vanished, third neoclassical monument here: the national theatre which succeeded the older one on Platía Theátrou. The remaining two neoclassical buildings – the relatively modest *dimarhío* (town hall) and more imposing headquarters of the Ethnikí Trápeza tis Elládos (National Bank of Greece) – face each other across an archaeological site: a section of ancient road, houses, shops and part of the Classical city's fortifications, all uncovered during the 1980s when excavation began for a car park.

Stadíou and Panepistimíou

The Germans who arrived in the mid-1830s, with architects and city planners in tow, envisioned an orderly, Central European style capital with wide boulevards and sweeping vistas from strategic points of the Acropolis. Omónia,

In a city not known for monumental modern art, you can glimpse a bold example by nipping across Stadíou and then down to Amerikís Street, where the headquarters of the Pireos Bank is home, in the entrance foyer, to Fernando Botero's Rape of Europa: one of his typically rotund figures serenely astride an equally squat Zeus-as-Bull.

BELOW: the City of Athens Museum, once the home of King Otho.

rather than Sýntagma, was to the be the official centre of town, and Stadíou was so named because it was to link Omónia with the ancient stadium some 1,700 metres (1 mile) to the southeast. But things got in the way, in the shape of the National Gardens and Royal Palace, so Stadíou never arrived at its namesake.

The parallel street, Panepistimíou (officially renamed Eleftheríou Venizélou, though absolutely nobody uses that designation), unfolded more according to plan. Another aspect of the German master-plan which was also honoured were the numerous shopping arcades, in imitation of the ancient stoas, which perpendicularly link the two boulevards. Most of these elegant pedestrian thoroughfares, often with a round atrium at the centre, have miraculously managed to survive post-World War II "redevelopment", and the shops in them still for the most part thrive. Though as in the central market area, they are organised according to a local rather than north-European logic: the elegant Stoá Orféos is almost completely devoted to upmarket luggage and handbag merchants.

Between Stadíou and Panepistimíou is the pedestrianised esplanade of Koráï, now enlivened by occasional art installations. The subterranean Asty art-house cinema at No. 4 endured a grim interval as a Gestapo interrogation centre during the German occupation of 1941–44.

If Stadíou is relentlessly commercial – with theatres, upmarket shops, a few hotels, and the headquarters of various banks on, or just off it – Panepistimíou is as monumental as the new post-Independence elite intended. (This aspect is not lost on the frequent demonstrations which march from Omónia to Sýntagma; it's the only boulevard in the centre wide enough to accommodate them.) At No. 12, opposite the massive Attica department store, is the **Iliou Melathron** ❻ (Palace of Ilium, ie Troy), built as a mansion for Heinrich Schliemann, the excavator of Mycenae and Troy, in 1878. After a chequered public history (including a spell as the main Court of Appeal), it is now the **Numismatic Museum** (open Tues–Sun 8.30am–3pm; admission charge). Even if you have no particular interest in the over 600,000 coins on the premises, it's worth stopping in to see Heinrich and Sophie Schliemann's domestic taste: frescoes, mosaics and coffered ceilings.

A bit further along the same side of the street, at No. 20, looms the imposing Catholic cathedral of **Ágios Dionýsios** (the Areopagite), patron saint of Athens, where Sunday services see foreign Catholic parishioners – mostly Poles and Filipinos – vastly outnumber the local Greek community, principally descended from Catholic islanders on Sýros and Tínos. On the corner of Sina stands the neo-Byzantine Ofthalmiatrío or Eye Hospital, designed by Theophil Hansen in 1845 as a sort of encore to his work on the nearby University.

The three "Temples of Learning" – the **University**, flanked by the **National Academy** and the **Library**❼ – are covered in detail in the neoclassical feature *(see pages*

BELOW: neoclassical decoration on the University.

160–3). In day-to-day life, they seem rather underused, because most university activity today is carried on in drab modern buildings a few blocks away. Only the Library continues to function as intended (with restricted access). The Academy is used mainly for special functions, and the University building is taken up by administrative offices. Pop out of the main Panepistimíou metro "rabbit hole", however, and you'll be left in little doubt that this is a focus of student life: in the broad square in front of the building there are invariably hunger strikers for the cause of the moment, leaflet booths or – when feelings run particularly high – banners and rallies.

Beyond the Library, before reaching Omónia, Panepistimíou offers most of the major (and a few minor) music-CD retailers in the city, yet another aspect of trade clustering.

Omónia

Omónia ❽, or Platía Omónias ("Concord Square"), marked the northern edge of Athens until after the 1870s. The concord was apparently that imposed by oath upon rival gangs of political thugs who fought it out here after King Otho's deposition in 1862. During King George I's reign (1863–1913) Omónia almost lived up to the city planners' ambitions for it, with fountains playing in the centre amid palm trees, a bandstand, and elegant hotels at the perimeter. It's hard to credit this when confronted with today's circular maelstrom of traffic – six major and two minor streets meet here – the few surviving neoclassical buildings amid the brutalist post-war architecture, and the slightly edgy human factor. And this is after a pre-Olympic clean-up drive banished most of the drug addicts, prostitutes and homeless Albanians who called the square home.

The redesigned, elevated parkland in the centre is shadeless and unattractive, and the businesses at the perimeter – including newsagents whose main stock seems to be hard-core porn – relentlessly downmarket, except for a handful of renovated mid-range hotels of interest mostly to certain businessmen. ❑

One of the surviving neoclassical features of Omónia Square.

BELOW: shopping on Ermoú.

RESTAURANTS & BARS

Restaurants

Monastiráki

Baïraktaris
Platía Monastirakíou 2
(metro Monastiráki)
Tel: 210 32 13 036
Open daily all day.
Cash only. **€–€€**
The assiduous touting outside here can annoy, and the take-away *gýros* or *souvláki* isn't a patch on Thanassis' (*see below*), but step inside the cosy dining area and opinions improve. Since its founding in 1879, everyone from a succession of prime ministers to actors and artists has eaten here, as photographs on the wall attest, and the *magireftá* is washed down by inexpensive barrel wine. Expect occasional spontaneous live music sesssions.

PRICE CATEGORIES

Prices are based on an average meal per person, including house wine:
€ = under €15
€€ = €15–25
€€€ = €25–40
€€€€ = over €40
Key: B = breakfast, L = lunch, D = dinner

Café Avyssinia
Kynéttou 72
(metro Monastiráki)
Tel: 210 32 17 047
www.avissinia.gr
Open Tues–Sat noon–2am, Sun noon–7pm.
Cash only. **€€€**
After browsing the flea-market at weekends, there's no handier or more atmospheric place to retire to than Café Avyssinia – a taverna rather than café, despite the name – for hearty, Macedonian-influenced food and a spot of bohemian entertainment courtesy of an accordionist and a singer. Upstairs tables, or those outside, are a bit quieter.

O Thanassis
Mitropóleos 69
(metro Monastiráki)
Tel: 210 32 44 705.
Open daily noon–midnight.
Cash only. **€**
Three hotly competing *souvlatzídika* (*souvláki* stalls) cluster here where Mitropóleos meets Platía Monastirakíou – be careful whose table you sit at, as annexes and turf-wars abound – but it's obvious which is the best from the numbers of folk queuing for a take-away or waiting for a table (you can't book).

Thanassis' specialty is kebab, a variation on *souvláki* where minced meat is blended with onion and spices. The dining room is crowded and noisy, the outdoor tables somewhat less so. Beware the side dish of chili peppers – most Greek food is bland but these will blow your head off.

Omónia

To Athinaïkon
Themistokleous 2
(metro Omónia)
Tel: 210 38 38485
Open Mon–Sat 11.30am–12.30am
Cash only. **€**
A traditional eaterie (established 1932), all dark wood, tiled floors, marble table-tops and framed memorabilia. It's popular with lawyers and businesspeople from the Omónia Square area, and a lively place to enjoy *mezédes* in an animated atmosphere. You can choose between a vast range of appetisers (technically this is an *ouzerí*) or a full meal.

To Diporto
Sokrátous 9, corner Theátrou (no sign outside)
(metro Omónia)
No phone.
Open Mon–Sat noon–6pm.
Cash only. **€–€€**
Located at the western edge of the central market district, To Diporto (meaning double entrance) is tucked anonymously under a disused shop, but attracts a huge range of clientele, from "suits" to market-stall-holders. They're here for the excellent, no-nonsense grub: grilled or fried fish of the day (often sar-

LEFT: Baïraktaris has a history stretching back to 1879.

dines or pandora), a stew or two, mountainous salads, some kind of bean dish and of course strong *retsína* with soda water to dilute its impact. Such is the place's popularity, and limited space, that you're expected to share tables with strangers. Go soon before it's gentrified into something much duller.

Guru
Platía Theátrou 10
(metro Omónia)
Tel: 210 32 46 530
Open: D Mon–Sat, closed late-Jul to late-Aug. **€€€**
Upmarket Thai restaurant, crowded mezzanine bar with small dance floor and top-floor jazz club all in one; the food is authentically spicy and savoury.

Iy Klimatarla
Platía Theátrou 2
(metro Omónia)
Tel: 210 32 16 629
www.klimatria.gr
Open: L Fri–Sun, D Mon–Sat, take-away noon–8pm. **€€**
Some of Iy Klimataria's endearing rough edges got filed smooth in a 2006 refit, but it's still an excellent source of hearty, mostly meat-based cooking – as the row of *gástres*, the traditional stewing apparatus of mountain shepherds, tells you as you enter. Prices are a tad bumped up for this category of restaurant, but they help support very competent live acoustic music, a world away from "Greek Night" travesties, performed Mon–Sat eve and Sun afternoon. Limited but well-priced wine list.

To Monastiri
upstairs at the Varvákio central meat market
(metro Omónia)
No phone.
Open 24 hours daily.
Cash only. **€**
Patsás (trotter soup) and *iskembé* (tripe soup) are the time-honoured Balkan hangover cures, and this is the best place to get them. Although it's open round the clock, it's at its liveliest between midnight and 5pm.

Pak-Indian
Menándrou 13, off Platía Theátrou
(metro Omónia)
Tel: 210 32 19 412
Open daily to 1am. **€€**
Many of the little Indian-subcontinent canteens in this part of Athens don't expect outsiders, especially female outsiders. This one's an exception, with handsome décor, careful cooking and occasional musical performances.

O Telis
Evripídou 86
(metro Omónia)
Tel: 210 32 42 775
Open Mon–Sat L and D to 1am. Cash only. **€**
The Greek-language listings magazine *Athinorama* is often a bit idiosyncratic, but in this case they've got it just about right: *Láos ke Kolonáki tróne me ta héria hiriná brizolákia* ("High life and low life chomp on pork chops without a knife"). The famous spicy salad tends to run out early, the menu is otherwise quite limited, the interior décor equally so, but the price is right and the outdoor tables pleasant.

Cafés/Bars

Aiolis
Eólou 23
(metro Monastiráki)
Tel: 210 33 12 839
Open daily 10am–2am
Restored neoclassical premises with tables out on the pedestrian walkway right opposite Agía Iríni church. Alcohol, hot drinks and desserts are on offer; romantically dim lighting after dark.

Eletheroudakis
Panepistimíou 17
(metro Panepistimíou)
The sixth floor of this bookshop has uneven ventilation and no great view, but it compensates with some of the best (and priciest) coffees in town, plus light snacks.

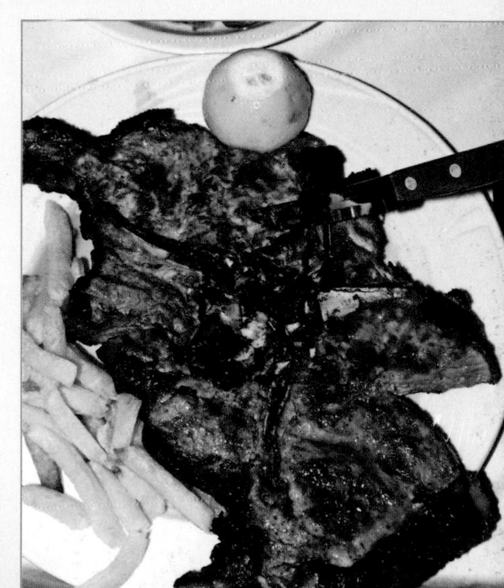

RIGHT: grilled chops and chips.

50

SÝNTAGMA TO KOLONÁKI

Sýntagma Square is the civic centre of modern Athens: in the vicinity are the parliament building, ministries, embassies and the National Gardens. Nearby Kolonáki is characterised by expensive apartments, upmarket shops and some fine museums

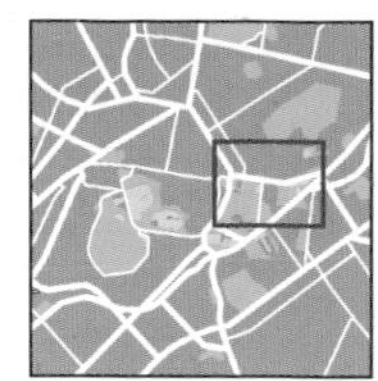

The hub of Athens is the open area called Sýntagma, or Constitution Square. Here is the centre of all activity, from the functioning of government to the meeting of friends, and all degrees in between. The square is hemmed in by busy streets but since the opening of the new metro station has received a facelift, with live music on some nights and well maintained gardens.

On the west side of the square there also are bus and trolley stops, banks and the inevitable McDonald's. The south side of the square is lined with offices and the street is named after Othonos (Otho), the first king of modern Greece. The north side has luxury hotels, notably the Plaza and Grande Bretagne. Leading off from here is the wide Vasilísis Sofías (also known as El. Venizélou) Avenue, lined with large neo-classical buildings, either foreign embassies (among them the French, Italian and Portuguese) or government ministries. Unfortunately the British Embassy, just off Sofías, looks fine from the front but like a brutal concrete fortress at the back.

The square is often a gathering point for demonstrations (which often end up outside the American embassy at the far end of Vasilísis Sofías) about everything from tax protests to election rallies; which means traffic comes to a complete halt, buses are re-routed and it is generally accepted that transport chaos reigns.

The **House of Parliament ❶**, a large lemon-coloured structure, occupies the high ground. It was built to be the Palace, but after the second of two serious fires, it was judged in 1935 to be unfit for royal occupation, and turned over to the Voulí or Parliament.

In front of the building is the **Tomb of the Unknown Soldier**,

LEFT: Kolonáki cafés.
BELOW: the square has received a facelift.

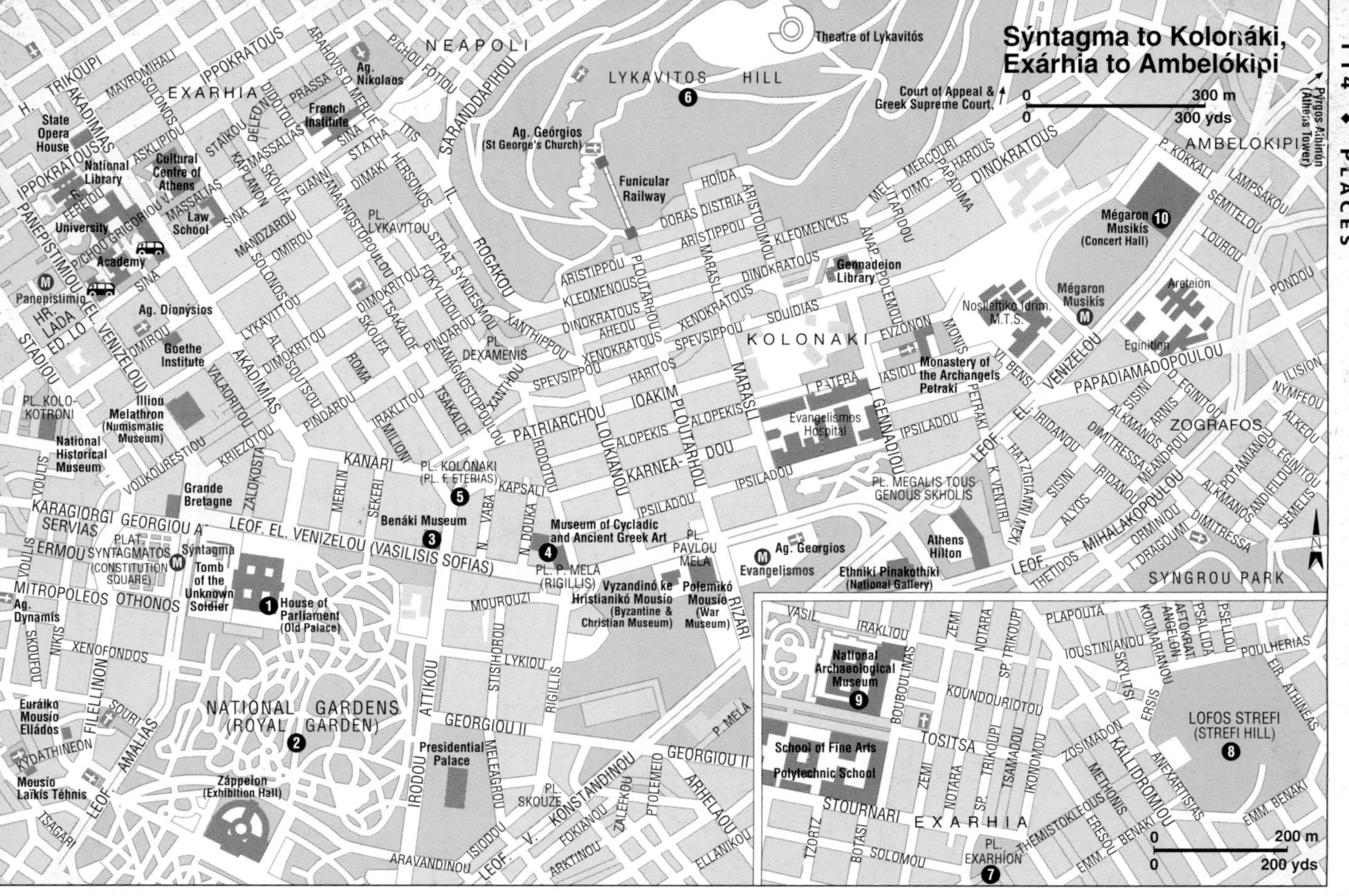

Sýntagma to Kolonáki, Exárhia to Ambelókipi
0 300 m
0 300 yds
0 200 m
0 200 yds
Pýrgos Athinón (Athens Tower)
Court of Appeal & Greek Supreme Court
Theatre of Lykavitós
LYKAVITOS HILL
Funicular Railway
Ag. Geórgios (St George's Church)
NEAPOLI
EXARHIA
KOLONAKI
AMBELOKIPI
ZOGRAFOS
SYNGROU PARK
Mégaron Musikís (Concert Hall)
Mégaron Musikís
Areteion
Eginition
Nosileftiko Idrim. M.T.S.
Monastery of the Archangels Petraki
Gennadeion Library
Evangelismos Hospital
Athens Hilton
Ethnikí Pinakothiki (National Gallery)
Ag. Georgios
Evangelismos
Polemikó Mousío (War Museum)
Vyzandinó ke Hristianikó Mousío (Byzantine & Christian Museum)
Museum of Cycladic and Ancient Greek Art
Benáki Museum
Presidential Palace
NATIONAL GARDENS (ROYAL GARDEN)
Záppeion (Exhibition Hall)
House of Parliament (Old Palace)
Tomb of the Unknown Soldier
Sýntagma
PLAT. SYNTAGMATOS (CONSTITUTION SQUARE)
Grande Bretagne
Ilíou Melathron (Numismatic Museum)
National Historical Museum
Goethe Institute
Ag. Dionýsios
Law School
Cultural Centre of Athens
National Library
University
Academy
State Opera House
Panepistimío
French Institute
Ag. Nikolaos
Ag. Dynamis
Euráiko Mousío Elládos
Mousío Laïkís Téhnis
LOFOS STREFI (STREFI HILL)
National Archaeological Museum
School of Fine Arts
Polytechnic School
PL. EXARHÍON
PL. KOLONAKI (PL. F. ETERIAS)
PL. DEXAMENIS
PL. LYKAVITOU
PL. KOLOKOTRONI
PL. P. MELA (RIGILLIS)
PL. PAVLOU MELA
PL. MEGALIS TOUS GENOUS SKHOLIS
LEOF. EL. VENIZELOU (VASILISIS SOFIAS)
AKADIMIAS
PANEPISTIMIOU (EL. VENIZELOU)
STADIOU
PATRIARCHOU IOAKIM
MARASLI
SKOUFA
SOLONOS
H. TRIKOUPI
IPPOKRATOUS
HERODOU ATTIKOU
AMALIAS
FILELLINON
LEOF. V. KONSTANDINOU
GEORGIOU II
LEOF. MIHALAKOPOULOU
VENIZELOU
PAPADIAMADOPOULOU
DINOKRATOUS
KLEOMENOUS
LOUKIANOU
PLOUTARHOU
KARNEADOU
IRODOTOU
RIGILLIS
ERMOU
MITROPOLEOS
OTHONOS
KARAGIORGI SERVIAS
STOURNARI
TOSITSA
KALLIDROMIOU
THEMISTOKLEOUS

where visiting dignitaries lay wreaths, and on major holidays, officials bury its marble step in flowers. The bas-relief of a dying soldier is modelled on a sculpture from the Temple of Aphaia in Aegina; the bronze shields on the wall represent the victorious battles in which Greek soldiers have fought since 1821. El Alamein, Crete and Korea might be names recognisable to English-speakers.

Keeping watch over the tomb are a pair of the élite soldiers called *évzones*, an honour guard which changes every hour. On Sundays and holidays these men wear the uniform of the Revolutionary mountain fighters, a short white *foustanélla* – a cotton kilt with 400 pleats – and white stockings, embroidered velvet jacket and heel-less red shoes with pom-poms, called *tsaroúchi*. On weekdays they wear a tan tunic in summer, navy blue in winter, but still perform their elaborate goose-step choreography as they change positions.

In the beginning

It was only after Athens became the capital of independent Greece in 1834 that this area was developed. The War of Independence bankrupted most Greeks: in 1832, Ermoú street was a wide dirt road lined with a few huts. Property vacated by the Turks was going for a song, often to the repatriated. Yet the rebuilding of Athens was strangely desultory. Only 160 houses had gone up, and deliveries of window glass and wood were few and far between.

At the time, Athens was ruled by King Otho, the teenage son of King Louis I of Bavaria. King Louis' large-scale planning of Munich created that city's graceful, classical style. Louis announced that Athens would rise again, in the "shade of the Acropolis", a new city to be raised on the ruins of the ancient, and the glory of the classical world restored.

It might have worked better to build a new city in an underdeveloped area instead of superimposing the plans on top of an old village, but architects and designers rallied to the task, the expatriate Greek Stamatis Cleanthes and his German colleague Edward Schaubert came from Munich.

Athenians objected strenuously. Expansive boulevards, would be too hot. It's all too big, too wide. The little streets are going to look like slums in contrast. Where is the shade? Where are the shops to be? They were, perhaps, accustomed to mazes of streets with plenty of hiding places.

There was dissension and the regent called on Leo von Klenze, another Munich architect, to sort out the mess. His revised plan was adopted on the same day in 1834 that Athens was declared the official capital of Greece.

Athenians, ever political, made an issue of it. The plans were altered. The green parks vanished.

Map on page 114

In Classical times, this area contained Apollo's Garden of the Muses, which gave the name "Square of the Muses" to the space on the town plans of the 1830s. Here Aristotle lectured his students as they walked, earning the nickname the "Ramblers" – the Peripatetics.

BELOW: the former palace on the east side of Sýntagma Square now houses the Parliament.

Sculpture in the National Gardens.

Streets that were meant to be wider became narrower instead. Stoas that looked elegant on paper ended as crooked alleys. The old narrow streets in the centre still criss-cross the wide avenues, making a web of little lanes that causes traffic control headaches, and accommodate hundreds of tiny shops.

The king and his new queen, Amelie, took up residence in the Papagarrípoulos house, near Klavthmónos Square, while they waited for the palace to be completed. In January 1840, the king threw a party for his builders on the day he laid the cornerstone. He didn't spare any expense: 50 roast lambs and 4,000 bottles of wine were consumed during the celebration.

By 1842 the Royal Palace was standing ready on the high ground of Perivoláki (Little Garden) Square, where Queen Amelie had been planting trees and flowers. The building has been described as hideous, dignified, clumsy, austere, ugly and a fine example of neoclassical architecture. King Louis professed himself satisfied that it was sufficiently imposing to impress the people, which was what what one wants of a Royal Palace. Now it houses the Parliament.

BELOW: *évzones* guard the Tomb of the Unknown Soldier.

A palatial hotel

The houses of the general public were small and mean compared to the fine public buildings or the houses of the wealthy. A Mr Demitríou applied for permission to build a mansion under the windows of the palace. Since the design was an elegant affair by Theofil Hansen, already a well-known name in the new Greek architecture, His Highness was pleased. Besides, it was a good location for extra guest rooms, which the king required for state visitors. So many stayed there that it was called the "Petit Palais".

For a brief while after the owner died, it was occupied by the French Archaeological Institute. Later, it was bought by a royal cook who had gone to Paris, became a master chef and wanted to run a hotel. Now dubbed the **Grande Bretagne**, the building was described by a guest as "among the greatest hotels of Europe, for its charming position, imposing building, well-ventilated rooms [it was Europe's first air-conditioned hotel], exceptionally good cuisine and architectural regularity". Until the 20th century, however, there was only one bathroom – in the basement.

In 1924 and again in 1930 the Grande Bretagne was enlarged, in harmony with the original design. During World War II it served in turn as headquarters for Greek, then German and then British officers. The building seems to be lucky: at one point, Greek soldiers mined it to blow up the Germans, but the task was unsuccessful. In 1944, during the Civil War, Communists lobbed a grenade at Winston Churchill who was inside conferring with the government: they missed.

Leafy romance

As the Royal Palace neared completion, Queen Amelie determined on an exotic **Royal Garden** ❷ nearby. Almost 40 acres were set aside, and the French garden designer François-Louis Barrauld was imported to make the plans. Soon the workers found themselves excavating a lost Roman site, and it was decided to leave the antiquities in place. A mosaic floor, tumbled columns and fragments of marble lend romance to the gardens even today.

Thousands of plants were laboriously brought in by cart from Italy and far flung parts of Greece. As usual, water was a serious problem; then a 6th-century BC aqueduct was found under the wilting shrubbery, which serves as a basis for the present watering system. Water now flows through channels throughout the gardens, occasionally passing through ponds where ducks, goldfish and turtles can be found.

The biggest duck pond is near a depressing zoo close to the centre of the gardens. The animals on show are mostly birds, and all, without exception, seem to be miserable. Wolves and even a pair of lions have been housed here in the past. There are hundreds of stray cats, fed by local animal-lovers. Of course, these gardens were for the use of the royal entourage, not open to the public. It wasn't until 1923 that the park was decreed the National Gardens.

The gardens make ingenious use of space, with little paths that wander among the leaves of 500 different varieties of plants under a canopy of trees. They open into flower circles where perhaps an ancient stone seat has been joined by wooden benches, or on to steps which lead under a rose arbour.The green avenues offer the illusion of privacy while birdsong fills the air. The gardens are open every day, from dawn until dusk.

The Záppeion

Between the National Gardens and the Temple of Zeus is the smaller park area called the **Záppeion**. It was a barley field when the Royal Gardens were designed, and only later was this area developed by the brothers Záppas: the handsome exhibition hall, designed by Hansen in the 1840s, was finally built in 1874–8. Although the gardens close at dusk, the area around the Záppeion is always open.

Next to the building is a pagoda-like structure with bright golden yellow walls and red-tiled roofs. This houses a popular, if expensive, café.

On the corner of Olgas and Amalías avenues stands a highly romantic statue of Lord Byron in the arms of the muse.

Kolonáki

Kolonáki is an area of distinguished museums and elegant, expensive apartments and shopping. The finest of them is the **Benáki Museum** ❸ *(see pages 122–5)*. However, scarcely less impressive is the **Museum of Cycladic Art** ❹ at 4 Neo-

Map on page 114

The Grande Bretagne was entirely rebuilt in 1956 still based on the Hansen design – but this time with bathrooms. It was completely renovated again in time for the 2004 Olympics and it is still the most luxurious hotel in the city.

BELOW: palms in the National Gardens.

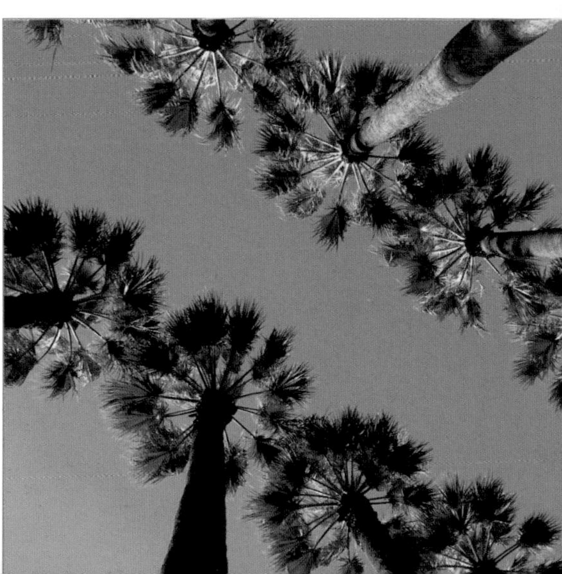

The back of the Parliament exits on to Iródou Attikoú, one of the most expensive and exclusive residential streets in Athens. Just after the green-house and caretakers' area is the barracks of the évzone *troops from which they emerge to march around the parliament to their stations. Opposite, also guarded by the* évzones, *is the President's House.*

fítou Doúka (open Mon, Wed–Fri 10am– 4pm, Sat 10am–3pm; entrance charge; www.cycladic-m.gr).

The museum is divided, by floor, into four sections, all beautifully displayed: on the first floor is early Cycladic art; on the second Ancient Greek art; on the third the Zintilis Collection of Cypriot Antiquities; and on the fourth the Politis Collection of Ancient Greek Art. On the ground floor is a very pleasant atrium café and the museum's excellent shop.

The real highlight of the museum is the wonderful collection of early Cycladic sculpture. These highly stylised but still strangely moving works were very influential on some 20th century artists, such as Picasso and Brancusi. Notable exhibits among the collection include a superb, near life-sized figure which is a distant prototype of Archaic sculpture, and the famous figure of the "cup bearer" with its rare example of an extending arm. The figures are overwhelmingly female, there is just one fragment of an evidently male figure, and just a couple of figurines, one a hunter or warrior. You can tell a surprising amount from the seemingly plain figures: one has striations on her belly, possibly indicating a recent childbirth. As well as the figurines and statues there are some beautifully worked vessels.

The Ancient Greek collection is more familiar but does have some very fine black- and red-figure vases and some wonderful bronze vessels. There is also an excellent marble statue of a boy (from Attica, 320–310 BC).

The Cypriot collection, on the third floor, is also well worth a look. Compare the rather odd cruciform (3,900–2,900 BC) and "plank-shaped" (*circa* 2,000– 1,800 BC) figures with the Cycladic statues on the floor below. There is also a powerful torso of a male figure (first half of the 6th century BC) and some beautiful examples of glassware.

The fourth floor has some excellent examples of Geometric pottery, two of which are particularly fine with figures of horses on their lids. There are also some well-preserved

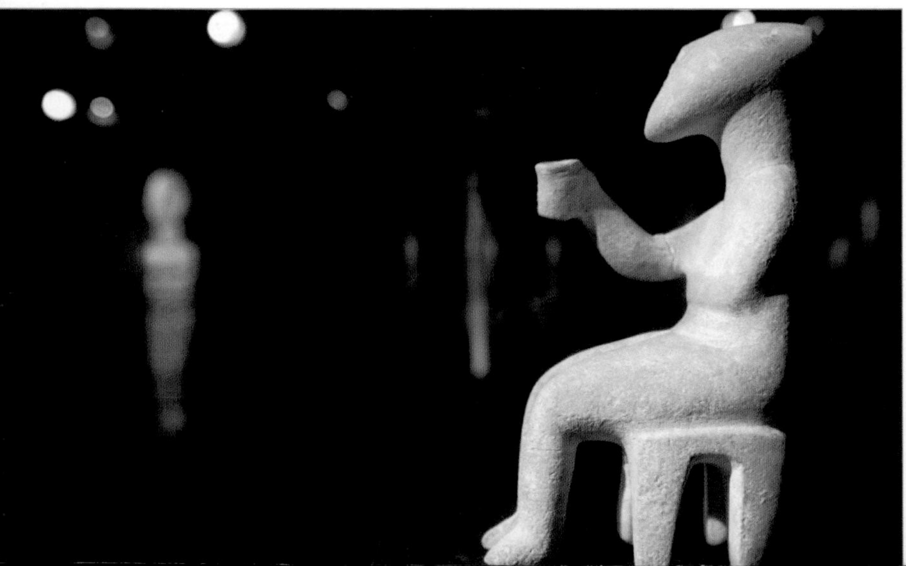

BELOW: the unusual "cup-bearer" in the Museum of Cycladic Art.

bronze helmets and a few Cycladic and Minoan pieces.

Posh neighbourhood

Beyond the two museums, **Kolonáki Square** ❺ (officially Platía Filikís Eterías) is the haunt of rich Greeks and foreigners. This is one of the most expensive neighbourhoods in Athens. Imported foodstuffs, designer clothing, and even a couple of embassies hold sway in the immediate vicinity; the British Council is here too at number 17. Find the *kolonáki* (little classical column) on the southwest side of the square, hiding under a tree. It is around Kolonáki Square that many of Athens' designer clothing and shoe shops are to found.

Just north, Platía Dexamenís supports pleasant cafés above and below a covered water depot begun by Hadrian. This, and a shady square next to the huge church on Skoufá, are the only other public spaces of note in Kolonáki. Villas at the corner of Fokylídou and Pindárou below Dexamenís are some of the most expensive in Greece.

Athenian stair-streets reach their apotheosis beyond Dexamenís as they scale the slopes of **Lykavitós** ❻. This is Athens' highest and most popular hill. Slightly to one side, at the very edge of Kolonáki, the British and American Schools of Archaeology, and the excellent Gennadion Library each hide in patches of landscaping. On Athens's highest street, Hoïdá, the zoned limit is four storeys, and this restriction means there are wonderful views down the steep streets over much of Athens and all the way out to sea.

The easiest way to get to the summit is by the funicular railway that starts from Ploutárhou Street, near Platía Dexamenís (runs every 20 minutes, in summer 8am–10pm, in winter 9.30am– 4.40pm). Though, if you are feeling energetic, there are plenty of paths up through the shrubbery and you may even see tortoises. The summit is graced by the white chapel of Ágios Geórgios and the magnificent view – Athens at its finest – best observed near sunset as the city lights up for miles far below. ❑

A few hundred metres northeast, tucked behind Lykavitós's secondary peak, is the Lykavitós Theatre, hosting fringe events during the Athens Festival. Directly below Ágios Geórgios, Pefkákia park is an extension of Lykavitós and makes for a pleasant walk down toward Exárhia.

BELOW:
Kolonáki by night.

RESTAURANTS & BARS

Restaurants

Filippou
Xenokrátous 19
(metro Evangelismós)
Tel: 210 72 16 390
Open noon–midnight Mon–Fri, L only Sat
Closed part of Aug
Cash only. **€**
This *estiatório*, founded in 1923, remains a firm favourite with all sorts of diners from across town – not just the *beau monde* of the neighbourhood – for the sake of honest, surprisingly low-priced fare such as baked sardines, steamed courgettes, or peas and potatoes with dill, washed down by excellent white or red bulk wine. Service is low-key but efficient; the dining-room had a welcome face-lift in 2005, but has kept a pleasantly retro air with proper table linen.

Kiku
Dimokrítou 12
(metro Sýntagma)
Tel: 210 36 47 033
Open D Mon–Sat
Major credit cards. **€€€€**
Arguably the best place to eat Japanese cuisine in Athens – certainly homesick Japanese tourists endorse it – Kiku sports a contemporary minimalist interior hiding discretely behind blinds. The food encompasses *sushi* (served at a separate bar), *sashimi* and *tempura*; and there are also some less common options like *udon* noodles and *yakisoba.*

To Kioupi
Platía Kolonakioú 4
(metro Sýntagma)
Tel: 210 36 14 033
Open Mon–Sat L and D (summer L only), closed Aug
Cash only. **€**
A classic basement *inomagerío* that is an open secret for those who live or work in the area. A light refit around the millennium exposed the original, attractively pointed stone walls. Durable standbys in the steam-trays include *gída vrastí* (stewed goat), *gouronópoulo* (suckling pig), baked fish, *angináres ala políta* (artichokes with carrots, potatoes and dill), *hórta* and beans, accompanied by palatable bulk wine.

Noodle Bar
Apóllonos 11
(metro Sýntagma)
Tel: 210 33 18 585
Open Mon–Sat L and D 11am–midnight, Sun B, L and D, 5.30am–midnight
Cash only. **€**
The exotic smells wafting out from the open-plan kitchen on to the pavement, with its hotly contested tables, lets you know you're on to a good thing here. The flagship franchise of a small local chain, Pláka's Noodle Bar delivers on its promise of "Polyasian Tastes": wok-tossed noodles, rice dishes from Indonesia to Thailand, chicken satay or sweet and sour, and imaginative salads. They're always packed – you may have to settle for diner-style seating inside – and do a bumping trade in take-away.

Ouzadiko
Karneádou 25–29
(metro Evangelismós)
Tel: 210 72 95 484
Open L and D Tues–Sat, closed Aug
Cash only. **€€**
Kolonáki's most established *ouzerí* reputedly offers more varieties of *oúzo* and *tsípouro* than anywhere else in Athens, to accompany almost-as-numerous platters like *lakérda* (white fleshed marinated bonito), *hortópitta* and *revythokeftédes*

PRICE CATEGORIES

Prices are based on an average meal per person, including house wine:
€ = under €15
€€ = €15–25
€€€ = €25–40
€€€€ = over €40
Key: B = breakfast, L = lunch, D = dinner

LEFT: cafés on Milióni street, Kolonáki.

(chickpea croquettes), as well as daily specials from the chalkboard. Crowded and convivial, it's a popular hangout for local movers and shakers.

Papadakis
Voukourestíou 47, corner Fokylídou
(metro Evangelismós)
Tel: 210 36 08 621
Open Mon–Sat noon–midnight
Major credit cards. **€€€€**
There's been a fish taverna of some sort for years here; the latest incarnation has relocated to Athens from Náoussa, Páros, where Papadakis established a reputation for fresh, well-executed seafood in a competitive waterfront environment. Here, expect creative renditions of monkfish, crayfish and *astakomakaronáda* (the island staple of pasta flaked with lobster) in a minimalist, linen-napery dining area.

Il Postino
Grivéon 3, pedestrian lane off Skoufá
(metro Panepistimíou)
Tel: 210 36 41 414
Open 1.30pm–1am Mon–Sat
Major credit cards. **€€**
The unpretentious menu at this genuine *osteria*, supervised by an Italian chef-proprietor with an illustrious track record at other establishments in Athens, comprises starters like marinated anchovies, pasta dishes, fish and meat entrées, and a full dessert/wine list. Tables in the quiet *cul-de-sac* outside are sought after, but the lower-ground-floor interior appeals too with its décor of old photos, newspaper clippings, and advertising posters, plus equally retro music on the sound system.

Cafés/Bars

Filion
Skoufá 34, Kolonáki
Landmark café right opposite the church of Ágios Dionýsios, serving light snacks and breakfast as well as coffees. Slightly older crowd.

To Kafenadaki tis Dexamenis
The walkway, Platía Dexamenís
(metro Evangelismós)
Tel: 210 72 32 834
Open daily until late (winter inside conservatory)
When this long-standing landmark closed temporarily around the millennium, there was an uproar; since the Olympic summer it has re-opened under new, slicker management, inevitably pricier but still a wonderful spot to sit in the shade and watch the world go by. Seafood titbits like cuttlefish with spinach, vegetarian starters like *mavromátika* and other rather small platters absorb the shock of your double *oúzo* – sized like a *karafáki* elsewhere.

Lallabai (ex-Aigli)
terrace of the Záppeio
(metro Sýntagma)
Tel: 210 33 69 302
Open daily to 2am
This Athens landmark had a sudden makeover under a new concessionaire in late 2005, and the more staid, elderly regulars must still be in a state of shock over the current young, hip, loud-soundtracked environment. The snack menu is outrageously priced but the sweets, coffee and juices are almost affordable and quite good.

Skoufaki
Skoufá 47–49, Kolonáki
(metro Panepistimíou)
Tel: 210 36 45 888
The cluster of cafés at the more student-y end of Skoufá are mostly much of a muchness, but this one – with a warmer interior than the others, and good music on the sound system – is friendly and unpretentious.

RIGHT: chefs at the Grand Bretagne Hotel, Sýntagma.

BENAKI MUSEUM

Athens' most exciting museum has a wonderfully eclectic collection of treasure from every period of Greek history – even El Greco is here

The Benaki Museum, on the corner of Vassilísis Sofías and Koumbári streets, can lay claim to being the best museum in Athens. Founded by Antonis Benaki, a wealthy Alexandrian cotton merchant, its wonderfully eclectic collection of treasures from all periods of Greek history includes jewellery, costumes and two icons attributed to El Greco. The museum has an excellent gift shop and a pleasant terrace restaurant (open Mon, Wed, Fri, Sat 9am–5pm, Thu 9am–midnight, Sun 9am–3pm; entrance charge; www.benaki.gr). A complex of neo-classical buildings located in the Keramikós district now houses its separate Islamic art collections *(see page 141)*.

ABOVE Antonis Benakis observing the gold Mycenean kylix (cup) from Dendra in the Argolid, in a photograph that has become almost a hallmark of the Museum.

RIGHT: Funeral portrait of a man (second quarter of the 3rd century AD) from Antinoöpolis, Egypt. Encaustic technique on linen.

Third Floor

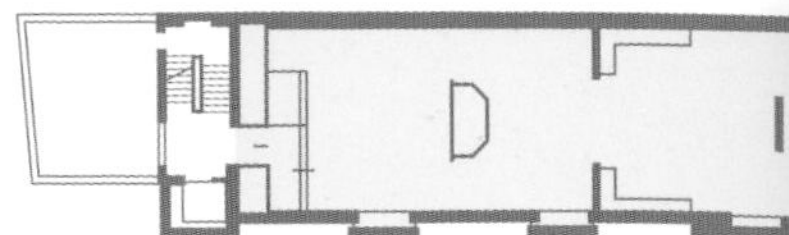

Second Floor

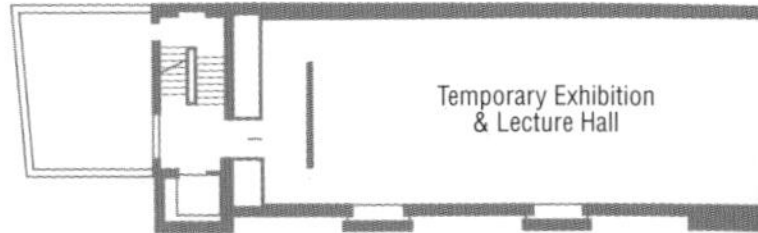

First Floor

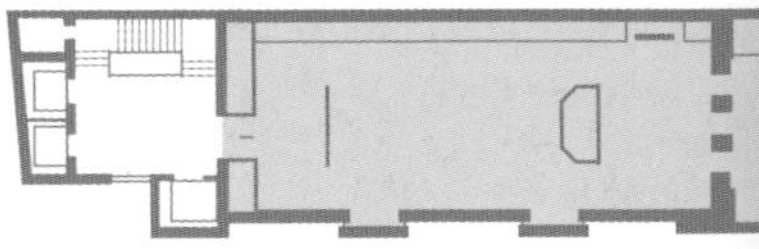

- Prehistory to late Roman period
- Byzantine Empire and early post-Byzantine centuries
- Development of Hellenism during the period of foreign domin
- Ecclesiastical Art during the late post-Byzantine period
- Culture, economy and society on the eve of the War of Indepe
- War of Independence to the formation of the Modern Greek S

Ground Floor

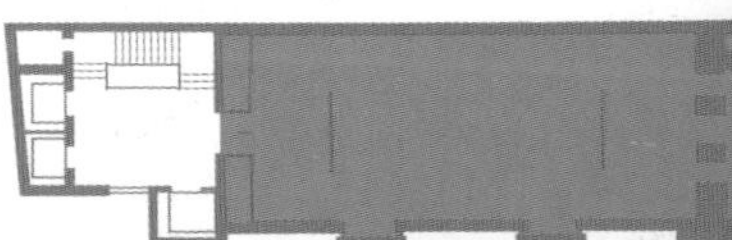

Benáki Museum

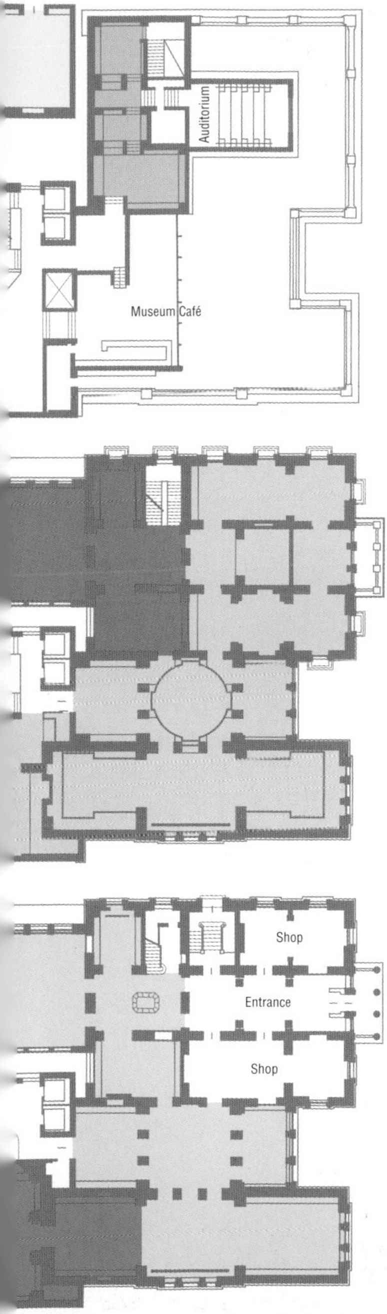

Auditorium
Museum Café
Shop
Entrance
Shop

HIGHLIGHTS

Ground Floor

Rooms 1 and 2 Neolithic-Cycladic-Mycenean. Extraordinary restored vases from 5th millennium BC. An excellent early Cycladic female 'crossed arm' figurine. Mycenean gold from the Thebes treasure', 15th–14th century BC.

Room 3 Priapic satyr on bowl 580 BC. Two exquisite gold sphinxes 6th–5th century BC

Room 5 Great pointy Arcadian bronze helmets.

Room 6 Delicate golden wreaths of oak leaves.

Room 7 Stunning gold medallion of Athene and mesh, to be worn over the hair at the nape of the neck

Room 8 Macedonian gold ivy and myrtle wreaths. A good collection of Romano-Greco glass. Amazing Coptic textiles from 3rd–6th centuries AD.

Rooms 11 and 12 hold part of the Benaki's extraordinary collection of icons. See the Renaissance-influenced Adoration of the Magi (16th century), attributed to Permeniatis, a Greek painter living in Venice; the cabinet of 15th–16th century Cretan icons; also the Virgin Hodegetria and Christ Pantokrator, 16th century from Ipieros, set in splendid 19th century wooden doors from a church in Caesarea.

ABOVE: Gallery 12. The tradition of the Byzantine East and the influences of the Renaissance West in the artistic enquiries of the first post-Byzantine period.

RIGHT: Oak Wreath, gold and gold sheet. Late Hellenistic or Roman period (200-100 BC), provenance unknown (Attica?).

Benaki Highlights (continued)

First Floor
The exhibitions here go under the rather pompous titles of 'The development of Hellenism during the period of foreign domination' and 'Ecclesiastical art during the late-post Byzantine period'.
Rooms 13, 14 and 15
A stunning collection of Greek costume running all the way through Greece, including Crete and Cyprus. It comprises: a wonderful embroidered dress from Crete (17th century) influenced by the Western Renaissance style; the fairytale bridal costume from Astypalaia (in the Dodecanese); and the fabulous 17th–18th century *sperveri* (a tent which covered the raised bridal bed) from Rhodes. Also here are some beautifully carved marble door frames (18th century) from Ios whose spiralling vine motif is from Renaissance models. Look for the fabulous pleating (dropping almost from the shoulders) on a female festive costume from Skópelos and, with both ancient and modern resonances, the baggy pantaloons and bolero of the female festive costume from Lesvos (Mytillíni). Some of the most colourful costumes – almost native American- or Tibetan-looking – hail from Thrace and Macedonia.
Room 16 Heavy jewellery from Istanbul and late-Byzantine gold.
Rooms 17 and 19 These have one of the great highlights of the museum: two fully reconstructed rooms from mansions, with all their wooden panelling and ceilings. The first is a reception room from a mansion in Kozani, Macedonia (mid-18th century). Wood-carved decoration with gilded, silver and painted decoration. It is a heady mix of neo-Hellenic, Central

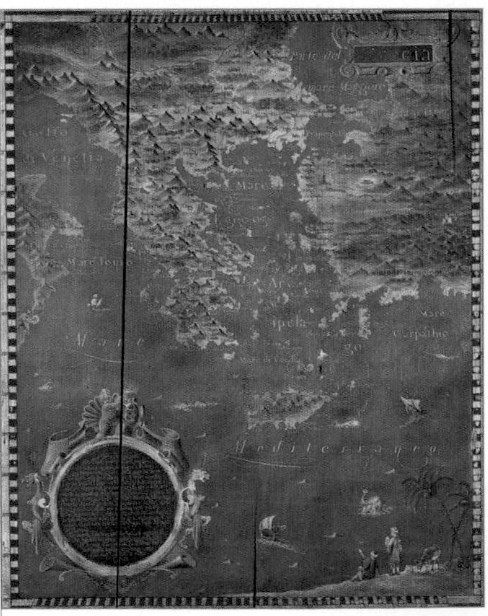

Above: Galleries 35–36 contain more of the Benaki's wonderful costume collection as well as covering the reign of Otho; Eleftherios Venizelos; territorial expansion and the Greek catastrophe in Asia Minor.
Right: Painted map of Greece post-1585, after Stefano Buonsignori. Egg tempera on wood.

ABOVE: Mid-18th century reception room from a mansion in Kozani, Macedonia. Wood-carved decoration with gilded, silvered and painted features. The décor was rescued by Alexandra Horemi, sister of Antonis Benakis, in the early 1930s and donated to the museum by her heirs.

ABOVE: The Adoration of the Magi (*circa* 1560–1567), by Domenicos Theotokopoulos (El Greco). Egg tempera on wood.

European, Ottoman and Byzantine influences, and the flowerpainting on the ceiling is quite exquisite. The second is also a reception room from Kozani (mid-18th century). This is quite different, however, with the most intricately carved wooden ceiling and panels. The exceptionally fine work draws on ecclesiatical traditions, with flower vases, flowers, birds and double-headed eagles all depicted. The two rooms are so splendid that you could almost miss the wonderful bridal embroidery on the walls (Epirus).

Room 20 Very rich and heavy jewellery (18th and 19th century) – all heavily Byzantine-influenced.

Room 21 Middle class urban life, beautiful Western-influenced costume.

Room 24 A more restrained but very elegant early-19th century Hydriot reception room of Ottoman-rococo style.

Room 27 The Aithousa Damianou Kyriazi Bequest of Icons and Ecclesiatical Decoration. Make sure you see the highly detailed and colourful 'Epí soi hairei…' (In thee rejoiceth…) by Theodoros Poulakis (2nd half of the 17th century), one of his finest works. Note the less-than-Christian zodiac surrounding the Virgin and Child at the centre of the work.

Second floor

Holds the museum's excellent café and space for temporary exhibitions. The Thursday night buffet (until midnight, book in advance) is well worth making time for. The Athenian great-and-good gather here to gossip, and it is lovely sitting out on the veranda overlooking the National Gardens. 335 euros pp, without drinks.

Third Floor

Items relating to the Greek war of independence.

BELOW: Gallery 34 documents the period from the reverse in Greece's fortunes up to the declaration of Greek independence and the dramatic end of Ioannis Capodistria.

EXÁRHIA TO AMBELÓKIPI

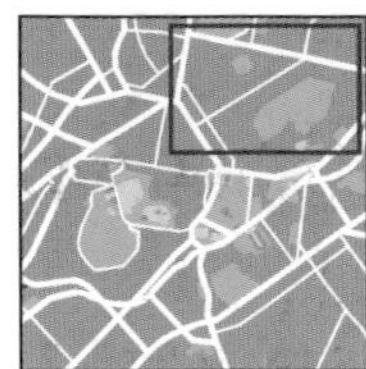

The Exárhia district takes its character from the university – lively, bohemian and politically active. At the foot of towering Lykavitós, Neápoli shares some of Exárhia's easy-going social style, while Ambelókipi contains law courts, nostalgic football grounds and the city's tallest building

Map on page 114

Beyond Akadimías – the third, parallel, broad boulevard just northeast of the Hansen brothers' neoclassical complex – one becomes aware of the **university**'s pervasive influence through the astonishing concentration of small bookstores and Greek-language publishers, mostly contained within the quadrangle bounded approximately by Akadimías itself, Sína, Themistokléous and Valtetsíou streets. This is also generally reckoned to be the start of the bohemian **Exárhia** district, which with its high student population has always had an organic link with the university. All told, Exárhia amounts to less than 200 square blocks on hillsides, stretching between the late-19th-century Pédion Áreos park, a typical venue for book fairs or Communist rallies, and the rarefied heights of Kolonáki, but it has long been one of the liveliest parts of Athens.

Bill-posting – particularly on and around the ugly **Law School** building at the corner of Sólonos and Sína – and spray-painted black anarchist graffiti on every available surface together reveal a passionate commmitment to various anti-imperialist causes, hunger-striking political prisoners and some stark summaries of life as they see it (EAT THE RICH – THEIR WEALTH IS OUR BLOOD; IMMIGRANTS ARE OUR BROTHERS; COPS=SWINE).

Foreign cultural institutes, whose language courses and scheduled events have long served as a window on the wider world for those young Greeks who desired one, also cluster here at the transition zone between Kolonáki and Exárhia: the Goethe Institute on Omírou, the French Institute on Sína and the more recently opened Cervantes Institute on Skoufá.

BELOW: cafés are buzzy in the university district.

After the colonels' junta closed down most of the intimate protest-song *boîtes* and more amplified music clubs in Pláka, they gradually resurfaced through the 1970s and 1980s in Exárhia, especially along Valtetsíou, Arahóvis, Methónis and Kallidromíou streets. Their successors are still there, and while limited student budgets mean that there aren't as many tavernas locally as you'd imagine, there are plenty of cafés at which the fine art of nursing a single expensive drink all night has been honed over many decades.

The epicentre of *frappádika* culture is the triangular **Platía Exarhíon ❼**, one of the less inspired results of the pre-Olympic city-wide facelift. Exárhia is also still home to the majority of Athens' surviving venues devoted to *rebétika*, the musical style whose post-junta revival peaked in the early 1980s *(see pages 64–5)*.

By day, Exárhia also throbs with life, not all of it high. There are some quirky clothing and music stores, a Saturday flea-market along Kallidromíou, and a disconcerting number of panhandlers, winos and junkies along both pedestrianised Tsamádou, north of the square, and on or around **Lófos Stréfi ❽** (Stréfi Hill), which dominates the neighbourhood to the northeast.

Were it not for disposed drug paraphernalia the landscaped hill would make for a delightful retreat with its walkways, terraces, mock-castle walling and fine views across towards Lykavitós. During summer a café-*ouzerí* operates just above Anexartisías Street. Unusually for Athens, security against break-ins is tight and many apartment blocks around Stréfi have seen fit to install heavy-duty grilles at the main entrance.

Just west of here, on Patísion street (also known as 28th October,

On Platía Exarhíon, take a look at the Bauhaus-inspired building which houses Floral café (established 1934) on its ground floor: this was Athens' first apartment block, built in 1932–3.

BELOW: Ágios Geórgios on Likavitós.

to commemorate General Metaxás' famous repulsion of Mussolini's attempted invasion in 1940), and close to Viktória metro station, stands the **National Archaeological Museum** ❾, one of the world's finest collections of antiquities *(see map on page 127 and photo feature on pages 132–5).*

Neápoli and Lykavitós

Beyond Kallidromíou to the east, Exárhia blends into Neápoli, a densely built neighbourhood which might best be described as populated by folk who have nominally outgrown their student days but can't bear to tear themselves away too far from the scene of their enactment. Accordingly there's a respectable sprinkling of art cinemas, tavernas, by-the-hour "love" hotels (for use more by young student couples with nowhere else to go than professionals) and a few unusual bars among the mix of neglected neoclassical houses and 1950s apartment blocks.

Multiple stair-streets, a striking feature which Athens shares with San Francisco, allow a 20-minute approach on foot heading southeast towards Lykavitós (Lycabettus) hill. The round theatre here, northeast of the summit, is a popular summer venue for well-known acts from abroad, as well as events during the Hellenic Festival.

It is possible to climb the hill from this side, though it is more usually accessed from the south side, by equally steep paths or the funicular that starts on Ploutárhou Street, near Platía Dexamenís *(see page 119)*. The summit itself (277m/909ft elevation) is graced by the originally 18th-century chapel of Ágios Geórgios, where seemingly half the city turns up for its name-day celebration on 23 April.

In mythology, Lykavitós hill resulted from a fit of pique on the part of the goddess Athena, who hurled a large rock at the daughters of King Kekrops, and missed; the missile, on landing, became the ridge. Guidebooks from the mid-1950s describe salient points of a view all the way southwest to the Argolid peninsula of the Peloponnese, but in our polluted era you'll be lucky to see beyond the Saronic island of Égina except on the very clearest winter days. Still, the prospects over the city at your feet are second to none.

Ambelókipi

Both Exárhia and Neápoli are delimited by west-to-east Leofóros Alexándras, which runs respectively past the main **Court of Appeal** and **Greek Supreme Court**, the national police headquarters, a crumbling block of 1930s social housing that has been listed and rescued from demolition, assorted hospitals and ministries, the **Apostolos Nikolaïdis football grounds** and the Craft microbrewery, en route to Ambelókipi.

The dilapidated Nikolaïdis pitch, otherwise known as Leofóros (The

Athens Polytechnic, the scene of a bloody seige in 1973.

Massacre at the Polytechnic

At the corner of Stournára and Patissíon stands the Athens Polytechnic, the *Polytekhnío*. For most Greeks of a certain age, it is an emotive name, synonymous with 1970s student idealism and the beginning of the end for the 1967–74 military dictatorship. In November 1973, months of anti-junta student demonstrations culminated in a barricaded occupation of the premises. As older citizens mobilised in support, smuggling in food and medicines, the military regime sent in tanks to break down the main gates, while sharpshooters fired down into the courtyard from surrounding buildings. Bullet holes are still visible on columns and steps and the mangled set of gates are kept as a memorial inside the current entrance. The number of students who died remains unknown; estimates range from 20 to 200. Although the rebellion failed in the short term, the outrage engendered forfeited the junta any lingering support and was a key factor in its collapse just eight months later. The nation's debt to the students is acknowledged in many streets or squares named Iróön Polytekhníon (Heroes of the Polytechnic),37 of them in Athens alone.

Avenue), was for decades home to one of Athens' most celebrated football clubs, green-liveried Panathinaïkós Athlitikós Ómilos (PAO for short), but it has stood unused since June 2005. However, you'd have to be blind to miss the still-ubiquitous green graffito ΘΥΡΑ 13 (Gate 13), here and in every corner of Athens, eulogising that entrance number which gave access to the home stands *(for more on Athens' football clubs, see page 254)*.

The name **Ambelókipi** means "vine gardens" and, before the 1920s influx of refugees, there were indeed extensive vineyards here, something hard to credit as you attempt to cross what must be the city's busiest junction at Alexándras and Vasilísis Sofías. Just southwest rears the 1960s-vintage **Pýrgos Athinón** (Athens Tower), at 27 storeys this earthquake-prone city's tallest structure (elsewhere the limit is generally seven floors, though the Hilton manages 12). The nearby metro station has brought a bit more life to a formerly humdrum area, with tavernas, cinemas, cafés and bars both along the main thoroughfares and on the back-streets in every direction.

Vasilísis Sofías heads southwest back towards the centre, past fountain-spangled Platía Mavíli – which is reckoned the transition between Ambelókipi to Ilíssia district – and two adjacent landmarks. The US Embassy, built in 1959–61 to a design by noted architect Walter Gropius, is now fortified to the hilt with anti-car-bomb measures, including closures of the side streets all around.

Next door stands the **Mégaron Musikís** ⑩ (Hall of Music), Athens' main concert venue for classical music, its first phase completed during the early 1990s (though two further, smaller halls have since been added). After standing half-finished through much of the 1980s, rumour had it that the US State Department discretely provided the funds for completion as the roof of the building site would have provided an ideal platform for a terrorist rocket attack on the adjacent embassy. ❑

Lykavitós, Athens' highest hill, looms over Neápoli.

BELOW: the city's main concert hall, Mégaron Musikís.

RESTAURANTS & BARS

Restaurants

Exárhia

Alexandria
Metsóvou 13
(metro Viktória)
Tel: 210 82 10 004
Open D Mon–Sat, closed Aug. €€
Nostalgiac semi-enclosed courtyard with patterned floor tiles, potted plants, ceiling fans and other Belle Époque touches. The menu has Egyptian dishes like *foul madamas* and generic Middle Eastern such as *baba ghanouj* and *felafel*.

Barba Giannis
Emmanouíl Benáki 94, corner Dervenίon
(metro Omónia)
Tel: 210 38 24 138
Open L and D Mon–Sat, L Sun, closed Aug
Cash only. €
One of the last surviving *inomagería* (wine-and-casserole-food kitchens) in this district, a perennially popular outfit serving consistently edible, if slightly stodgy, fare in big portions. On any given day there's likely to be *fáva*, *giouvarláki* (rice-&-meat rissoles), stewed okra, or baked mackerel. The tables on pedestrianised Dervenίon fill first in summer.

Fasoli
Emmanouíl Benáki 45
(metro Omónia)
Tel: 210 33 00 010
Open L and D Mon–Sat
Cash only. €€
Since it opened in 2005, Fasoli has quickly grabbed a big share of the local market, even with penny-pinching students, thanks to excellent value and trendy yet utilitarian décor. The food's solid Greek with creative twists: lentil salad, *biftéki* roulade, light pasta dishes, good bread, the usual starters. Consult the blackboard for daily specials and desserts.

Giandes
Valtetsíou 44
(metro Omónia)
Tel: 210 33 01 369
Open daily noon–1am
Credit cards. €€€
The name means "wishbone" in Greek, but poultry breast is probably the last thing you'll find at Exárhia's premier "modern Greek" restaurant, with "modern" courtyard and vaguely industrial-chic interior to match. The menu changes seasonally, according to the strictly organic ingredients, but typically include wild greens, monkfish, lamb and sun-dried tomatoes, or *tas kebab* Asia Minor stew.

Iy Kriti (alias O Takis)
Veranzérou 5, off Platía Káningos
(metro Omónia)
Tel: 210 38 26 998
Open L and D daily
Cash only. €€
This little Cretan *stéki* has become so popular that it's expanded across the arcade into overflow premises – expect to wait for a table. Regional dishes such as *hiroméri* (smoked pork) and *marathópita* (fennel pie) have pride of place, along with more usual titbits like fresh *bakaliáros* and, of course, Cretan *rakí*. A bit pricey for the setting, but portions quite large.

Iy Lesvos
Emmanouíl Benáki 38
(metro Omónia)
Tel: 210 38 14 525
Open daily noon–late
Cash only. €€
Clinical 1970s atmosphere at this strictly seafood *ouzerí* which sets out tables under concrete overhang facing a parking lot. But those tables are always full for the sake of patently fresh scaly fish, a few shellfish like *kydónia* (cockles), the usual fried starters and a wide range of *oúzo*.

O Skoufias
Lóndou 4
(metro Omónia)
Tel: 210 38 28 206
Open L and D Tues–Sat, L Sun. Cash only. €
The proprietors of this popular bohemian hangout are Cretan, and it shows in the regularly changing, handwritten menu, though the kitchen is open to many Armenian, Turkish and peninsular Greek delicacies like *mercemek kófte* (lentil-based rissoles), Circassian cold chicken and *hunkar beyendi* (aubrgine-based stew). Craft beer and *rakí* at attractive prices.

Tria Tetarta
Ikonómou 25
(metro Omónia)
Tel: 210 82 30 560
Open daily Oct–May
Cash only. €€
A "creative" *mezedopolío*, one of Exárhia's oldest, which operates inside an old house; the multi-level, frankly wacky interior is much of the attraction, as the rich, heavy food can be hit-and-miss. Good wine list selected by proprietor Taxiarhis.

Neápoli

Iy Lefka
Mavromiháli 121
(no nearby metro)
Tel: 210 36 14 038
Open D to 2am Mon–Sat
Cash only. €
The last survivor of Neápoli's traditional courtyard-and-barrelled-wine tavernas, working in its present incarnation since 1937. Popular and good value for *mezedákia*, meat grills and

PRICE CATEGORIES

Prices are based on an average meal per person, including house wine:
€ = under €15
€€ = €15–25
€€€ = €25–40
€€€€ = over €40
Key: B = breakfast, L = lunch, D = dinner

specialties like lamb-offal platter, all washed down by inexpensive organic bulk wine.

O Pinaleon
Mavromiháli 152
(no nearby metro)
Tel: 210 64 40 945
Open D, late Sep–mid-May
Cash only. **€€**
This well-loved old-house taverna has acquired a cult following since the late 1980s for the sake of its rich hot and cold *mezédes* (offered on a *dískos*) – including unusual items like chicken livers with rocket and sun-dried tomatoes – mains such as smoked pork loin, own-brewed red wine in preference to *oúzo*, and *mastíha* (a Hiot drink) as a digestif. It's usually lively, with close-packed tables and taped *rebétika* music so it's prudent to book.

Ambelókipi

O Karvouniaris
Vatopedíou 9
(metro Ambelókipi)
Tel: 210 84 28 371
Open L and D Mon–Sat. **€**
One of the last old-style tavernas in this neighbourhood, with standard starters encompassing *fáva*, cabbage-carrot salad or *hórta* preceding mains such as *marídes*, cuttlefish in sauce, baked *pérka* (comber, not perch) or mackerel, meatballs and sausages, washed down by barrelled wine.

Koutouki tou Liafou
Panórmou 54, entrance from Evrytanías 58
(metro Ambelókipi)
Tel: 210 69 25 086
Open D daily, closed summer. Cash only. **€**
A *koutoúki* in Greek is a locally patronised hole-in-the-wall, and this atmospheric, subterranean spot qualifies on all counts. The food's resolutely old-fashioned, but for a slice of bygone Athens at literally bargain-basement prices you can't complain.

O Papasideris
Évrou 98, corner Farandáton
(metro Ambelókipi)
Tel: 210 77 73 220
Open daily noon till late
Cash only. **€**
The oldest and arguably best of several *inomagería* along this stretch of Évrou, founded in 1933 and now run by the grandson of the founder. A pre-Olympic makeover resulted in folk embroidery curtains and patterned wallpaper (even on the ceiling), but hasn't much affected prices or the quality of the casserole fare or charcoal grills, the latter offered at lunch too. You can combine the two, i.e. *keftédes* with perfectly executed *bámies* (okra).

O Vlassis
Páster 8, Ambelókipi
(metro Mégaron Mousikís)
Tel: 210 64 63 060
Open L and D Mon–Sat, L Sun, closed Aug. **€€**
Vlassis sticks to its time-tested formula of large-portioned, rich, "modern Greek" cooking. *Mezédes* like cabbage *dolmádes* are selected from the *dískos*, while one waits for mains such as suckling pig or grilled *thrápsalo* (sweet, deep-water squid). The place is full most evenings, so booking is wise.

Cafés/Bars

Craft
Leofóros Alexándras 205
(metro Ambelókipi)
Tel: 210 646 2350
Open daily to 1.30am
The striking blue industrial façade of this building – shared with a government ministry – conceals the main outlet of Greece's only microbrewery. The recessed ground-floor premises currently purvey lager in three grades (blonde, "smoked" and black) as well as a red ale, by the glass or in measures up to 2 litres. There's a limited menu of pricey snacks, mostly international munchies like *quesadillas*, burgers, spring rolls and won ton but also some token Greek platters like *dákos* salad.

Kapetan
Mihalis Fidíou 3, corner Genadíou
(metro Omónia)
Tel: 210 38 20 073
Open noon–late Mon–Sat
Cash only. **€**
Very characterful Crete-themed *kafeníon* with old photos and posters on the wall which pushes the limits of its operating licence, and the capacity of a two-hob stove, to offer salads, seafood *mezédes* and stews suitable for a full meal – or you can just have *rakí* plus *mezédes* for a few euros.

TAF
Emmanoíl Benáki 9
(metro Omónia)
Tel: 210 380 0014
Tiny outlet of a French chain, with *dégustation* of quality African and Asian coffees at the bar or upstairs in the tiny loft. Basically a shop, with shop hours, selling both beans and a small range of teas in bulk.

Archaeological Museum

Nowhere else in the world can you see such treasures from Greek antiquity. The sculptures and artefacts here are the key to all Western art

North of Omónia (close to Viktória metro station), the National Archaeological Museum has reopened after lengthy renovation, fresh from a redesign and crammed with treasures from every period of antiquity. Its fabulous collection of ancient art and artefacts provides a survey of the various artistic styles of Greek antiquity unrivalled in the world.

Don't be intimidated by the apparent size of the collection but, at first, concentrate on certain key rooms. In the basement you'll find the museum shop with its good – if pricey – replicas, as well as an adequate café. Statues salvaged from the Antikythera shipwreck adorn the courtyard.

Open Mon 12.30–5pm, Tues–Fri 8am–5pm, Sat–Sun 8.30am–3pm; entrance charge.

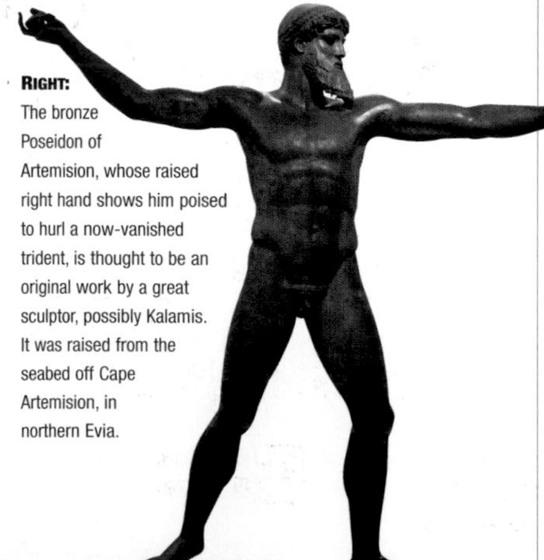

Right: The bronze Poseidon of Artemision, whose raised right hand shows him poised to hurl a now-vanished trident, is thought to be an original work by a great sculptor, possibly Kalamis. It was raised from the seabed off Cape Artemision, in northern Evia.

Above: The bronze Jockey of Artemision, found in pieces in the vicinity of a shipwreck, must once have held the reins of his horse in his left hand and a whip in his right. **Below:** Gold mask from the grave circles at Mycenae. **Above Right:** Rooms 8–13 are a good hunting ground for *kouroi* (statues of male youths) and *korai* (their female counterparts).

Museum Highlights

Ground Floor

Room 4 Mycenean gold from the grave circles at Mycenae. Apart from the famous gold masks, there is a wonderful repoussé *pyxis* showing lions chasing a deer and antelope. Also here are an exceptionally ornate, carved marble vase, lots of hammered gold jewellery and wonderful gold cups. The highly decorated jugs and vases are sometimes overlooked but they also show a high degree of craftsmanship. The wall paintings, such as that of the 'Mycenean Lady', a serious-looking goddess, are also exceptionally fine. Don't miss the small but exquisite ivories from the Mycenae acropolis. Some of the earliest writing appears on the Linear B tablets from Pylos.

Room 6 Cycladic. Here are the famous figures of a harpist and a male playing a double flute (from Keros, 2,800–2,300BC). Three-dimensional sculpture was formed very early in the Cyclades and here is the largest known Cycladic sculpture, a near life-sized female statue (from Amorgos, 2,800–2,300BC). Perhaps the most extraordinary pieces are the fragments of frescoes from Phylakopi III (16th century BC); those of the flying fish are particularly charming. A unique find is the silver diadem embellished with animals and birds found at Kastri on Syros (3rd millennium BC).
Room 8 *Kouroi*, especially the huge votive offering to Poseidon at Sounion (circa 600BC).
Room 15 Trident-throwing Poseidon. Most of the rest of the Classical sculpture is known from 2nd-century AD marble copies, a number of which can be seen here (namely the majority of the marble monumental sculptures).
Room 19 Many 2nd-century AD marble copies of earlier bronzes.

National Archaeological Museum

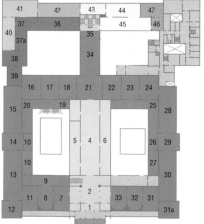

Ground Floor

41 42 43 44 47 37 36 45 46 40 37a 35 34 38 39 16 17 18 21 22 23 24 15 20 19 25 28 14 10 5 4 6 26 29 10 27 13 9 30 2 11 8 7 33 32 31 12 1 31a

1st Floor

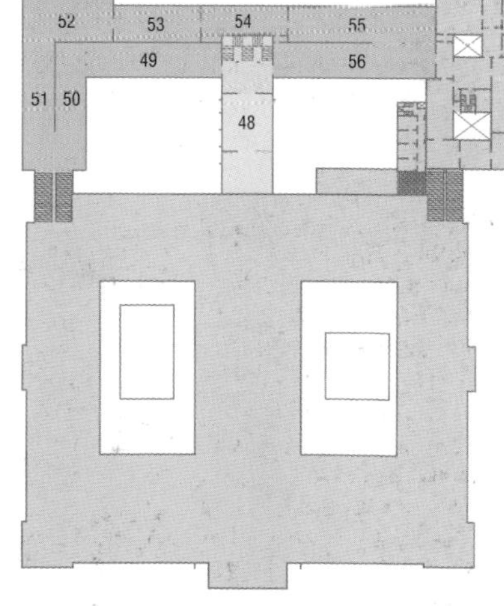

Prehistoric Collection
Sculpture Collection
Bronze Collection
Egyptian Collection
Collection of Pottery and Miniature Objects
Temporary Exhibitions
Conference Room
Vestibule

At the centre of the room is the bronze of the Horse and Young Jockey (140BC).

Room 37 A stunning selection from Olympia including the votive offering of a head of Zeus from a monumental statue (520–510BC). Wonderful animal decorations from cauldrons (8th century BC) and a fascinating selection of finds from the Athenian Acropolis.

Room 38 An exceptional collection from the 2nd century BC Antikythera shipwreck showing the intriguing Antikythera Mechanism, thought to be a device for calculating the position of the moon, sun and planets.

Room 39 Chiefly given over to the imposing, larger-than-life bronze known as the Lady of Kalymnos (circa 2nd century BC), discovered by fishermen in 1994.

Room 20 The 3rd century AD copy in miniature, the best surviving, of Pheidias's Athena Parthenos (originally 438BC and approximately twelve times larger).

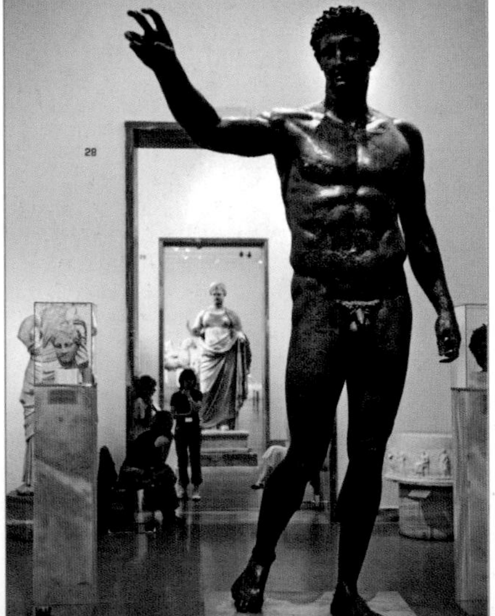

Room 28 A bronze statue of a young athlete found in the sea off Marathon, one of the masterpieces of the late Classical period (340–330BC), from the school of Praxiteles. Also, the bronze statue of a youth from the Antikythira Shipwreck, once thought to be Perseus holding the head of the Medusa but more likely to be Paris awarding the apple to Aphrodite. Attributed to Euphranor (circa 340–330BC).

Room 29 More treasures including the bronze portrait head of a philosopher, found in the Antikythira Shipwreck, with the original eyeballs and irises made of glass paste preserved.

MAIN PICTURE: The first floor is largely given over to a rich vase collection. **ABOVE LEFT:** Heads from the museum's vast marble holdings. **ABOVE:** Hellenistic gold wreath. **LEFT:** Thought to be Paris, the youth from Antikythera represents the finest in Peloponnesian bronze sculpture.

First Floor

Room 48 Akrotiri on Thíra (Santoríni), destroyed in the Late-Cycladic (16th century BC). Most importantly, the wall paintings are back on display after the long period of restoration that followed the 1999 earthquake. Covered first with clay and straw, then a thick layer of plaster, then with a series of thinner layers of plaster – the initial design and then paint was applied to a wet layer. The three on display are The Boxing Children, The Antelopes, and Spring. Spring has lovely depictions of swallows and shows Thira's landscape before the volcanic eruption. Also look for the delightful *kymbe* (long, open vessel) decorated with dolphins, which betrays a Minoan influence. The same motif can be seen on, among other items, a plaster tripod offering table.

Room 49 Wonderful mid-late Geometric *pyxis* (round flat dishes with a lid) on which there are models of horses. Extraordinary late-Geometric pitchers covered with 'geometric' decoration.

Room 50 A lovely female figurine from Boeotia with a bird-like face and moveable legs. Used as the mascot for the 2004 Olympics. Opposite is the Mistress of the Animals, a pithos-amphora decorated with a mother goddess figure surrounded with animals (680–670 BC).

Room 51 Large, impressive vases of the 'orientalising period' – with influences picked up on trading voyages – showing many animals: sphinxes, centaurs, griffens and chimeras, also lions, panthers and wild goats, all dominated by the earth goddess. The large relief pithos from a Cycladic workshop is particularly impressive (7th century BC).

Room 54 As we get into the Mature Archaic (570–530 BC) the black figure designs become more complex and less stylised. Some of the pieces are just wonderful: see the lovely depiction of a male deer scratching its nose (mid-6th century BC). Exceptional Attic vases form the bulk of the collection. With the Late Archaic (530/480–475BC) comes the emergence of the red-figure style, more playful in subject matter. There is a beautiful *kylix* of a man singing (the distich by Theognis, 'O most beautiful child') while he has his hand nuzzled by a rabbit.

Room 55 By the early Classical (480–475/50BC) a more severe and stylised ethos comes into play. It is refined by the Classical (450–415BC) to become one of the ancient world's most stunning accomplishments, at its best in the more detailed miniature work. Later work loses this clarity and sense of form, although it is often enlivened by added colour.

ABOVE RIGHT: Depicting two boxing boys, this wall painting from Akrotiri would have once decorated the interior wall of a house in the ancient city. **ABOVE LEFT:** Geometric amphora detail. **LEFT:** Minoan vase.

THISÍO TO ROÚF

This section of the city, previously working class and run down, is now home to a thriving nightlife scene and has a number of attractions from an excellent museum of Islamic art, to the reworked grounds of the city's old gas works

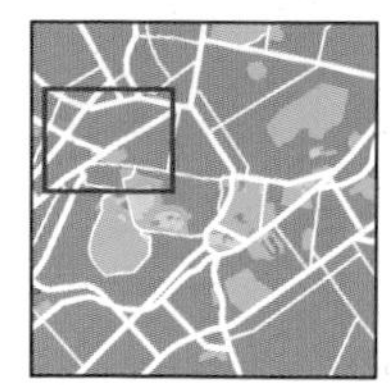

The modern, compact district of Thisío, and its metro/ISAP station, take their name from the Temple of Hephaistos (sometimes called the Theseion) on the north side of the Ancient Agora *(see pages 87–8)*. It's dominated by the **Hill of the Nymphs** – essentially the north end of the Filopáppou ridge – on whose summit sits the 1842-built **National Observatory** ❶ (www.noa.gr; open first Fri of month), designed by Theophil Hansen (he of the National Library). Despite the city's nocturnal airglow – inimical to any serious star-gazing – it still functions as a serious research entity, in tandem with a free-standing domed telescope a short way to the south.

Just below stands the unusually attractive and popular neo-Byzantine church (1922) of **Agía Marína**, built next to an older Byzantine chapel of that dedication and the focus of a festival for a few days either side of the saint's day, July 17. In the Greek countryside, she is normally a patroness of crops, but here she is the protector of expectant mothers – a link possibly with an ancient rock-slide just below, worn smooth by generations of women using it as a remedy for sterility. Still further downhill is an empty rocky slope which on close inspection turns out to have extensive ancient building foundations and carved steps; local tavernas used to set out tables on the handy flat surfaces until the archaeological authorities chased them out and fenced the area off.

Where Akámantos, Níleos and Iraklidón converge at Apostólou Pávlou – the latter pedestrianised as part of the pre-Olympic improvement of the central archaeological zones – a lively nightlife district has sprung up since the mid-1990s. There are, however, few nightclubs

Map on page 138

LEFT: looking down from Filopáppou ridge. **BELOW:** the National Observatory.

The Herakleidon Museum's aim is to offer visitors an understanding of both the work and life of their featured artists. Preliminary sketches, photographs, personal effects and explanations of the artist's various techniques are all exhibited, building up a context with which visitors can connect.

per se, merely surplus-to-requirements *frappádika* – indistinguishable, posey cafés specialising in *kafés frappés* (despite the Frenchified name, a uniquely Greek concoction of whipped, iced Nescafe) and *freduccino* (the same process applied to cappuccino). The only local cultural sight is the privately run **Herakleidon Museum** ❷ at Iraklidón 16 (www.herakleidon-art.gr; daily 1–9pm; admission charge), with a café and exceptionally well stocked shop. Their permanent collection comprises rotating items from holdings by M. C. Escher, the Hungarian Victor Vasarely and American Carol Wax, plus over 100 of the earliest photographs of Athens.

For the truly committed, at the far west end of Iraklidón on Platía Aféas, there's the **Haridimos Museum of Shadow Puppetry** (Tues–Sun 9am–1pm, 5–9pm, not Sun eve; admission charge) on the ground floor of the **Politistikó Kéndro tou Dímo Athinéon Melina Merkouri** (Melina Mercouri Municipal Cultural Centre), with examples of this all-but-vanished art from the puppet collection of the family who ran the Haridimos Shadow Theatre in Pláka until the late 1980s.

Psyrrí

The north end of Apostólou Pávlou frays into a number of attractive walkways – some through the *álsos* or grove of Thisío – which re-unite to cross over the ISAP lines to a *platía* containing the three-apsed, 11th–12th-century Byzantine *Ágii Asómati* (the "bodyless saints", ie angels), its dome supported on four columns. A generous swath of parkland around it allows you to admire the carved crosses on its external masonry which, as on most of Athens' early churches, is its most noteworthy feature.

The square and church also mark the southwest corner of, and a main

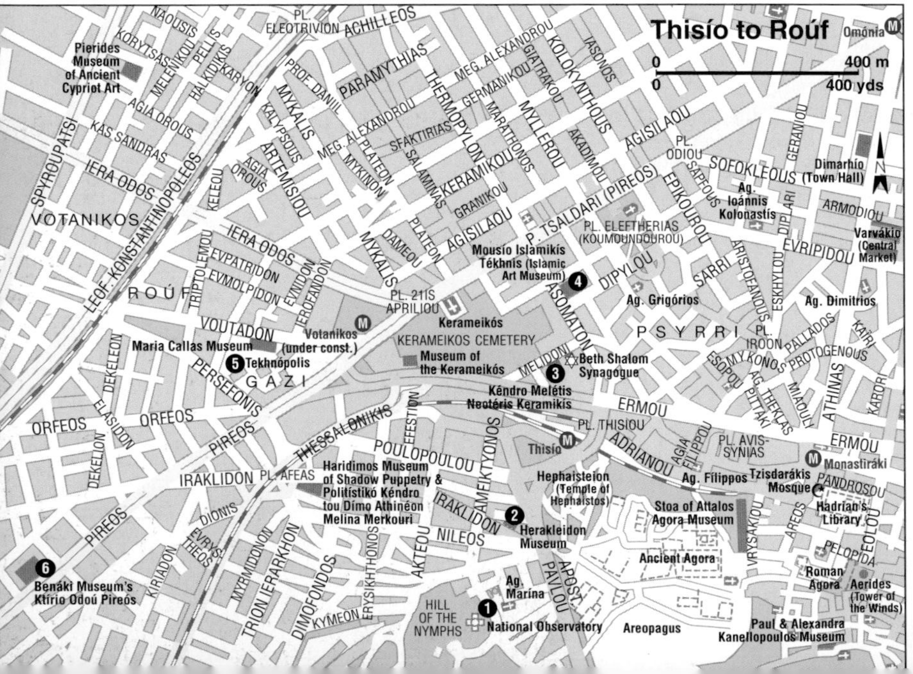

gateway to, **Psyrrí**, a pentagonal, somewhat shabby maze bounded by the ancient Keramikós site plus Athinás, Evripídou and Ermoú streets. All the narrow lanes within these limits converge on Platía Iróön; just who the "heroes" of the name were is not made clear by any inscription or statue. Historically it has been a light-industry and crafts area, and by day it still retains this character, including: ropes, candles, metalwork, basketry, household wares, barbeques fasioned ingeniously on Tournavítou from spent pressure chambers of hot-water heaters, and an acoustic instrument-maker on Louká Níka.

But sharp-eyed strollers will spot the shuttered premises which metamorphose after dark into honeypots for young and not-so-young Athenians intent on a good time. Rather before Thisío, early in the 1990s, Psyrrí emerged as the city's top destination for trendy nocturnal activities. The seriously, self-consciously hip, always in search of the cutting edge, now disdain the neighbourhood as hopelessly passé, but reports of its demise as a venue have been greatly exaggerated. It's far too convenient – especially given its own portal of Monastiráki metro station – and frankly still too characterful, though prices at most of the crammed-in tavernas, themed clubs and cafés are eye-watering.

The district actually has some literary cachet: Lord Byron lodged with the Makris family here in 1809 (at a house on the site of Agías Théklas 11), and his *Maid of Athens* is modelled on one of their daughters, Teresa, with whom he apparently fell in love. By the first decades of the 20th century – though Piraeus always eclipsed it in this respect – Psyrrí had become a haunt of the *mánges* (wide boys) and *rebétes*, and a celebrated music club (Zefyros) flourished here during the late 1920s.

There are few great sites or monuments in central Psyrrí, though the Hamam Café on Platía Agíon Anagýron does appear to have once been a (Christian, post-Independence) baths, and just on the far side of Evripídou stands the ancient church of **Ágios Ioánnis Kolonastís** (St John of the Column; usually open daylight hours), with a Roman-era Corinthian colum sprouting right through the roof. In the old days, on the August 29 feast of the Baptist's beheading, *ex votos* were wrapped around it as pleas for cures from malaria, against which the saint was guardian.

Like most other bazaar districts in the Balkans, Psyrrí was home to local religious minorities, and the architecturally undistinguished but distinctive conically-domed **Ágios Grigórios** Armenian Apostolic church (locked) stands tall on Kriézi, although today most of Athens' Armenian community worships at four churches in distant Néos Kósmos and Kokkiniá (two of them following the Apostolic rites, the other two the Catholic tradition).

Agía Marína is celebrated in a festival around her saint's day, July 17.

BELOW: Agía Marína.

At the Beth Shalom temple, as in all Greek synagogues (and Orthodox synagogues across the world), female members of the congregation sit upstairs in the balcony.

Athens' remaining Jewish community of about 3,500 is served by the **Beth Shalom Synagogue** at Melidóni 5, a neoclassical, marble-clad structure erected in the late 1930s to replace the older synagogue of Etz Hayyim across the way at No. 8, still found inside what's now the community offices. You can visit Beth Shalom's interior (Mon–Fri 10am–noon), with its unusual layout – the *bema* or speaker's platform is together with the *ehal* or Torah-scroll cabinet, rather than at opposite ends of the interior as is usual – but security will be tight; Melidóni itself is barricaded against would be car-bombers, with a guard-booth outside No. 8.

These days there are certainly more Muslims and Africans in and around Psyrrí than Jews or Armenians. West Africans circulate through the nocturnal crowds, peddling pirate CDs to a ready audience baulking at normal retail prices of €16–20 per disc. On the northern margins of the district, around Evripídou, are numerous Bengali storefronts offering cut-rate phone calls to the Subcontinent and butchers catering to a frugal Asian clientele with decidedly humble offal. At the west end of Evripídou, Platía Koumoundoúrou was, before the general pre-Olympic cleanup, the site of a cardboard-box encampment of homeless Kurdish refugees shunning the dubious charms of their Lávrio holding camp. It is still the haunt of rent-boys after midnight, who service kerb-crawlers. But visually the square – named after a late 19th-century prime minister, and also known as Platía Eleftherías – is unrecognisable compared to before, since its re-landscaping and the planting of dozens of new shrubs and trees.

Pysrrí Museums

On the very western edge of Pysrrí are two more conventional attractions. The **Kéndro Melétis Neotéris Keramikís** ❸ (Centre for the Study of Modern Pottery) at Melidóni 4–6 is in fact a museum (Mon–Fri 9am–3pm, Sun 10am–2pm; admission charge) highlight-

BELOW: murals in Gázi.

ing folk and art pottery from the 19th century onwards, with a temporary exhibition space, a café and a shop selling quality products.

Just around the corner at Asomáton 22, on the corner of Dipýlou, is the **Mousío Islamikís Tékhnis** ❹ (Islamic Art Museum; www.benaki.gr; open Tues–Sun 9am–3pm, until 9pm Wed; admission charge), an annexe of the Benaki Museum. Hundreds of works collected by Emmanouil Benaki are arranged over four floors, ranging chronologically from the 8th to the 19th centuries (while in the basement a large section of 4th-century BC defensive wall, which augmentede Themistocles' Long Walls, is on view). If nothing else, the galleries demonstrate the startling variety of techniques and mores over time; representations of animals and musicians from 11th-century Fatimid Egypt, illuminated Persian miniatures, 12th-century Iranian oil-lamps in the form of rodents and a Turko-Mongolian warrior figure as a candlestick mock any notions of Islamic prohibitions on figural depiction.

Painted ceramics from Mesopotamia to Iberia are thoroughly represented: Iznik ware from the 16th and 17th centuries – its heyday – contrasts sharply with the almost Delft-like Iranian pieces from 200 years earlier; 19th-century Iranian tile panelling is far more refined than the almost naïve 19th-century Kütahya ware, which – executed mostly by Armenian craftsmen – supplanted Iznik ware. As the economy of Egypt and Syria declined during the 15th and 16th centuries, engraved or embossed metalwork replaced earlier, more costly inlaying with precious materials such as gold or silver.

Otherwise, singling out items in such a treasure-house is invidious, but highlights include 8th-century tapestries from Egypt, carved Ummayad double doors from Iraq, medieval chessboards with ivory and bone pieces, a solid-stone *mihrab* with a kufic inscription around the edge, a Shi'ite processional standard for Ashura (the first ten, penitential days of Muharram), a tulip-motif saddle cover in predominantly red

An exhibit at the Islamic museum.

BELOW: looking out through the Benaki's window.

Bursa velvet, and an inlaid floor, complete with central fountain, from the 17th-century Cairo mansion of a minor Ottoman official.

An installation at Tekhnópolis inspired by fishing floats.

Gázi and Rouf

From Platía Agíon Asomáton west, Ermoú is attractively pedestrianised as it heads towards intersection with busy Pireós; here strollers are brought up short by exceptionally lurid (and well-executed) graffiti-murals on the wall of the trolley-bus depot, besides the Keramikós site museum. Just across the boulevard are the landmark stacks, lattice-cradled tanks and brick warehouses of a factory and former gas depot which functioned from 1862 to 1984, and lent its informal name (**Gázi**) to the neighbourhood immediately behind.

The whole site was transformed around the millennnium into the **Tekhnópolis** ❺ (grounds open all day), which now hosts changing "trash art" exhibits and avant-garde performances, especially grunge/electronica/rock concerts in the ample cobblestoned courtyards during an annual October festival. Besides the headquarters of a radio station and administrative offices (in two ex-tanks) and a worthwhile café *(see page 145)*, the only permanent installation, towards the north edge of the complex, is the **Maria Callas Museum** (open Mon–Fri 10am–3pm; free) containing displays of letters, archival photos and a few personal effects that will primarily interest devoted fans.

The streets of Gázi, and just beyond it Roúf, are being slowly gentrified as the ambitious Tekhnópolis project has had a ripple effect, though not particularly for any intrinsic charm of their own. By day at least it's difficult to understand the attraction for trend-setters other than sheer novelty – especially compared to more attractive districts of the city – and it's impossible to say where one area ends and the other begins. Roúf takes its name from a Bavarian officer in the Othonian court, and subsequently from a now-closed army camp just the other side of major thoroughfare Konstantinopóleos. Until the 1960s,

BELOW: icons of modern Athens – *frappé* (iced coffee) and mobile phones.

modest yet occasionally stylish one-storey neoclassical cottages here were home to poorer Greeks who worked in the two wholesale produce markets which bracketed the whole district. When the markets were demolished – one is still commemorated by the Paleá Lahanagorá bus stop by Tekhnópolis – the working-class Greeks moved out to be replaced by Muslim gypsies, Pomaks and Turks from Thrace, and developers destroyed many of the original houses.

None of the alternative theatres and clubs here, and few of the tavernas, are open at midday (except at weekends), so Gázi-Roúf really only comes into its own after 10pm. The narrow streets, while often gritty, are safe enough, but after-dark parking is predictably so difficult that you'll probably want come by public transport (frequent buses along Pireós), taxi or scooter.

The other renovation project which also helped kick-start an upswing in the area's fortunes and reputation is the **Benaki Museum's Ktírio Odoú Pireós** annexe ❻ (open Wed–Thu, Sun 10am–6pm, Fri–Sat 10am–10pm, admission fee; www. benaki.gr). An almost windowless, box-like former Lada dealership has been refitted as three floors of gallery space arrayed around an atrium and linked by graceful ramps. There are usually up to a half-dozen temporary exhibitions on at any one time, and you buy tickets for some or all of them on an *à la carte* basis.

The programme for late 2006 – The Unknown Artistotle Onassis, with personal effects and archival material; Yiannis Mitarakis (painter, 1897–1963); and Voula Papaïoannou, Greece's first woman photographer and chronicler of the Occupation famine – gives an idea of the curating sensibility. Rumour has it that Emmanouil Benakis' enormous collection of warehoused artefacts from Africa and Asia will soon find a permanent home here. On the ground floor of these enormous premises are a high-quality shop peddling contemporary Greek jewellery and a popular café with windows facing the boulevard.

Across Konstantinopóleos in **Votanikós district** – hopelessly remote from any public transport until and unless the Votanikós metro station opens – is one further industrial-conversion project, arguably the most successful thus far: the Polýhoros Athináïs at Kastoriás 34–36 (www.athinais.com.gr), housed in a 1920s silk factory. This complex comprises a gallery space, a concert hall, a cinema screening old classics, a theatre, conference centre, two upmarket restaurants and a bar. Also on-site is the **Pierides Museum of Ancient Cypriot Art**, effectively an annexe of the namesake museum in Lárnaka (open daily 9.30am–1pm; admission fee), with predominantly glass and ceramic treasures dating from as early as the 9th century BC. ❑

Map on page 138

At the start of the 20th century, the new Athináïs factory was heralded as a landmark of the modern age, with an enviable reputation for its high-quality silk. But postwar technological advances turned the industry on its head: it was the advent of rayon that finally brought about the factory's demise in the mid-1950s.

BELOW: the Benáki Museum's Ktírio annexe in Gázi.

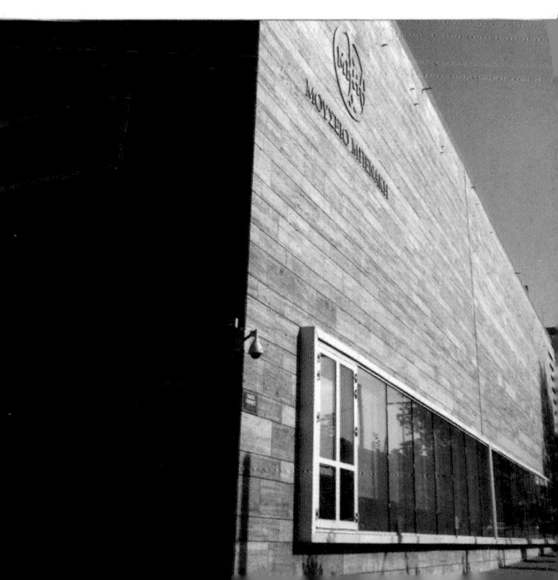

Restaurants & Bars

Restaurants

Bengal Garden

Korínis 12, off Platía Koumoudoúrou, Psyrrí (metro Monastiráki)
Tel: 210 32 53 060
Open daily 10am–10pm
Cash only. €€

Despite the name, this offers plenty of dishes from all over the Indian Subcontinent, such as lamb-based *biriyani*, *dahl*, *sabze* and beef-based *garu masala*, with *nan* and *chapati* to mop up sauces. Finish off with spiced Indian *chai* (tea).

Inomagirio

Dekeléon 32, Roúf (no nearby metro)
Open: see below. €

Inconspicuous basement premises underneath the co-managed Beduin Bar. Very inexpensive *magireftá*, but erratic trading hours – you're most likely to find it open at weekends, with live music sessions on Sunday afternoon (featuring clarinet instead of the usual *bouzoúki*).

O Nikitas

Agíon Anargýron 19, Psyrrí (metro Monastiráki)
Tel: 210 32 52 591
Open noon–6pm Mon–Sat
Cash only. €

Probably the oldest taverna in Psyrrí (founded in 1967), O Nikitas has built its reputation on a short but sweet menu comprising a few *mezédes*, *souvláki*, pork chops, *fáva* and daily specials like oven-baked cheese pie or broccoli. Drink is confined to beer or *oúzo*, and usually there are no sweets. Nonetheless for good value you can't beat it, especially if you get an outdoor table under the trees on the pedestrian walkway by Agíon Anargýron church.

Ta Psarakia

Orféos 34, Roúf (no nearby metro)
Tel: 210 34 69 995
Open L and D daily, may close part August
Cash only. €

A new (opened in mid-2006) and thus very keen *ouzerí* doing only seafood (as the name implies – *psári* means "fish") – and a few *mezédes*. The quality is high, prices relatively low and portions fair-sized; the cuttlefish with spinach is excellent, and the beets come with their greens.

Sardelles

Persefónis 15, Gázi (metro Thisío)
Tel: 210 34 78 050
Open L and D daily. €€

One of the more reasonably priced of this area's trendy eateries, Sardelles concentrates on the humbler varieties of seafood like, well, *sardélles* (sardines) and other small fish. There's outdoor seating right opposite the back gate of Tekhnópolis, and modern subdued décor inside.

To Steki tou Ilia

Eptahalkou 5
Tel: 210 34 58 052
Thessaloníkis 7
Tel: 210 34 22 407
(metro Thisío)
Open D Mon–Sat, L Sun; may close Mon outside of summer. Cash only. €€

On any given evening (plus Sunday lunch), one or other branch (200m apart) of this enterprise will be open and packed with locals who've come for the house specialty: a big pile of grilled lamb chops. Starters are competent, service is quick, and barrelled wine is very reasonable at under €5 euro per litre. You'll sit indoors under the wine barrels if you haven't booked one of the popular tables out on the pedestrian lane.

Taverna tou Psyrri

Eskhýlou 12
(metro Monastiráki)
Tel: 210 32 14 923
Open daily noon–1am.
Cash only. €

Trendy, overpriced eateries are ten a penny in Psyrrí; this is one of the few normal-fare, normal-

LEFT: lunch *al fresco* in Psyrrí.

PRICE CATEGORIES

Prices are based on an average meal per person, including house wine:
€ = under €15
€€ = €15–25
€€€ = €25–40
€€€€ = over €40
Key: B = breakfast, L = lunch, D = dinner

priced traditional tavernas, and accordingly popular (you can't book, so show up early). The menu is strong on fish and seafood, but there's also plenty for vegetarians. Choose from the steam trays with an eye to the daily specials on the chalkboard outside – and bear in mind that portions are huge. There's a garden out back, but the wall décor inside is well worth a look: old photos and gravures of Athens, folk art, aphorisms. The only minus: service can be brusque.

Skoufias
Vasiléou tou Megálou 50, Roúf
(no nearby metro)
Tel: 210 34 12 252
Open D daily
Cash only. **€€**
This is the sister restaurant to the Skoufias in Exárhia – though the menu here is more traditional. This Skoufias is housed in a fine old house opposite the church of Ágios Vasílios.

Thalatta
Vítonos 5, Roúf
(no nearby metro)
Tel: 210 34 64 204
Open D Mon–Sat
Major credit cards. **€€€**
Upmarket "modern Mediterranean", seafood-strong restaurant in resolutely downmarket surroundings, though the nearby Benaki Museum annexe and Tekhnópolis will change that. Pleasant internal courtyard for summer, nautical décor inside.

Cafés/Bars

Filistron Apostólou
Pávlou 23
(metro Thisío)
Tel: 210 34 67 554
Open Tues–Sun, evening only summer, afternoon–evening winter
An alternative to the rather gormless *frappádika* (places specialising in iced Nescafé) just down the street, Filistron offers *mezédes* platters, a high-quality Greek wine list, *tsípouro*, *oúzo* and specialty digestifs like *vin santo* from Santoríni. The summer roof terrace has in-your-face views of the Acropolis.

Omilos Gastoni
Tekhnópolis, Gázi, Persefónis Street entrance
(metro Thisío)
Open: daily 8am until late
The main café of the Tekhnópolis complex has plenty of sleekly restored industrial machinery in situ to admire as you sip your drinks.

Iy Revekka
Miaoúli 22, corner Palládos
(metro Monastiráki)
Open daily
Lively, popular *kafeníon* with marked *ouzerí* tendencies, and very reasonably priced for the area. Beside the usual *karafáki* of *oúzo* and *mezédes* platters, the specialty is *rakómelo* from Amorgós island served hot in a *bríki*. Good acoustic *rebétika* sessions on guitar and *bouzoúki* Sat and Sun afternoons.

Stavlos
Iraklidón 10
(metro Thisío)
Tel: 210 34 67 206
www.stavlos.gr
Open noon–2am most days
Housed in what were the royal stables (and thus the Greek name) during the 19th century, and one of the first cafés to colonise the area during its mid-1990s gentrification. Stavlos also comprises a stone-and-wood trimmed bar, a "club" of sorts, an art gallery and a generic Mediterranean restaurant, all much more accomplished than the typical *frappádiko* on this street.

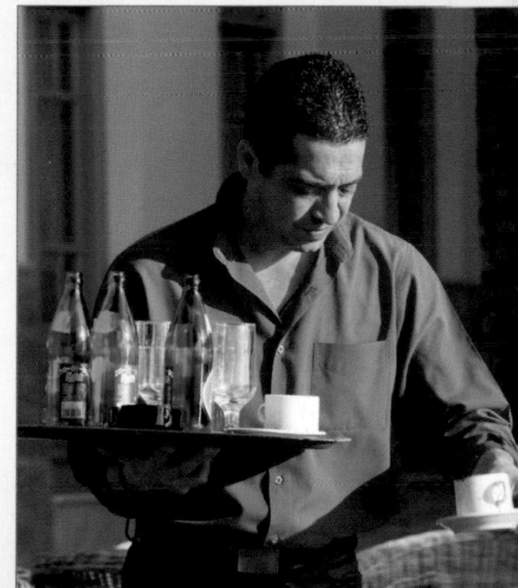

RIGHT: waiter service in Thisío.

PETRÁLONA TO PANGRÁTI

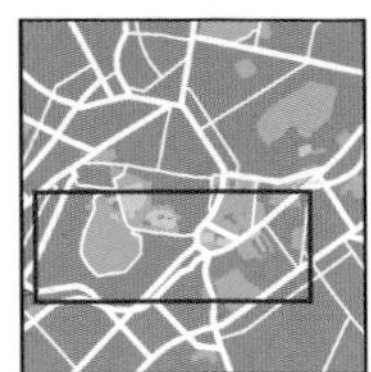

To the south and southwest of the Acropolis are some up-and-coming districts – former working-class areas and refugee ghettos that are benefiting from Athens' cleaning and greening campaigns. Further west, comfortable Pangráti contains three of the city's most interesting museums

Ano Petrálona, a long, narrow grid of streets on the western slopes of Filopáppou Hill, tucked between the ISAP train lines, Thisío district and Kallirróis boulevard, is historically working-class and was for many years overlooked. But being so close to the centre, with good transport links by trolley-bus and the *elektrikó* (as Athenians call the pre-metro ISAP train), it was only a matter of time before the neighbourhood was "discovered". By the early 1990s good-value tavernas were multiplying, especially along Tröón, Dimofóndos and their perpendiculars. The doyen of these, in business since the 1960s, is 'I' Askimopapo at Ionón 61 (winter only).

Rents began to inch up as the savvy discovered the virtues of a quiet, modest yet convenient bolthole here. Especially at the Thisío end of things, some streets have been attractively pedestrianised, and the already sparse traffic calmed with diversions and narrowings. Lower down towards the train lines, modern blocks of flats predominate, but further up the slope there's a good sprinkling of low-rise interwar houses and a few neoclassical specimens.

Arriving by No.15 trolley-bus, you'll alight at **Platía Amalías Merkoúri** (honouring Melina Mercouri's grandmother), with a tiny, fenced-off archaeological zone in one corner. More of these have helped to suspend in aspic a last surviving cluster of refugee shanties just northeast, between Kallisthénous and Apolloníou. In these humble shacks, each room originally housed a family, with several sharing a water-tap, privy and a courtyard. Their wealthier descendents would pull some down only to discover ancient foundations, tombs or other structures underneath, and the

BELOW: the monument to Caius Philopappos.

archaeological service would put a stop to any construction.

Just east of this lingering reminder of the Asia Minor Catastrophe is the southwestern tip of Filopáppou Hill with its **Dora Stratou Theatre ❶**, where most summer evenings see performances of Greek folk dance *(see page 246)*.

Filopáppou Hill

The ancient "Hill of the Muses" is a wonderful expanse of greenery in a city with a dire need of such. It is more usually known as **Filopáppou Hill** after the ancient monument at the summit on the southeast flank. This rectangular tomb was completed in AD 116 for one Caius Julius Antiochus Philopappos, a Syrian prince and Roman consul, portrayed on a frieze driving his chariot, who so loved Athens that he was made an honorary citizen and interred here.

But most people make the climb not to pay their respects to the deceased but to enjoy the views – the best possible of the Acropolis, especially towards dusk – to jog, walk their dogs and generally take the air. On the first Monday of Lent, children still fly kites from the ridge as their families picnic, weather permitting. The grading of the paths and the satisfying, half-wild mix of indigenous cypress, pine, shrubs and flowers is the work of distinguished landscape architect Dimitris Pikionis (1887–1968), who between 1953 and 1957 carried out the first improvement of the Acropolis and Filopáppou zones.

Northeast of the peak, on the slope facing the Odeon of Herodes Atticus, is a Classical troglodytic dwelling known with far more poetic licence than truth as the Prison of Socrates; in Hellenistic or Roman times the subterranean chambers were used as tombs. About 50m north, across a main walkway, sits the mid-15th-century church of Ágios Dimítrios Lombardiáris, with a lavishly frescoed interior. Because of its site and aesthetics it's a popular Saturday venue for weddings and baptisms.

Since antiquity, the hill has had a rather chequered career. During the 1687 Venetian siege of the Ottoman-held Acropolis, from near the summit the fateful shot was fired that ignited the powder magazine held in the Parthenon and blew nearly half of it to bits. During their 1967 coup the colonels parked their tanks at the foot of the hill, and in 2002 angry local residents tore down newly erected perimeter fencing which would have restricted access to their favourite park.

It's worth walking to the top of Filopáppou Hill

Makrygiánni to Syngroú

East and south of Filopáppou, as far as Leofóros Syngroú, lie the contiguous neighbourhoods of Makrygiánni and Koukáki. **Makrygiánni** still lies very much within the tourist ambit, and this tendency will only increase with the completion of the new Acropolis Museum; the numer-

BELOW: lunch in Petrálona.

Outside the National Gallery in Pangráti stands Droméas (the Runner), made of shattered plates of glass.

ous hotels here all mandatorily sport post-Olympics roof-gardens for ogling the Acropolis.

Makrygiánni's one conventional attraction is the **Atelier-Museum Spýros Vassilíou** ❷ at Webster 5a (www.spyrosvassiliou.org; open Tues, Thu, Fri 10am–8pm, Wed 10am–10pm, Sat–Sun 10am– 3pm; admission fee), exhibiting some 40 works of this versatile artist (1902–1985) in his former studio and family dwelling. Vassilíou's long career encompassed initial discipleship to Nikolaos Lytras stage design, posters and a later preponderance of acrylic on canvas; his idiosyncratic vision is not easily pigeonholed, though bus-stops and sewing-machines are recurring motifs in his portraiture (mainly of his family) and landscapes.

Koukáki is very much more local, with its own metro station (Syngroú-Fix) and bracketed by two lively pedestrian zones – Márkou Drákou and Georgíou Olympíou – both replete with bars, cafés and eateries. The higher up the gradient you climb towards Filopáppou, the more desirable the address, with self-employed professionals to be seen bent over drawing-boards at second-floor windows, and entire terraces of neoclassical dwellings awaiting restoration.

Descending towards Syngroú, matters become progressively frowsier; auto-spares dealers begin appearing along Falírou and, across Syngroú in the districts of Kinosárgous and Néos Kósmos, completely dominate commerce for blocks on end. You can – at a pricc – find almost any used or new part for models of the past three decades.

Along with autos comes eroticism (though fortunately not the two in combination): the upper reaches of high-speed, four-lane Leofóros Syngroú have long been known as a gay/transvestite cruising zone, and

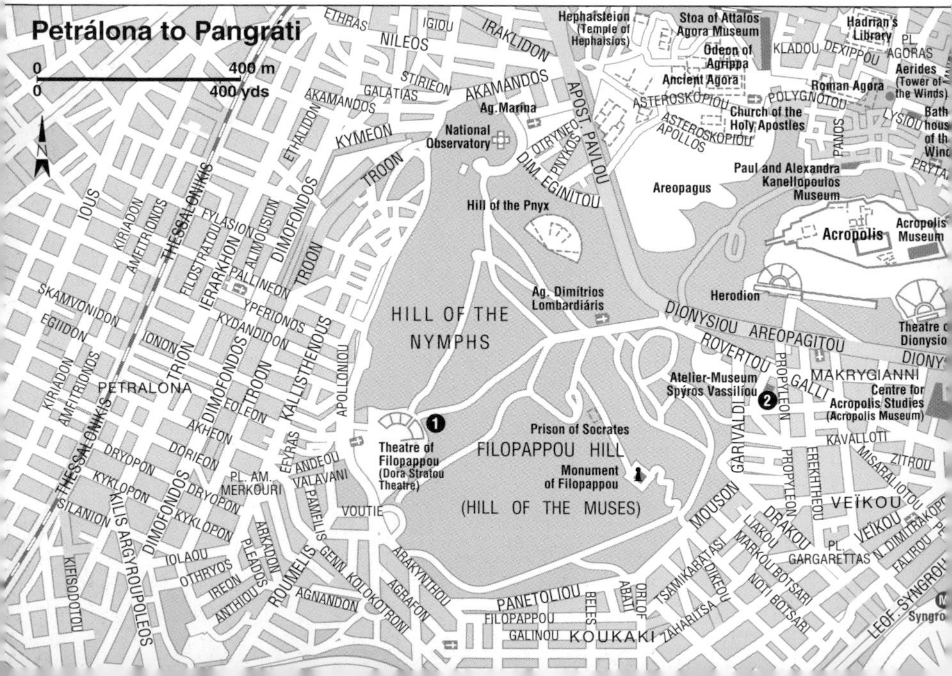

Petrálona to Pangráti

0 400 m
0 400 yds

two of the oldest gay clubs in the city sit a few doors apart on Lembési. Lately, however, there's a crop of more conspicuous hetero strip clubs – staffed in the main by central European women – and sex shops down near the old Fix brewery, which ceased operations in 1980.

Around the millennium this stark structure was saved from certain demolition by briefly housing the National Museum of Contemporary Art. But plans for upgrading and reopening it have stalled indefinitely, and the collection – such as it is – occupies temporary quarters at the Mégaron Musikís. The only trace of its short independent existence are some photovoltaically propelled propellers and winking lights in the Syngroú-Fix metro station.

Across the Ilissós to Mets

First as Ardittoú and then Kallirróis, the roaring boulevard separating Makrygiánni from Mets and now traced by the new tram line, follows exactly the line of the ancient river Ilissós. Its only remaining uncapped section lies southeast of the Temple of Olympian Zeus, before it disappears into a modern culvert under Kallirróis, made after repeated, destructive flooding in the modern era *(see also page 78)*.

Before World War I, **Mets** was known as Gefýria (Bridges), after the rickety little ones that used to cross the then free-flowing Ilissós. The current name, the Greek rendition of Metz in Alsace, comes from a pro-Entente café which traded here after 1914 (a pointed jibe at the pro-German Greek royal family). After World War I the neighbourhood became an artists' quarter, then declined during the Depression before coming to the attention of foreigners during the 1960s as expatriates were priced out of their former favourite haunts on the slopes of Lykavitós hill.

Known for a brief period – and by all fans of blues, jazz and world music – as the Blues Hall, this Mets venue has been renovated and relaunched as Planet Music (44 Ardittoú; tel: 923 7109). This time round, acts from the international indie circuit join the jazz and blues roster.

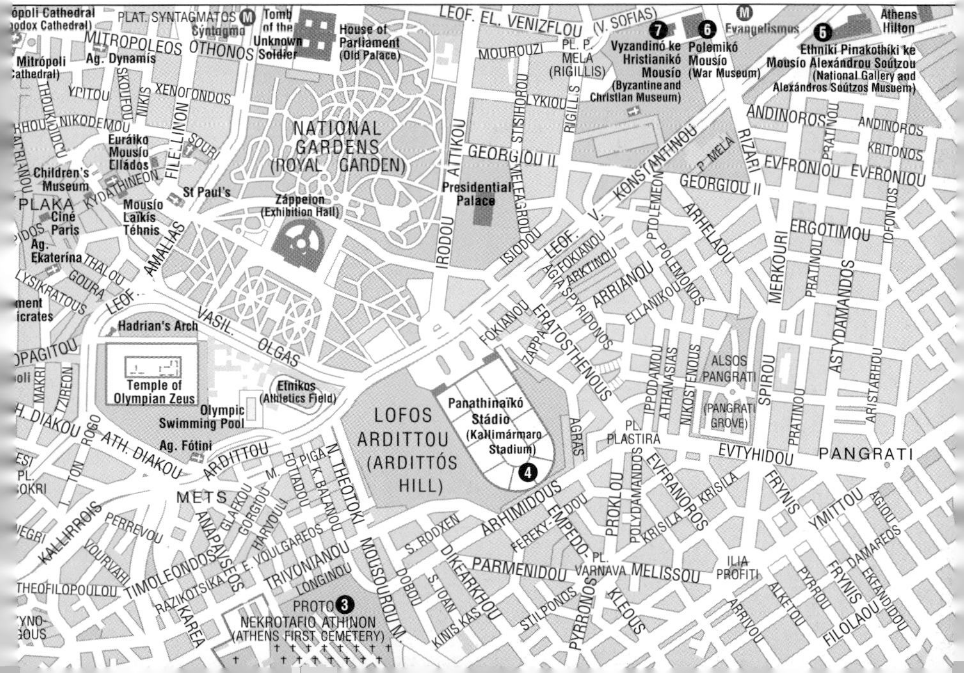

In Athen First Cemetery, a sculpture of an emaciated, supine figure whose title translates as "The Mother of the Occupation, 1941" serves as a harrowing reminder of the 100,000 Greeks (of which 40,000 Athenians) who starved to death during the winter of 1940–41.

It's a small, roughly square district some seven blocks on each side, but seems much larger if you're hoofing it up one of the many car-free stair-streets. The elevation and seclusion are the main selling-points, not the architecture which is largely modern. Even before "redevelopment" the area took quite a knock during December 1944, when ELAS forces bombarded British headquarters at Sýntagma from these slopes and those of Ardittós hill adjacent. On Nikifórou Theotóki, the street adjoining the hill, a few old, ungentrified, mud-brick houses are still bullet-scarred.

Mets had its last moment in the sun during the 1980s, when the main thoroughfare Márkou Mousoúrou and certain perpendicular streets hosted the first wave of "updated" Greek tavernas, and a number of small pensions catered to long-stay, academic and artistic visitors. But its star declined as first Petrálona's, then Psyrrí's rose. Both the lodgings and eateries are long gone, the area is now rather staid, and after dark Mets seems as dead as the denizens of the cemetery that dominates the area to the southeast.

BELOW: view of the Acropolis from Filopáppou Hill.

First Cemetery

Imagine a blend of Washington DC's Arlington, Paris's Père Lachaise and London's Highgate cemeteries without, respectively, honour guards, groupies at Jim Morrison's grave, or dangling moss, and you'll get an idea of the place that **Próto Nekrotafío Athinón** ❸ (Athens First Cemetery) holds in local society. When well-connected Athenians – or any other worthy Greeks – die, their cortège processes up Anapávseos (Eternal Rest) street, climbing a slight gradient past shops devoted to every aspect of funerary culture. Besides florists and marble-monument carvers, there are storefronts displaying sample ceramicised memorial portraits – a Greek obsession – usually featuring the most famous of the recently departed.

Immediately inside the main gate, grandiose mausoleums of prominent Hellenes and philhellenes – Emmanouil Benaki, Georgios Averof, Harilaos Trikoupis, Theodore Kolokotronis, Heinrich Schliemann among others – confront you, but these miniature neoclassical temples soon yield to more intimate family tombs. The most famous of these, high in popular affection, is the *Kimoméni (Sleeping Maiden)* by the Tiniot sculptor Giannoulis Halepas (1851–1938), a pre-Raphaelite, post-Romantic effigy on the Afendákis family plot, some 300 metres in on the right. Although the 18-year-old-girl so idealised has been gone a century and more, there are still likely to be fresh flowers left on her lap. Conversely, 1930s dictator Ioannis Metaxas, though dying in an odour of sanctity after defying the Italians, has a simple, almost anonymous slab-tomb in the rear-centre section. Hunt more diligently and you'll find just about everyone else who was anyone in modern Greek life: both elder Papandreous, Nobel-winning poets George Seferis and Odysseas Elytis, thespians Melina Mercouri and Manos Katrakis, plus Alexandros Panagoulis (the army officer and later politician who attempted to assassinate junta Colonel Papadopoulos in 1968).

There are separate sections for Orthodox, Jews (full and no longer used), Protestants, Catholics and – high up on the east side – a small zone set aside for free burial of impecunious cultural and literary figures. All other plots have long since been exhausted, filling during the 1960s for tens of thousands of dollars.

The great and the good are not exhumed as Orthodox doctrine stipulates after five years, but lesser mortals are, thus the huge ossuary just to one side of the main gate, with thousands of skeletons kept in metal boxes. Many of these were buried in less prestigious cemeteries, but subsequently lodged here, a macabre example of posthumous social climbing. More cheerfully, the relatives of the not-yet-dug-up deceased treat graveside visits as a dignified weekend excursion: picnicking, sweeping and changing flowers, and leaving *kólyva* (boiled wheat and other seeds, a very ancient custom) on tombs and handing it out to passers-by. Outsiders are also welcome to treat the peaceful, cypress-studded grounds as a park for strolling, as long as they are unobtrusive. Formal escorted tours (with a commentary in Greek) are conducted periodically.

Ardittós and the Kallimármaro

Ardittós is perhaps not so famous as other Athenian hills, but it's the most thickly vegetated, and to protect the dense pine groves from summer arsonists, it has long been securely off-limits. On the slopes there was an ancient shrine to the demigod of the Ilissós River, and another to the goddess Tyche. The forests are said to be haunted, either by the unquiet spirits of those executed and buried here by the Nazis during World War II, or by something much older.

Commemorating the site of the first modern Olympics.

BELOW: the Kallimármaro ("beautifully marbled") Olympic stadium.

Cradled in a cavity of the northewest flank of Ardittós is the stadium known as the **Kallimármaro** ❹, built in 330 BC to stage the Panathenaic Games (thus the offical name of Panathinaïkó Stádio). It was adapted by the Romans for their blood-sports, and refurbished handsomely by Herodes Atticus in AD 140. The conveniently ready-cut Pendelic marble slabs from the 60,000 seats were systematically pilfered by Byzantine and medieval builders, but in 1895 the stadium was restored to its former dazzling glory by Alexandrian Greek Georgios Averof (honoured by an adjacent statue), in time to serve as the main venue of the first modern Olympics in 1896.

The ancient stadium is not really right for modern athletics, the bends are too tight and the length (at just over 200m) is awkward. During the 2004 Olympics, the only events to be staged here were the archery and the finishes of both the men's and women's marathons.

Pangráti and its museums

East of the First Cemetery and Ardittós Hill, the district of **Pangráti** is considerably livelier than Mets but solidly, pleasantly middle-class; conferring enough anonymity on local residents that it was the ideal place for top cadres of now disbanded terrorist group Dekaeftá Novemvríou (November 17) to blend in, keeping a *giáfka* or safe-house here on Damáreos Street until their unmasking in July 2002. Arhimídous Street just behind the Kallimármaro makes a good introduction to the neighbourhood, with one of Athens' largest *laïkés agorés* (street markets) every Friday.

Platía Varnáva, with its benches, central fountain and greenery, together with the pedestrianised approach from Arhimídous, was one of the first and more successful examples of the mid-1980s "greening" of Athens under the early PASOK municipal administrations. There's a concentration of tavernas for all tastes in the streets around, as there also is east of Eratosthénous, the busy gateway boulevard that divides Pangráti roughly in half, with Mets-like stair-streets on the slopes to either side. Eratosthénous leads up to Platía Plastíra, with its landmark neoclassical *kafeníon* Iy Ellas dominating it from a slight elevation.

From here more eccentrically angled streets lead to other plazas and over to the Álsos Pangráti (Pan-

BELOW: *Carmeni, Santoríni* by Konstantinos Maleas.

grati Grove), the area's largest green space. Vasiléos Konstantínou delineates the district on the northwest and leads up to a trio of worthwhile museums at the point where Pangráti, Kolonáki and Ilíssia meet, all a short walk from the Evangelismós metro station.

The National Gallery

The **Ethnikí Pinakothíki ke Mousío Alexándrou Soútzou** ❺ (National Gallery and Alexándros Soútzos Museum; open Mon–Sat except Tues 9am–3pm, Sun 10am–2pm; admission charge) at No. 50 takes you on a quick chronological and thematic gallop through Greek painting and sculpture from just before Independence to the 1990s – doing a good job of placing the art in its social context – and also hosts worthwhile temporary exhibitions, though the single section of foreign art is distinctly second-rate.

The so-called Ionian School was spurred by the fall of Crete in 1669, and the progressive Italianisation of society and artistic conventions of these islands. Early post-Independence Greek portraiture charts the rise of an indigenous bourgeoisie, while the historical-propagandistic canvases of Munich-trained Theodoros Vryzakis (1819–1878), such as Lord Byron arriving at Mesolónghi, may be familiar to some from textbook reproductions. The first great painter of the post-Othonian period, Nikiforos Lytras, is represented by *The Milkman*, plus the sequential *The Waiting* and *The Kiss*, while an original, non-derivative style emerges under Nikolaos Gyzis (1842–1901), with his hyper-realistic group (*The Children's Betrothal*) and individual portraits, many of the latter commissioned by the new bourgeoisie generated by the prosperity of the Harilaos Trikoupis years. Gyzis also prefigured symbolism with his *Idou O Nymfios Erhetai* (*The Celestial Bridgroom*), while others dabbled in orientalism, though the few Greek practitioners of Impressionism chose to go abroad as the pitiless Aegean light seemed not to be congenial to it.

The upper floor introduces "Modernism" (arbitrarily pegged at 1900–25), when for the first and apparently last time Greek landscapes and townscapes were celebrated by the leasing painters Konstantinos Maleas and Konstantinos Parthenis, both heavily influenced by Fauvism. The 1930s saw a retrenchment in many respects, but also the emergence of a stellar generation who would dominate Greek painting for the next four decades, even as they went their separate ways: Spyros Papaloukas, Spyros Vassiliou (*see page 148*), the surrealist Nikos Engonopoulos (1907–85), the portraitist Yiannis Moralis (1916–), still-active illustrator Alekos Fasianos, Ioannis Tsarouhis (d. 1990) and – probably the only one who is internationally known – Nikos Hatzikyriakos-Ghikas, long resident in Paris and Ýdra. He gets

Romantic 19th-century couple in the National Gallery.

BELOW: "Ionian" portraits in the National Gallery.

As well as weaponry and photographs, the War Museum has uniformed mannequins of officers and men from every era in full-dress regalia, including, curiously, several "diplomats". There are also pilots' flying suits from three decades, including a fur-and-leather one from the 1919–22 Asia Minor war.

an entire room for his bracing, synthetic-cubist take on all genres evolving into his semi-abstracts of the 1950s to 1970s. But the other luminaries are scandalously under-represented, and sculptor Giannoulis Halepas – he of the *Kimoméni* in the First Cemetery *(see page 150)* – has only a single series of rough-hewn mythological studies to account for his career.

Probably the single most striking modern work, however, opposite two scenes by naïve painter Theofilos, is the secular altar-screen – for want of a better term – by the neo-Byzantine painter Fotis Kontoglou (1895– 1965), which he made for his own house. This decidedly eclectic composition encompasses figures ranging from ancient philosphers and his own relatives to an Indian fakir (clearly modelled on Orthodox Saint Onofrios) and a cannibal king (his panel was famously reproduced on a CD cover by avant-garde group Mode Plagal, who are to folk music what Kontoglou was to iconography). The galleries conclude with a mixed bag of contemporary artists working in various media. An indigenous 1950s–1960s non-figurative movement was squashed by the colonels, but works now reflect most prevailing international trends. Just in front of the museum, in the traffic circle opposite the Hilton, stands a prime example: *Droméas (The Runner)*, fashioned from stacked plates of shattered glass and long resident in Platía Omónias.

BELOW: the rape of Greece as depicted in the National Gallery.

The War Museum

The **Polemikó Mousío** ❻ (War Museum; open Tues–Sat 9am–2pm; Sun 9.30am–2pm; free) on Rizári, corner Vasilísis Sofías, is tainted by its status as the sole "cultural" foundation of the colonels' junta. It is also labelled mostly in Greek only, and tends to be overrun by groups of noisy schoolchildren brought here on educational/indoctrinational visits. For some or all of these reasons, most visitors to the city shun the place, but what they miss are excellent displays on Greece and the Greeks during World War II. Documentation of child famine-victims in particular will bring viewers up short, Greece lost 620,000 civilians or 8 percent of its population through the war, especially during the winter of 1941–42, the highest proportion in Axis-occupied Europe. The activities of the Egypt-based Ierós Lóhos (Sacred Battalion) are chronicled with newspaper clippings of their successful actions. Quite rare photos show resistance groups ELAS (leftist) and EDES (rightist) in the hills; their one successful joint operation, the severing of the Gorgopótamos rail viaduct; and captured German General Kreipe being bundled off Crete to Egypt.

These actions – and assorted proclamations – are matched by chilling images of the inevitable Nazi reprisals and edicts. Interestingly, given the original ultra-right-wing impetus for the museum, various personal effects of ELAS General Stefanos Sarafis are featured, but the civil war (still too controversial) gets passed over in silence, and the Cyprus Hall is a clumsy propaganda exercise attempting to prove the eternal Greekness of that unhappy island, and glorifying the armed group EOKA.

There's a rather incongruous gallery of foreign swords and armour – even a full samurai suit – while the forbidding exterior is surrounded by assorted artillery pieces, both Greek and captured as booty. A collection of aircraft to the west includes a suspended life-size model of the Daedalus biplane, one of the first-ever military aircraft, used in the 1912–13 Balkan Wars.

The Byzantine and Christian Museum

The **Vyzandinó ke Hristianikó Mousío** ❼ (Byzantine and Christian Museum; open Tues–Sun 8am–7.30pm; admission fee) at Vasilísis Sofías 22 ranks as one of the city's top museums for clarity and quality, following a thorough 2004 revamp. It is housed partly in a 19th-century villa (summer concerts are staged in the courtyard) that once belonged to a wealthy French philhellene, the eccentric Duchesse de Plaisance. The displays are wisely grouped both chronologically – beginning in the basement – and thematically, with ample attention paid to secular life and contemporary crafts, such as glass, ceramic and metal vessels. The workmanship and taste of exquisite gold jewellery inlaid with semi-precious stones seems utterly timeless, and indeed is imitated by the best contemporary Greek craftsmen and -women.

Perhaps the museum's most valuable aspect is how it demonstrates the gradual transition from, and continuity of, Roman and pagan religion and sensibilities. The "new" sacred architecture is shown to be an outgrowth of Roman public buildings, with the mosaic floor of the Ilissós basilica as an example. Although pagan artefacts and shrines were Christianised as often as they were destroyed, funerary practices are

Outside the War Museum.

BELOW: the Byzantine and Christian Museum is one of the best designed in the city.

One of the Byzantine and Christian Museum's unboubted assets is its setting, centred on a peaceful, courtyarded villa in the Tuscan–Renaissance style.

little changed in the early Christian era, with ancient relief-carved sarcophagi used until the 11th century, goods still buried with the deceased and funerary banquets conducted at the graveside. Floor-mosaic motifs echo those of Hellenistic times, and rather Asiatic marble altar-screen carvings include a lion attacking a stag and two other lions rampant before the Tree of Lion.

The Hoard of Mytilene – gold jewellery, coins dated AD 602–626 and household objects hastily buried to protect them from 7th-century Arab raids – includes a silver bath-pan with a nude Aphrodite in relief on the handle. In the display on maritime trade, Poseidon rides an aquatic monster while hoisting a ship and trident, in the middle of a silver-and-gilt 12th-century dish; nearby a centaur is seen on a slightly earlier altar-screen fragment.

The Christian Egypt section features the oft-reproduced icon of St George slaying a dragon that seems to be only playing dead, and a silk-embroidered liturgical robe plus other superb Coptic textiles. Iconoclasm, in its two 8th- and 9th-century phases, is shown as a mere blip in the continuity of Orthodox practice, arguably a panicky reaction to the success of image-less Islam and the troubled preceding centuries of barbarian raids, thought to be God's punishment for some doctrinal deviation. Icons, all dating from after this contentious period, include many double-sided specimens designed for use in processions. Osía María (Blessed Mary of Egypt) is shown early in her career as a courtesan, rather than in her usual depiction as a withered desert ascetic; there's a rare 13th-century mosaic of the Panagía Glykofiloússa (Virgin Sweetly Kissing), and an obviously Venetian-influenced 14th-century Crucifixion from Monemvasiá.

These, however, are arguably overshadowed by legions of mostly 13th-century frescoes removed from nearby locales, wonderfully expressive because they are so late, subject to westernising artistic currents brought with the Fourth Crusade. You'll notice a typically tonsured St Stephen from Náxos; a haunting Pantokrator from Skhimatári; a nicely dishevelled, gimlet-eyed John the Baptist; improbably long-winged angels; and a crowded Dormition with clearly differentiated saints attending the Virgin's bier.

A masonry *témblon* (altar screen) has been re-erected on-site, with an unusual iconography of saints above and the Virgin and Christ below. There's a special wing, appropriately devoted to "Attica as a Byzantine Province", whose highlight is the re-mounted art from Ágios Nikólaos Spiliá Pendélis (1233), with a doe-eyed Christ Pantokrator in the dome and unusually wide-eyed saints below – strongly reminiscent of similar Romanesque reliefs in western Europe from just a century before. ❑

BELOW: a harpist depicted in the Byzantine Museum.

RESTAURANTS & BARS

Restaurants

Petrálona

T'Askimopapo
Ionón 61
(metro Petrálona)
Tel: 210 34 63 282
Open D Mon–Sat Oct 1 to mid-Jun. Cash only. €
Founded in 1968 by leftist actor Antonis Voulgaris, who treated government ministers or labourers without distinction, this bohemian taverna is now run alternate days by his daughters. The multi-roomed interior is lined with old theatre photos and pen-and-ink or charcoal sketches donated by admirers (many from eastern Europe). The food – a mix of meat-based *magireftá* and vegetarian starters – is plainly presented but well-priced and wholesome. There's Limnos white wine or Neméa red to wash it down.

Chez Lucien
Tróön 32
(metro Petrálona)
Tel: 210 34 64 236
Open D Tues–Sat until 1am
Cash only. €€
Tiny, French-run bistro where you share tables indoors or out and no bookings are taken; the minimally Hellenised fare is at French prices, and the owner-chef has a habit of standing over you and explaining his dishes ad infinitum, which may not be to everyone's taste.

To Koutouki
Lakíou 9
(metro Petrálona)
Tel: 210 34 53 655
Open D daily. Cash only. €€
Occupying one of the more substantial houses on a lane of refugee dwellings by a flyover, To Koutouki specialises in meat grills with a few *mezédes* preceding. In summer you sit on a roof terrace, with unbeatable views of Filopáppou hill and the city; in winter you're inside a Tardis-like, stepped interior. That said, the food, while decent, isn't quite up to the atmosphere.

Ikonomou
Kydandídon 32, corner Tróön
(metro Petrálona)
Tel: 210 34 67 555
Open D Mon–Sat
Cash only. €
The crowded pavement tables rather than the tiny sign over the door announce you've come to this *inomagerío* which does just a handful of dishes per day, with no menu per se: *laderá*, roast meat, a limited repertoire of *orektiká* in big portions, semolina *helvá* on the house to finish. The *retsína* is cheap but average quality; the red wine is better. The décor – old coloured engravings of Attica and Athens, caricatures of wine-drinkers, new tiling – has gone slightly upmarket since a change of proprietors in 2003, without affecting prices.

To Therapevtirio
Kydandídon 41
(metro Petrálona)
Tel: 210 34 12 538
Open daily noon–1am except Sun eve and part Aug
Cash only. €€
This *mezedopolío* does a bumping trade while nearby rivals are empty, despite a less than inspiring interior and waits for a table outside. The menu, sensibly, is limited and stresses seafood (you should confirm prices of fish beforehand) plus *mezédes* like *hórta* and *tyrokafterí*.

Makrygiánnni–Koukáki

Amvrosia
Márkou Drákou 3–5
(metro Syngroú-Fix)
Tel: 210 92 20 281
Open L and D daily
Cash only. €
This pedestrianised street leading up from the metro "rabbit-hole" towards Filopáppou hill is crammed with bars and restaurants. Amvrosia is perhaps the best value for a meaty feed, whether a takeway *souvláki* or a sit-down meal at a table, out by the planter boxes in fine weather. There's also a full range of starters, and bulk wine or beer.

Apanemia
Erekhthíou 2, corner Veïkoú
(metro Syngroú-Fix)
Tel: 210 92 28 766
Open 1pm–1am Mon–Sat
Cash only. €
Competent *ouzerí* offering standard platters like *keftédes*, *hortópita* (vegetable turnover) and *saganáki* (fried cheese), all with palatable, well-priced Límnos bulk wine in addition to *oúzo*. It's okay just to have a *pikilía* (medley) of *mezédes*. Walls of exposed recycled brick and pointed masonry provide atmosphere.

Diva
Márkou Drákou 13
(metro Syngroú-Fix)
Tel: 210 92 16 790
Open L and D daily, closed Aug. Cash only. €€
Very hygienic, mid-range Italian *trattoria* which sets tables outside a long, narrow premises.

PRICE CATEGORIES

Prices are based on an average meal per person, including house wine:
€ = under €15
€€ = €15–25
€€€ = €25–40
€€€€ = over €40
Key: B = breakfast, L = lunch, D = dinner

RESTAURANTS & BARS

The menu encompasses all the usual pasta and pizza choices, plus chicken and a few *polpette* dishes.

Edodi
Veïkoú 80
(metro Syngroú-Fix)
Tel: 210 92 13 013
Open D Mon–Sat, closed summer.
Major credit cards. **€€€€**
One of the best "nouvelle" restaurants in the city, this intimate, eight-table affair is tucked away on the upper floor of a neoclassical house. The international fusion menu changes regularly but might include dishes such as duck in cherry sauce or smoked-goose carpaccio. The attentive staff ensure that you see the basic ingredients and understand what will be done to them. Save room – and bank balance – for the wine list and creative desserts.

Evvia
Georgíou Olymbíou 8, Koukáki
(metro Syngroú-Fix)
Tel: 210 92 41 816
Open L and D daily
Cash only. **€**
Trendy bars and tavernas come and go like mushrooms on this pedestrianized artery of Koukáki, but this warhorse *ouzerí* has been here since the year dot. There are all the expected starters – mostly fried – plus seafood options and bulk wine, but also (unusually) a couple of *magireftá* of the day, such as chicken soup in winter.

Iy Gardenia
Anastasíou Zínni 29
(metro Syngroú-Fix)
Open Mon–Sat to 8pm winter, 6pm summer
Cash only. **€**
The last surviving (and very friendly) *inomagirío* in the area, a cavernous, predominantly white-marble premises doling out sustaining, well-executed, not overly oily *magireftá* – with plenty for fish-lovers and vegetarians – plus bulk wine.

Manimani
Falírou 10
(metro Akrópoli)
Tel: 210 92 18 180
Open D Tues–Sat, L Sun
Major credit cards. **€€€**
Inconspicuously tucked away on the top storey of a 1930s building, this 2006-opened eatery takes its name from the Mani peninsula, but the food is in fact pan-Greek-mainland: meaty mains, salads, *mezédes*, rare cheeses, a few desserts – though not fish. Willing staff, a decent wine list and a scarcity of nearby eateries of comparable quality mean that booking is mandatory, especially at weekends.

PRICE CATEGORIES

Prices are based on an average meal per person, including house wine:
€ = under €15
€€ = €15–25
€€€ = €25–40
€€€€ = over €40
Key: B = breakfast, L = lunch, D = dinner

Mets–Pangráti

Kalimarmaron
Evforíonos 13
(metro Evangelismós)
Tel: 210 71 19 727
Open L and D Tues–Sat, L Sun. Cash only. **€€**
This taverna tastefully done-up with old photos and engravings stresses island and regional recipes. Lots of off-menu daily specials will be recited to you, though the permanent menu – stuffed baked sardines, sausages, island recipes like Corfiot *sofríto*, courgette pie, bean dishes – have wide appeal. There's decent bulk wine from Neméa, and a limited range of desserts such as soft *myzíthra* cheese with candied raisins.

O Karavitis
Arktínou 33 & Pafsaníou 4
(metro Evangelismós)
Tel: 210 72 15 155
Open D daily
Cash only. **€€**
O Karavitis is one of the oldest classic 1930s tavernas in Pangráti relying on baked casseroles, a few *mezédes* and grills, washed down with bulk wine from the Mesógia (inland Attica), though the wine barrels which occupy an entire wall are now only decorative. Traditional desserts like quince or semolina *hélva* are available; outdoor seating in a lovely garden across the street.

O Kostas
Ekális 7, Pangráti
(no nearby metro)
Tel: 210 701 1101
Open D Mon–Sat, closed Aug. Cash only. **€**
For decades found just off Platía Varnáva in a warren-like shack, this endearing neighbourhood local moved to this converted 1920s house around the millennium, keeping the same brief menu featuring meatballs, sardines and bean soup, the same popular prices and the same loyal clientele. If anything, the cooking's now better, with Kostas' son-in-law now in charge. There's not more than 30 seats indoors and out on the narrow terrace, so best reserve at weekends.

Ke Ftais
Ippodámou 31, corner Platía Plastíra
(no nearby metro)
Tel: 210 75 13 296
Open L and D daily
Cash only. **€**
Tiny hole-in-the-wall *ouzerí*

which stresses *politikí kouzína* (Constantinopolitan cuisine): *flogéres* (cylindrical fried *börek*), stuffed mushrooms, taboulleh, various croquettes. It shares tables with the Kafenio Hellas, and is best at lunchtime.

Spondi
Pýrronos 5, Pangráti
(no nearby metro)
Tel: 210 75 20 658
www.spondi.gr
Open D daily, closed Aug
Major credit cards. **€€€€**
With the kitchen under the command of a French chef, this Michelin-starred restaurant (one of just three in the city) is among the best special-occasion eateries, with seating inside a neoclassical house and out in its stone courtyard. Creative – often improbable – fusion cuisine, in a menu changed twice yearly, combines continental and Pacific influences in herb- or truffle-flavoured duck, meat and fish dishes followed by decadent dessert concoctions prepared under the supervision of a Parisian *pâtissier*.

Stavros
Ivýkou 7, off Eratosthénous, Pangráti
(metro Evangelismós)
Tel: 210 71 16 747
Open D daily. Cash only. **€**
The area's cheap-and-cheerful *ouzerí* has an unbeatable setting on a leafy, triangular park; the menu is almost entirely seafood plus the usual starters, though the price and environment are at least as attractive as the food.

Sushi Bar
Platía Varnáva, corner Stílponos
(no nearby metro)
Tel: 210 752 4354
Open D Mon–Fri, L and D Sat–Sun. Cash only. **€€€**
Part of a small Athens-based chain, the most central outlet has a wood-floored, high-ceilinged dining area with a few tables, though they're equally geared up for take-away orders. All the *sushi* standards are on offer, plus a few *tempura* snacks as well.

Vyrinis
Arhimídous 11, Méts
(no nearby metro)
Tel: 210 71 12 021
Open L and D daily except Sun eve. Cash only. **€€**
Much-loved neighbourhood taverna, now being managed by the grandsons of the founder. They've made the décor more contemporary with butcher-paper table coverings, ugly double-glazing and a large, swooping awning in the summer garden, but the *mosaïko* floor and elevated wine barrels have stayed – as has the good-value fare, mainly salads, *mezédes* and creative mains. Live jazz sessions Sunday afternoon.

Cafés/Bars

Fellos
Márkou Drákou 5, Makrygiánni
(metro Syngroú-Fix)
Tel: 210 92 48 898
Dark, wood-trimmed wine bar that gets lively and popular after dark; wide range of bottled vintages, plus Craft beer on tap.

Kafenio Hellas
Platía Nikoláou Plastíra, Pangráti
(no nearby metro)
A recent, rather insensitive restoration slightly dented the atmosphere of this sumptuous neoclassical premises, but it's still a great place for a drink, indoors or out on the elevated terrace above the traffic.

Vyni
Márkou Drákou 10, Makrygiánni
(metro Syngroú-Fix)
Tel: 210 92 26 225
Possibly the largest selection of imported beers – mostly Belgian and German – in town, and you pay dearly for them, as you do for the perfunctory snacks. Pleasant interior for winter, tables on the pedestrian way in summer.

RIGHT: carving *gýros* from the spit.

NEOCLASSICAL ARCHITECTURE

When Athens was elevated to capital status, a whole new city had to be built: it was German Neoclassicism that provided the inspiration

When Athens was designated capital of modern Greece in 1834, King Otto required a city fit for a king, not the existing dusty little Balkan village of crooked lanes and low, mean structures. The Bavarian royal entourage, especially architect Ernst Ziller, took as their cue the long-standing Germanic admiration for classical Greek culture, and Othonian Athens became a reflection of this; not so much in its overall layout – much less grandiose in fact than the original city plan envisioned by disciples of Friedrich von Schinkel, the classical revivalist – but in the details of the individual structures, both public and domestic.

The more imposing the building, the more likely it was to sprout (neo-) classical elements, to wit some or all of the following: pilasters at the corners, colonnades at the summit of entrance stairways, pediments (*metopés* in Greek, often with reliefs of mythical figures in the tympanum) over the colonnade, and a shallowly pitched canal-tile roof with *akrokérama* (ceramic, stylized acanthus patterns or Medusa heads) at the corners. Windows and doors, usually double-leaf, adhered as much as pos-

ABOVE: this fine griffin is on the pediment of the Library, one of the splendid buildings that makes up Athens' "neoclassical trilogy".
RIGHT: neoclassicism was not restricted to architecture, as this sculpture from the City of Athens Museum attests. Classical motifs, as here, were a great source of inspiration.

ABOVE: the Benaki Museum's collection is housed in this splendid neoclassical mansion. No expense has been spared in its restoration and it is one of the best examples in the city of how these fine buildings can find a new use. In the basement is a section of the Themistoclean wall; the Classical meets the neoclassical.

ABOVE: the Záppeion in the National Gardens was designed by Hansen in the 1840s as an exhibition hall, a function it still fulfills today. Close by is a popular café.

BELOW: the University building of the "neoclassical trilogy" on Panepistimíou is perhaps the finest example of neoclassical architecture in the city.

sible to the classical *Hrysí Tomí* (Golden Section or Golden Mean) in a height-to-width ratio of 1.62:1; while house doors sported knockers with inscrutable classical female visages.

Meanwhile, the existing, Balkan/Ottoman vernacular architecture was to neoclassical construction as the demotic spoken language was to the classicizing *katharévoussa* *(see page 263)* imposed on the population: something to be improved upon, filtered for "corrupting" influences, or if necessary supplanted in the interests of recapturing a lost Golden Age – of which the new arrivals and the foreignly-educated Greek upper crust were the authoritative interpreters.

The most obvious trio of surviving neoclassical public projects stand close together along Odós Panepistimíou, designed in this case by Danes rather than Germans. At the centre is the original University, the 1842 work of Hans Christian Hansen. It sports an Ionian-order colonnade modelled on the Parthenon's Propylaion, and a little beyond, frescoes of King Otto in the company of ancient gods and heroes. Just southeast looms the Academy of Arts and Sciences (1859) by Hansen's younger brother Theophilus, with statues of Apollo, Athena, Plato and Socrates at the front and pediment friezes – again echoing the Parthenon – by Leonidas Drosos. Northwesternmost and most sober of the three is the National Library, done in 1902 by an elderly Theophilus in homage to the Temple of Hephaistos in the ancient agora.

We know from pigment traces on ancient statuary that they were often garishly coloured, not unlike Hindu temple idols – a far cry from the chastely natural marble tones the classical-idealizers had in mind. However, over time the arbiters of nineteenth-century taste got used to

RIGHT: the Frissarás Museum in Pláka (Monis Asterlou 3 and 7; www.frissaras.com) is housed in an elegant neoclassical building. The museum holds rotating, temporary exhibitions of painting and sculpture.

the notion of painting the new structures, the preferred pigments being vermillion, yellow and powder-blue – interestingly, much the same as the Ottoman *louláki* (powder blue), ochre and rust-magenta.

Neoclassicism prevailed from the 1830s to the 1890s. Between 1890 and 1912, the style morphed into Art Nouveau or at the very least acquired Art Nouveau embellishments such as curves and rounded corners. Until well after World War II – during which central Athens sustained minimal damage – much of the original angled grid of streets laid out by the Bavarians was still studded with Neoclassical items, cheek by jowel with a few Art Nouveau, Art Deco and Internationalist examples dating from the 1900s to the 1930s.

ABOVE: the debating chamber of the Old Parliament building, now part of the National Historical Museum. Foreign philhellenes were chiefly responsible for pushing the city's classical heritage.
RIGHT the Goulandris Museum of Cycladic Art in Kolonáki includes this wonderful example of a patrician neoclassical mansion. The interior has been preserved giving the visitor a wonderful insight into how life in these elegant buildings must have been.

ABOVE: the Old Parliament building, now the National Historical Museum, shows how the fledgling state used its classical past in nation-building.
LEFT: the National Bank of Greece building. Many of the grander buildings and houses still retain their magnificent wrought-iron balconies, the older ones of these being marble slabs or at the very least supported on marble corbels (or, less commonly in Athens, cast-iron supports in intricate patterns).

BELOW: as well as the balconies (clearly seen below) neoclassical buildings also have decorative *akrokérama* (toothed tiles) running all the way along the roofline, not just at the corners, giving it a crenellated look akin to battlements.

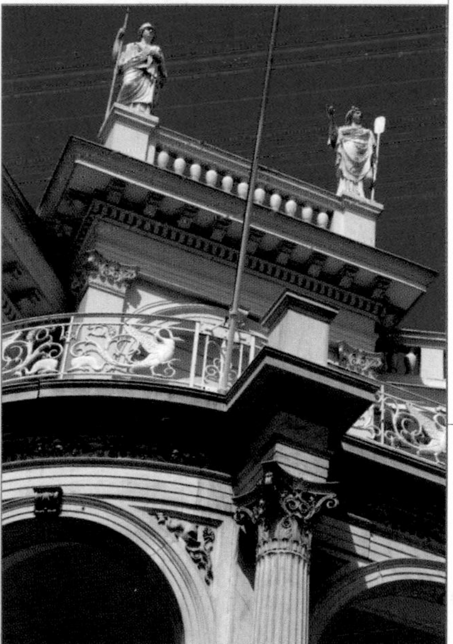

LOSS OF HERITAGE

What doomed most of the neoclassical heritage was the law of *andiparohí* introduced in the mid-1950s. It was triggered by massive internal migration from the provinces during and after the civil war, and by a desire to solve the problem of hundreds of thousands of refugees and their descendants, who, three decades after the events in Asia Minor, were still often housed in squalid shanties. In exchange for granting a developer free of charge the land on which your house stood, you were given flats in the apartment building built on your site, equally free. Typically, the number would be three apartments, say, in a 16-unit building (the extra two coming in handy as dowry for your daughters); but in a cheap-and-nasty block built from reinforced concrete. Moreover, the law made no distinction between a tumbledown shack and a frayed-at-the-edges but still reparable neoclassical mansion. Thousands of the latter crumbled under the wrecking ball as the 19th-century fabric of Athens – and many other provincial towns – was shredded.

Since the early 1990s surviving neoclassical specimens have been strictly protected by law; any such semi-derelict building is likely to be swathed in scaffolding and protective netting, pending availability of funds to complete restoration. Some of the more spectacular renovated examples include the splendid Art-Nouveau hybrid at Navárhou Nikodímou 24, in Pláka; a more puristic specimen at Apóllonos 36, and a very grand one in the Thissío nightlife district, at the corner of Iraklídon and Apostólou Pávlou. There are also entire terraces of much older, humbler one- or two-storey neoclassical houses along the higher streets of the Pláka. Many of these display the Venetian-slat shutters which can also be seen elsewhere in Greece – for example on Corfu, as well as in Návplio *(see page 217)* and Galaxídi *(see page 224)*.

RIGHT: a monumental sculpture of a philospher outside the "neoclassical trilogy". Taking inspiration from the works of the past, sculptors sought to recreate a mythical golden age by populating the city with classicising statues.

NNER 1

PIRAEUS

The main port of Athens since the 5th century BC, Piraeus is the home base of the world's largest merchant fleet. But this is much more than just a commercial port. A lively cosmopolitan population, attractive quayside restaurants and some exceptional museums make it well worth a day trip from the capital

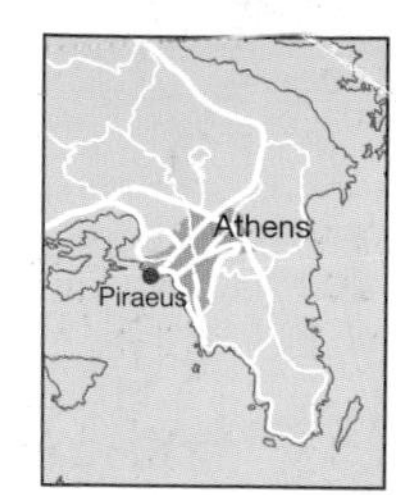

Most tourists, even those who retain a sentimental image of Piraeus' earthy cafés and waterfront inspired by the film *Never on a Sunday*, never get a chance to explore this seaside town. Guidebooks tend to regard Piraeus (Pireás) as Athens' untidy, noisy port through which travellers are obliged to pass on the way to the islands. They caution that Piraeus is devoid of charm and there is no reason to spend any time in the area, unless one is dining in the touristy harbour of Mikrolímano. On the contrary, Piraeus is well worth at least a day trip to explore its three harbours, its museums and its charming quayside restaurants.

It is most easily reached by metro (line 1; allow around 45 minutes for the journey from the centre of town), alternatively, a bus leaves from Sýntagma, but this can be very slow. An express bus runs direct to Piraeus from Athens' new airport (the E96), and stops outside the Port Authority (OLP) passenger building on Aktí Miaoúli street.

An ancient settlement

Piraeus has a rich history, although few of its monuments remain. Of the people who appeared on Piraeus' shores, the first to settle were the Minyans, a warlike seafaring people. They worshipped the goddess Artemis Munychia, whose temple was on the hill now known as Kastéla. The church of Profítis Ilías (the Prophet Elijah) stands on the site today.

Another remnant of prehistoric civilisation is the Serangeion or Pareskevas' Cave, behind Votsalákia Beach below Kastéla. The original houses near the cave had been turned into baths during Roman times. After World War II, the cave

Map on page 166

PREVIOUS PAGES: the port of Rafína on Attica's east coast.
LEFT: a ferry tied up in Piraeus.
BELOW: a waitress in a Pireaus café.

You can explore the prehistoric Pareskevas Cave, but you need rubber-soled shoes (it's slippery) and a torch.

was converted into a small club which featured the famous performers of the day.

In the early 5th century BC, when the Persian Empire threatened invasion by sea *(see pages 25–6)*, Themistocles persuaded the Athenians to enlarge their navy and use Piraeus as its base (instead of the sandy bay at Phaleron). The shipyard owners of Piraeus returned the favour by building about 100 galleys a year for the new fleet.

After the Persian Wars, Piraeus quickly developed into a progressive trade centre. By 460 BC the port had been fortified and the Long Walls built, extending from the base of Munychis (modern-day Kastéla) to Athens. In about 450 BC, the architect Hippodemus of Miletus created a unique town plan for Piraeus based on a gridiron, which became one of the great achievements of the "Golden Age".

After the Spartans defeated the Athenian fleet in 405 BC, Piraeus, was captured and its fortifications destroyed. The Athenian leader Conon rebuilt them and the Long Walls in 393 BC but Athens was on the decline and the walls fell into

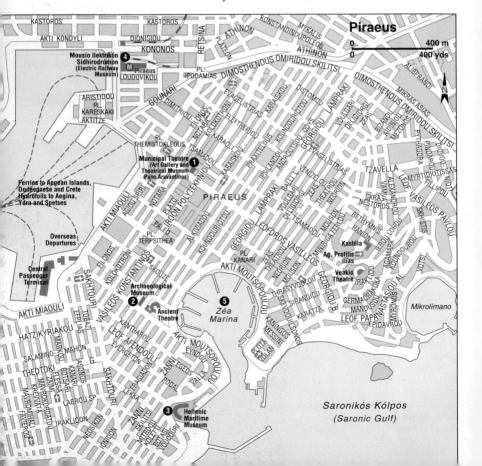

Piraeus

0 400 m
0 400 yds

Mousío Ilektrikón Sidhirodrómon (Electric Railway Museum) 4

Municipal Theatre (Art Gallery and Theatrical Museum Pano Aravantinos) 1

Archaeological Museum 2

Hellenic Maritime Museum 3

Zéa Marina 5

Ferries to Aegean Islands, Dodecanese and Crete
Hydrofoils to Aegina, Ydra and Spetses

Overseas Departures

Central Passenger Terminal

Ancient Theatre

Kastéla

Ag. Profítis Ilías

Veakio Theatre

PIRAEUS

Mikrolímano

Saronikós Kólpos (Saronic Gulf)

ruin. In 86 BC, the Roman general Sulla razed Piraeus and destroyed the harbours. The port lost its commercial significance and became virtually uninhabited.

In the Middle Ages, Piraeus was known as Porto Leone, a reference to the imposing 3-metre (10-ft) marble lion that had guarded the harbour entrance since classical times. In 1688, Venetian general Francesco Morosini, not content with having blown up a much of the Parthenon, decided to confiscate the lion and take it home to Venice as a souvenir.

Immigration from Greece

In 1834, the new Greek government began a reconstruction of Piraeus. Stamatis Cleanthes and Edwardo Schaubert, the architects who created the Athenian city plan, made one for Piraeus as well. The first settlers were 106 refugees who had emigrated to Sýros from Híos after an island massacre during the War of Independence. They came to Piraeus in 1835, just one year after Athens had become the capital of the new state. Piraeus was nothing more than a wilderness with the ruined monastery of St Spyridon as the sole edifice.

The government offered land on favourable terms in the hope that they would service the needs of the new capital. The immigrants, who settled around the harbour, dreamed of creating a "New Híos". Their keen grasp of mercantile and industrial development established Piraeus as an independent commercial town rather than merely an Athenian satellite.

Piraeus absorbed many further immigrations, beginning with the Hydriots in 1837, followed by Cretans during the rebellion of 1866–9, Peloponnesians in various movements during the second half of the 19th century and refugees from Asia Minor in 1922. The population rapidly increased from 2,400 inhabitants in 1840 to 10,000 in 1870. By 1920, Piraeus had a population of 130,000, a number which almost doubled after the "great catastrophe" of Asia Minor. The figure has now levelled off at slightly less than 200,000, according to a recent census.

Industrialisation began with the Hydriots; the first factory was founded in 1847. By the turn of the century there were 76 steam-powered factories, or one-third of the total in Greece, earning Piraeus the international label "the Greek Manchester".

Piraeus' cultural life developed in tandem with its economic growth. The splendid Municipal Theatre was built in the 1880s. The town's reputation as a literary centre flourished when *Apollo* magazine was launched in 1892 and was enhanced by the debut of *Our Magazine*, the first modern Greek literary publication which printed articles written by well-known Athenians.

After 1900 the literati of Piraeus began to show a preference for

Map on page 166

Piraeus is Greece's busiest port.

BELOW: amulets for warding off the "evil eye".

The Olympiakós football team came about largely thanks to the backing and efforts of some of Piraeus' biggest names in commerce. Most instrumental among them was the Andrianopoulos family, from which no less than five brothers played together in the team.

Athens. Writers were lured into the capital by publishing houses and daily newspapers. By the 1920s, Piraeus had been relegated to a commercial hub, while Athens became the cultural centre.

Of more importance to a large segment of the population was the establishment in 1925 of Olympiakós, a football (soccer) team to rival Panathinaikós of Athens. Olympiakós is still one of the most popular teams in Greece, and inspires fervent loyalty.

Piraeus became increasingly unfashionable between the two world wars. Social and cultural life stagnated; it was home to mostly the working and lower-middle classes. During the 1920s and '30s, refugees from Asia Minor brought their subculture with its own lifestyle, dress and music, which came to symbolise Piraeus itself. The port was bombed extensively during World War II, a fate Athens escaped, and much was rebuilt.

From 1951 to 1971, Piraeus' population decreased by three percent while the population of Athens increased by 55 percent. Even worse, during the junta years the municipality embarked on an ill-advised campaign to modernise Piraeus. Many of the town's historic buildings were destroyed and replaced by tasteless monstrosities. At the same time, the charming wooden *períptera* (kiosks) were torn down and ugly corrugated metal boxes erected.

Modern Piraeus

Piraeus has now become known as a banking and insurance centre but even more, its identity is linked to the sea and the shipping trade. This is the home port for the world's largest merchant fleet, and there are more than 600 or so shipping offices in the town.

A sense of community pride has been boosted by the renovations carried out by recent mayors in the form of parks, greenery and the exclusion of traffic from certain streets. In the neighbourhoods behind Zéa Marina and on Kastéla hill some of the graceful neoclassical houses have been lovingly

BELOW: Zéa Marina.

restored. Piraeus' multinational mixture of permanent and temporary residents – ship-owners, office workers, seamen, yacht brokers, chandlers, shopkeepers and factory workers – adds a cosmopolitan flavour to the town.

The **flea-market** (every Sunday morning near Platía Ipodamías, at the top end of Goúnari, behind the train station) offers an eclectic mixture of household items, second-hand clothes, electronic equipment, video cassettes, sports clothes and occasional white-elephant treasures. Be sure to bargain.

Good antique shops are located on the block bounded by Alipédou, Plataíon, Skylítsi and Ippodamías Square. Half a dozen shops specialise in old furniture, jewellery, lamps, icons, copper and bronze and embroideries. The shop at 2 Pílis and Skylítsi is one of the most interesting. The back wall of this crowded space is a section of one of the 5th-century Long Walls.

The Theatre and Musems

The **Municipal Theatre ❶**, located on Agíou Konstantínou across from the prefecture, is a magnificent 800-seat neoclassical structure that was built between 1884 and 1895. Based on the plans of the Opéra Comique in Paris, its acoustics are said to be the best in the Balkans. The theatre houses the **Municipal Art Gallery** and the **Theatrical Museum of Panos Aravantinos** (open Mon–Wed 4-8pm, Thu–Fri 9am–2pm; free). The museum has attractive paintings and models of theatrical sets from the artist's career when he worked mainly in Germany.

Piraeus Archaeological Museum ❷ (Harílaou Trikoúpi 31; open Tue–Sun 8.30am–3pm; entrance charge) is highly regarded by both scholars and tourists. Its prize exhibits are two bronze statues found by workmen digging a drain in the 1950s: a magnificent 6th-century BC *kouros* (figure of a young man), the earliest known life-sized bronze, and a 4th-century helmeted Athena, looking oddly soulful for a warrior goddess. Both are thought to have come from a shipment of loot that was overlooked by Greece's Roman conquerors in the 1st century BC.

There is a further superb bronze of Artemis dating from the mid-4th century BC. Also impressive, on the ground floor, is the restored mausoleum of an Istrian merchant.

The **Hellenic Maritime Museum ❸** (Aktí Themistokléous; open Tue–Sat 9am–2pm; entrance charge) has 13,000 items on display – scale models of galleys and triremes, Byzantine flags, figureheads, uniforms, shells, documents, and actual sections of famous boats. One interesting exhibit highlights part of the "Long Walls" which happens to be incorporated right into the building's foundation. Sections of the walls run along Aktí Themistokléous.

Tucked away in one corner of the Piraeus ISAP station is the 2005-inau-

Map on page 166

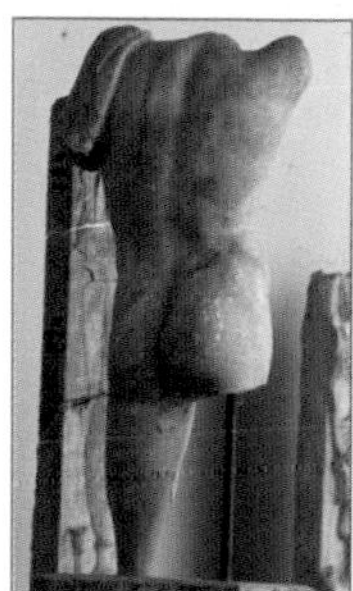

Piraeus Archaeological Museum

BELOW: Piraeus Archaeological Museum

Map on page 166

Hydrofoils shuttle to and from the nearby islands.

BELOW: a Piraeus local.

gurated **Mousío Ilektrikón Sidhirodrómon** ❹ (Electric Railway Museum; daily 9am–2pm; free), two floors crammed full of items, lovingly collected by retired railway employees, related to the Piraeus–Athens railway that was electrified in 1904. Labelling is thus far in Greek only, but you don't have to be a train-spotter to enjoy the archival photos, mocked-up ticket windows, enamelled signs in laboured *katharévousa* Greek, track switches, ammeters, dials, logos, bells, uniforms for every rank and electrical widgets straight out of a mad scientist's lab. It's probably the best use of time in Piraeus if you've 20 minutes or so to spare before catching a boat or hydrofoil to the Saronic Islands.

The highest point of Piraeus (87m/285ft above the sea) is **Kastéla**, with a spectacular view of the Saronic Gulf and islands. On top of the hill stand the church of Profítis Ilías and the open-air municipal **Veakio Theatre**. The church is the focal point for an annual festival on July 20, the saint's day of Ilías (Elijah), which is celebrated by the whole of Piraeus. The theatre is a thriving cultural centre in summer, the setting for productions by Greek and foreign theatre companies, an annual dance festival and all manner of folk music.

The lesser harbours

The winding coastal area known as Pirikí (along which are remnants of the Long Walls) leads to **Zéa Marina** ❺, Piraeus' largest yacht harbour. In the 5th century BC, it held 196 triremes; now it has berths for 365 yachts. In Ottoman times the harbour was called Pasalimani ("Pasha's Harbour") because the Turkish pasha used to moor his flagship here. The area is lined with restaurants, bars, yacht supply shops and ships' offices.

Mikrolímano ("Little Harbour") was also used by the Ancient Athenian navy. Today it is a charming but much-visited crescent-shaped bay, a pleasant place to dine under awnings at the water's edge. There are at least 22 restaurants in this little cove, all of whose menus are fairly similar. ❑

Coping with the Port

If you're heading on for one of the Greek islands after your stay in Athens, a ferry or catamaran trip can be more enjoyable – and cheaper – than a flight. But be prepared to be confused by Piraeus' commercial harbour and its many quays. Get there one hour before sailing time, so that you have half an hour to find the right quay before the boarding deadline as ships do really leave on time. But unless it's high summer or you require a berth, don't worry about booking in advance: you can buy tickets from one of the dockside agencies. The ticket agent will be able to tell you which quay your ferry departs from. As a general guide: ferries to the Cyclades depart from the quays opposite the metro station, and also from the other side of Platía Kareskáki (south of the metro); boats to Crete (the largest ferries) leave from Aktí Kondýli on the northern side of the port; large catamarans to most island groups and Flying Dolphin hydrofoils to the Argo-Saronic islands depart from the quays close by Platía Kareskáki; and the islands of the Dodecanese are served by the quays near Aktí Miaoúli. ❑

RESTAURANTS

Ahinos
Aktí Themistokléous 51
Tel: 210 45 26 944
Open daily
Major credit cards. **€€€**
This split-level *ouzerí* built against a seaside cliff, with a terrace overlooking the beach, is strong on seafood, offering good value in a somewhat touristy area near the Maritime Museum. Scaly fish is more expensive, but you can fill up instead on good-value vegetarian and seafood platters.

Dourambeis
Aktí Protopsálti 29
Tel: 210 41 22 092
Open L and D daily
Major credit cards. **€€€**
Going since 1932, this cult seafood taverna underwent a major refit in early 2006, emerging with tasteful wood, stone and white-cloth decor. Starters like rocket, lettuce and cress salad, coarse-grained white *taramosaláta*, razor-clam *saganáki* and fried crayfish nuggets can be better than the mains, where the grill may struggle to get the fish exactly right. For dessert: apple pie or spoon sweets.

Kollias
Nikoláou Plastíra 3, Tamboúria district
Tel 210 46 29 620
Open L and D Mon-Sat, L Sun; closed two weeks Aug
Major credit cards. **€€€**
It's worth the trek to this out-of-the-way seafood specialist hidden behind an apartment block. Owner-chef Tassos Kollias sources shellfish and other delicacies from the sea, such as sea urchins, oysters and barracuda from all over Greece for *mezédes* to accompany more usual scaly fish.

To Palio Roloï
Dimosthénous 5
Tel: 210 41 73 730
Open daily. **€€**
It's rare to have a combination *psistariá-ouzerí* that does meat and fish equally well, but To Palio Roloï (alias To Rebetadiko) manages it, with excellent baked sardines and heaping portions of *kontosoúvli*. Curiously, the cramped interior can be more popular than the tables out on the cobbles. The *oúzo* is stiffly priced, though – how the management makes its money. Live music (thus the alias) on weekend nights/afternoons.

Terzian
Palamidíou and Vlahákou
No phone
Open 5pm–midnight Mon–Sat. Cash only. **€**
A tiny Armenian-run takeaway *psistariá* (you can also eat at the counter) specialising in various Anatolian kebabs, such as: shish, spicy Adana, *giaoúrtlou* (with yogurt and tomato sauce), *soutzoúki* sausage, all at various tongue-heats – check first as they can be hot. Having evolved next to Muslim sensibilities, all the kebabs are based on beef and lamb, not pork as elsewhere.

Vasilenas
Etolikoú 72
Tel: 210 46 12 457
Open D Mon-Sat, closed Aug
Major credit cards. **€€€**
Half a century ago, the restaurants founder Thanasis Vasilenas introduced the concept of set-price *table d'hôte* to Greece. His descendants continue the tradition, bringing on 16 platters in sequence (€30, drink extra) though recently they've been made more elaborate, with meat choices joining old classics like fish soup and *taramosaláta*.

The interior has been overhauled as well, without losing the original charming touches like old bottles and the marble serving counter.

PRICE CATEGORIES

Prices are based on an average meal per person, including house wine:
€ = under €15
€€ = €15–25
€€€ = €25–40
€€€€ = over €40
Key: B = breakfast, L = lunch, D = dinner

RIGHT: iced coffee *(frappé)* by the waterside.

FÁLIRO TO VÁRKIZA

There are beaches and resorts within a few miles of Athens city centre – and the Athenians take full advantage of them. Other features of the west coast of Attica include the white elephant that was once the main airport and a remarkable hot lake beside the sea

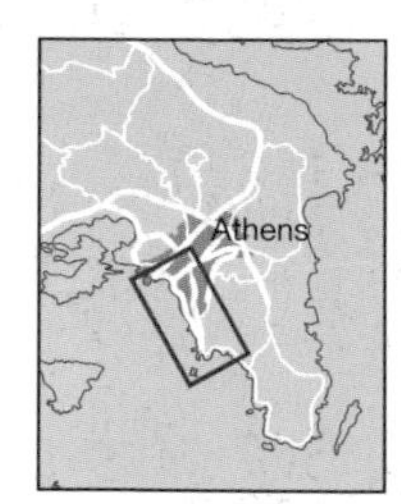

The main road from the city centre to the west coast of Attica is properly called Leofóros Posidónos but more commonly known as the Paraliáki ("Seaside Street"). The traffic can be horrendous at weekends (leaving town in the morning, returning in the evening) as Athenians flock to re-affirm their historical link with the sea.

Paleó Fáliro Ⓐ is the closest in of the beachside suburbs, and as such constitutes a desirable address, with a couple of comfortable hotels and a scattering of restaurants. The only real "sight", however, is the **Thoriktó G. Avérof/ Battleship Averoff** permanently anchored at Trokadéro-Flísvos marina (www.bsaveroff.com; open Jun–Sep Mon–Fri 9am–1pm, also 5–7pm Mon, Wed, Fri; Sat–Sun 11am–3pm; Oct–May Mon–Fri 9am–1pm, also 3–5pm Mon, Wed, Fri; Sat–Sun 10am–2pm; admission charge). Built in 1910, it was for years afterwards the fastest and biggest ship in the Greek navy, and instrumental in ensuring that the east Aegean islands of Sámos, Híos, Lésvos and Límnos fell easily to Greece in the First Balkan War, during autumn 1912.

The Averoff served in both subsequent World Wars before being decommissioned in 1958. Most of the restored battleship is open for visits (except for the quarters of a few naval personnel who still live aboard), with displays detailing the ship's illustrious career. Next to it is a hand-built replica of an ancient trireme (*triíris* in Greek), which brought the Olympic flame ashore from its tour of the islands in summer 2004.

Álimos Ⓑ, the next suburb, hasn't any special distinction other than the largest yacht marina on the Attic coast, dwarfing the more naturally protected Zéa and Mikrolímano marinas in Piraeus. **Ellinikó**, next

LEFT: Glyfáda is a popular resort with young Athenians. **BELOW:** the trireme at the Maritime Museum.

Delphi
Delfí
Itéa
Galaxídi
Dístomo
Karakolithos
Livadiá
Orhomenós
Lamía
Evoikós Kólpos
Ágios Ioánnis
Akréfnio
Paralímni
Loukissia
Halkída
Stenós
Ósis Loukás
Elikón Óros
Elikónas
Korónia
Evangelistria
Mavrommáti
Movriki
Ktipás
Limniliki
Thebes
GR 1
Kólpos Antikíras
Motsára
1526
Ágía Ána
Thespiés
Vágia
Thíva (Thebes)
Leontári
Assopía
Thísbi
Korinthiakós Kólpos (Gulf of Corinth)
Ákr. Agiá
Paralia
Neohoráki
Léfktra
Ágios Ioánnis
Kaparéli
Erithrés
Dáfni
Likoporiá
Alikí
Píli
Skoúrta
1409
Kithairón Óros
Pirgos
Xilókastro
Aigósthena
Vília
Sikéa
Patéras Óros
Káto Alepohóri
Psátha
Phyle
Diminio
Kiáto
Souli
Akr. Iréo
Perahóra
Mándra
Mánna
Yeránia Óri
1351
Sikióna
Vélo
Loutráki
Elefsína
Eleusis
Asprópi
Néa Péramos
Megara
Kórinthos
Corinth
Corinth Canal
Kastráki
Faneroméni
Salamína
Pérama
Dafní
Psári
Arhéa Kórinthos
Kryá Vrýsi
Ágios Theódori
Kólpos Megaron
Pireás (Piraeus)
Galatás
Eándio
Selinia
Athíkia
Peristéria
Salamína
Neméa
Arhéa Neméa
Ágios Vasílios
Sofikó
Saronikós Kólpos (Saronic Gulf)
Tripolis
Mycenae
Kórfos
Mykínes
Trapezona
1137
Koutsopódi
Límnes
Dimena
Mesagrós
Égina
Kariá
Arahnéo
Angístri
Páleohóra
Aphaia
Agía Marína
Árgos
Skála
Néa Epídavros
Tiryns
Pórtes
Égina
Krionéri
Ligoúrio
Paleá Epidávros
Náfplio
Kólpos Epidavrou
Kounoupitsa
Skafidáki
Epidauros
Hersónissos
Drépano
Karathónas
Mavrovoúni
Trahiá
Méthana
Neohóri
Rómvi
Platia
Káto Dolianá
Parálio Irion
Iria
Póros
Dídimo
Póros
Zoödóhou Pigís
Parálio Ástroa
Dídima
Adéres
Trizina
Ástros
Galatás
Argolikos Kolpos
Psíli
Parálio Agia Andréou
Kiláda
Saronida
Thermisía
Ermióni
Kranídi
Ágios Andréas
1935
Ágios Panteleimon
Parnon
Portohéli
Dokós
Ýdra
Ýdra
Profítis Ilías
Spétses
Spétses
Mirtó Pélago
Leonídio
Spetsopoúla
Trikéri
Paleohóri
Pláka

up, has a small, privately-run beach but is best known is known as the site of the old airport, which closed in March 2001.

Suitably converted, the former terminal building saw brief use as the venue for Olympic handball and basketball competitions, and baseball and softball were played in fields laid out on the former runways, but since then it has become the whitest of the Olympic white elephants. Although out-of-service jets are occasionally seen mothballed here, its days of public aviation use are over.

Observers might well wonder why it couldn't continue operating as a low-frills airport for the proliferating no-frills airlines of Europe, after all, Milan, Paris, Istanbul and Berlin each have a pair of airports, and London has no less than four (five if you count Luton). The answer is a little-known law rammed through Greek parliament in the year 2000, forbidding any other airport from operating within 70 air-miles of Elefthérios Venizélos, as the new airport's administration wanted no competition for lucrative landing fees.

Vaguely mooted plans to convert the ex-airport to parkland are unlikely to come to fruition. A more probably outcome, despite a ban on the sale of Olympic facilities to private developers, is precisely that. The Olympic sailing events were held at the small Ágios Kosmás marina across the road, and this plus its associated sports centre continue to function as intended.

Good-time Glyfáda

Beyond the ex-airport zone, **Glyfáda** ❸ is the first coastal suburb with a resort and good-times atmosphere. It has been indelibly marked by its long history – which ended only in the early 1990s – as a bedroom community for dependents

The battleship Averoff, for years the pride of the Greek navy, now moored in Fáliro.

On the quay at Glyfáda you'll find a Rescue Centre for the rehabilitation of injured sea turtles, run by ARCHELON (Sea Turtle Protection Society of Greece). The centre also acts as a venue for environmental education programmes and free tours are provided.

of the substantial American military presence at Ellinikó's air force base. It has accordingly always been the most westernised part of Athens in its tastes – quite literally so in the proliferation of more or less authentic outlets for Mexican, Chinese, Italian and Texas-style-ribs-and-burgers cusine.

If you arrive by tram, this takes you right into the heart of the action, **Leofóros Dimárhou Angélou Metaxá**, with shopping malls lining it and most of the more popular eateries and watering-holes to either side. There's a small marina here too, as well as a golf course. And, on summer weekends, seemingly half the population of Athens.

Voúla

The next borough is **Voúla** **D** – for that is what they are, each a self-governing municipal unit within Greater Athens – marginally posher than Glyfáda but merely a taster for seriously exclusive Vouliagméni. Certainly the greenest of the coastal suburbs, Voúla's pines drape themselves over a complicated topography of headlands and peninsulas encompassing **Kavoúri** and **Lemós** sub-districts. There are two beaches on the coast here, Voúla Próti, near the Asklipío Hospital, and Voúla Déftera, about 2km (1 mile) south

The survival of these forests is apparently the result of most local land being still owned by the Orthodox Church, who would long ago have sold or leased most of it to developers if they hadn't been opposed by the local mayor. The *Lemós* (Neck) which protects the central **Vouliagméni Bay** on its west terminates in the controlled-access Astir Palace luxury compound, where because of the ideal security arrangements – no riff-raff need apply at the gatehouse – inter-

BELOW: the Glyfáda tram.

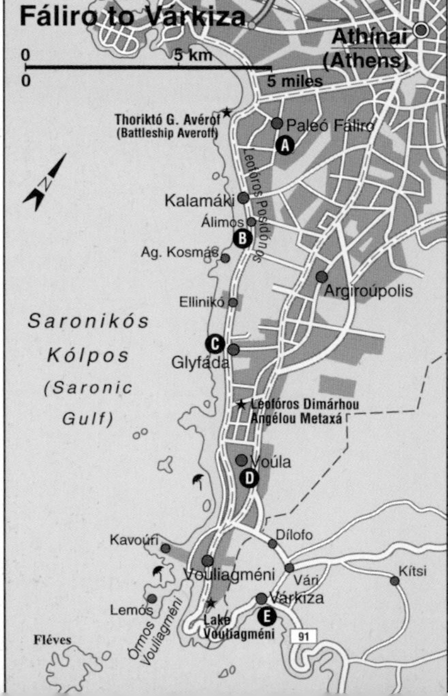

national diplomatic conferences have been held. The west end of the bay has the area's longest beach, fairly short on any amenities but still popular with younger Athenians.

The other local curiosity, just off the highway south out of town, is **Lake Vouliagméni** (open summer daily 7am–8pm; winter 8am–5pm; admission charge). As much a spa as a swimming hole, this was once a huge cavern, whose roof collapsed during an earthquake, probably during the Middle Ages. It is only about 50cm (20 ins) above sea-level (*Vouliagméni* means "sunken") and is constantly overflowing, but is replenished by underground hot springs, which keep the water at a constant 24°C (75°F) year-round. The brackish, emerald-green water is considered ideal for a variety of ailments by the somewhat geriatric clientele; accordingly, behind the shoreline café, there's a small hydrotherapy centre.

South of Vouliagméni, 20km (12 miles) from the city centre, you officially leave Greater Athens, but the urban bus line continues another 6km (4 miles) along the convoluted coast to **Várkiza** **E**, the site of a fateful conference in February 1945, where an agreement formally ended the December 1944 Battle of Athens between ELAS on one side and right-wing Greeks plus British troops on the other. The treaty – violated by each side in various particulars – provided for a plebiscite on the king resuming his throne, and subsequent elections, within a year, after ELAS, which was promised an amnesty for "political" crimes, had disbanded and surrendered much of its armament.

Today Várkiza is a middle-class beach resort, described in full (like all others noted here in passing) over the page. Just one word of advice: at the main bus stop, the fare structure changes over to that of the long-distance Attica bus service; woe betide anyone caught by frequently-appearing ticket inspectors riding beyond this point on an urban ticket or day-pass, as these are not valid.

For restaurants along this stretch of coast, *see page 187*. ❑

The tree-lined coast near Voúla.

BELOW: one of Voúla's two beaches.

BEST BEACHES

When it's time to head for the beach, you need to know which way to go. Here's a guide to popular sandy and rocky spots within easy reach of the city

For quick beach escapes around Athens look to the west-facing Saronic Coast down towards Cape Soúnio (the eastern Attica coast is covered on pages 180–7). Although there are designated, recognised beaches from Pálio Fáliro southward, relatively few people go in the water before Ellinikó, and even at its best, the sea is never quite as pristine as the open Aegean.

The more popular stretches of sand are a vision of wall-to-wall bodies on summer weekends (and weekdays for that matter), many engaged in paddle-ball games to the detriment of those interested in a peaceful lounge. This applies whether they are one of the (increasingly rare) unrestricted, public, free beaches or a privately run fenced concession where one pays between €5 and potentially as much as €15 for admission to a groomed, amenitied area with sunbeds (usually on a first-come-first-serve basis), beach volleyball, tennis courts, kids' playgrounds and snack bars to hand. Controlled-access beaches are generally open from just after sunrise until an hour after sunset; public beaches around the clock for that midnight dip.

Be mindful of the prevailing heavy-traffic patterns on the coastal Leofóros Posidónos: out of Athens on weekend mornings, back into town in the later afternoon and evening. Parking four-wheelers at most of the beaches is a nightmare, but there are some exceptions.

TOP: subathers take shelter under umbrellas on the beach at the ironically named Edém (Eden) Paleó Fáliro. This public beach is free – hence often packed. Facilities are available at private beachside hotels.
ABOVE: you can swim or wade to the rocky islet and its ancient ruin at Megálo Kavoúri in Vouliagméni. Although the facilites are fairly limited here, this beach is a firm favourite of young Athenians.
BELOW: the most attractive and upmarket beach on the east Attic coast is Pórto Ráfti, a natural harbour well protected by small islets.

BELOW: the Athenians take full advantage of several resorts and stretches of beach within just a few miles of the centre of the capital. Glyfáda, shown here, is the first coastal suburb with a resort.

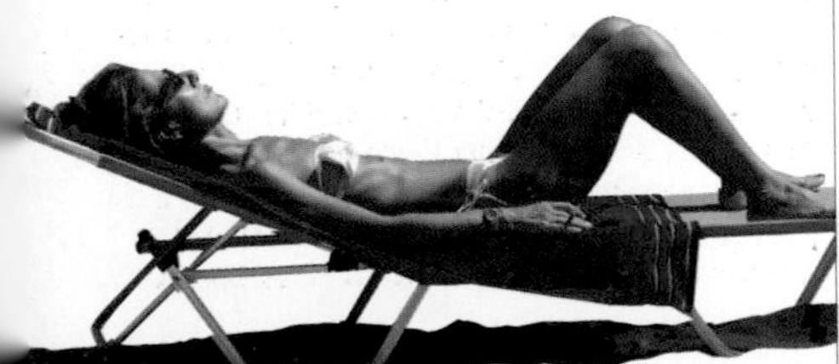

ABOVE RIGHT: the privately run beach at Aktí Alímou Álimos has basic but decent facilities and good transport links, hence its enduring popularity among local sun-worshippers.
BELOW: holidaymakers enjoy the relative tranquillity of upmarket Glyfáda. Amenities at this chic resort include a range of watersports, a pool and ball courts.

THE CITY'S BEACHES (NORTH TO SOUTH)

Edém Paleó Fáliro/Álimos boundary "Eden" it isn't quite, but it is a free, public, sandy beach with amenities available at the Hotel Poseidon's private section, which includes a taverna. Tram from Sýntagma.
Aktí Alímou Álimos Ex-EOT premises now let to a private concessionaire, with (cold) showers, snack-bars and sunbeds. Hard-packed sand. Tram or bus.
Ágios Kosmás Ellinikó Small, privately run beach secluded from boulevard traffic, nestled in between fenced-off sports facilities. Clean water, low-key activities on shore, relatively low fee. Tram or bus to 'Défteri Agíou Kosmá', then short walk.
Aktí Astéros (Astéria) Glyfáda. The biggest beach so far, pricey and upscale with extensive gardens. Amenities include ball courts, a pool and low-tech watersports. Tram to Glyfáda's Platía Katráki and a long walk, or A2/E2 bus to Grigóri Lambráki and a shorter walk.
Voúla Próti, near the Asklipío Hospital, and **Voúla Déftera**, about 1800m south. These ex-EOT beaches represent good value with low admission fees, beach volleyball, and manageable crowds. Déftera has the more generous gardens. A1, A2, E1 buses to both.
Megálo Kavoúri Vouliagméni. Medium-sized with facilities limited to a couple of wooden-platformed cafés behind the hard-packed sand and a little islet offshore, with an ancient ruin, to which you can swim or wade. You can picnic in the pines just inland, and there's plenty of parking behind the cafés. Bus #114.
Attica Vouliagméni The west end of Vouliagméni's bay has the area's longest beach. Free, public, without any amenities, it attracts a young, trendy crowd. The eastern portion is another ex-EOT fee concession but good-value with ball-game courts. Bus #114.
Vouliagméni Rock Lido Alight a bus at the stop closest to the lake by a tiny, often wind-buffeted pebble cove that's perennially full. Carry on 150m south and you'll find paths leading down to a rock shelf from which a mixed crowd dives in. No facilities, no shade.

THE EAST COAST

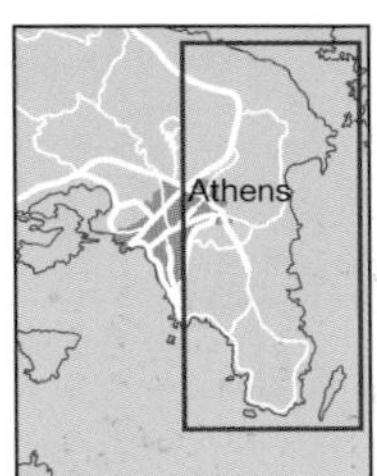

Attica to the east of the capital is notable for the site of a momentous battle, some impressive remains from the Classical period and some peaceful, secluded countryside

Map on page 182

From the northeastern tip of Greater Athens, near Ágios Stéfanos just beyond Kifisiá, a choice of roads heads either directly to Marathónas or over the saddle of Mt Pendéli in a more roundabout course. The latter is the most spectacular route, and would be even more so if forest fires had not denuded most of the mountain during the late 1990s. Marble quarries on Pendéli's southwestern slopes supplied all of the stone for the Periclean public-works projects of 5th-century BC Athens, though in modern times only a quarry on the north-facing slopes has marble extracted from it.

The saddle-road drops in curves to the edge of **Néa Mákri**, a dull seaside settlement, originally of post-1922 refugees, whose most interesting feature is its name, nostalgically recalling Makri of Asia Minor (now Fethiye, opposite Rhodes). The giant naval air-station just overhead is now staffed exclusively by Greeks following the departure of American forces in the 1990s.

From here, or from Ágios Stéfanos, roads converge on modern Marathónas, the direct northerly foothill route passing the giant **Marathon reservoir** (Límni Marathónos), retained by the world's only dam made from marble. Before the Mórnos aqueduct project from the mountains of Vardoússia in central Greece was completed in the late 1950s, this collected all of Athens' drinking water, and is still used as an auxiliary holding facility. Near the east side of the huge dam there's a café, To Fragma (also working as an expensive restaurant by night), from where you can admire the view over the pine-cloaked slopes and water.

BELOW: the east coast.

Ancient battlefield

However you arrive, the modern, nondescript village of Marathónas is inevitably overshadowed by the plain of **ancient Marathon** Ⓐ some 2.5km (1½ miles) seaward on the road to Néa Mákri. Here, in late summer 490 BC, occurred one of the crucial battles of antiquity, which saw a force of about 10,000 Athenians and 1,000 Plataeans trounce, through superior tactics, the Persian army of 25,000 that had recently landed on the nearby coast *(see page 25)*. Some historians, however, consider that the odds were not so lopsided, and that the Persian force was scarcely bigger than the Greek army, though the invaders did have the advantage of cavalry.

A fanciful story goes that a messenger called Pheidippides, was dispatched to Athens, 42 km (26 miles) distant, to report the wonderful news. Having covered the distance in superhuman time, he expired after announcing the victory to his fellow citizens: thus the footrace of that name, and the regulation distance. In fact there's no contemporary evidence for Pheidippides' feat, and the distance of the modern marathon was arbitrarily set at the 1908 London Olympics (26.2 miles from Windsor Castle to White City Stadium). Nevertheless, both men's and women's marathons in the 2004 Olympics began here, and followed what theoretically could have been Pheidippides' course to the Kallimármaro stadium.

The only surviving evidence of the battle, other than a lengthy, often tendentious account by Herodotus, are the two burial mounds scattered across the plain, one for each Grek army. The 192 Athenian casualties, including their commander Miltiades, were cremated and interred in the **Týmvos** mound (open Tues–Sun 8.30am–3pm; admission charge), 9m (30ft) high and some 50m (55 yds) in diameter, just off the Néa Mákri Marathónas road. The 11 Plataean dead were buried in another mound some ways west, next to a small archaeological museum (same hours) which has finds mostly from Mt Pendéli's Cave-Sanctuary of Pan. The Persian

The coast is well signposted.

BELOW: a memorial commemorates the battle of Marathon.

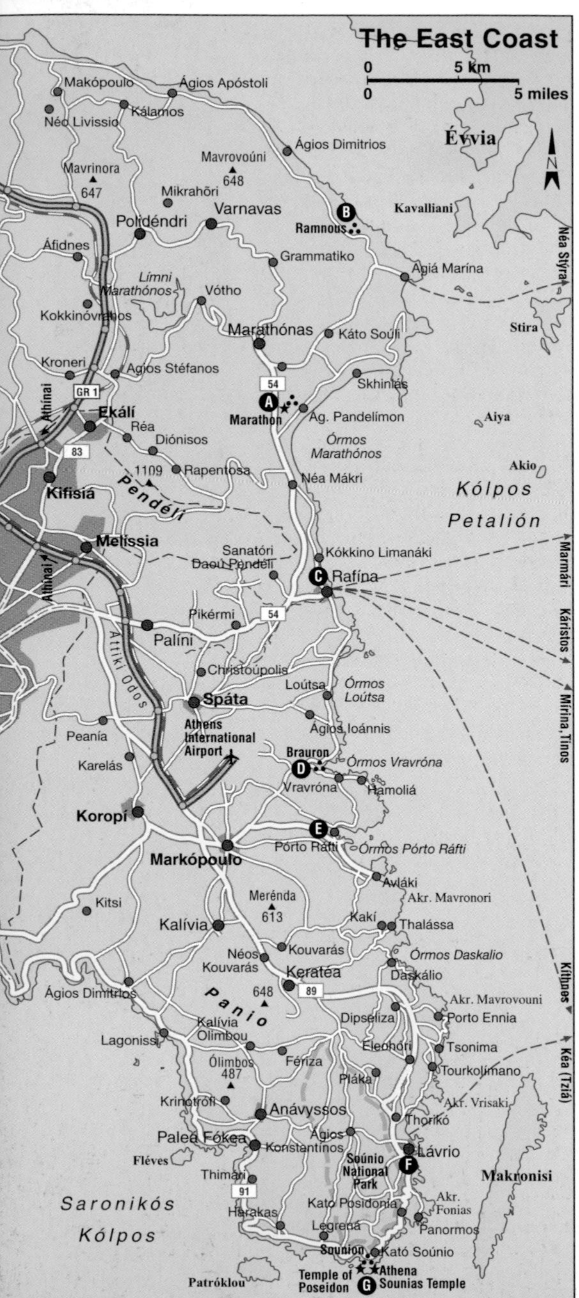

deceased – related by Herodotus to number 6,400, though this is now thought a vastly exaggerated figure – are thought to have been buried near the site of the modern church of Panagía Mesosporítissa, though there is no mound to be seen. The plain is legendarily supposed to be haunted; Pausanias, writing in Roman times, claimed that "every night at Marathon are heard the neighing of [the Persians'] horses and a clamour similar to that made by combatants."

Beaches of Marathon Bay

The coastal road near the Týmvos heads east-northeast, past the little beach resort of **Ágios Pandelímon** with its tavernas, and the anchorage point of the Persian fleet, towards **Skhiniás**, a long strand of hard-packed, muddy sand, separated from a vast wetlands by equally extensive pine groves; all of this now a protected natural reserve despite being somewhat sullied by the disused Olympic rowing facilities amidst the marsh. Although the beach here isn't brilliant, it is eminently scenic, with views south over the entire east Attic coast, and relatively sheltered from the winds which afflict it. The western end of things is developed, with private sports concessions and sunbeds, but the eastern half is relatively pristine – paved roads are forbidden in the pine groves – with just a half-dozen very rustic tavernas doing business between the trees and the water (open daily in summer, weekends only otherwise). There is no public transport out to here, or to Ramnous just beyond.

Ancient Ramnous

From near the centre of Skhiniás's frontage road another minor road leads, via the village of **Káto Soúli**, into a secluded, uninhabited valley planted thickly with olives and vines, past a single well-sited taverna, to the site of ancient **Ramnous** **B** (Ramnoúnda in modern Greek; open mid-Jun to mid-Sep daily 8am–5pm, otherwise Tues–Sun 8.30am–3pm; admission charge). The site – with views across to the island of **Évvia** – is magnificent, especially in the light of late afternoon. It was always a strategic point guarding the straits, with a Classical-era garrison town 800m (½ mile) downhill by the water (mostly off-limits for excavations).

For most visitors, however, the highlight will be the suprisingly evocative foundations of a Doric Temple of Nemesis (built *c.* 435 BC), goddess of retribution. Pausanias, rounding off his account of the Battle of Marathon, notes that the Persians certainly provoked the goddess by bringing along a giant block of marble on which they intended to commemorate their impending victory. Instead they met their nemesis on the marshy plain and the victorious Greeks sensibly used the raw material to carve a suitably reverent thanks-offering. Remains of a smaller shrine dedicated to Themis, goddess of justice, are found adjacent, and both are accessed from the gatehouse by a patch of uncovered ancient road (which continued down to the seaside fortifications). As well as the Taverna Ramnous overlooking the nearby vineyards, there's another one at the port of **Agiá Marína** 8km (5 miles) east, from where several daily ferry boats (more in the evenings) ply to Néa Stýra on Évvia.

Rafína

The shore road south from Néa Mákri passes through increasingly featureless coastal development before arriving at **Rafína** **C**, much the largest place on the east Attic coast. Its main role in life is as Athens' second ferry port after Piraeus (though Lávrio may eventually outstrip it in this respect), with services to the eastern and central Cyclades, as a weekend-home venue for wealthier Athenians, and as a place to go for a seaside meal in one of the numerous tavernas which overlook the harbour on the left, as you face the Aegean. There's

Rafína is a major ferry port.

BELOW: everything you need for the beach in Rafína.

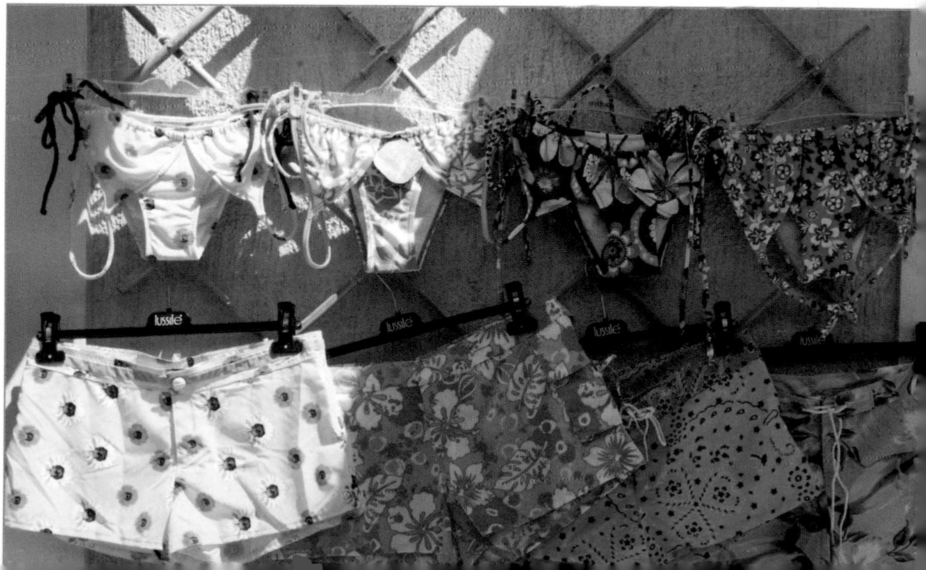

Sounion

The archaeological site at **Sounion** (Soúnio), a place once dedicated to Poseidon and Athena, is one of the most impressive in Greece (open 9.30am–sunset; entrance charge). Even without the dramatic Classical remains, it is a spectacular headland with tremendous views of the Aegean; which may explain why it was originally chosen as a sanctuary to the sea-god Poseidon.

"Holy Sounion, the headland of Athens" is mentioned in Homer's *Odyssey* as the place where Menelaus stopped on his return from the siege of Troy to bury his helmsman, Phrontes Onetorides. By the 7th century BC organised worship was taking place at two spots on the promontory: in the *temenos* (holy precinct) of Poseidon at the southern edge, and the sanctuary of Athena about 500m to the northeast.

Votive offerings have been found from the 6th century BC, but both sanctuaries remained fairly modest affairs until the beginning of the 5th century, when the Athenians began the construction of a grand temple in the *temenos* of Poseidon. It was never completed; the temple and most of the the sacred offerings were destroyed by Xerxes' army in 480 *(see page 26)*. In the decades following the Persian Wars, Sounion, like the rest of Attica, flourished, and an important building project was undertaken at both sanctuaries. The results can still be seen today.

The imposing temple of Poseidon, completed around 444 BC, measured 31m x 13.5m (100ft x 44ft) with slender Doric columns, of which 16 remain. Its design has been attributed to the anonymous architect responsible for the Hephaisteion in Athens.

Thanks to its size and position, the temple was – and still is – an important landmark to sailors, the last sight of their city for Athenian mariners as they left their native shore, and the first sight to greet them on their return home. In the mid-2nd century AD, the geographer Pausanias remarked on it as he approached Attica from Asia Minor; though he mistook it for the temple of Athena. More recent travellers to be impressed by the building include Lord Byron, who sacriligeously carved his name into one of the columns.

Not much remains of the sculptural decoration of the temple. The frieze of the east side depicted a battle against Centaurs, and the east pediment (of which only a seated female figure is preserved) probably showed the fight between Poseidon and Athena for the domination of Attica.

The smaller temple of Athena, to the northeast, has scholars arguing about its origin. Some maintain that it was built from scratch in the late 5th century BC, while others believe that the cella (inner chamber) was an Archaic 6th-century construction that survived the ravages of the Persians, and had an outer colonnade of Ionic columns added later. Either way, there's not much to see now except the foundations. An even smaller Doric temple just to the north of Athena's shrine is even more problematical. Nobody knows when it was built or which deity was worshipped there.

Cape Sounion was fortified in 412 BC during the Peloponnesian War. The fortifications stretched down to the sea, where a small harbour was built to shelter warships. Inside the fortress, excavations have brought to light part of a central street, and the remains of houses and water cisterns. ❑

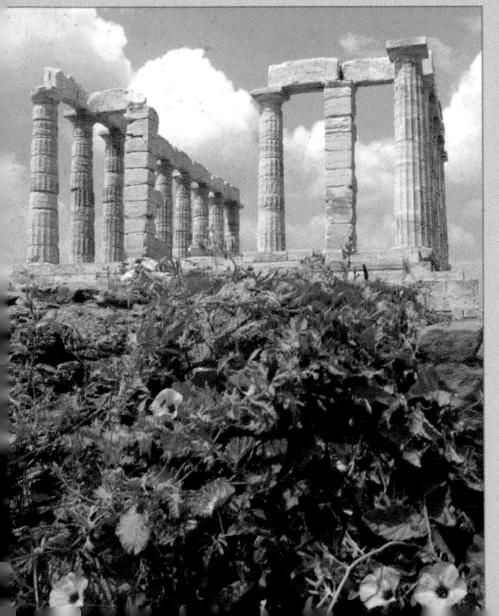

LEFT: Poseidon's temple, a landmark for sailors.

absolutely nothing else to see in the relentlessly modern town, and the town beach arc-ing off to the right is often rendered unusable by fierce winds. You'll have better bathing north of Rafína at Blé Limanáki (1km/½ mile away) or Kókkino Limanáki (2km/1 mile distant), the latter with tavernas and some shade. These are not served by public transport, though central Rafína is, by regular KTEL bus from the Mavromatéon terminal near the Pédion Áreos in central Athens.

Brauron and Pórto Ráfti

South of Rafína, the road passes through more drab seaside development around **Loútsa** to the site of ancient **Brauron** D (modern Vravróna; open Tues–Sun 8.30am–3pm; admission charge), reachable only with your own transport. This isolation only adds to the charm of the bucolic, tree-shaded site, a Classical sanctuary of Artemis, goddess of hunting and childbirth, mistress of wild animals. The remains – most prominently the reconstructed 5th-century BC Stoa of the Little Bears with a baker's dozen of columns upholding some architraves – occupy a marshy, low-lying locale where yellow irises emerge in spring, frogs croak in the pool of the sacred spring, and scops owls hoot at twilight. In ancient times the sea, now a few hundred metres on the east, must have lapped the site, which also included an Artemis temple (now merely foundations, just downhill from a locked post-Byzantine chapel).

The "little bears" in question were the apprentice priestesses of Artemis, young, high-born girls under 10 years old, who participated in a quadrennial festival honouring the goddess by dressing up as bears – long linked with maternity in European folklore – and miming the movement's of Artemis' favourite animal in dance. About 1500m (1 mile) down the road, the site museum (same hours; separate admission charge) contains some statuettes of the young girls with bear-masks, and marble reliefs of others coming to offer sacrifices at the festival.

Your closest opportunity for lunch – discounting the little snack bar at Hamoliá bay – is 6km (4 miles) south at **Pórto Ráfti** E. This is much the most attractive, and upmarket, place on the east Attic coast, a natural harbour admirably well-protected by small islets. The convoluted shoreline of the main bay is, however, densely developed with villas, apartments and five tavernas. The name – the "tailor's port" – is derived from the presence of a Roman-era female statue on one of the islets; her vanished arm once held the first crops that were dedicated to the shrine at Delos, but in medieval times she was thought to have been wielding shears.

A 400-metre-long (¼-mile) beach with clean water and mixed sand and pebbles (though somewhat

Map on page 182

The old port captain's office in Lávrio.

BELOW: Pórto Ráfti bay is densely developed but still attractive.

exposed to the prevailing wind) lies just to the southeast at **Avláki**. It's somewhat less built up, though there are several tavernas here as well as a few discrete nightclubs.

Lávrio F, at the southern end of the eastern coast, is a rather nondescript town which is chiefly useful as a jumping-off point for the island of Kéa. However, if you have some time to spare pop into the small Archaeological Museum (open daily 10am–3pm; admission charge) which contains artefacts from the excavations at nearby **Sounion** G *(see page 184)*.

Relaxing on the beach.

The annual Festival of Mediterranean Documentary Film, which used to be staged in Sámos in October, is now going to be staged in Lávrio every July from 2007. The rationale is that Lávrio is the closest thing Greece ever had to Italy's Cinecittà: between the 1930s and 1960s hundreds of movies were shot on location in the triangle formed by Lávrio, Soúnio and Anávyssos. Screenings are planned to take place in a former film-studio warehouse.

BELOW: fresh octopus by the sea.

Kéa (Tziá)

The closest of the Cyclades to Attica, **Kéa** (or Tziá in local dialect) is an eminently logical destination from Lávrio, with four or five ferries or catamarans daily in each direction. This proximity means that – like much of the Attic coast – it becomes a virtual Athenian suburb at weekends and all summer, and the number of villas on the gentler western slopes of the island increases yearly. But away from the functional port of Korissía and the busy yacht anchorage of Vourkári, Kéa has a more alluring interior stippled, unusually, with large oak trees, and an attractive hill capital, Ioulída, with red-tiled pitched roofs on neoclassical dwellings rather than the usual Cycladic flat ones on vernacular houses.

The village has been "discovered" in recent decades, and has the best-quality tavernas on the island and (for somewhat staid Kéa) the liveliest nightlife in its bars and cafés. After a stroll along the flagstoned lanes, you might wander a few minutes' north of the village to the 6th-century BC "Lion of Kéa", carved from the living rock and about 6m (20ft) long, with a suitable Archaic-enigmatic expression on its bewhiskered face.

Kéa had four city-states in antiquity, when it was known as Keos, but little of them is visible today other than a crumbling, square Hellenistic watchtower at Agía Marína, the fenced-off Minoan settlement of Agía Iríni near Vourkári, and foundations of an Apollo temple at ancient Karthaia in the far southeast. Kéa's scalloped-edge coastline is not the greatest when it comes to beaches. The only serious ones, on the southwest shore, are at **Písses**, **Koúntouros** and **Kambí**, all with tavernas. Public transport is limited, so you're best advised to bring a car on the boat from Lávrio, or be prepared to pay over the odds in Korissía for a hired scooter. ❑

RESTAURANTS

Restaurants

China
Dimárhou Angéllou
Metaxá 11, Glyfáda
Tel: 210 89 46 252
Open daily 11am–2am
Cash only. **€**
On the whole, Athens' few Chinese eateries aren't particularly distinguished, with the exception of Noodle Bar *(noted on page 120)*. This is another standout. Eat at little tables, or take away, at this quick-serving outfit in the Stoa Arian. The menu includes the usual (won ton, spring rolls) and the less usual (spicy chicken with basil, rice-flour noodles with Chinese mushrooms, pork in honey-garlic sauce).

Gri-Gri
Paralía Skhiniás
Tel: 229 40 63 266
Open L and D daily Jun–Sep, otherwise weekends only
Cash only. **€–€€**
Of the half-dozen fairly indistinguishable *exohiká kéndra* (rural tavernas) at the east end of this beach, Gri-Gri is one of the more sympathetic, with reasonable seafood (often frozen in low season), a selection of *mezédes*, and bulk wine.

Iy Kali Kardia
Kostí Palamá 12, Rafína
(200m behind the town hall)
Tel: 229 40 23 856
Open D Mon–Thu, L and D Fri–Sun
Cash only. **€€**
An oddity for a port: a meat specialist, though there are some token fish dishes. Pleasant untouristed environment inside and out, in a gazebo surrounded by palm trees, though it's no cheaper than the waterfront places. Other pluses are their own (expensive) bulk white wine, and good hand-cut potatoes.

Louizidis
Iásonos 2, corner Ermoú, Vouliagméni
Tel: 210 89 60 591
Open daily noon till late
Major credit cards. **€€**
Founded in 1961, this is one of the few traditional Greek tavernas in this posh suburb, though prices are stratospheric for fish (€60/kilo) and grilled meat. *Magireftá* and *mezédes*, which have a good reputation, are more normally priced. Undeniably convenient – just one block in from the beach.

Psaropoúla-Bibikos
Far end of Avláki beach, Pórto Ráfti
Tel: 229 90 71 292
Open L and D daily.
Cash only. **€€€**
A bit pricier than Raftopoula, but renowned for its seafood *mezédes* and scaly-fish mains. A good position behind the sand, and (usually) no parking problems.

Iy Raftopoula
Esplanade, inner bay, Pórto Ráfti
Tel: 229 90 87 870
Open L and D daily
Major credit cards. **€€**
Pórto Ráfti, conveniently close to ancient Brauron, is a favourite destination for a weekend-afternoon fish lunch. Iy Raftopoula is one of the bettter of a half-dozen eateries which line the very protected inner port here, popular with the boating set. Scaly fish is fairly pricey (€48–53 a kilo and climbing), as it is everywhere in Attica, but the quality is high and there's a vast array of cheaper *mezédes* like dips and boiled vegetables, as well as humbler fish like *atherína* (sand smelt) and sardines to choose from. Service copes fairly well with the crush.

Syrtaki
2km (1 mile) along Soúnio–Lávrio road
Tel: 229 20 39 125
Open L and D daily
Cash only. **€€**
A simple waterside taverna with both seafood and spit-roasted meat, served on a split-level terrace with sweeping views. Their signature dish is *astakomakaronáda* (pasta with lobster flesh flaked in).

Vincenzo
Gianitsopoúlou 1, off Platía Esperídon, Glyfáda
Tel: 210 89 41 310
Open daily 1pm–1.30am
Major credit cards. **€€**
Very authentic thin-crust pizzas baked in a wood oven, also some pasta dishes. Seating is either in a busy front terrace or calmer back garden.

O Vrahos
Platía Tahydromíou, Rafína
Tel: 229 40 22 307
Open L and D daily
Cash only. **€€**
Probably the best value available at the line of seafood places which overlook the harbour, though again expect to pay €45–50 per kilo for fish.

PRICE CATEGORIES

Prices are based on an average meal per person, including house wine:
€ = under €15
€€ = €15–25
€€€ = €25–40
€€€€ = over €40
Key: B = breakfast, L = lunch, D = dinner

KIFISIÁ TO DAFNÍ

Spend some time in one of Athens' most glamorous and expensive suburbs, then head for the hills. The nearby mountains provide good walking trails and spectacular views – and there are a couple of memorable monasteries in the area

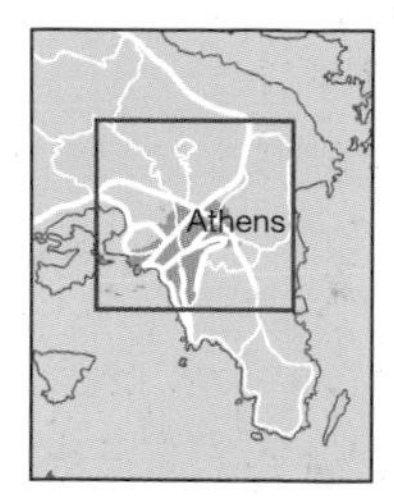

The leafy suburb of **Kifisiá** ❶, some 9km from downtown Athens on the western feet of **Mt Pendéli**, has always been a place of refuge. At just under 1108m (900 ft) elevation, it's considerably higher – and cooler – than the centre of town, a fact not lost on (among others) Herodes Atticus, who had a villa here. Ancient writers praised its lush groves, oddities then and now in barren Attica. Pendéli on the east may block some morning sunlight, but in compensation sunsets can be spectacular, and the springs surging forth from the base of the mountain created the oasis and indirectly provided its name: Kifissia, a water nymph. The main spring or *kefalóvryssi* near Metamórfosis Sotíros church has lent its name to the neighbourhood of Kefalári. It was long thought to be the primary source of the River Kifissós but is actually that of a main tributary, the Angólfi.

Kifisiá in history

Under the Ottomans, Kifisiá was a large village of some 1,500 inhabitants – half Christian, half Muslim – again unusual in an era when the latter rarely settled in rural areas. After independence, the "better" Greek families began taking advantage of its virtues. From the 1860s onwards, aristrocratic or upper-middle-class Athenians spent the summer here, making the perilous journey up by horse-carriage until, in 1882, Kifisiá was linked to Platía Attikís in Athens by a steam-powered train dubbed the Thirío or "Monster". This remained in service until 1938, and after a long gap the ISAP or *elektrikó* finally arrived in 1957.

By 1900, Kifisiá had acquired an international reputation, in part because it had the only hotels of (for the time) luxury standard in Attica,

Map on pages 174–5

LEFT: Kessarianí Monastery.
BELOW: bird watching on Párnitha.

Wealthy Athenians built incongruous villas in a variety of styles in Kifisiá.

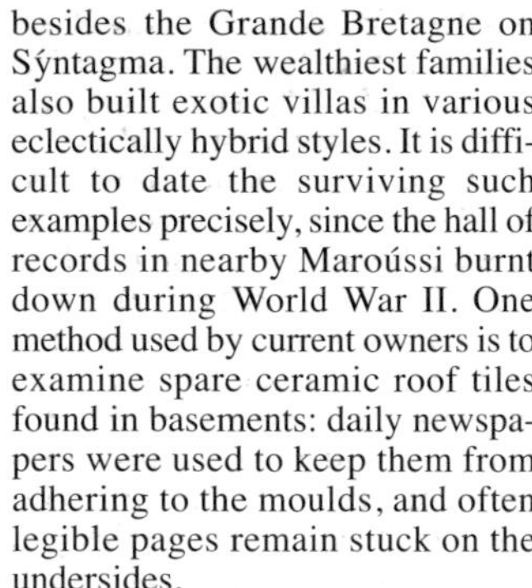

besides the Grande Bretagne on Sýntagma. The wealthiest families also built exotic villas in various eclectically hybrid styles. It is difficult to date the surviving such examples precisely, since the hall of records in nearby Maroússi burnt down during World War II. One method used by current owners is to examine spare ceramic roof tiles found in basements: daily newspapers were used to keep them from adhering to the moulds, and often legible pages remain stuck on the undersides.

Between the world wars the community continued to flourish; politicians Eleftherios Venizelos and George Papandreou endowed many schools, and the Asia Minor disaster caused only a ripple here. The abundant local water irrigated many market and ornamental gardens, the latter developed by the Moulidis family, former landscapers to the Ottoman sultan. Thus began Athens' flower market, and Kifisiá is still noted for its many plant nurseries. The elegant Álsos (Grove) which still greets you as you step out of the metro station is another result of this horticultural tradition. In keeping with this bucolic theme, eminent conductor Dimitris Mitropoulos staged an outdoor performance of Beethoven's Pastoral Symphony here in 1937. But this was the twilight of Belle Époque, Art Nouveau and Art Deco culture, and the era soon ended abruptly. At 3am on 28 October 1940, the Italian envoy Grazzi delivered his country's ultimatum to Greek dictator Ioannis Metaxas at his recently purchased villa on Kefallinías Street. Metaxas' apocryphal "*Óhi*" (No) reply – it was actually the mutually understood *Alors, c'est la guerre* – precipitated Greece's entry into World War II on the Allied side.

Modern Kifisiá

Today Kifisiá is a bustling town of nearly 60,000 people, engulfed by Athens' urban sprawl during the 1970s. Traffic is just as congested as downtown, parking a car can be nearly as impossible as in the city centre, and the metro is still the most relaxing way to get here, though there are also buses from the centre (A7, E7, B7). At the rear of the Álsos, the name of Platía Platánou is the only trace of the monumental *plátanos* (plane tree) which succumbed some decades ago to the ravages of paving, pruning and traffic.

Kifisiá's glory days may be over, but it is still one of the most glamourous and expensive Athenian suburbs. The streets leading east from Platía Platánou to Kefalári – in particular Kassavéti and its continuation Kolokotróni – are lined with designer shops, cafés or clubs to be seen in and restaurants. **Kefalári** district itself is home to most of the facilities – including some recommended hotels – that a visitor might want.

For a glimpse of old Kifisiá, follow Tatoïou Street north from the ISAP station; the first blocks, up to

BELOW: a designer shop in upmarket Kifisiá.

the football pitch, are lined with a half-dozen surviving interwar villas. The prominent Pezmazoglou family stayed at No. 25 of perpendicular street Pesmázoglou, which sports several other grand residences. Elsewhere, 19th-century prime minister Harilaos Trikoupis had premises at Benáki 13, while Emmanouil Benaki (he of the museum) had digs at No. 42 of the same street. One of the most ornate residences is the Giorganda-Kolokotroni mansion at Kolokotróni 7, while the simplest – and perhaps the first – villa is that of Trikoupis' perennial rival, Theodoros Deligiannis, at Levídou 19 near the centre of Kifisiá.

The one villa to which you are guaranteed admission is at Levídou 13, now home to the private **Mousío Goulandrí Fysikís Istorías** (Goulandris Museum of Natural History; open Mon–Sat 9am–2.30pm, Sun 10am–2.30pm; admission charge), founded by the ecologist and painter Niki Goulandris with her husband in 1964. There's appropriately good coverage of Greece's fauna, including endangered species like the monk seal and loggerhead turtle, plus a collection of nearly 250,000 botanical specimens, along with a café and decent shop selling publications and wildlife-related souvenirs. Just around the corner at Óthonos 100, the affiliated **Kéndro Géa** (Gaia Centre; same hours as Goulandris; advantageous joint ticket available) is good for kids, with three floors of often interactive displays on environmental issues and natural phenomena. Most of the labelling is Greek-only, so you'll probably want an audio-guide.

Mount Párnitha

The most extensive, tallest (1,413m/4,636ft) and most heavily vegetated of the mountains surrounding the city, **Mount Párnitha** ❷ is also the best target for a long-day (or even multi-day) walking trip. Despite the presence of numerous springs, midsummer is probably a bit too hot for comfort at this relatively modest alpine altitude – you have to pity the participants in the 2004 Olympic mountain-biking competition which

Card-operated pay phones can be found everywhere.

BELOW: street art in Kifisiá.

was held here – but late winter and spring are usually idyllic, with all manner of bulb-flowers pushing their way up through the snowdrifts that can lie late on the north flank of the peak. Early autumn is also very pleasant, but you have to contend with short daylight hours.

Flowers are abundant on Mt Párnitha.

Much of Párnitha is a national park, established in 1961 and totalling 38 sq km (15 sq miles), which guarantees a decently maintained network of proper hiking trails, marked in a variety of colour conventions with metal tree-badges, blazes and the like. There have, however, been some bad wildfires on the lower slopes – thus the large number of fire-lookout towers – and you must avert your eyes from the military and telecommunications paraphernalia that crown every major summit of the range, and dodge a number of roads, paved and not, which garland the alpine zone. The best map is the 1:35,000 product published by Anavasis; you'll notice that many of the place names are Albanian, a legacy of the medieval settlement of this area by Arvanítes or Orthodox settlers from what is now Albania.

The completely sedentary and car-bound might instead consider a visit to the half-ruined but still-impressive Classical 4th-century BC fort of Phyle, seven twisty kilometres (4 miles) above the modern Párnitha-foothill village of **Fylí** (best known by its Arvanitic name Hasiá). In the village there are a large number of *psistariés* (meat grills) at which to fill up. About 3km (2 miles) above Hasiá sits the convent of Kímisi Theotókou Klistón, originally 14th-century but insensitively restored since. The view from slightly above in the Goúra gorge, of the premises nestling inside its fortification wall, is more impressive than anything to be seen close up.

Hiking with a vehicle

If you have a car, the best strategy is using it to gain elevation on the hairpin road which climbs from the north-Athenian suburb of Thrakomakedónes to the vicinity of the adjacent chapel of **Agía Triáda** and the Chalet Kyklamina, serving

BELOW: much of the lofty Párnitha plateau is a national park.

snacks and drinks (at 1,000m/ 3,250ft), and leaving it here at the hub of a number of trails which can be combined into loop-walks with a minimal altitude change. The following classic circuit takes in the best the summit area has to offer, avoiding for the most part the ring-road around the peak.

From Agía Triáda, head east 800m (½ mile) along this until you meet the junction with the access drive serving the somewhat seedy, smoky Mont Parnes casino (open 24 hours if the idea appeals). Pick up the red-marked path heading north, more or less parallel to the ring-road, until you arrive, after 45 minutes, at the Báfi Refuge (1,160m/ 3,800ft; tel 210 24 69 050; open Fri evening to Sun evening all year, also weekdays in mid-summer). This is a substantial two-storey structure where you can sleep and eat (their bean soup is renowned) if necessary. From Báfi, continue north, with a brief stretch of road-walking, until you find the onward trail (still red-blazed) signposted for "Móla". This threads a saddle between the secondary peak of Órnio (1,350m/ 4,430ft) with its telecom tower and Karámbola summit (1413m/ 4,635ft), topped by a clumsily camouflaged radar "golf ball".

About half an hour beyond Báfi, having descended from a small chapel through thick forest, you'll reach a junction: right heads down within 20 minutes to the Móla recreation area, with its ancient chapel of Ágios Pétros, but for now bear left instead, following blue trail-markings towards the Skípiza spring, reached in just under an hour. The way there skims spectacularly along the north flank of the peak, with sweeping views over central Greece on a clear day.

Skípiza ("the eagle's place" in Albanian, 1,200m/3,935ft), at the heart of the range, is a four-way junction. The completion of the recommended walking circuit involves heading southeast on a yellow-blazed trail for another hour to the Paleohóri spring on the ring road, just 15 minutes' walk from Agía Triáda chapel. This gives a total walking time on the day of just

Poppy field on the mountains.

BELOW: the summer festival on Párnitha.

under four hours, not counting rests or meal-stops at Báfi.

Hiking with public transport

Buses for the southern foothills of Párnitha depart fairly regularly from a terminal at Aharnón 10 in central Athens, near Platía Váthis. There is often a change of coaches in Aharnés (aka Menídi). If for any reason this service is not available, you'll have to settle for bus No.714, which departs only at dawn and early afternoon from Márni Street, also off Platía Váthis. The Aharnón 10 services should eventually bring you to the edge of Thrakomakedónes, while the 714 passes the base of the cable-car up to the casino before climbing up to Agía Triáda and the casino itself. There are more frequent services on Sundays, but generally the last 714 bus down is at about 4pm.

Hardened cases might care to leave either bus at the base of the cable-car for the classic approach to the mountain. This may involve negotiating a welter of dirt tracks for 15 minutes northeast to where trail-marking picks up at the mouth of the spectacular **Hoúni Ravine**. The path, now clear and well-trodden, climbs from typically Mediterranean scrub to firs at a junction just over an hour along.

Bear right if you want to head for Párnitha's other staffed refuge, **Flamboúri** (1,160m/3,805ft; tel 210 24 64 666 or 24 61 528), reached after another 80 minutes' challenging but scenic walking through forest. Keep left for the Báfi refuge, reached in a similar amount of time. From Flamboúri to the region of **Móla**, a two-hour trip, the route tangles repeatedly with jeep tracks; the itinerary via Báfi is shorter and more straightforward.

Whichever way you go, bear in mind the time of the last bus down from Agía Triáda, and the likely difficulty of hitching a lift off the mountain. If it looks as if you'll be stranded, and have enough daylight in hand, the best strategy is probably to descend from Móla on a blue-marked path to Sfendáli rail station, from where hourly trains run back to Athens until quite late. The route down is attractive, following the course of a stream valley for the most part. The only drawback is that nearly half the three-hour descent is on dirt track, once you're past the spring at Paliomílesi.

Cypress and firs on the upper slopes of Párnitha.

BELOW: a marble rams-head fountain at Kessarianí monastery.

Mount Ymittós

Mount Ymittós ❸ is the third mountain, after Párnitha and Pendéli, to enclose Athens, on the east rather than the north. Its scrubby, herby vegetation has historically proved ideal for bee-keeping and honey – mostly heather-flavoured nowadays – and at sunset the long ridge changes successively from magenta to a deep purple, which led the ancient poet Pindar to dub it *iostefanos* or "violet-crowned". In modern times, alas, Ymittós has been increasingly scarred by cement quarries which provide the raw materials for Athens' mushrooming growth.

A new ring road loops around the mountain to Peanía on the eastern side, just above which is the entrance to the **Koutoúki cave** (open daily 9.30am–4.30pm; admission charge), discovered in 1926 by a goat-herd looking for a lost animal. The interior contains suggestively shaped stalagtites and stalagmites, as well as varicoloured rock curtains, all ingeniously illuminated.

Kessarianí Monastery

Tucked into a fold on the west side of Ymittós, just 5km (3 miles) or so from the city, the monastery of **Kessarianí** (open Oct–May Tues–Sun 8.30am–3pm; Jun–Sep may open until 7pm, also on Mon; admission charge) offers a very convenient escape from city life. It lies at the far eastern end of Leofóros Ethnikís Andistáseos, the main thoroughfare of modern Kessarianí neighbourhood, at the point where it bends to become the road up to the summit of the mountain. Without transport, take a No. 224 bus from the centre and then be prepared to walk for 20 minutes. Parking your own transport is limited and often complicated by the presence of various tour-buses.

The walled monastic complex dates from the 11th century, and incorporates a refectory and kitchen, monks' cells, and pre-existing Byzantine bathhouse (none of these open to visits at present), as well as the central, cross-in-square church to one side of the flagstone courtyard. The *katholikón* or main church, and the post-Byzantine narthex and side-chapel, are all decorated with vividly coloured frescoes by one Ioannis Ypatios, dating back mostly to 1682. Highlights include, in the conch, the *Virgin Enthroned* flanked by the *Communion of the Apostles*; the vaulting contains scenes from the life of Christ, including the Baptism, the Last Supper, the Entry to Jerusalem and the Transfiguration, while the narthex displays assorted miracles. Unlike Dafní, Kessarianí monastery was inhabited continuously from its foundation until the Greek War of Independence, because its monks agreed to submit

Kessarianí's dome is supported by four columns taken from a Roman temple.

BELOW: Kessarianí monastery.

to Latin authority in the person of the Franks' Catholic bishop after 1204.

The monastery was established just below Kylloú Péra, one of the sources of the River Ilissós, celebrated since ancient times (by Ovid among others), and spring-water is still channelled into a fountain (always accessible) behind the church, with a replica, carved-ram's-head spout (the original is in a mid-town museum). For centuries Athenians used to collect the water here, but unfortunately it's no longer drinkable.

However the local supply is perfectly adequate to nurture – as it always has – thriving gardens all around, which are available to enjoy even when the monastery is closed. The grounds were, admittedly, much neglected and abused in the century-plus following the place's abandonment in 1821, but after World War II a group known as the Friends of the Trees, working with distinguished landscape architect Dimitris Pikionis, set to work rehabilitating the environs of Kessarianí. Besides the masoned terraces and stairways leading up from the ram's-head fountain, tens of thousands of native trees and shrubs were planted on the hillside, and paths graded to various signposted points of interest.

If time is short, the best single target for a walk is the hill of **Taxiárhis**, which has the eponymous chapel (locked) and the half-ruined Byzantine monastic church known as Ágios Márkos Frangomonastírou. From here a network of trails – very popular with joggers and dog-walkers – continue onwards towards the top of Ymittós, affording unlimited views west over the city. Another path, marked for "Análipsi", ends at a former medieval cistern adapted as a chapel, its interior festooned with modern icons.

Christ looks down from the dome of Dafní's church.

BELOW: the ancient and sacred settlement of Eleusis.

Dafní Monastery

Situated just 11 km (7 miles) west of Athens, **Dafní** ❹ lies about halfway along the Sacred Way, the ancient route taken by revellers from the city to the pagan centre of worship at Eleusis. The site, at the foothills of the mountains Aigáleo, Poikilón and Korydallós, had once been occupied by a sanctuary to Daphneios, but in the 5th century this temple was torn down by Christians and the materials used to erect a basilica on the same spot. This was in the hope of winning over to the ways of Christ curious pagans on their way to celebrate the Eleusinian Mysteries.

In the 12th century an octagonal church was built to replace Dafní's older basilica. This church, embellished with mosaics and marble, was crowned by a glorious dome. The immense height of the dome, over 16 metres (52 ft) high at the centre, flooded the church with light pouring through its 16 windows.

Dafní (closed for the foreseeable future for ongoing restoration) is distinguished from other Byzantine churches in the Athens area by its collection of mosaics. Looking down is a rather severe Almighty, clutching a Bible to his chest with great, elongated fingers. Just beneath this figure, and positioned between each window, are 16 prophets, much like the statues from the Acropolis in attitude and posture. In the four corners of the dome four religious festivals are depicted: the Annunciation, the Nativity, Baptism and Transfiguration.

Glowing in soft blue and gold colours, the dome is so transfixing that it's hard to look away to the smaller paintings, or to escape the feeling of being judged by a glowering Christ. These wall paintings are scattered throughout the monastery, 76 themes in all, which illustrate the teachings of the church in the 11th and 12th centuries.

Dafní can be reached in less than an hour by public bus. The attractive ruins of ancient **Eleusis** (open daily 8am–6pm; admission charge), 11 km (7 miles) further on, are unfortunately surrounded by very heavy industry. The cult of Demeter took hold here in the Mycenaean age (around 1200 BC).

Eleusis rose to wider importance in the 8th century BC and by the time of Solon it was the site of one of the most important Attic festivals. Among the ruins still to be seen today are the Sacred Court with altars for offerings to Demeter and the two propylaias, the older a copy of the one on the Acropolis, both dedicated to the goddess. The museum at the site, with finds from excavations here, is well worth a visit (open Tues– Sun 8am–6pm, Mon 11am–6pm; admission charge). ❑

The ritual ceremonies performed at Eleusis were known as the Mysteries and participants forbidden to reveal their contents on pain of death. By the 5th century BC, the cult had evolved into an annual festival attracting up to 30,000 people from all corners of the Greek world.

RESTAURANTS AND CAFÉS

Koutouki tou Othona
Kimíseos Theotókou 11, Kessarianí
Tel: 210 75 11 241
Open nightly. Cash only. €
Occupying the ground floor of an old mansion, this *koutoúki* is adorned with photos of poets (mostly of a leftist persuasion), actors and shadow-puppet figures. The food is *ouzerí* fare, such as *bakaliáros skordaliá*, sausages, Smyrna-style meatballs, fried peppers, *gígantes* (baked haricot beans), and the *retsína* or red wine is cheap. The clientele is local and very mixed, who come especially at weekends to hear pick-up *rebétika* music sessions.

Stelios (Iy Trata)
Platia Anagenisseos 7–9, Kessarianí
Tel: 210 72 91 533
Open L and D daily, closed Aug. €€€
The longest established of a handful of equivalently priced (and pricey) seafood restaurants around the district's pedestrianised central square, Stelios combines the virtues of freshness with efficient service, especially at crowded Sunday lunches. There's fish soup as well as the usual grilled and fried seafood.

Monippo
Drosini 12, Kifisiá
Tel: 210 62 31 440
Open L and D Mon–Sat, L Sun. Cash only. €€
One of the few genuine *ouzerís* in Kifisiá boasts a vast range of recipes from across Greece, plus a few from Asia Minor and Constantinople, served in a contemporary environment. Examples include *spétzofaï* (Piliot sausage and pepper stew), *politikí kebáb* (Constantinopolitan kebab), stuffed *psaronéfri* (pork medallions) and cheese turnovers. Live music most Fri and Sat nights, plus Sun afternoon.

Tike
Krítis 27, corner Hariláou Trikoúpi, Kifissiá
Tel: 210 80 14 584
Open L and D daily. €€€
Turkish-style kebab is all the rage in Greece now, and this branch of an Istanbul-based chain meets the needs of the fan-base in the northern suburbs. The fare – various kebabs, *lahmacun* (Arabic pizza) and traditional starters – is rooted in the southeastern regions of Turkey, but the décor is strictly modern, with the grill *(oçakbashi)* and domed oven *(tandir)* centre stage.

Varsos
Kassavéti 5, off Platía Platánou
A vast, long-established, old-fashioned café-*zaharoplastío* which, despite trendy nearby competition, is still a favourite meeting-point. Renowned for its own-made yoghurts as well as the usual range of West Asian sweetmeats and European cakes.

THE SARONIC ISLANDS

You don't have to travel far from Athens to experience Greek island life. The five islands in the Saronic Gulf are within easy reach by ferry or hydrofoil, and popular with day-trippers. Each one is distinctive, rich in history and remarkably attractive

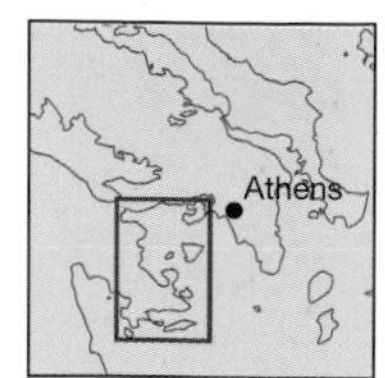

The islands scattered in the Saronic Gulf (Saronikós Kólpos) between Athens and the Argolid peninsula provide the closest and easiest escapes from the capital. Journey times from Piraeus can be as little as 45 minutes, making the nearer ones good options for a day-excursion.

Island-hopping, practised with greater ease elsewhere in Greece, can be tricky here: there are very few connections between Égina and the remoter islands beyond Póros; Angístri is linked only with Égina and Piraeus; while Salamína is connected only with Pérama, an industrial district of Piraeus. Nonetheless, it is strongly recommended that you avoid the heavily promoted "three-islands-in-one-day" cruises which maximise the amount of time you spend on board and allow perhaps 90 minutes on Égina, Póros and Ýdra apiece. With careful planning, you'll do better (and possibly cheaper) yourself.

Salamína (Salamis)

The ancient name of **Salamína** ❺ is redolent with history: in 480 BC, the (briefly) united Greek city-states defeated the Persian navy in the straits between Salamis and Perama through superior seamanship, despite being outnumbered three to one. Though there's still a naval base facing the straits, Salamína has come down in the world since that moment of glory. Its alias is now *Kouloúri* (breakfast-biscuit) – perhaps because of its shape – and trendy Athenians like to disparage the island for its working-class flavour. Nonetheless, "Biscuit Island" makes for an enjoyable day-trip, especially if you hire a scooter or car in Athens and take it across on the RO-RO ferry from Pérama (which runs

Map on pages 174–5

PRECEDING PAGES: Ýdra's charming harbour. **LEFT:** the splendid Temple of Aphaia on Égina. **BELOW:** Ágios Nektários, Égina.

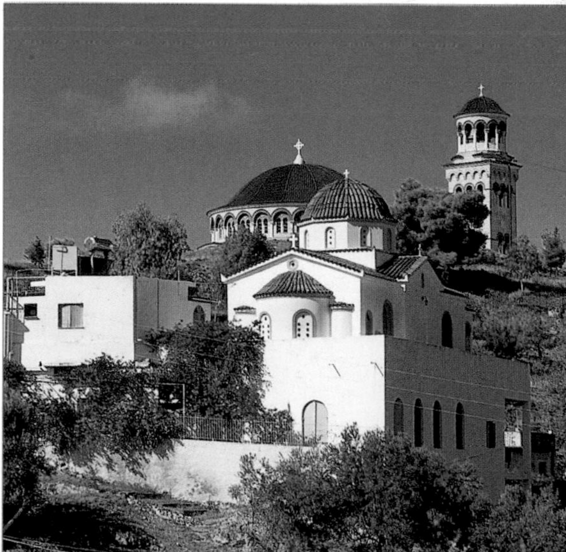

from 5am to 1am). There are only three modest hotels here but good tavernas and surprisingly hygienic bathing options considering the proximity of gritty Pérama.

The major sight, in the far northwest of the island and 6km (4 miles) beyond the capital of Salamína Town, with its many *ouzerís*, is the monastery of Faneroméni, originally founded during the 13th century and now home to 25 nuns. The *katholikón* or monastic church was restored and vividly frescoed in the decades immediately after 1670.

Rocky Salamína is easily reached from Athens.

Nearby, occupying the former monastic boathouse, is the so-called Kellí Sikelianoú or "Cell of (Ángelos) Sikeliános", conceded in 1941 to that illustrious modern Greek poet for use as a retreat. He wrote some of his finest work here until his death in 1952, and there are plans to restore the *kellí* as a museum.

The island's best beaches are in the southern limb of the "biscuit", at Perània and Peristéria. The latter also has a very pretty little harbour.

BELOW: Égina Town is a popular port for yachtsmen.

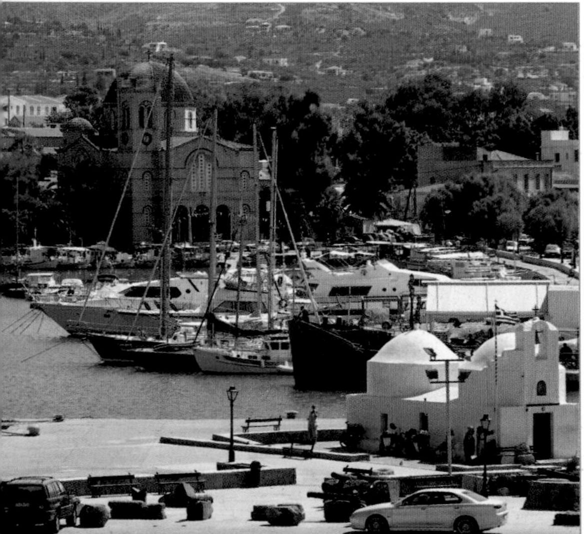

Égina (Aegina) and Angístri

Égina ❻ too was prominent in ancient times. For a while during the 5th century BC it rivalled Athens in wealth and seafaring activities until the Athenians defeated the Aeginots in two naval engagements. However it has not declined quite so much as Salamína: for a few years from 1828 the main port served as the first capital of modern Greece, a period which has left an elegant neoclassical townscape as its legacy, quite obvious as you disembark at Égina Town.

There is plenty here to keep you occupied, including three cinemas and lively nightlife, for the duration of a weekend, a fact not lost on well-heeled Athenians, many of whom have second homes in town or scattered across the countryside as do large numbers of expatriates. The promontory north of the main anchorage, staked out by a single surviving column of an Apollo temple, has been occupied since the early Bronze Age, as the very good adjacent **archaeological museum** (open Tues–Sun 8.30am–3pm; entrance charge) ably documents.

Some 2km (1 mile) further along the coast in the same direction, you'll find the **Mousío Hrístou Kaprálou** (Chrístos Kaprálos Museum; open June–Oct Tues–Sun 10am–2pm and 6–8pm; Nov–May Fri–Sun 10am–2pm; entrance charge), occupying the summer atelier of that prominent Greek sculptor and painter, whose monumental frieze *The Battle of the Pindus* adorns one wall of the parliament building in Athens (a copy is displayed here).

The principal trans-island road heads east, served by frequent buses, past some of the pistachio-nut groves for which Égina is famous. Some 8km (5 miles) further, it reaches the Byzantine capital of **Paleohóra** on a rugged hillside.

After Greek independence and the decline of piracy, Paleohóra was completely abandoned in favour of Égina Town, and the only surviving buildings are about 30 (usually unlocked) churches – a number of them engagingly frescoed.

The road continues another 4km (2 miles) to the Doric 5th-century Temple of **Aphaia**, one of the best-preserved such structures in Greece, atop a pine-clad hill. The obscure dedication honours a Cretan nymph who, fleeing the lust of King Minos, fell into the sea, was rescued by some fishermen and brought to ancient Aegina, where her cult was established in the late Bronze Age. Another 3km (1½ miles) further brings you to **Agía Marína**, a rather down-at-heel ex-package resort with many vacant premises and Égina's sandiest beach – but rather shallow, dubious water offshore.

In fact there is nowhere on Égina that offers brilliant swimming. **Pórtes** 8km (5 miles) south is about the best, with several seafood tavernas, although **Marathónas** and **Eginítisa** on the west coast, also on a fairly regular bus line, are tolerable.

For cleaner water and somewhat better beaches, head off to the pine-forested islet of **Angístri** to the west, with plenty of accommodation and tavernas in the two northerly villages of **Skála** and **Mýlos** – both, like Égina Town, very busy at weekends and all summer. A scooter or mountain bike is sufficient to explore the rest of the island as far south as the village of **Limenária**, with a popular taverna and farm-products shop in the centre. More secluded, part-naturist beaches are found at **Dragonéra** on the west coast, and at **Halikiáda** (path access only) on the east coast.

Póros

There's more healthy pine forest on volcanic **Póros** ❼, which lies less than 500m (550 yds) off the Argolid Peninsula – *póros* meaning "ford" in Greek. Frequent car-ferries cover the distance from dawn until late at night, as do even more regular pedestrian-only shuttle-launches (you must leave four-wheelers at the car park by the

At Pérdika stands a small, cylindrical, wood-clad steel building, the vision of a Viennese architect and artist/film-maker duo. It's a 21st-century take on the camera obscura, as commissioned by the Aegina Academy. Light enters the interior through 12 openings producing a panoramic image of the landscape outside, upside down and reversed on a screen.

BELOW: Aegina's landscape is green and rolling.

Hydra backstreets.

ferry jetty on arrival). This storm-proof access ensures that the island is popular with Athenian weekenders as well as tourists, almost uniquely in the Saronic Gulf, with package holidays (mostly Swedish). Póros is actually two very hilly islands: Sferiá, almost completely covered by Póros Town, and linked by bridge over a shallow canal to Kalávria, about 10 times the size.

The shelter afforded by the narrow channel makes Póros Town a sailor's haven – the quay will be lined with yachts as far as you care to walk. Aside from the famous hilltop clocktower which a maze of stepped lanes leads to for predictably stunning views, the only real sight is a two-room **archaeological museum** (open Tues–Sun 8.30am–2pm; entrance charge) featuring finds from every era from both the island and the Argolid sites opposite.

A scooter or car is useful for exploring Kalávria, though there is a reasonable bus service along its south coast. To the east, **Askéli** is the first beach resort reached, hopelessly packed out in summer. **Monastiríou** beach further along is better, with two acceptable tavernas just inland. The "monastíri" in question is peaceful 19th-century **Zoödóhou Pigís** about 765 yds uphill, next to one of the only springs in these islands, and tenanted by four monks.

Backtrack slightly to find the paved loop road that climbs forested ridges to the site of ancient **Kalaureia** (always open; free) and the foundations of its 6th-century BC temple of Poseidon, where the Athenian orator Demosthenes committed suicide in 322 BC rather than surrender to Macedonian forces. The Swedish Institute of Archaeology has been digging here on and off since the 19th century – thus the nationality of most vacationers on Póros.

The circuit road passes the turning for **Vagioniá**, the best of the north-facing beaches, before tracing an arc back down to **Kanáli** at the channel. West of this lie more small resorts, like Mikró Neório and Megálo Neório with protected but hard-packed, stony beaches and watersports facilities. At the end of the bus line and paved road is the Roussikós Stathmós or "Russian Naval Station", dating from the late 18th century and the time of Count Orloff, a paramour of Catherine the Great who tried unsuccessfully to foment a Greek anti-Ottoman rebellion.

BELOW: Hydra museum exhibit.

Ýdra (Hydra)

Ýdra ❽ (Hydra) is easily the most celebrated of the Saronic Gulf islands, a reputation that has been accruing since World War II. During the 1950s and early 1960s it became a fashionable bolthole and bohemian colony for everyone, from the Greek painter Hatzikyriakos-Ghikas to the Canadian singer-songwriter Leonard Cohen, drawn here by the perfectly preserved har-

bour town of 18th- century stonebuilt mansions. These architectural riches were the result of maritime prowess well before the War of Independence, at a time when Albanian-speaking Ydriot captains and crews provided much of the Greek navy's fleet.

Today, despite evolving into a mainstream resort, Ýdra Town exists in a sort of time-warp: a strict preservation code ensures that there are no multi-storey modern hotels (and thus no package tours), and the main conveyances – aside from a few miniature garbage trucks and earth-movers – are donkeys.

All of which makes it a supremely relaxing retreat, once the day-cruises have departed, and a surprisingly affordable place as long as you're not interested in buying real estate, jewellery or a coffee on the waterfront. While accommodation prices are high year-round owing to the patronage of Athenian weekenders and the aforementioned restrictions on hotel construction, taverna meals in the back streets can be reasonably priced, and commercial life in the covered market just in from the waterfront reassuringly normal.

Some of the former captains' and ship-owners' mansions on the hillsides flanking the achingly photogenic port have been pressed into service as two museums, a merchant- navy college and an artists' hostel; but for the most part the pleasure of the town resides in just strolling around.

If you can arrange a place to stay, Easter is a wonderful time to be here: on the eve of Good Friday, at the fishermen's parish of Ágios Ioánnis at **Kamíni** hamlet, the *Epitáfios* or symbolic bier of Christ is carried into the shallows to bless the boats and ensure smooth sailing.

Speaking of the sea, there are few good beaches on he island, though the water is generally clean and taken advantage of by the local scuba outfitter. The best coves are considered to be **Limnióniza**, a steep 75-minute path-walk from town on the southeast-facing coast, eminently scenic but with no reliable facilities; and **Bísti** or **Ágios**

Hydra Museum, in a former ship-owner's mansion.

BELOW: catching up on the news in Ýdra town.

Nikólaos at the southwest tip of the island, served in season by water-taxis from the port and furnished with sun-beds and *kantínas*.

Vlyhós, some 45 minutes' walk southwest of town on a good, wide donkey track, is the only other significant settlement on Ýdra, with a graceful bridge, tavernas and a few rooms to rent, though the beach is average. En route, people also swim at **Kastélo**, just beyond Kamíni.

Flying the local flags.

Walks inland are also rewarding, especially up the hill from the port to the convent of **Agía Evpraxía** and to the monastery of **Profítis Ilías** just above, the latter approached by what must be the longest stairway in Greece. Water and *loukoúmi* (Turkish delight) are hospitably left outside the main gate to revive hikers who arrive during the daily noon-to-4pm closure.

Really hardened trekkers can strike out towards the agricultural hamlet of **Episkopí** in the far southwest, just over two hours distant (one-way); or make for the monastery of **Panagía Zourvás** at the northeastern end of Ýdra, in a similar time.

BELOW: Byzantine mosaic from Hydra Museum.

Spétses

Of all the Saronic Gulf islands, **Spétses** ❾ is the furthest from Athens and thus beyond the reach of any day-cruises. Given the cost and duration of travel, you really should allow for a long weekend here. Like Ýdra, the island played a significant role in the Greek War of Independence, contributing fleets to the cause. Here too, the population is concentrated in one large town along the north coast, straggling several kilometres between the ports of Baltíza and Dápia, leaving the rest of the island sparsely developed and with just a smattering of holiday villas.

Unlike Ýdra, Spétses has been a fashionable resort for upper-crust Athenians since the 1890s, and it shows, especially in the eye-watering price of some tavernas. There is plenty of modern construction in among the traditional architecture, as building regulations are laxer; and, while four-wheel traffic is restricted, two-wheelers, trikes and horse-drawn charabancs are not, making Spétses Town a hazardous and noisy experience for pedestrians.

One of the Spetsiot admirals was Laskarína Bouboulína, a wealthy, colourful widow who commanded her own frigate (the *Agamemnon*) and was reputedly so unattractive that she had to seduce lovers at gunpoint. In 1825 she was gunned down by the father of a girl her son had eloped with. A depiction of her sternly directing a gunnery crew on deck used to adorn the now-retired 5,000-drachma note. Just inland from the Dápia, one of her family mansions is kept as a private **museum** (half-hour tours daily; entrance charge).

Another 18th-century mansion now houses the worthwhile local **historical museum** (open Tues–Sun 8.30am–2pm; entrance charge), its prize exhibits the carved polychrome wooden ships' prows from the insurgents' fleet.

The author John Fowles lived during the 1950s on Spétses, which provided the setting for one of his most famous novels, *The Magus*. He taught at the Anárgyros Korgialénios College just west of town, endowed (like the massive Edwardian Hotel Poseidonion on the waterfront) by Sotírios Anargýros, a wealthy Spetsiot who made his fortune in America and who also replanted the island's pine forests, destroyed by centuries of shipbuilding.

Walking east of town, you'll pass the monastic church of **Ágios Nikólaos**, overlooking the least glamourous of the town harbours, Palió Limáni. Vast pebble mosaics – *votsalotá* in Greek – spread out in front; inside, a plaque commemorates philhellene Paul-Marie Bonaparte, nephew of Napoleon, who died fighting with the Greeks in 1827 and was embalmed here for five years in a barrel of rum until his remains could be safely shipped home. The road ends at Baltíza inlet, chock-a-block with pleasure craft, though a few boatyards on the far side continue to build wooden *kaïkia* in the time-honoured fashion.

The paved loop road around the island can easily be negotiated by hired scooter, or somewhat more strenuously by mountain bike. It gives access to the side-turnings for the best and most scenic beaches of the Saronic islands. Heading anticlockwise (east), the first good one, with amenities, is **Ligonéri**. Near the western tip of Spétses is clothing-optional **Kórbi**, accessible in ten minutes by a steep path. **Agía Paraskeví**, a bit west as the road heads back to town, is possibly the island's best beach, with pines backing the pebbles and a full-service taverna.

Ágii Anárgyri, about halfway around the island, is a full-blown resort behind a mostly sandy beach, with windsurfing and water-skiing available. If it's too busy, carry on a little to the side-track down to **Xylokériza**, with just a snack bar lining the mixed sand-and-gravel strand. Continuing back to town, you'll see the privately owned islet of Spetsopoúla just offshore; this belongs to the heirs of the shipping magnate Stávros Niárchos. ❑

Local boat at dusk.

BELOW: the old Poseidonion Hotel on Spétses harbour.

RESTAURANTS & BARS

Restaurants

Égina/Angístri

Estiatorion Economou
Dimokratías, waterfront, Égina Town
Tel: 22970 25 113
Open daily 9am-midnight
Major credit cards. €€
Portside taverna with a blue canopy about midway along the waterfront. Serves some meat dishes but specialises in seafood: grilled fish and the lemony fish soup are recommended. Grilled local lobster is sometimes available – but expect to pay as much as €60 per kilo.

Ippokampos
Faneroménis 9, south edge of Égina Town by football stadium
Tel: 22970 26 504
Open D daily until 1am
Cash only. €€
Lebanese-run *mezedopolío* with rich fare, such as pork roulade and stuffed squid served in a peaceful courtyard slightly at odds with the surroundings.

Lekka
Kazantzáki 4 (north waterfront), by tiny town beach, Égina Town
Tel: 22970 22 527
Open L and D daily
Cash only. €
Renowned for its vegetarian dishes and well-sourced meat grills, accompanied by excellent sherry-like *hýma* wine.

Parnassos
Village centre, Metóhi, Angístri
Open D daily
Cash only. €– €€
The welcoming couple who run this hilltop taverna make their own cheese and source good bulk wine to accompany the few dishes of the day plus the usual grills and starters.

Yeladakis (aka Tou Steliou or Iy Agora)
Behind covered fish market, Égina Town
Tel: 22970 27 308
Open daily 11am–midnight
Cash only. €– €€
The first-established (around 1962), much the best, and the least expensive of three rival seafood *ouzerís* on this cobbled lane. Accordingly, it's usually mobbed and you may have to wait for a table outside or up in the winter loft inside as they don't take bookings. Their stock-in-trade is grilled octopus, sardines, prawns, plus a few vegetarian starters. As ever, price-band straddling reflects the fact that sardines are cheapish, prawns expensive.

Póros

Karavolos
inland from Cinema Diana
Tel: 22980 26 158
Open D daily
Cash only. €– €€
Follow the hand-painted signs up from the front to this little *ouzerí* which has snails (*karavólos* in one Greek dialect) on the menu as well as a lot more. Large portions and fair prices.

Oasis
Harbour, Poros Town
Tel: 22980 22 955
Open daily 11am-midnight
Cash only. €€
This taverna has traded on the harbourside since the mid-1960s. Indoor and outdoor tables, excellent fresh fish and cheerful staff. One not so traditional item on the menu: pasta with lobster.

Platanos
Platía Agíou Georgíou, up from north quay
Tel: 229 80 24 249
Open D daily
Cash only. €
Run by a local butcher, and with tables under the plane tree of its name, this is the spot for meat grills accompanied by rosé retsina, a rarity. Shame about the prefab chips, though.

Ýdra

Kondylenia
Kamíni waterfront
Tel: 229 80 53 520
Open Orthodox Lent–Oct

LEFT: *gýros* – pork carved from the spit.

PRICE CATEGORIES

Prices are based on an average meal per person, including house wine:
€ = under €15
€€ = €15–25
€€€ = €25–40
€€€€ = over €40
Key: B = breakfast, L = lunch, D = dinner

11am–midnight
Major credit cards. €€
With an unbeatable view over the sea from its verandah, this taverna could easily rest on its laurels. Fortunately the food, with an emphasis on seafood, is good, with the grilled *thrápsalo* (sweet deep-water squid) being particularly recommendable. Especially outside of meal times, it's okay to just have an *oúzo* or coffee here.

Manolis & Hristina's (To Gitoniko)
inland lane beyond Bratsera Hotel and Xeri Elia Taverna
Tel: 229 80 53 615
Open L and D daily
Cash only. €€
Perhaps the best all-rounder on the island, doing *magirevtá*, fish, grills and starters equally well. Regrettably, portion size has shrunk of late, but there's still friendly service and seating either downstairs or up on the roof terrace.

Marina's Taverna (aka Iliovasilema)
Vlyhós, on the rocks west of Kamíni swimming area
Tel: 22980 52 496
Open daily noon–11pm
Cash only. €€
You can reach Vlyhós at night by water-taxi from Ýdra Town – worth the €10 fare just to watch the sun go down (*iliovasílema* means "sunset"). The food's good, too: basic traditional fare prepared by Marína, with excellent *tirópita* and *spanakópita* (filo pies with cheese and spinach respectively), and the occasional quirky main such as sea-urchin spaghetti cooked in seawater.

To Paradosiakon
100m inland from quay, by Hotel Amaryllis
Tel: 22980 54 155
Open L and D daily until midnight
Cash only. €€
The best *mezedopolío* on the island, and thus very popular. Limited terrace tables, and sometimes glum service from trying to cope with the crowds who scoff down *fáva*, salads and seafood.

Spétses

Kafenio
Dápia port, next to Alpha Bank
Open daily all day
Cash only. €
Pebble mosaics underfoot and sepia photos on the walls attest to the antiquity of this, the island's first – and still most versatile – watering-hole. Sparrows beg for crumbs from your well-priced English breakfast; later in the day there's a full range of *mezédes* – or just have a drink while waiting for a hydrofoil.

Nykhthimeron (To Amoni)
Baltíza port
Open D daily
Cash only. €€
The alias means "the forge", and chef Nektários' father and grandfather used to run the local smithy out of this characterful building, now an exceptionally reasonable (especially for Spétses) *ouzerí*. Seasonal fresh seafood titbits, vegetarian appetisers, a few grills and homemade *tyropitákia* are typical offerings.

Patralis
Kounoupítsa waterfront, 300m before the Spetses Hotel
Tel: 229 80 72 134
Open L and D daily Feb–Oct
Major credit cards. €€
The most upmarket, white-tablecloth venue on the western side of town, with excellent service. Their *psári a la Spetsióta* (fish in ratatouille sauce) is made with tuna or amberjack. There's good bulk wine (plus an arrestingly priced wine list), and baked apple for dessert.

RIGHT: eating on Égina's waterfront.

THE ARGOLID

The peninsula across the Saronic Gulf from Athens contains some of Greece's most famous ancient sites – the remains of Bronze Age Mycenae, the Theatre of Epidauros and monumental Tiryns – as well as some mighty Venetian fortifications and the pleasant port of Návplio, modern Greece's first capital

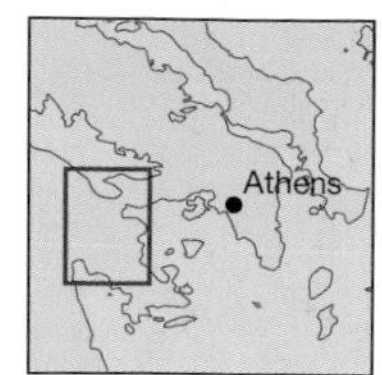

Especially if you avail yourself of a hired car, the northeastern corner of the Peloponnese peninsula – just an hour or so's driving from greater Athens on the motorway – is a logical and tempting excursion. Concentrated into a very manageable area are some of the earliest sites that Greece has to offer, plus (on the way in, a short way beyond the canal-riven Isthmus) the Roman ruins of Corinth, also a key locus in the history of early Christianity.

It's too much ground to cover in a single day, so make at least a weekend of it, using the elegant seaside town of Návplio as a base, though you'll have plenty of company and advance arrangements for lodging are strongly recommended.

The Corinth Canal

Geographically if not officially (in an administrative quirk, the province of Korinthía extends a bit into Attica, around Loutráki spa and Perahóra), you enter the Peloponnese as you cross the engineering marvel that is the **Corinth Canal ❿**, which cuts 6km (3½ miles) through the narrow isthmus dividing the Saronic Gulf from the Gulf of Corinth.

Sailing around the Peloponnese has always taken considerable time and exposes ships to some of the most dangerous waters in the Mediterranean, around Cape Maleás and Cape Ténaron (wrecks and groundings still occur there almost yearly, during winter storms). The idea of cutting a canal through the isthmus was first mooted in the Roman era, but Emperor Nero's efforts to inaugurate excavations (with a silver shovel) in AD 67 came to nothing. From then on until the late Byzantine period, to avoid the hazardous

BELOW: the ancient theatre at Epidauros
BELOW: the entrance to the fortress at Corinth.

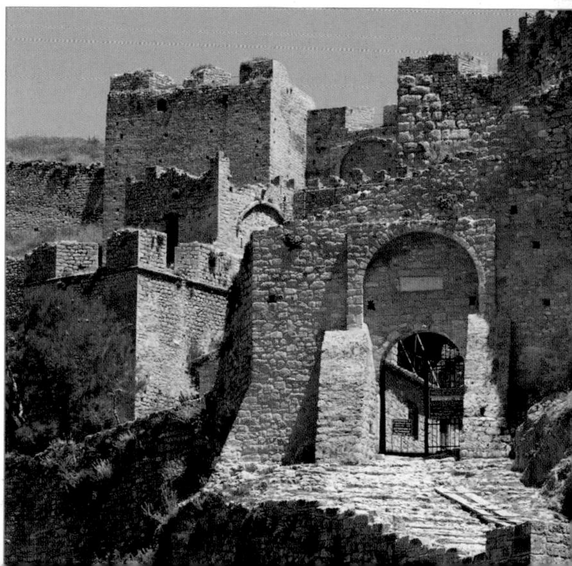

trip round the Peloponnese, ships were divested of their cargo and dragged across land between the two gulfs along a slipway called the *diolkos*, the remains of which are most visible at the northwest end of the canal (open summer Mon noon–7pm, Tues–Sun 8am–7pm; winter Tues–Sun 8.30am–3pm).

Finally, in July 1893, after 11 years of digging, a channel was opened measuring 70m (230ft) deep, 25m (80ft) wide, with 8m (25ft) of water, and admitting a single ship at a time. Its modest dimensions, however, rendered the canal obsolete almost immediately, and the equally modest revenue from tolls meant that it never made a profit either. In the contemporary era of supertankers it's even more of an anachronism, though several smaller craft still squeeze through every day.

A Roman marble from Corinth Museum.

Near the south end of the canal, by the village of **Krýa Vrýsi,** stand the remains of ancient Isthmia, renowned for its shrine of Poseidon and quadrennial Isthmian Games, which were second in prestige only to the Olympic Games at Olympia. The site (closed for restoration work), with sparse foundations of the Poseidon temple, is rather less impressive than the contents of the local museum (also temporarily closed), which feature superb *opus sectile* panelling – like ancient stained glass – recovered from an earthquake-collapsed Byzantine warehouse at the ancient port of Kenkhreai to the east.

Corinth

In ancient times the city-state of **Corinth ⓫**, 7km (4 miles) southwest of its drab modern successor Kórinthos, rivalled Athens in power and influence. Poised between two gulfs on the main trade routes between the Adriatic and the southeastern Mediterranean, and between northern Greece and the Peloponnese, it could not help but prosper; and be the focus of various battles or sieges. The layout of Corinth mimicked that of Athens – a town radiated out from the base of a rocky pinnacle that housed a temple of Aphrodite – though Acrocorinth

BELOW: the Temple of Apollo in ancient Corinth.

is much higher and more imposing than the Acropolis.

Corinth was a going concern from the 8th century BC onwards, and a keen rival of Athens. It sided with Sparta against Athens in the Peloponnesian Wars (431–404 BC). During the Hellenistic period the city remained wealthy despite political turmoil, and was a leading member of the Achaean League of Peloponnesian city-states, formed to resist Roman hegemony. After surprising initial success, in which Roman legions were cleared from most of mainland Greece, the superior resources of Rome eventually prevailed. In 146 BC Corinth was razed to the ground and its inhabitants sold into slavery, as a warning to others who might contemplate resisting Roman power.

The site was unoccupied for just over a century, until Julius Caesar began to rebuild the city on a grand scale in 44 BC. A revitalised Corinth soon became the capital of the Roman province of Achaea, and acquired a reputation for the beauty and sensuality of its women, hundreds of whom served as sacred prostitutes at Acrocorinth's Temple of Aphrodite.

The city developed two ports (Kenkhreai to the east, which it shared with Isthmia, and Lekhaion immediately north), and at one of these Saint Paul arrived in AD 50. He stayed 18 months, attempting to combat the perceived immorality of the inhabitants, though he mainly succeeded in provoking riots and being arraigned in front of the Roman authorities. Nonetheless, Paul left behind a small community of believers to whom he later addressed two of his more famous epistles. Cornith suffered major earthquakes in 375 and 521, interspersed with barbarian raids, after which the lower settlement spiralled into decline.

The ancient site (open summer 8.30am–7pm, winter 8am–5pm; admission charge) is dominated by its oldest relic, the splendid 6th–5th-century Doric **Temple of Apollo**, with seven columns and some architraves intact. Most other remains date from the Roman era, including the ornate facade of the Fountain of Peirene, where you can still hear the water flowing through chambers at the rear on its way to supply the modern village of Arhéa Kórinthos, and the marble-paved Lekhaion Way, with cart- and chariot-wheel-ruts deeply grooved into the slabs.

The *bema* or speaker's platform (the term is still used in both Jewish synagogues and Orthodox churches), traditionally believed to be the site where St Paul preached, is situated to the south side of the agora. The site **museum** (same hours) contains a frieze depicting the labours of Herakles (Hercules), plus some superb mosaics from Hellenistic and Roman villas.

The magnificent site of **Acrocorinth**, standing sentinel above, is the linchpin of ancient Corinth's

Map on pages 174–5

A Byzantine carving on Acrocorinth.

BELOW: mosaic floor with the head of Dionysus in the Corinth Museum.

fortifications, which extended down to enclose the port of Lekhaion and totalled 15km (9 miles) in circumference during the Roman era. Long after the lower city was abandoned definitively in the 12th century, the Byzantines, Franks, Venetians and Ottomans assiduously elaborated the walls of the upper citadel, which are entered via a series of three gates.

The ancient Lion Gate at Mycenae, Europe's oldest monumental sculpture.

At or near the summit are the remains of the Temple of Aphrodite, an Ottoman fountain Christianised with carved relief crosses, an early Christian basilica, Byzantine cisterns, a Frankish tower and a mosque. The views are out of this world, and inspired one of modern Greek poet Angelos Sikelianos's more memorable works in the 1920s, entitled simply *Akrokórinthos*.

Ancient Mycenae

From the mid-16th to the mid-12th century BC, this rocky peninsula – the "thumb" of the Peloponnesian land-mass "hand" – was one of the key centres of the eastern Mediterranean, with ancient Mycenae the seat of a Late Bronze Age empire which grew to encompass Crete and other Aegean islands, as well as the mainland. The exploits of the Mycenaeans and their leader Agamemnon, as related in Homer's *Iliad*, were thought to be myth until – during the 1870s – the German amateur archaeologist Heinrich Schliemann embarked on a mission to establish the factual basis of the Homeric epics, by uncovering the (until then) strictly legendary sites of Troy and Mycenae.

Schliemann found the remains of ancient **Mycenae** ⓬ (open daily summer 8am–7.15pm, winter 8.30am–4.45pm; admission charge) buried under millennial debris in a sheltered valley about 30km (19 miles) southwest of Corinth. It had been forgotten in popular memory and thus remained miraculously unplundered. His team found ample evidence for the Homeric epithets of "well-built Mycenae, rich in gold". As they dug through the ruins of what is now dubbed "Grave Circle A", the tombs of several

BELOW: Grave Circle A at Mycenae.

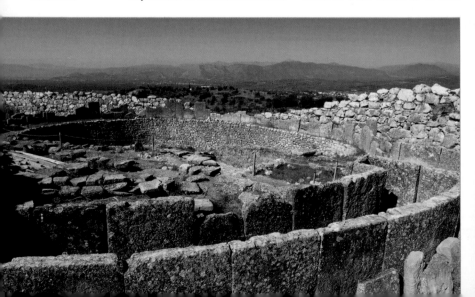

Map on pages 174–5

members of the local ruling dynasty were discovered. One skull was covered in a solid gold funerary mask, prompting Schliemann to cable King George I of Greece: "I have gazed upon the face of Agamemnon!"

In fact the burials are too early to be those of a historical Agamemnon and his followers, supposedly murdered by Queen Clytemnestra and her lover on their return from the Trojan War in about 1220 BC, but they were certainly those of nobility. Exquisite statuary and intricate jewellery found in nearby family tombs show a softer side of these enigmatic Bronze Age people. All the artefacts from the site were taken to Athens and many are now on display in the National Archaeological Museum *(see pages 132–5)*.

The main citadel of Mycenae, naturally defended on two sides by ravines and supplied securely with water by a cistern-spring at the far eastern end of the precinct, accessed by a steep stairway, is enclosed by an irregularly shaped circuit of walls dating from about 1250 BC. Their masonry – huge rough-hewn, polygonal blocks joined very precisely without use of mortar – was dubbed "Cyclopean" by later Greeks who couldn't credit mere mortals with this construction and attributed it to the mythical one-eyed giants.

Apart from a discrete postern gate near the cistern, the only entrance to the fortified town is through the **Lion Gate**, so called after the sculpted pair of lions on the lintel, the earliest known monumental sculpture in Europe. These were apparently the insignia of the ill-starred Atreid dynasty, whose misadventures were enshrined for posterity in the trilogy of tragedies by the Classical playwright Aeschylus. The heights of the citadel are taken up by the presumed palace, with rooms identified as a throne room, *megaron* (reception hall) and apartments.

Only Mycenaean royalty dwelt inside the fortified citadel: commoners lived unprotected outside, to the west, where merchants' houses have been revealed next to the modern access road. More impressive, however, are three examples of the Late Bronze Age *tholos* (domed tomb shaped like a beehive), the best and most intact of these being the Treasury of Atreus, otherwise known as the Tomb of Agamemnon, built in about 1300 BC and entered via a 15-metre *dromos* or passageway. The masonry – again constructed without the use of mortar – is superb, as is the reverberating echo inside. The actual funerary chamber is off to one side.

The beehive-shaped Treasury of Atreus is made of 33 superimposed rings of ashlar (hewn stone blocks), each ring carefully positioned so as to slightly project beyond the edge of the one above it.

Two more ancient cities

Some 14km (9 miles) south of Mycenae (including the 2km/1 mile from the main road to modern Mykínes village and the ancient

BELOW: the roof of the Treasury of Atreus, a huge beehive-shaped chamber.

The ancient theatre of Argos was built during the 3rd century BC and, as a festival venue, was used for musical and theatrical contests, and later for hunts and gladiator fights following renovation during the Roman period. At a later stage, a pool was even built on the orchestra to accommodate naval fights and aquatic games.

site) stands **Árgos**, claimed to be the longest continuously inhabited town in Greece (about 5,000 years), and the one that has given the peninsula its name.

Despite this illustrious history, there's little here today to delay the visitor other than a good **archaeological museum** in the centre (open Tues–Sun 8.30am–3pm; admission charge), with both Mycenaean and Roman artefacts, and the remains of **ancient Argos** (open Tues–Sun 8.30am–3pm) about 1km (½ mile) south of town on the road towards Trípoli, which include one of the largest ancient theatres in the Greek world, which held 20,000 spectators in its day.

A different road leads southeast towards Návplio, passing en route the relatively little-visited site of ancient **Tiryns** (open summer daily 8am–6.45pm; winter 8.30am–2.45pm; admission charge). This fortified town offers even more spectacular "Cyclopean" masonry than Mycenae, nearly a kilometre's worth of walls enclosing a small hillock which during the Bronze Age would have been a seaside promentory; the coast has since receded by several kilometres.

BELOW: the traffic-free old town, Návplio.

Although parts of the Tiryns remains are off-limits, so as not to disrupt ongoing excavations, what is visible more than justifies a stop – in particular the entrance ramp, wide enough to admit chariots but ingeniously designed so that any hostile visitors were compelled to expose their unshielded right side to defenders perched above. The gateway is nearly as spectacular as that at Mycenae, though missing its lintel stone and any relief above it.

A famous theatre

Some 22km (14 miles) east of Návplio lies another, later ancient site also renowned for its acoustics. The extraordinarily well preserved **Theatre of Epidauros** ⓭ (Epídavros; open daily 8am–7pm, winter closes 5pm; admission charge) was built in the late-4th century BC and could accommodate an audience of 12,000 people. It has startling acoustics: you may not be able to hear the proverbial pin drop in the centre of the stage while you are sitting in an upper row of the 54 tiers of seats, but you can certainly hear whispered speech. Performances are staged here during summer on Friday and Saturday nights, as part of the Hellenic Festival.

The theatre was part of a much larger Sanctuary of Asklepeion, one of the most important centres of healing in ancient Greece. There were several such *asklepeia* in the Greek world, all dedicated to Asklepios, the son of Apollo and god of healing, and generally sited next to natural springs. The Epidauros sanctuary endured for several centuries until being sacked and razed in 86 BC by the forces of the Roman consul Sulla; thus only foundations of the various buildings, scattered across the wooded site, remain.

Besides being an early "health spa", Epidaurus hosted a quadrennial festival, including drama in the theatre and games in the gymnasium, baths and stadium whose traces have been identified.

The curative functions of the site are most evident in the Abaton, where patients would sleep to await a dream-visit by the demigod Asklepios in the form of a serpent (at some monasteries in modern Greece the unwell still sleep in cots around the central church, hoping for saintly intervention). The nearby round *tholos*, the most distinctive structure here, has a labyrinthine ground-plan which may, it is thought, originally have had a snake-pit at the centre. The priests of Asklepios possibly bred and released harmless snakes to "visit" patients in a more corporeal form than they might have imagined.

Návplio

The port town of **Návplio** ⓮ (alias Nauplia or Návplion) makes the perfect base for touring the Argolid. Unlike most other Greek resorts, it is busy all year round, especially at weekends when Athenians flock here, and accordingly hotel rates are little different from those in the capital.

Set in the northern lee of a striking promontory on the south coast of the Argolid, Návplio has been a strategic point for centuries, sporting no less than three castles dating from Byzantine and Venetian times on the towering rock of Palamídi, a fourth on Akronavplía ridge, plus a fifth on an offshore islet. The old town up against the rock preserves much of its Venetian and Ottoman heritage, and served as the capital of the newly independent state from 1829 until 1834, with King Otho in residence for the last two years.

The hub of the architecturally protected old town is the vast, marble-paved Platía Syntágmatos (Constitution Square), flanked on its west side by a former Venetian building which is now the **archaeological museum** (open Tues–Sun

Map on pages 174–5

Turkish-style balconies are characteristic features of Old Návplio.

BELOW: the Palamídi, the fortified complex built by the Venetians above Návplio.

Venetian-style shutters on an old Návplio house.

8.30am–3pm; admission charge). Within walking distance are three former mosques: one, at the south-east corner of the *platía*, works sporadically as a cinema; another nearby sheltered the country's first parliament; while the third, on Odós Plapoutá, is now the cathedral but was originally built as a Venetian Catholic church.

In the same neighbourhood are two Ottoman fountains with calligraphic inscriptions: one on the south wall of the theatre-mosque, the other opposite the steps of Ágios Spyrídon church, the spot where Ioannis Kapodistrias, the first president of independent Greece, was assassinated in October 1831. The inscription on one of the fountains refers to the Shia martyrs of the battle of Kerbala who supposedly died of thirst, indicating that a Bektashi – an offshoot of Shi'ism, and the "house religion" of the janissaries – probably commissioned it.

There are also a few minor museums in the grid of part-pedestrianised streets to seaward of the above monuments – in particular the **Peloponnesian Folklore Foundation Museum** (daily except Tues 9am–3pm, closed Feb; admission charge) on Vasiléos Alexándrou. However, in truth the main pleasure of Návplio is strolling about, absorbing the atmosphere imparted by the handsome old buildings with their pastel paint-jobs and Venetian-style slatted shutters.

Of a summer evening, the seaside promenade flanked by smart cafés is the main venue for a *vólta*, though the port is quiet now, no longer handling any scheduled passenger traffic, only the odd cruise ship or freighter being loaded with citrus.

BELOW: the fortified island of Boúrtzi, off Návplio.

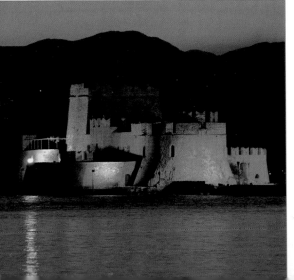

Venetian fortifications

Offshore is the tiny island of **Boúrtzi**, fortified in 1473 by the Venetians, who also equipped it with a chain that could be stretched across the strait to halt shipping during times of war.

By contrast, the biggest fortress complex is the **Palamídi** overhead, comprising three self-contained castles built by the Venetians from 1711 to 1715. They were a key focus of the Greek War of Independence, being taken by Kolokotroni after a year's siege, and later serving as harsh prisons. Very steep steps, or for the lazy a road, lead up to them, and their intricacy and excellent state of repair well repay a visit.

The Its Kale (Turkish for "Inner Citadel") of Akronafplía is in comparison of limited interest, though the lowest bastions now enclose the local Xenia Hotel.

For a seaside resort, Návplio has few beaches immediately to hand, but from either the Palamídi or Akronafplía you can easily spy, to the south, the long expanse of **Karathónas** beach less than 3km (2 miles) distant. ❑

RESTAURANTS & BARS

Restaurants

Ta Fanaria

Staïkopoulou 13, Návplio
Tel: 27520 27 141
Open L and D daily
Cash only. €€

This long-running favourite, a reliable option in an otherwise tourist-trap area, offers outdoor seating under a vine-shrouded pergola; indoor seating is limited and for winter only. Really best for lunch when *magireftá* such as *moussakás* and *soutzoukákia* emerge fresh from the oven. Good bulk *retsína*, unusually from Mégara, on offer.

To Koutouki tou Parelthon

Profítis Ilías 12, east of the Árgos-bound road, Návplio
Tel: 27520 29 930
Open L and D daily
Cash only. €

If you're willing to forego the charms of the old town in favour of a humdrum modern setting, you'll do well to head for this friendly *ouzéri* in an attractive old stone house with a courtyard. It serves unfussy *mezédes*, superbly executed, to a local clientele.

Leonidas

Lygourió village centre
Tel: 27530 22 115
Open L and D daily
Major credit cards. €€

This is the time-honoured (since 1953) place to have supper after a summer performance at the Epidaurus theatre, just 4km (2 miles) away. You'll need to book on such evenings to join the ranks of famous patrons – actors and politicans – whose photos adorn the walls. The fare is hearty country Greek: all the usual grills and *magireftá*. Garden seating as well.

Omorfo Tavernaki

Vassilísis Ólgas 16, Návplio
Tel: 27520 25944
Open L and D daily; summer weekends D only
Cash only. €€

Flanking one of the old town's narrower lanes is this taverna installed in a neoclassical building. Specialities include *kolokotroneïko* (pork in wine sauce), *bekrí mezé* (pork morsels in red sauce), and *spetzofáï* (sausage and pepper stew), plus the more usual grills and seafood. Reliable quality and speedy service are big pluses, with tables both inside and on the lane.

Savouras

Leofóros Bouboulínas 79, Návplio
Tel: 27520 27 704
Open daily noon–11pm
Major credit cards. €€€

This *psarotavérna* (fish restaurant) has operated on the palm-lined waterfront for over 20 years. Fresh fish featuring today's catch attracts Greeks as well as tourists. Specialities include *mýdia saganáki* (mussels cooked with cheese in tomato sauce). On summer weekends, it can get crowded. Booking recommended.

Cafés/Bars

Stathmos

Old railway station, Návplio
Open daily 9am–midnight
Cash only. €

Drinks, ice-cream and snacks in or outside the old station, with its elaborate wooden trim. Popular with high-school kids in the holidays, but otherwise a quiet haven away from the touristy areas.

Noufara

Sýntagma Square, Návplio
Open daily 9am–midnight
Cash only. €

Established on the main square 25 years ago, Noufara's outside tables are a great place for people watching. Light Greek and Italian dishes and especially good coffee.

PRICE CATEGORIES

Prices are based on an average meal per person, including house wine:
€ = under €15
€€ = €15–25
€€€ = €25–40
€€€€ = over €40
Key: B = breakfast, L = lunch, D = dinner

RIGHT: aubergine *mousaká* with sheep's cheese.

DELPHI

The ancient Greeks regarded this holy site as the centre of the world, and utterances made by the oracle here were followed as divine truths. Quite apart from its spiritual resonance, Delphi is in a stunning location on the slopes of Mt Parnassós, and makes an understandably popular trip from Athens

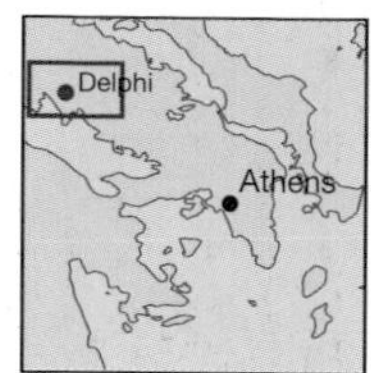

The ancient site of **Delphi**, the spiritual centre of the classical world, is by far the most popular choice for an excursion from Athens (178km/111 miles). Its stunning location overlooking valleys and fertile olive groves makes for an extremely pleasant day out.

The journey can be tiring, however, and organised trips allow at most two hours for a visit to both the site and the museum. Overnight accommodation can be arranged in the nearby village of Delphi (Delfí).

It is claimed that, in antiquity, Delphi was the "navel" of the world, the spot where two eagles released by Zeus at opposite ends of the earth chose to meet. Zeus's son Apollo is given credit for having founded the sanctuary which bears his name, although recent evidence implies that the site might have had earlier inhabitants, perhaps from Crete, around the 8th century BC. Very few early sources give a complete picture of Delphi during its heyday, for the simple reason that the oracle was so famous throughout Greece that little documentation was necessary. People travelled from all over the Greek-speaking world for consultations.

Interpretations of Apollo's prophecies – delivered through the medium of an old woman called the Pythia – were notoriously inaccurate but Delphi became rich and powerful on the back of their reputation. Despite a fair number of muddled predictions Strabo was moved to write: "Of all oracles in the world [Delphi] had the reputation of being the most truthful."

The road to Delphi

Setting off from Athens, the present-day route leads first to the ancient city of **Thebes**. In Archaic and Classical times this was the largest city-state in the region of Boeotia.

LEFT: the *tholos* at the sanctuary of Athena Pronaea, Delphi.
BELOW: Ósios Loukás.

Birds on a mosaic floor in the Delphi museum.

Mythologically speaking, it was the birthplace of Dionysios, the seat of King Creon (Heracles' father-in-law) and the hometown of Oedipus, with his unfortunate family problems. Historically, it was a rival and often an enemy of Athens (especially as an ally of Sparta in the Peloponnesian Wars) and home of the poet Pindar. Thebes (Thíva) is now a fitful modern town surrounded by gypsy encampments.

Beyond the workaday town of **Livadiá** (noted for its clocktower presented by Lord Elgin) the road west begins to climb into the foothills of Mt Parnassós. The precise spot where Oedipus is said to have inadvertently killed his father is often pointed out by tour guides. Whether this is the site of an early regicide which gave rise to the Oedipus myth remains anyone's guess, but certainly it is an isolated, even moody view of the valley, perfectly suited for a tragedy.

The left turn for Dístomo village and the **Monastery of Ósios Loukás** ⓯, dedicated to a local 10th-century ascetic named Luke, is clearly marked. The monastery (open May–mid-Sep 8am–2pm, 4–7pm; otherwise 8am–5pm; entrance charge) commands a wonderful view over a secluded valley in the shadow of Mt Elikónas. The smaller chapel of the Virgin (on the left) dates from the 10th century; the 11th-century *katholikón* or main church contains superb mosaics, survivors of a1659 earthquake. The best and easiest to view, including a Resurrection and Washing of the Apostles' Feet, are in the narthex.

The village of **Aráhova** clings to the toes of Parnassós. Formerly a bastion of pastoral culture, it has now woken up to a new life as a ski resort, with Athenian-weekender chalets sprouting rapidly on the outskirts. Tourist souvenirs, including

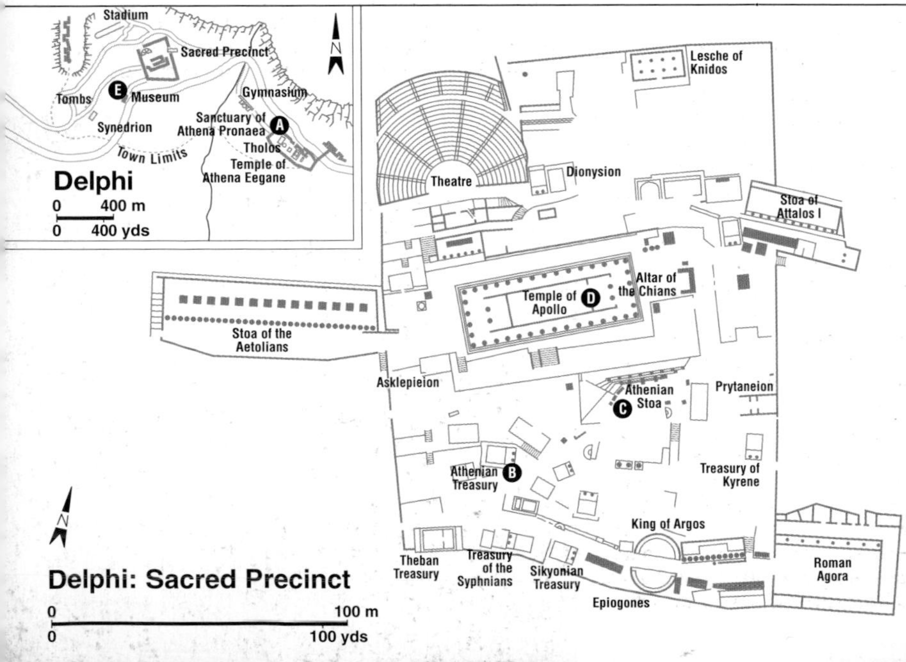

Delphi

Stadium
Sacred Precinct
Tombs
E Museum
Gymnasium
Synedrion
Sanctuary of Athena Pronaea A
Town Limits
Tholos
Temple of Athena Eegane
N
0 400 m
0 400 yds

Delphi: Sacred Precinct

Lesche of Knidos
Theatre
Dionysion
Stoa of Attalos I
Altar of the Chians
Temple of Apollo D
Stoa of the Aetolians
Asklepieion
Athenian Stoa C
Prytaneion
Athenian Treasury B
Treasury of Kyrene
King of Argos
Theban Treasury
Treasury of the Syphnians
Sikyonian Treasury
Epiogones
Roman Agora
N
0 100 m
0 100 yds

various types of noodles and the almost-purple wine particular to the area, are pitched more at Greeks than foreigners.

The ancient site of **Delphi** ⓰ is 11 km (7 miles) further along, built on terraces at the base of sheer cliffs, the whole poised to topple over into the Plístos Gorge. Since its excavation by the French towards the end of the 19th century, Delphi has ranked as the most popular, memorable ruin on the mainland, attended as well by gliding birds of prey launching themselves from the palisades. A visit involves steep climbs rewarded by ever-changing viewpoints and new monumental treasures.

Exploring the site

The first locale, on the south side of the road, is the so-called **Marmaria** (open daily same hours as main site; free), comprising a gymnasium (complete with a straight track and a round bath) and the **sanctuary of Athena Pronaea** Ⓐ. Pronaea means "guardian of the temple" and ancient visitors passed first through this shrine. The original 7th-century BC temple was destroyed by the Persians, and replaced by the present complex. The most interesting structure here is the circular, 4th-century *tholos*, whose purpose remains unknown.

On the north side of the road gushes the **Castalian Spring** (open daily; free). Parts of the older, rectangular fountain right next to the road date to the 6th century BC, although thin marble slabs on the floor are Hellenistic or early Roman. All pilgrims had to perform ritual ablutions here.

The main sacred precinct at Delphi is the **Sanctuary of Apollo,** above the road past the Castalian Spring (open daily 7.30am–7.30pm; entrance charge). Many of the ruins exposed today date from Roman times, but just as many monuments, including the stadium and main temple, are earlier. For the casual visitor, highlights include the Athenian Treasury, the Athenian stoa and the Temple of Apollo.

The Doric-order **Athenian Treasury** Ⓑ (late 6th- or early 5th-century BC) was pieced together by French archaeologists in 1904–6, using the inscriptions covering its surface as a guide. The late-6th-century **Athenian Stoa** Ⓒ, today retaining three complete Ionic columns before a polygonal wall, was a roofed area protecting souvenirs from various Athenian naval victories, including the defeat of the Persians at Salamis in 480 BC. An inscription reads: "The Athenians have dedicated this portico with the arms and bow ornaments taken from their enemies at sea."

The **Temple of Apollo** Ⓓ just above the Athenian Stoa is the third confirmed temple to have stood here, and there are literary rumours of three even earlier ones; two 7th- and 6th-century predecessors were done for by fire and earthquake respectively. What you see dates from 369–329 BC, and is impressive

Maps: Area 174 Plan 222

The stadium, a long narrow oval north of the sanctuary, is well worth the steep walk to reach it. It retains 12 rows of seats on the north side and six on the south. You will easily find the starting and finishing lines, the limestone starting blocks complete with grooves for the runners' toes.

BELOW: the 5th-century Charioteer in the Delphi museum.

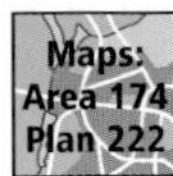

enough, measuring 66 by 26 metres (215 x 85 ft): six columns were re-erected by the French.

The god Apollo was associated, among other things, with prophecy, his main function here. His oracle resided under the temple flooring in the *adyton* chamber, where a chasm in the earth belched forth noxious and possibly mind-altering vapours. It was here that a petitioner's question would be relayed to the god Apollo by a priestess known as the Pythia, who would squat over a tripod, to the modern eye a rectangular rock approximately one metre long with three primary and a few secondary holes chiselled in it. She could hear Apollo's answer only when she was in a trance, induced, conveniently enough, by residing in the vapour-filled *adyton*.

The small 4th-century theatre above the temple, thoroughly restored during the Roman era, seats 5,000 people and has marvellous acoustics.

Her ravings could be understood only by the sanctuary's priests, who interpreted them for the supplicant – often ambiguously – for a suitable fee. One of the oracle's more memorable pronouncements was that Oedipus would kill his father and marry his mother, thereby giving the world its most tragic hero and Freud his most famous complex.

Delphi's **museum** Ⓔ (open Tues–Sun 7.30am–7.30pm, Mon noon–6.30pm; entrance charge), renovated in time for Olympics and now splendid, contains finds from the ancient city, the sanctuaries and the general area of Phocis. Among the collection of fine 6th- and 5th-century sculptures, the two most outstanding are the winged Sphinx of the Naxians (565 BC), and the Charioteer, a life-size, lifelike bronze (note the immaculate toenails) made in 475 BC. Look out also for two huge 6th-century *kouroi*, the votive, life-sized bull made from hammered silver sheets, and the Siphian frieze with scenes from the Trojan War and a battle between the gods and the titans.

The Gulf of Corinth

Below Delphi and its namesake modern, touristic village, a vast plain of olive trees stretches south towards the Gulf of Corinth. Literally gritty **Itéa** was once the ancient port of Delphi and still ships out the odd cargo of purple-red bauxite, strip-mined from the flanks of Mt Gióna to the west. But the real star of this often bleak coast is little **Galaxídi**. With its Venetian-influenced mansions, the place seems closer in style to Koróni or Návpaktos further along the coast, than the rough-hewn village houses of Fokída.

Local shipowners prospered during the 18th and 19th centuries when Galaxídi was, amazingly, the fourth-busiest harbour in Greece – thus the elaborate mansions. But captains refused to convert to steam after the 1890s, and the place sank into obscurity until being rediscovered by wealthy Athenians looking for a pleasant weekend bolt-hole. Foreign tourists are thus few, but there are plenty of comfortable lodgings and decent restaurants along the south harbour quay. ❑

BELOW: night descends over the Temple of Apollo.

RESTAURANTS

Albatross
On the ridge street between the two churches, Galaxídi
No phone
Open D daily
Cash only. €
The cheapest – and many say the best – taverna in town offers well-executed *magireftá* from a brief daily-changing menu. This might include octopus, spinach/cheese pie, pale *taramosaláta* or *samári* (pancetta in savoury sauce). Limited quantities are cooked, and no reservations taken, so arrive early to avoid disappointment. Admire the illuminated church belfries from the outdoor tables.

PRICE CATEGORIES

Prices are based on an average meal per person, including house wine:
€ = under €15
€€ = €15–25
€€€ = €25–40
€€€€ = over €40
Key: B = breakfast, L = lunch, D = dinner

Barko Maritsa
Far northeast end of Iánthi quay, Galaxidi
Tel: 22650 41 059
Open L& D daily (weekends only in low season)
Major credit cards. €€
One of the most durable tavernas on the main (southeasterly) harbour occupies a tastefully decorated old house, almost a museum in itself. The menu features savoury, non-greasy *pítes* (turnovers) and an approximation of seafood risotto that is the best you'll get in provincial Greece. Ordering bulk wine keeps bills within the indicated price category.

To Maïstrali
One block inland from Iánthi quay, Galaxídi
No phone
Open L and D daily
Cash only. €
An inexpensive seafood *ouzerí* in an atmospheric alley; the fare is fried but fresh, and the experience is apt to be free of the rip-offs which sometimes attend the more prominent places on the water.

Iy Skala
Up stair-street opposite Hotel Sivylla, modern Delfí
No phone
Cash only. €–€€
Tavernas in this rather touristy village are generally undistinguished; this purveys honest fare, mostly *magireftá*, at honest prices.

Panagiota
Near Ágios Geórgios church, Aráhova
Tel: 22670 32 735
Open L and D daily Oct–Apr, weekends only Jul–Sep, closed May–Jul
Cash only. €€
This is the place to sample local specialities in a white-tablecloth environment, away from the commercialisation of the main through road. Dishes include chicken soup, stewed lamb, and (appropriately for a pastoral community) cheese-based recipes.

BELOW: *tzatziki.*

TRANSPORT

GETTING THERE AND GETTING AROUND

GETTING THERE

By Air

Olympic Airlines is the national carrier of Greece, though perennnially threatened with closure due to its serious financial troubles. It operates flights to Athens from London (Heathrow and Gatwick), Manchester, New York and Toronto. From the UK, **British Airways** flies to Athens from London Heathrow and London Gatwick; **Air Scotland** from Glasgow; and **easyJet** from Luton and London Gatwick. From Ireland, **Malev Airlines** offers direct flights from Dublin from March to October.

From North America, **Delta** is the only other carrier flying directly to Athens, from both New York and Atlanta. Otherwise you'll arrive via a European hub on such airlines as Lufthansa (www.lufthansa.com), KLM (www.klm.com), British Airways (www.ba.com) or Alitalia (www.alitalia.com). There are no direct flights from Australia or New Zealand to Athens; the most likely advantageous providers of multi-stop flights include Singapore Airlines (www.singaporeair.com), Gulf Air (www.gulfairco.com), Emirates (www.emirates.com), Qantas (www.qantas.com) and Air New Zealand (www.airnewzealand.co.nz).

The Airport

Elefthérios Venizélos airport, opened in 2001, lies 27km (18 miles) from Sýntagma Square in the heart of Athens; it is claimed to be the second largest in the world by area, if not (yet) by air traffic. Its size means you should adhere more or less to suggested check-in times and intervals between flights, otherwise missed connections are very likely. The airport has Schengen (no border controls for arrivals from 15 European countries) and non-Schengen zones, and domestic arrivals/departures tend to be towards the northeast end of the complex, but otherwise it's not useful to generalise.

The Departures concourse has a respectable number of shops, including two bookstores/newsagents, two bank ATMs, a music shop and assorted fashion outlets, but is divided into two zones – one for holders of boarding passes only. There are a number of overpriced food and drink outlets on the general concourse, with a deficient amount of seating at some; the canny will notice that meal prices are noticeably lower (though the range of choice is smaller) in the lower-tax, passenger-only areas.

At Arrivals level there is a post office, pharmacy, another music shop, more bank ATMs, and car hire booths (including all the multinational chains) – but no left-luggage facility owing to security considerations. The two levels are linked by escalators or several somewhat inconspicuous elevators/lifts.

DIRECT FLIGHTS

Olympic Airlines
Tel: 801 11 44 444 (Greece)
Tel: 0870 606 0460 (UK)
Tel: 800 223 1226 (US)
www.olympicairlines.com

British Airways
Tel: 801 11 56 000 (Greece)
Tel: 0870 850 9850 (UK)
Tel: 1-800-AIRWAYS (US)
www.ba.com

Air Scotland
Tel: 0141 222 2363 (UK)
www.air-scotland.com

easyJet
Tel: 210 35 30 300 (Greece)
Tel: 0905 821 0905 (UK)
www.easyjet.com

Malev Airlines
Tel: 210 32 41 116 (Greece)
Tel: 01 844 4303 (Ireland)
www.malev.com

Delta
Tel: 80044 12 9506 (Greece)
Tel: 0845 600 0950 (UK)
Tel: 800 221 1212 (US)
www.delta.com

By Car and Ferry

The overland route to Greece from western Europe has long been problematic because of difficulties transiting the former Yugoslavian countries. However you can drive to the Italian ports of Venice, Ancona, Brindisi or Bari and take an overnight ferry to Igoumenítsa or Pátra on the Greek mainland, the latter just a three-hour motorway drive to Athens.

The following companies currently offer a trans-Adriatic service between Italy and Greece:

Agoudimos Lines
www.agoudimos-lines.com
ANEK
www.anek.gr
Fragline
www.fragline.gr
Maritime Way
www.maritimeway.com
Minoan Lines
www.minoan.gr
Superfast
www.superfast.com
Ventouris
www.ventouris.gr.

Arrival

On arrival in Greece, cars with EU number plates are no longer stamped in but, assuming that road tax remains valid for that period, and that all registration and insurance papers are also current and with the vehicle, have just six months free circulation in the country before they have to be officially exported – or re-imported. Keep your ferry ticket in the vehicle, as this will be considered sufficient proof of the car's entry date if demanded by police at traffic controls or harbour authorities upon departures. Stiff fines, up to and including impounding of the vehicle pending payment, are levied against violators.

The official importation procedure is unnecessarily burdensome, with Greece being in violation of EU directives by charging up to 200 percent of the assessed value of the car in import duties, but so far recourse to the European Court in Strasbourg by litigants – and a succession of rulings against the Greek state – has not yet secured an adjustment of attitude.

Rules of the Road

As in most countries, seat-belt use in the front seats is mandatory. The speed limit in built-up areas is 50km/h (31mph), on the open road 80 or 90km/h (50 or 56mph) depending on local posting, and on motorways (such as the Attikí Odós) 100 or 120km/h (62 or 75mph), again depending on signage.

Speed limits, other provisions of the Greek highway code and plain common sense are widely ignored, thus it's hardly surprising to learn that Greece has one of the highest accident rates in the EU. Uninsured, unlicensed, underage and drunk drivers are all potential hazards you might encounter (especially on motorbikes and/or weekend nights), despite police crackdowns on same.

If you are caught committing a moving or parking violation, you do not pay the officer but have a certain number of working days to do so at a dedicated municipal department, after which evidence of payment must be forwarded to the police precinct that issued the ticket. It's illegal to leave the scene of an accident involving another vehicle – or to move either vehicle before police officers arrive on the scene. They will take down all details of the incident, with driver statements, and give a copy to all registered vehicle owners to be used for insurance purposes (or forward a copy to the rental company if your car is hired).

By Rail

This method is also not popular because of disrupted services through the former Yugoslavia; in any case, it is not possible to buy a return fare from the UK or Ireland to Greece. Rail services from western European capitals can link with the ferries at Ancona or Brindisi for onward sailing to Pátra and rail transfer to Athens. It only really makes sense to arrive by train if you're on a longer tour of many European countries, and have a rail pass. In the UK, contact **Rail Europe**, tel: 0870 584 8848, www.raileurope.co.uk, for discounted youth rail fares and InterRail passes.

GETTING AROUND

From/to the Airport

Public transport links are provided by express bus lines (all prefixed "X") to and from Sýntagma Square, Kifisiá and the port of Piraeus around the clock, as well as (more expensively) by the metro and taxis.

In the Arrivals hall, there are helpfully placed plasma screens profiling the comings and goings of all the numbered X express buses (Nos. 92–97), with times of the next departure. They also track the unnumbered ones to Lávrio and Rafína.

Bus line X95 (24 hours) will take you directly from just outside arrivals to Sýntagma Square in

USEFUL NUMBERS

Athens Airport
Tel: 210 35 30 000
OASA (Athens Public Transport)
Tel: 185
OSE (Hellenic Railways)
Tel: 1110
Larissa Station
Tel: 210 52 97 777
Peloponnisou Station
Tel: 210 51 31 601
ELPA breakdown service
Tel: 10400
Port of Piraeus
Tel: 210 42 26 000–4
or 210 41 47 800

just over an hour if traffic is light (it can take almost two hours in heavy traffic). Departures are every quarter-hour during the day, half-hourly between 11pm and 6am. At peak traffic times, and with light luggage, you might consider using the X94 bus which stops at the Ethnikí Ámyna metro station and continuing your journey into town from there. This usually works out quicker and cheaper than using the infrequent (half-hourly) light-rail/metro combination which has its own inconspicuous airport station next to the Hotel Sofitel.

If you're heading out straight to the islands, or a beach suburb, it makes most sense to use the X96 express bus, which links the airport up to three times hourly with Karaïskáki Square in Piraeus via Vári, Voúla, Glyfáda and Paleó Fáliro. The X92 line provides service all the way to Platía Platánou in Kifisiá, a somewhat long walk from our accommodation recommendations in Kefalári district. There is also an unnumbered direct service between the airport and the ferry port of Rafína 12km (7 miles) away, useful if you plan to visit some of the Cyclades islands before or after a stay in the city.

Fares

The fare for all express buses is €3.20 and the ticket is only valid for a single journey to or from town, without using the metro part-way. Buy your ticket at the kiosk outside the Arrivals hall and validate it on the appropriate machine as you board the bus – checks for fare-dodging by plain-clothes inspectors are frequent. The light-rail/metro combined ticket (you don't have to change cars, as ones specially adapted for both systems make the trip) costs €6, or €5 per person for groups of 2 or more.

A taxi will take just about the same time as the X95 bus and will cost roughly €26 from the airport to Sýntagma Square. They will also follow the the same route as the X96 bus to Piraeus and charge not more than €30, unless you happen to be unlucky enough to be caught in a late-afternoon traffic jam along the coast road as half of Athens returns home from the beaches. These figures should include the typical airport surcharge of €3 and per-boot-luggage charge of 50c.

By Metro

The 2001-inaugurated metro (officially Attikó Métro) is clean, fast and glitch-free, and you will find it is the best way to travel around Athens. The old, pre-2001 subway (now Line 1 of the joint system), called the ISAP after the entity which administers it, runs from Piraeus to Kifisiá. Attikó Métro's Line 2 runs between Ágios Dimítrios and Ágios Andónios. Line 3 runs between Monastiráki and Doukísis Plakendías, but two special cars per hour, clearly marked, continue beyond to the airport on the light-rail line of the suburban railway system or Proastiakós (otherwise of limited use to most visitors). None of the metro system operates between midnight and 5.30am. Extensions to the lines – and the opening of the currently half-built stations at Agía Paraskeví and Nomismatokopío – are likely within the lifetime of this guide.

A single ticket costs 80c and is valid for a single one-way journey on the metro only. For single one-way journeys on Line 1 only, tickets are 70c. There's also a 90-minute ticket, valid also for a transfer to/from buses or trams, for €1. A 24-hour ticket valid for all means of transport – buses, tram, metro – costs €3, while a week pass – good for 168 hours from the minute of validation – is outstanding value at €10. Tickets are purchased at metro stations, either from coin-op machines or an attended window.

Fines for fare-dodging are a stiff 60 times the amount of the single fare evaded. Rules are complicated and changeable, so unwitting violations occur. The main trip-ups for newcomers are attempting to switch from the airport bus to the metro once in town (not allowed) or forgetting to validate tickets. So do be careful: omitting to pay the €3.20 fare on the airport express bus could cost you €192!

INTERNAL FLIGHTS

Air travel within Greece, to and from Athens, is provided by the national carrier and the private airline Aegean:

Olympic Airlines
Tel: 801 11 44 444
www.olympicairlines.com

Aegean Airlines
Tel: 210 35 30 101
www.aegeanair.com

City Buses

An extensive bus network, run by OASA, connects many places that the metro doesn't reach. Regular city buses run from 5am–11.45pm roughly every 20 minutes per route. They can be crowded, so for short journeys it may be more comfortable to walk or get a taxi. Tickets (60c) can be purchased individually or in bundles of 10 from news kiosks and special booths at bus-route start-points. Most buses have been upgraded to air-conditioned models with digital destination placards up front, a few of the newest arrivals even being disabled-compatible.

Augmenting these blue-and-white buses are electric trolley buses, formerly all dull yellow but now likely to be emblazoned with colourful adverts. Fares and tickets are the same for these.

As a general guide, bus numbers beginning with 0 operate in central Athens; those beginning with 1 operate in the southern coastal suburbs as far as Vougliaméni; 2 to the south-central suburbs; 3 and 4 to southeastern and central Attica; 5 to Kifisiá and the northern suburbs; 6 and 7 to the northwest; 8 westwards towards Daphni; 9 towards Piraeus. At every bus stop there will be a helpful placard, showing the numbered routes serving it, frequencies and the entire stop sequence (in Greek only).

The Tramway

The 2004-inaugurated tramway (tickets 80c) is a fun way to get from the centre to the beach suburbs. The track system forms a schematic "T", with the split near Paleó Fáliro, leaving effectively three routes: #1, from Sýntagma to the Stádio Irínis ke Filías in Néo Fáliro; #2, from Sýntagma to Glyfáda; and #3, from Glyfáda to Néo Fáliro. The tram runs until 1am Sunday to Thursday, and (funding permitting) all night on Friday and Saturday.

Taxis

Taxis are numerous and affordable (they are painted yellow and have an illuminated "TAXI" sign atop the vehicle). Meters are to be set at the start of each journey (don't board a taxi if the meter isn't visible, and set to zero). A "1" by the fare display indicates regular fare, "2" indicates the rate between midnight and 5am. Prices are posted by the taxi rank at the airport, and basic charges also appear on a laminated sheet mounted on the dashboard. Fare-fiddling with foreigners is not unknown – often using sophisticated electronic devices to subtly speed up the digital meter – so the following sample "1" charges are useful: a short hop across the centre, €3–6; centre to Piraeus, €12. Trips to or from air/seaports have a surcharge, and luggage in the boot gets charged 50c each. The flag falls at €1.20, and phoning for a taxi also adds about €1.20 to the total.

Drivers are not obliged to take you anywhere you ask – extra long or short distances tend to be unpopular. Nor is there any certification requirement akin to The Knowledge of London cabbies; if you're going somewhere obscure, expect to direct the driver, with your street atlas in hand.

Shared Taxis

A particular Athenian institution is the shared taxi, especially at rush hours when free cabs are scarce. Drivers will pick up a sequence of fares all headed in vaguely the same direction – this explains would-be passengers lined up and shouting their destination at kerb-crawling taxi drivers. If he (very rarely she) decides you're suitable, they'll stop and take you in (up to a maximum of four passengers per car, three in the back). The catch is that everyone pays as if they were riding alone, so you must view and memorise the meter reading on boarding, and pay the diffence wherever you alight (bearing in mind the €1.20 minimum).

Some Athens taxi services:
Athina 1, tel: 1203
Dimitra, tel: 210 55 46 993
Express, tel: 210 99 34 812
Ikaros, tel: 210 51 52 800
Kosmos, tel: 18300

Driving

(see also Rules of the Road, page 227)

Car Hire/Rental

Athens is a very congested city with a critical (and expensive) parking situation, as well as tolls (€2.70) on the peripheral Attikí Odós. The main tourist attractions are concentrated in such a small area that it makes little sense to hire a car. If you want to visit some Saronic Gulf islands, it is easier to take the metro to Piraeus, which terminates within walking distance of the appropriate quay – and of course cars are not carried on hydrofoils or catamarans.

CAR HIRE AGENCIES

Autorent, Syngroú 11, 117 43 Athens, tel: 210 92 32 514, www.autorent.gr
Avance, Syngroú 40–42, 117 42 Athens, tel: 210 92 40 107, www.avance.gr
Bazaar, Syngroú 27, 117 43 Athens tel: 210 92 28 768, www.bazaarrac.gr
Budget, Syngroú 8, 117 43 Athens, tel: 210 92 14 771, www.drivebudget.com
Kosmos, Syngroú 9, 117 43 Athens, tel: 210 92 34 695, www.kosmos-carrental.com
Reliable, Syngroú 3, 117 43 Athens, tel: 210 92 49 000
Thrifty, Syngroú 25, 117 43 tel: 210 92 43 304, www. thriftygreece.gr

However, there are a few conventional ferries to Póros and Égina, where a car may be of use, and if you plan to spend a few days touring the Argolid (just across from Póros, with a cheap car-ferry link) or to head for Delphi, a car will definitely be an asset.

Those intending to hire a car should carry an international driver's licence if from the US, Canada or Australia (in these cases national licences alone will not be valid). Alternatively all European Economic Area national driver's licences are accepted, provided that they have been held for one full year and the driver is over 21 years of age (sometimes 23 years for certain agencies). You will also need a credit or debit card to avoid fronting a large cash deposit. Some brochure rates can seem too good to be true because they may not include personal insurance, collision damage waiver (CDW) or VAT at 19 percent.

Most agencies have a waiver deductible of between €400 and €600 – the amount you're responsible for if you smash a vehicle, even with CDW. Given

Greek road conditions and the high accident rate noted above, it is strongly suggested you purchase extra cover (often called Super CDW or Liability Waiver Surcharge) to reduce this risk to zero. Alternatively, there is an English company that specialises in insuring you from waiver deductibles: **Insurance 4 Car Hire** (www.insurance4carhire.com). For an advantageous yearly premium, you're covered for any outrageous charge the hire company may subsequently make on your credit card.

You will find all the major international chains represented in the arrivals concourse of the airport. In central Athens, almost all hire companies, including reputable small local ones, have their offices at the very beginning of Syngroú Avenue in Makrygiánni district, and comparison shopping for quotes a day or so before you need a car can be very rewarding. In our case, quotes for a four-day, small-car rental in May produced per-day rates varying from €27 to €36, with €30–32 being the average.

Ferries, Catamarans, Hydrofoils

Daily services operate to all the Saronic Gulf Islands from contiguous Aktí Tzelépi and Aktí Miaoúli in Piraeus. This is just a 10-minute walk from the end of Metro Line 1, even less from the terminus of the X96 bus from the airport. For details of all services, contact **Piraeus Port Authority**, tel: 210 42 26 000–4 – however English is not guaranteed to be spoken, and you may just get a long, far-from-comprehensive recorded recitation of departures.

If you have internet access, it's better to check at www.hellenicseaways.gr (on which tickets can be booked, to be picked up at the harbour) or ring the operators listed below, which along with Hellenic Seaways control all craft to the Saronic islands.

For an idea of fares, a hydrofoil or catamaran ticket economy class to Ýdra is currently €20 – though slightly more (€21.70); Spétses is a few euros more, Póros a bit less. Égina is the cheapest destination – you can get a ticket on a slow *symvatikó* (conventional) ferry for about €7.

The box below gives more information on ferries, cats and hydrofoils, and includes a rough idea of the timetables and approximate sailing times.

Getting to the Saronic Gulf Islands

All seagoing services to the Saronic Gulf islands, whether conventional ferry, catamaran or hydrofoil, depart from Aktí Tselépi in Piraeus – slower craft from the Posidónos side of Tselépi, faster conveyances from the Miaoúli side, neither more than 10 minutes' walk from the metro station.

There are frequent departures at weekends (Fri–Sun) and far fewer from October to June. Hydrofoils or catamarans are twice as fast, and twice as expensive, as the *symvatiká* or conventional craft. Égina is the most frequently served destination over the longest time range (hourly in season 7am–9.45pm to Piraeus, 6am–9pm from Piraeus). Car ferries on the Piraeus–Égina–Póros–Ydra route run at best once daily, usually at around 7.30am. There is no conventional ferry service between Spétses and Piraeus. Neither are there any hydrofoil/catamaran links between Égina/Angístri and the other Argo-Saronic islands.

At busy times – in particular Sunday afternoon and evening – hydrofoils back to Piraeus often fill quickly so buy a return ticket in Piraeus or see to it immediately upon arrival on your chosen island; many car-drivers have been stranded on Égina in particular until Monday noon owing to inattention on this matter.

Contact details for the various companies currently running departures are as follows. (Hellenic Seaways tickets can be bought on-line, but the "e-ticket" must actually be issued before travel at one of their authorised agencies.)

Hellenic Seaways
(ferries, hydrofoils and Flying Cat to all points)
Tel: 210 41 99 000
www.hellenicseaways.gr

Vasilopoulos Flying Dolphins
(to Égina only)
Tel: 210 210 41 19 500

Agios Nektarios Eginas
(car ferry to Égina only)
Tel: 210 42 25 625

Euroseas (Eurofast catamaran to Póros, Ídhra, Spétses)
Tel: 210 41 32 105

Keravnos (small catamaran to Égina, Angístri)
Tel: 210 41 13 108

Travel times and frequencies

Piraeus–Égina (Égina Town): 12–15 daily ferries, 1hr 30min–2hr; 26-30 hydrofoils daily, 45min.

Piraeus–Angístri: 2-3 daily ferries, 2hr 30min; 4–5 daily catamarans, 60–70min.

Piraeus–Póros: 4–6 daily ferries, 3hr; 7–9 daily hydrofoils or catamarans, 1hr.

Piraeus–Ýdra: 5–7 weekly ferries, 3hr 45min; 10–12 daily hydrofoils or catamarans, 1hr 15min–1hr 30min.

Piraeus–Spétses: 8–10 daily hydrofoils or catamarans, 2hr 30min.

Póros–Ýdra–Spétses: 4–6 daily, 40min–1hr 30min.

ACCOMMODATION

SOME THINGS TO CONSIDER BEFORE YOU BOOK THE ROOM

Choosing a Hotel

The Greek National Tourist Organisation oversees the classification of all hotels in Athens, from De Luxe down to the almost-extinct E class. These ratings are slowly being replaced, against some proprietor resistance, by a star system of five down to zero.

A hotel's rating is determined by the number of rooms it has and the amenities it offers in the common areas, not necessarily the quality of the rooms themselves – a C-class hotel may have rooms just as comfortable as those of a nearby B- or A-class.

Generally, D-class hotels must have en-suite baths; C-class hotels must provide breakfast in a designated area; B-class hotels should have a restaurant and business facilities (conference room, internet access etc); an A-class hotel should have a restaurant and a separate bar, a spa/gym, rooftop or garden pool, and off-street parking. A De Luxe hotel will be essentially a self-contained resort, with a multiplicity of all the aforementioned facilities.

Olympic Refits

In the run-up to the 2004 summer Olympics, scores of aging, uncompetitive Athens hotels received a thorough going-over, emerging (often only just) in time for the Games as stunning boutique hotels adhering to the most contemporary design values – at equally stunning prices, which have stayed high and indeed crept up annually ever since.

That hasn't deterred the clientele, and many of the more successfully executed designer lodgings are enjoying nearly 100 percent occupancy rates, with or without the attentions of tour companies (many of our listings are no strangers to organised groups, but are rarely monopolised by them).

Any high-end Athens hotel worth its salt will now offer rooms with data-ports, marble-trimmed baths sometimes larger than the sleeping area, parquet or wood-laminate floors, and themed colours – a far cry from the jail-like rooms of the 1970s and 1980s, with their mosaic or thin-moquette floors, hospital-green paint-jobs, cheap MDF furniture and closet-like bathrooms. Another trend is the emergence of small local groups of hotels; their advantage is that, if one member of the mini-chain is full, they'll happily refer you to an affiliate which does have a vacancy.

Rates and Booking

In the following listings, arranged by district or mini-chain, we give a realistic price (not necessarily the inflated official one) for a standard double room in high season. Where it is worth paying extra for a superior double or a suite, we've indicated the difference.

You will find that most of the higher-class hotels are present on generic travel websites such as Expedia, and booking with them can yield substantial discounts off the official rates. Especially in peak season – which in Athens means May–June and September, the most pleasant months to visit, as well as mid-summer – many hoteliers levy a 10-percent surcharge for stays of less than three nights. You do not have to take breakfast except in the plusher hotels (B-class and above), where it should be included in the room rate. VAT and municipal tax are also generally included.

Unless otherwise stated, the price guides for the listings below are for a standard double room for one night without breakfast:

€ = under €70
€€ = €70–€120
€€€ = €120–€200
€€€€ = more than €200

TRANSPORT ACCOMMODATION ACTIVITIES A – Z LANGUAGE

SÝNTAGMA

Esperia Palace
Stadíou 22, 105 64 Athens.
Metro Sýntagma.
Tel: 210 32 38 001
Fax: 210 32 38 100.
www.esperiahotel.com.gr
A classic mid-town businessmen's hotel (despite a lack of internet data-ports), the Esperia Palace retains a 1930s air (especially in the marble-trimmed corridors) even after the pre-Olympics refit. The standard rooms are good sized at about 23 sq m (25 sq ft), whilst the suites are a hefty 45 sq m (485 sq ft). Both grades have mock-antique furnishings, French curtains and double glazing (units facing the side street Eduárdou Ló are inherently quieter). Bathrooms vary between tiled and marble-clad, with a preponderance of tubs. There's no pool, gym or roof garden – though the coffee bar/lounge is pleasant, and the ground-floor Athinaios restaurant is sufficiently respected to get walk-in clientele. 184 rooms. €150–250 but look for specials on the website. Major credit cards. **€€€**

Grande Bretagne
Platía Syntágmatos north side.
Metro Sýntagma.
Tel: 210 33 30 000
Fax: 210 32 28 034.
www.luxurycollection.com
Perhaps the most famous hotel in Athens, oozing history and class, the Grande Bretagne is a neoclassical building dating originally from 1846 set directly on Sýntagma Square. A 2002–03 renovation restored every period detail – from the swag curtains to the cutlery and china – to its Belle Époque glory. "De luxe" (as opposed to "standard") doubles at 35–40 sq m (375–430 sq ft) are like junior suites elsewhere, with multicoloured marble trim and two basins in the bathrooms. Common areas are equally sumptuous: there's a seventh-floor pool garden, an eighth-floor restaurant converted to all-year use in 2006, a ground-floor restaurant (GB Corner), a ballroom (popular for wedding receptions) and conference halls, plus a basement spa with a palm court, and large (14 x 5m/45 x 16ft) pool with a water folly, *hamam* and sauna. If the rates – which are never much discounted from €280–400 depending on room grade – preclude staying here, just have a drink in the Alexander Bar with its 18th-century tapestry of Alexander the Great. 262 rooms and suites. Major credit cards. **€€€€**

King George II Palace
Platía Syntágmatos north side.

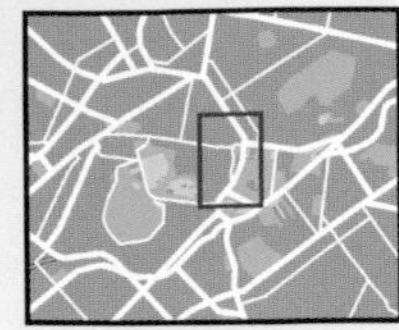

Metro Sýntagma.
Tel: 210 32 22 210
Fax: 210 32 50 504.
www.grecotel.gr
The "other" 19th-century neoclassical hotel on the square was temporarily a royal residence in the 1840s, then a private mansion with added upper storeys before conversion to accommodation. Having come back to life after a 17-year closure, the King George II Palace seems a more intimate, scaled-down version of the Grande Bretagne next door. There are the same swag curtains and antique Second Empire furnishings, plus parquet flooring in the large (30 sq m/320 sq ft) standard rooms, which jars a bit with the flat-screen TVs (internet access through them), recessed adjustable lighting and contemporary sound systems. Bathrooms are palatial, with marble trim, tubs and shower stalls. The hotel is actively pitched at a business clientele, who often book it out for conferences. There's a gym and spa (but no pool) on the lower ground floor, and a seventh-floor restaurant. 110 rooms and suites. €250 (standard double) – €430 (full suite). Major credit cards. **€€€€**

BELOW: the Grande Bretagne spa pool.

PLÁKA

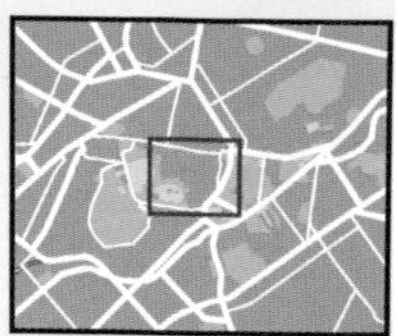

Acropolis House
Kódrou 6–8, 105 57 Athens.
Metro Sýntagma.
Tel: 210 32 22 344
Fax: 210 32 44 143.
www.acropolishouse.gr
This was Athens' first (1963) conversion of a neoclassical mansion to a pension-hotel, and in many respects it shows. The building's status as a listed monument prevents its creaky rooms getting a much-needed facelift, though for many patrons that's part of the charm. Acropolis House offers a mix of units, both en-suite and not, most of them with high ceilings (some of these with murals) and all with TV and phone. The hotel is non-smoking except for a designated area, due to fire hazard. An academic and student-ish clientele swop books and use the communal fridge in the lobby. There's a small breakfast room too. 19 rooms. No credit cards. **€€**

Athos
Patróöu 3, 105 57 Athens.
Metro Sýntagma.
Tel: 210 32 21 977
Fax: 210 32 10 548.
www.athoshotel.gr
Rooms at this low-key designer hotel vary considerably in both outlook and price, though they share a wood, olive and gold décor, tasteful wall art and ADSL dataports. Second- and third-floor units have no views to speak of and are classified as "standard"; fourth- and fifth- floor rooms, with their balconies and Acropolis views, are rated "superior"; plus there's a fifth-floor suite, just under the roof garden. Other common facilities include a pleasant ground-floor breakfast salon and a laundrette. €100 for standard rooms, €130 for superior, suite rate negotiable. Major credit cards. **€€**

PRICE CATEGORIES

Unless otherwise stated, price guides are for a standard double room for one night without breakfast:
€ = under €70
€€ = €70–€120
€€€ = €120–€200
€€€€ = more than €200

Ava Apartments and Suites
Lysikrátous 9–11, 105 58 Athens.
Tel: 210 32 59 000
Fax: 210 32 59 001.
www.avahotel.gr
Athens' most central apartment-hotel, renovated in 2004, is ideal for families or businessmen who need more independence than a de luxe hotel affords. Units vary from a small studio-with-patio on the ground floor to large two-room suites with kitchenette, via one-bedroom apartments, the front ones having Acropolis-view balconies. There's ADSL internet access and cable TV, as well as a communal breakfast room for those who can't be bothered to cook for themselves. €110 (studio); €170 (one-bed apartment); €330 (two-bedroom suite with view). Major credit cards. **€€€€**

Central
Apóllonos 21, 105 57 Athens.
Metro Sýntagma.
Tel: 210 32 34 357
Fax: 210 32 25 244.
www.centralhotel.gr
Italian designer furniture and wood-laminate or risum flooring set the tone for this revamped hotel (part of a small chain with affiliates on Ýdra and Skýros), with warm-toned soft furnishings in the slightly airless, soundproofed, smallish rooms, including a mix of double and twin beds and a few interconnecting family quads. Bathrooms are lit by glass partitions and have marble-clad showers. Some front rooms have balconies, but those at the back may have an Acropolis view. There are four conference rooms, limited parking on a first-come-first-serve basis, plus an Acropolis-view roof-bar with a planked sundeck and small spa. Major credit cards. **€€**

Electra Palace
Navárhou Nikodímou 18–20
105 57 Athens
Metro Sýntagma
Tel: 210 33 70 000
Fax: 210 32 41 875.
www.electrahotels.gr
The only real luxury/businessmen's outfit in the Pláka, the neoclassical Electra Palace – part of a small chain of Greek hotels – is an oasis, literally so with its lawn garden just outside the olive-and-brown-décor breakfast area. Choose among four grades of rooms: standard, superior with guaranteed balcony and Acropolis view (worth the extra amount), junior suites and full suites. Dark wood floors and oriental rugs adorn the comfortable suites, which have jacuzzis and bidets in the stylish bathrooms; all units have ADSL access with a fee card. A new wing, with a rooftop pool, should be ready some time in 2007; for the moment there's a small pool in the pleasant basement spa. Various meeting rooms and restaurants cater to the business clientele. Check the website for offers, usually well under the official rack rates. 131 rooms. Major credit cards. **€€€€**

John's Place
Patróöu 5, 105 57 Athens.
Metro Sýntagma.
Tel: 210 32 29 719.
One of the last survivors amongst the backpackers' pensions which used to fill Pláka until the 1980s, in a fine, well-kept Belle Époque building. Double, triple or quad rooms have original parquet floors, air conditioning and sinks, but no ensuite baths – there are only one or two of these per floor. No breakfast facilities (though there's a

Above: a comfortable bed in the St George.

decent independent restaurant downstairs). No credit cards. €

Kimon
Apóllonos 27, 105 57 Athens. Metro Sýntagma.
Tel: 210 33 14 658
Fax: 210 23 14 203.
The only real fair-standard budget hotel in this part of Pláka, the Kimon – if you accept a total lack of communal facilities like a breakfast room – isn't bad at all. The rooms have been all converted to en suite format, painted cheerfully and provided with mock-antique furniture (eg iron bedsteads), as well as TV and phone. 14 rooms. No credit cards. €

Metropolis
Mitropóleos 46, 105 63 Athens Metro Sýntagma or Monastiráki.
Tel: 210 32 17 469/871.
www.hotelmetropolis.gr
You'll recognise this interwar 1930s building of some architectural distinction by the bougainvillea vigorously scaling the front. There are two non-ensuites per floor in this well-kept budget hotel, the rest being en-suite rooms. All have air-con, phones and bland pine furnishings. Most units have balcony views over a grassy square to the Acropolis. The best are two "retirées" on the roof, where a breakfast bar is planned for 2007. No credit cards. £

Nefeli
Angelikís Hatzimiháli 2, corner Yperídou.
Metro Sýntagma.
Tel: 210 32 28 044
Fax: 210 32 25 800.
This 1970s veteran was finally redone in 2005, and has a breakfast area and a lift to its credit. The en-suite rooms, few with balconies, get some street noise (upper ones are quieter), but fill quickly as the price is right. Price includes breakfast. 18 rooms. No credit cards. €

Phaedra
Herefóndos 16, corner Adrianoú, 105 58 Athens.
Metro Acropolis.
Tel: 210 32 38 461
Fax: 210 32 27 795.
Quietly sited at the intersection of two pedestrian lanes, the Phaedra was rescued from dilapidation well before the Olympics and now offers the best budget value in Pláka. Although not all the cheerfully tile-floored rooms are en-suite, each has an allocated bathroom and TV, while some have balconies looking onto the square with its Byzantine church of Agía Ekateríni. Breakfast (optional) is served in a pleasant ground floor salon. 21 rooms. No credit cards. €

The **Stathopoulos Group** of four mid-range lodgings (three B-, one C-class) was one of the earliest-formed of the small local hotel groups, and arguably kick-started the trend for modish hotels with their 2001 remodellings. All of them (with the arguable exception of the Arion) share the same design sense, and to some extent layout, with breakfast (much the same at all four) invariably served in a dedicated mezzanine area. High (ie UK-compliant) safety standards make the Hermes and Plaka particularly attractive to organised tours. All also tend to yield up to 30 percent discounts off similar official rates for internet or direct bookings.

Achilleas
Lékka 21, 105 62 Athens.
Metro Sýntagma.
Tel: 210 32 33 197
Fax: 310 32 16 779.
www.achilleashotel.gr
With its tall, narrow frontage, the Achilleas is the least obvious of the Stathopoulos hotels – and probably the least distinguished, especially the bathrooms. There's the usual mezzanine breakfast room, and some family quads; most rooms from the fourth floor on up have balconies. 39 rooms. Major credit cards. €€

Arion
Agíou Dimitríou 18, 105 54 Athens. Metro Monastiráki.
Tel: 210 32 40 415.
www.arionhotel.gr
Yet another member of the Stathopoulos Group, this hotel – the only savoury one in the heart of Pysrrí – has perhaps the most boldly designed rooms of the four, with a vaguely Japanese theme to the good-sized rooms: lattice-mesh closet doors, modular headboards, square light fittings, but no balconies (though there is a common roof terrace). It's quiet despite being walking distance from the area's many *ouzerís* and bars. In theory you can park on the street outside, but frequent nocturnal break-ins mean it's best to use a secure covered car-park nearby. 51 rooms. Price includes breakfast. Major credit cards. €€

Hermes
Apóllonos 19, 105 57 Athens.
Metro Sýntagma.
Tel: 210 32 35 514
Fax: 210 32 22 412.
www.hermeshotel.gr
The Hermes has all-marble baths (variable in size) in the oak-effect-floored rooms, which also vary; front-facing ones are smaller but have a communal terrace, which is due to be partitioned into private spaces during 2007. The rear ones don't but are larger, some with sofas – though there are twin beds only. The breakfast room is on the mezzanine, decorated with professional photographs of the 2004 Olympics by group manager Dorína Stathópoulou. The relaxing street-level lounge-bar is naturally lit by a light well. 45 rooms. €90–120 by season. Major credit cards. **€€**

Plaka
Kapnikaréas 7, corner Mitropóleos, 105 56 Athens.
Metro Monastiráki.
Tel: 210 32 22 096
Fax: 210 32 22 412
www.plakahotel.gr
The Plaka resembles its stablemate the Hermes in many respects: twin beds only (though there are some adjoining family units), no minibars (you're welcome to stock the fridge with your own drinks), internet access, variable-format bathrooms. But all 2001-redone rooms here have balconies, with half facing the Acropolis and the rest the street. The roof-garden was one of the first in that particular craze and still one of the best (its bar operates until midnight, you can take your breakfast up there). The mezzanine breakfast salon is exceptionally cheerful, plus there's a small lounge on each floor. 45 rooms. Major credit cards. **€**

Makrigiánni and Koukáki

Acropolis Select
Falírou Street 37–39, 117 42 Athens.
Metro Acropolis.
Tel: 210 92 11 611
Fax: 210 92 16 938.
www.acropoliselect.gr
This 2003-renovated hotel scores points as much for its helpful staff and prime location as for its pleasant if dark-toned lounge-bar and plush breakfast area with a light well. Rooms have green carpets and big beds, as well as wi-fi access (hourly fee). Somewhat plain bathrooms are white-tiled with marble sink-tops. Off-street parking, but no roof garden; 13 rooms on the topmost three floors of six have Acropolis views. 72 rooms. Major credit cards. **€€€**

Price Categories

Unless otherwise stated, price guides are for a standard double room for one night without breakfast:
€ = under €70
€€ = €70–€120
€€€ = €120–€200
€€€€ = more than €200

Acropolis View
Webster 10, 117 42 Athens.
Metro Acropolis.
Tel: 210 92 17 303
Fax: 210 92 30 705.
www.acropolisview.gr
Many rooms at this small hotel on this quiet street near the Acropolis live up to their name, as does the popular roof garden. The stark white-with-dark-trim rooms and marble baths are on the small side, but were lightly redone in 2004 (with most attention being paid to the common areas). Wi-fi access and unusually low rates in high summer are further benefits. 32 rooms. €60 winter, €75 Jun–Aug, €95 May & Sep. Major credit cards. **€€**

Art Gallery
Erehthíou 5, 117 42 Athens.
Metro Syngroú-Fix.
Tel: 210 92 38 776
Fax: 210 92 33 025.
www.artgalleryhotel.gr
This small pension-hotel, named after the artwork on the walls of the common areas, got a much-needed 2004 makeover, which meant refreshed furnishings and all-new bathrooms with stall-showers for the parquet-floored rooms, some with balconies, though the two family-sized suites on the roof were less affected. Unusually for an establishment of this size, there's an elevator, plus a pleasant breakfast bar (with an Acropolis-view terrace. 22 rooms. Discounts for long stays. Major credit cards. **€€**

Athenian Callirhoe
Kalliróis 32, corner Petmezá, 117 43 Athens
Metro Syngroú-Fix
Tel: 210 92 15 353
Fax: 210 92 15 342.
www.tac.gr
Athens' very first (2002) "boutique" hotel was refreshed again in 2004, though its self-description as "hyper-hip exclusive" might put off as many clients as it attracts. It offers three grades of designer-

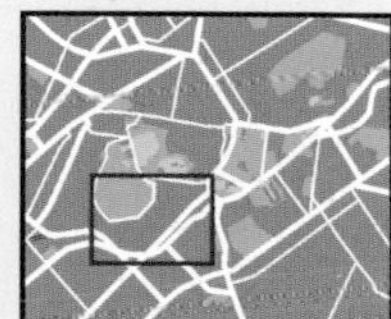

tweaked rooms (including non-smoking), with glass partitions, leather and metal trim, internet access and double glazing (essential as Kalliróis is a busy boulevard). Common facilities include an oriental theme bar – very popular for private functions – a small gym and a branch of the superb Corfiot-Italian restaurant Etrusco, serving on the roof with Acropolis views during summer, downstairs inside otherwise. A consolation for being confined without the view is that master chef Ectoro Botrini is in charge during the cooler months rather than an apprentice. 84 rooms. Major credit cards. **€€€**

Divani Palace
Parthenónos 19–25, 117 42 Athens.

Metro Acropolis.
Tel: 210 92 80 100
Fax: 210 92 14 993.
www.divaniacropolis.gr
The main advantage of this popular business-and-conference hotel, member of a medium-sized nationwide chain, is its vast common facilities, though the underground restaurant is surprisingly gloomily lit. Equally subterranean are exhibited sections of the Themistoclean Long Walls, discovered when the hotel was built. Rooms are a good size, and uniform throughout the building; there's also a small pool area, off-street parking and summertime rooftop garden with a restaurant, just outside one of the main conference venues. 250 rooms. Major credit cards. **€€€€**

Hera
Falírou 9, 117 42 Athens.
Metro Acropolis.
Tel: 210 923 6682.
www.herahotel.gr
Yet another result of the wave of pre-Olympic upgradings, the Hera has perhaps the best roof-garden in the area, with (unusually) a heated bar-restaurant for all-year operation up top. Individual rooms themselves are on the small side but have everything you'd expect in this (A) class. It's worth an extra supplement for the fifth-floor suites with bigger balconies (though bathrooms are much the same throughout). The dome-lit atrium-breakfast room, and friendly staff, are further assets. 38 rooms. €150 standard, €200 suites. Major credit cards. **€€€**

Herodion
Rovértou Gálli 4,
117 42 Athens.
Metro Acropolis.
Tel: 210 92 36 832
Fax: 210 92 11 650.
www.herodion.gr
The Herodion scores most points for its common areas: the café-restaurant with patio seating shaded by wild pistachios – more pleasant, perhaps, than the minimalist breakfast salon up front – and the roof garden with two 2006-installed jacuzzi tubs and the Acropolis a stone's throw away. Functional (ISDN lines) but fair-sized rooms, some with disabled-friendly baths and Acropolis views, have coco-fibre mattresses. If they're full, you'll be referred to their somewhat more modest sister hotel, the Philippos (see below). 90 rooms. Major credit cards. **€€€**

Marble House
Alley off Anastasíou Zínni 35,
117 41 Athens.
Metro Syngroú-Fix.
Tel: 210 922 8294 or 694 5756383
Fax: 210 92 26 461.
www.marblehouse.gr
This welcoming, family-run pension has an enviable location on a quiet cul-de sac where there's some chance of parking a hired scooter or car. Simple but tidy upstairs rooms, most with bath and balcony (a few have facilities across the hall), are done up in blonde pine furniture and white tiles, though the hall floor feature some striking mosaics. There are two slightly larger – if darker – studios on the ground floor, behind the marble-clad lounge where breakfast may be taken. Fridges and air con, but no phones, in the rooms, which were redone in stages 2001–2004. Very good value and thus hugely popular in season, so book well in advance. Late arrivals should obtain the front-door security code in advance, as reception is unstaffed 8pm–8am. 16 rooms. Credit cards for reservation deposit only. **€**

Philippos
Mitséon 3, 117 42 Athens.
Metro Acropolis .
Tel: 210 92 23 611
Fax: 210 92 23 616.
www.philipposhotel.com
The cheerful rooms at this B-class/3-star outfit have green carpets and ochre/tan décor, though bathrooms are a bit basic compared to the Herodion's. Fifth- and sixth-floor units have Acropolis views; there's no roof garden here. There's a ground-floor breakfast area and skylit atrium lounge with internet access, though other meals must be taken at the affiliate Herodion. 48 rooms. Major credit cards. **€€€**

PSYRRÍ AND THE BAZAAR

Attalos
Athinás 29, 105 54 Athens.
Metro Monastiráki.
Tel: 210 32 12 801
Fax: 210 32 43 124
www.attalos.gr
This friendly, C-class/two-star hotel offers good value if not many frills in a central location, and is thus popular with groups. Lightly touched up before the Olympics, it retains many "period features" (including basic baths which could still use some attention), but the rooms themselves – about half of them balconied – have modern furnishings, double glazing against street noise and parquet floors. Common facilities include the standard mezzanine breakfast salon, free use of a wi-fi hotspot and a very popular roof terrace operating from 6.30pm until late. Breakfast included. Major credit cards. **€€**

Carolina
Kolokotróni 55, 105 60 Athens.
Metro Panepistimíou or Monastiráki
Tel: 210 32 43 551
Fax: 210 3243 550.
www.hotelcarolina.gr

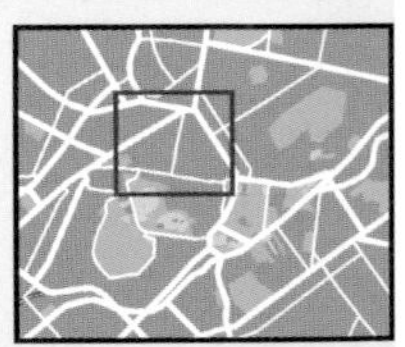

After some years of closure, the Carolina is back in business with very keen management and a variety of completely refurbished rooms which vary from singles to quads but share the same pastel decor, cheery floor tiles and mid-brown furniture. The best – if potentially hottest – ones are the fifth-floor "retirées" up on the roof garden; all others have balconies, and rear-facing units have limited Acropolis views. The only common area is a breakfast salon where a copious buffet meal is served, and a contiguous, inexpensive internet café. Best deals are bookable on the website. 31 rooms. Major credit cards. €€

Cecil
Athinás 39, 105 54 Athens. Metro Monastiráki.
Tel: 210 32 17 079
Fax: 210 32 18 005.
www.cecil.gr
A well-restored 1850s vintage mansion has become one of the most characterful small hotels in this area, right down to its iron-cage, inter-war elevator. For preservation reasons, varied-décor rooms have no balconies – unless you count the ornamental ones out front – but they offer parquet floors, iron bedsteads, double glazing, pastel colours on a blue base, and retiled baths. Common areas are limited to a first-floor breakfast room with its original wooden floor and painted ceiling, and a street-level café. 39 rooms. Major credit cards. €€

Delphi Art
Eridanus Pireós 78, 104 35 Athens. Metro Thissío.
Tel: 210 52 05 360
Fax: 210 52 00 550.
www.eridanus.gr
Although this hotel at the edge of Psyrrí is within walking distance of trendy Gázi and Thisío as well, it's primarily a business hotel located on a rather noisy boulevard, and gets primarily an international business clientele. There are five grades of soundproofed room in this adapted neoclassical mansion: standard, deluxe, Acropolis view, junior suite and penthouse. Common to all are spacious, green-marble bathrooms, most with hydro-massage jets; decor is contemporary without being rebarbative and internet access is through the TV. Original painted ceilings adorn many of the common areas, which include a small fitness centre and steam bath. Reasonable pricing for the facilities reflects the less than prestigious location. 30 rooms. €120–200. Major credit cards. €€€

Fresh
Sofokléous 26, corner Klisthénous 105 52 Athens; metro Omónia.
Tel: 210 52 48 511
Fax: 210 52 48 517
www.freshhotel.gr
Probably the most startling of Athens' handful of cutting-edge "design" (as opposed to just "boutique") hotels, the Fresh (*left*) leaves few observers neutral – you'll either love it or hate it. Detractors find the lollipop colour scheme, everywhere from the reception to the balcony partitions, off-putting. Chrome, leather and glass are much evident in bathrooms and sitting areas; on a more natural note, there's plenty of oak and walnut fooring and trim, while six superior rooms have private Zen rock gardens. Futuristic features include bedside remote control of windows and plasma TV. The rooftop pool-and-bar is pre-

BELOW: aspects of the Fresh Hotel.

PRICE CATEGORIES

Unless otherwise stated, price guides are for a standard double room for one night without breakfast:
€ = under €70
€€ = €70–€120
€€€ = €120–€200
€€€€ = more than €200

ABOVE: the rooftop bar at Fresh.

dictably a big hit. Off-street parking (for a fee). 133 rooms. Major credit cards. **€€€**

Tempi
Eólou 29, 105 51 Athens.
Metro Monastiráki.
Tel: 210 32 13 175
Fax: 210 32 54 179.
www.travelling.gr/tempihotel
For those who don't want the multi-bedded rooms of Athens' few (and generally indifferent-quality) hostels, this is the next notch up: a mix of proper if basic double rooms, all with air conditioning and double glazing (much less needed now that Eólou has been pedestrianised). The best rooms have views of the Agía Iríni flower market. Communal facilities are limited to a book exchange, a self-catering kitchen and a handy in-house travel agency. Some rooms en-suite, others (even cheaper) bathless. No credit cards. **€**

THISÍO

Erechtheion
Flammaríon 8, corner Agías Marínas, 118 51 Athens.
Metro Thisío.
Tel: 210 34 59 606.
Budget hotel located superbly yet quietly for the nearby nightlife, though you get what you pay for: somewhat pokey en-suite rooms overstuffed with old furniture, and sometimes glum management. No credit cards. **€**

Phidias
Apostólou Pávlou 39, 118 51 Athens.
Metro Thisío.
Tel: 210 34 59 511.
ephidiasa@otenet.gr
This small hotel on the Thisío pedestrian zone had just a light touch-up for the Olympics, and relatively modest prices reflect this. The lobby and breakfast area are still 1970s relics, the rooms on the small side but perfectly adequate, with new showers and flooring. The front eight balconied units have Acropolis views that

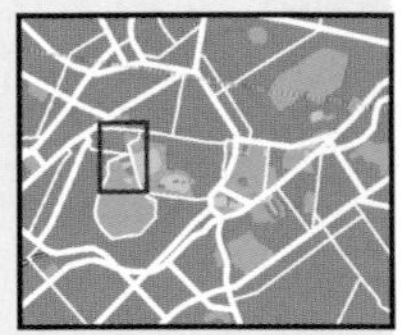

you'd pay double for elsewhere. Breakfast included. 15 rooms. No credit cards. **€€**

EXÁRHIA AND MOUSÍO

Art Athens
Márni 27, 104 32 Athens.
Metro Omónia
Tel: 210 52 40 501
Fax: 210 52 43 384.
www.arthotelathens.gr
Installed in a 1930s Art Nouveau/neoclassical building rescued from dereliction, this boutique hotel offers one-of-a-kind rooms which share only wood flooring, double glazing, original wall art and hi-tech gadgets like individual climate control. Colour schemes vary from grey to black to ochre, and bathrooms are also uniquely laid out and marble-clad to head height, though most have chrome basins. Common areas include a basement events hall, a low-ceiling breakfast area with more wall art, and a stunning reception atrium with a circular light well. The staff are helpful and clued-up, while "realistic" pricing reflects the less-than-stellar neighbourhood off gritty Platía Váthys, though you are still within walking distance of the National Museum and Exárhia. 30 rooms. Major credit cards. **€€**

Best Western Museum
Bouboulínas 16, 106 82 Athens. Metro Omónia.
Tel: 210 52 38 038
Fax: 210 52 31 548.
www.hotelsofathens.com
Since being acquired by the Best Western chain in 2001, the Museum has had its original rooms redone and a new wing of larger units added. The standard rooms are on the small side, inevitably with the feel of an American hotel, but the junior suites are spacious, and their bathrooms are a notable improvement on the standards.

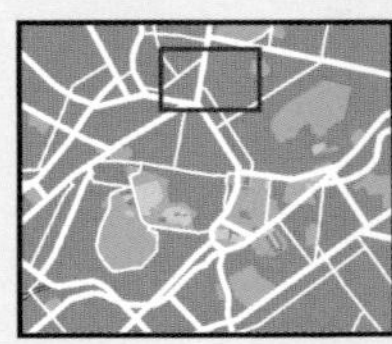

The executive suites will suit most tastes, with bathrooms completely marble-clad. Perks include free high-speed internet connection and free orange juice in the slightly-below-ground-level bar. 58 rooms, from €75 (standard) to €160 (executive); internet offers on the website are particularly good value applied to the executive units. Major credit cards. **€€**

Exarchion
Themistokléous 55, 106 83 Athens. Metro Omónia.
Tel: 210 38 00 731
Fax: 210 38 03 296.
www.exarchion.com
The frankly dated rooms of this 1960s high-rise, with their lino floors and ominously dark furniture, are ripe for redecoration, but they do have fridges, air conditioning and TVs. Given the price, and the location in the heart of Exárhia's nightlife district, you can't really complain. The mezzanine breakfast room is cheerful enough (buffet breakfast €4 extra), as is the roof terrace. 49 rooms. No credit cards. **€**

Orion/Dryades
Emmanuíl Benáki 105/ Dryádon 4, 114 73 Athens. Metro Omónia
Tel: 210 33 02 387
Fax: 210 38 05 193.
orion-dryades@mail.com
These co-managed, almost adjacent hotels (joint reception for them both is in the Orion) serve a youngish crowd who've outgrown hostels, and those on extended stays who take advantage of the fully equipped self-catering kitchens in each well-maintained building (the Orion's has a particularly stunning city view). The Orion has only washbasins in the rooms, with baths in the hallways, while the pricier Dryades (its security entrance monitored from the Orion) is fully en-suite with 2004-fitted baths, though its rooms with their dark wood panelling are on the gloomy side. Some units have balconies, with views either to Lófos Stréfis park (source of the odd mosquito) or over Athens. 38 rooms jointly. Major credit cards. **€**

KOLONÁKI

Hilton
Vassilísis Sofias 46, Kolonáki/Pangráti/Ilísia border. Metro Evangelismós.
Tel: 210 72 81 000.
www.athens.hilton.com
Athens' first real de-luxe hotel was built in 1962, and for years had no rival. Initially controversial, its arc-shaped design (by a local architect) is now recognised as a landmark, and the views to Ardittós hill, the Acropolis and Lykavitós hill from the upper floors are unbeatable. Following the pre-Olympics refurbishment, the rooms – many of them 34 sq m (365 sq ft) in area – are irreproachable and lack nothing for the business traveller. Common facilities include no less than three pools (one outdoors, unique in the centre), a large spa, and the acclaimed seafood restaurant Milos. Rack rates are predictably stratospheric, but rooting about on the website you can find off-peak specials for about €100. 534 rooms. Major credit cards. **€€€€**

Periscope
Háritos 22, 106 75 Athens. Metro Evangelismós.
Tel: 210 7297200
Fax: 210 72 97 206.
www.periscope.gr
Unlike many Athens hotels, the lounge and common areas at the Periscope – a member of the Yes! chain – are minimal as well as minimalist. Unusually, most of the renovation effort of the long-defunct Haritos Hotel has gone into the arresting black-, white- and grey-toned rooms, which are aimed at a business clientele. Wall- and ceiling-art comprises aerial photos of the city, plus there are real-time projections of the skyline relayed by a periscope! The higher in the building you go, the better the rooms (most people will insist on superior double as a minimum standard), culminating in airy suites with balconies, and a rooftop jacuzzi. All units have wood floors and flat-screen TVs, CD/ DVD players, plush bedding with a choice of pillows, and angle lighting. The somewhat clinical bathrooms are due for a refit but do include complimentary slippers, bathrobes and botanically based toiletries. 22 rooms, from €150 (stan-

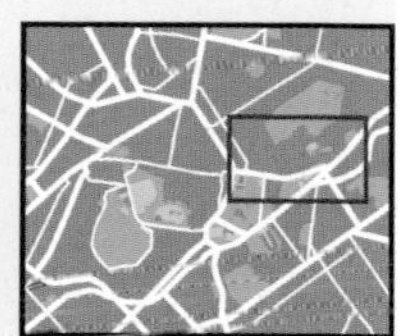

PRICE CATEGORIES

Unless otherwise stated, price guides are for a standard double room for one night without breakfast:
€ = under €70
€€ = €70–€120
€€€ = €120–€200
€€€€ = more than €200

BELOW: the pool at the St George.

ABOVE: luxury products at the St George.

dard double) to €260 (junior suite). Major credit cards. **€€€**

St George
Lycabettus Kleoménous 2, 106 75 Athens.
Metro Evangelismós.
Tel: 210 72 90 711
Fax: 210 72 90 439.
www.sglycabettus.gr
This medium-sized hotel, the highest in Athens, sits at the foot of Mount Lykavitós. Rooms either have a piney hill view north, or (more sought-after) look south over the city, as well as a few dis-advantaged ones facing the interior courtyard. Their decor varies by floor, from plush to minimalist, though they all feature broad beds and micro-tiled bathrooms with nice touches like the loo-roll suspended on a chain. The hotel is technically switched-on with CD players and wi-fi access, plus three large conference venues. In the basement there's a jacuzzi, sauna, massage studio and a small gym. Other facilities include two restaurants, a roof pool, a popular bar (Frame) and free parking. 157 rooms and suites, ranging from €140 (hillside or courtyard standard), through €200 (city view standard), to €300–370 (suites). Major credit cards. **€€€**

Xenos
Lycabettus Valaorítou 6, 106 71 Athens. Metro Sýntagma.
Tel: 210 36 06 000
Fax: 210 36 05 600.
www.xenoslycabettus.gr
This small, modernised but not cutting-edge hotel is the haunt of savvy shoppers and businesspeople who appreciate the buzz of the swank pedestrian zone just outside, especially the very popular café and restaurant on the ground floor. Breakfast is taken in a mezzanine salon. The rooms, with narrow balconies, have subtle beige and brown-hued décor; the bathrooms are large with marble cladding and tubs. 25 rooms. Major credit cards. **€€€**

AMBELÓKIPI

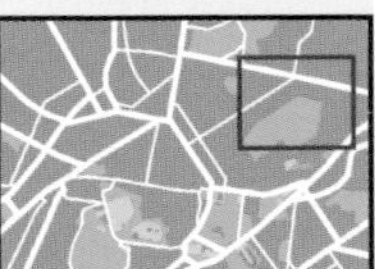

Airotel
Alexandros Timoléontos Vássou 8, 115 21 Athens.
Metro Ambelókipi.
Tel: 210 64 30 464
Fax: 210 64 41 084.
www.airotel.gr
Located on a little square behind a chapel which helps shield it from busy Vasilísis Sofías, the Airotel Alexandros offers comfortable accommodation with modern furnishings which counteract a slightly forbidding exterior. The high-ceilinged lounge is flanked by the brick-and-pastel-panelled breakfast salon, which later in the day doubles as the Don Giovanni restaurant. There are also three conference rooms much favoured by business folk, though probably not much used by the Spanish tours that also like this hotel. Most rooms have subtle grey-beige-white décor; free off-street parking. 96 rooms. Major credit cards. **€€**

Ambelókipi
Zafolia Leofóros Alexándras 87–89, 114 74 Athens.
Metro Ambelókipi
Tel: 210 64 49 012
Fax: 210 64 42 042
www.zafoliahotel.gr
This businessmen's A-class/4-star hotel, renovated in 2000 and well priced for its class, is a bit inconvenient for the metro, but is easily accessible by No. 7 or 8 trolleybus along Alexándras or Ippokrátous, and is handy for the tavernas and cinemas along Alexandras and in Neápoli district. Common areas include a roof garden with pool and view to Lykavitós, restaurant-bar, conference facilities, fitness centre and sauna. Rooms, while hardly cutting-edge in design, are spacious and comfortable with individual climate control. 191 rooms. Major credit cards. **€€**

Andromeda
Timoléontos Vássou Street 22, 115 21 Athens.
Metro Ambelókipi
Tel: 210 64 15 000
Fax: 210 64 66 361.
www.andromedaathens.gr
Set on a quiet side street off Vasilísis Sofías, the Andromeda was one of the earliest boutique hotels in the city. The common areas strive to impress, with an African theme to the lobby and oriental-kitsch-plus-Second-Empire décor in the first-floor restaurant and breakfast salon. Standard rooms lack balconies, but suites have them at both front and back. Furnishings are innocuous if a bit dated – the apartments across the way are better. 21 standard rooms, 10 suites, 12 apartments in a separate wing. Major credit cards. **€€€**

COASTAL SUBURBS

Best Western Premier Coral
Leofóros Posidónos 35, 175 61 Paleó Fáliro; access by tram.
Tel: 210 98 16 441
Fax: 210 98 31 207.
www.coralhotel.gr
Possibly a bit overrated as an A-class hotel, but comfortable enough and right on the seafront, with beaches, tavernas, cafés and of course the tram just over the road. Common areas include conference facilities, a gym and indoor whirlpool with countercurrent. Free wi-fi access throughout. 88 rooms. Major credit cards. **€€€**

Poseidon
Leofóros Posidónos 72, 175 62 Paleó Fáliro; access by tram
Tel: 210 98 72 000
Fax: 210 98 29 217
www.poseidonhotel.com.gr
A bit plusher, more keenly priced and more daring in room design than its nearby rival, the A-class Poseidon offers a private patch of Edém beach across the avenue, a rooftop restaurant, outdoor pool and extensive conference/event facilities. 91 rooms. Major credit cards. **€€€**

The Margi
Litoús 11, 166 71 Vouliagméni.
Tel: 210 89 29 000
Fax: 210 89 29 143.
www.themargi.gr
Superb taste in earth-tone soft and hard furnishings – starting with the skylit atrium and its cushioned divans – make The Margi a very home-like environment, and its loyal repeat clientele seem to treat it as a home from home. Their favourite haunt seems to be the small pool deck studded with brass and copper lanterns. The oriental theme is extended in the 2006-added Malabar poolside lounge. "American breakfast" is served in a somewhat dark, low-ceilinged area with white high-backed chairs, and white napery, though it does look out on the pool. An à la carte bar-restaurant is separately managed. There are two function rooms for The Margi's significant wedding and corporate clientele. As for the pleasant, carpeted, balconied rooms, you've a choice between street/oblique sea-view or (quieter) forest-view to rear. The lower two floors, comprising standard doubles, aren't quite up to the tone of the common areas. It's worth the extra for the "executive" rooms on the upper two storeys, which have been overhauled more recently and offer ADSL connection and CD players. 90 rooms. Major credit cards. **€€€**

Divani Apollon Palace & Spa
Agíou Nikoláou 10, corner Ilíou, 166 71 Vouliagméni, Kavoúri beach.
Tel: 210 89 11 100
Fax: 210 96 58 010.
www.divanis.gr
Much the best of the Divani chain hotels in Athens, it's hard to believe this was an ex-US military R&R facility until 1999 – it's now one of the largest spa hotels in Europe. Of the three grades of units, standard rooms are like superior elsewhere with their green-marble bathrooms (internet facilities are through the TV if you haven't a laptop). Superior rooms are larger, and have CD players as well. Suites have faxes, fireplaces and two sound systems, and are larger than many in-town apartments. Both executive rooms and suites have a guaranteed full-on sea-view. Common areas include two salt-water pools, two restaurants (Mythos tis Thalassas abuts a private section of sandy Kavoúri beach), ample conference facilities, a small gym with indoor pool, and of course the spa of the name. This is simply streets ahead of any other hotel spa in Athens, with every imaginable kind of thalassotherapy including another subterranean seawater pool heated to 32°C, sauna and *hamam* attached to the restaurant. 286 rooms and suites. Major credit cards. **€€€**

PRICE CATEGORIES

Unless otherwise stated, price guides are for a standard double room for one night without breakfast:
€ = under €70
€€ = €70–€120
€€€ = €120–€200
€€€€ = more than €200

Avra
Arafinídon Álon 3 (shore road), 190 09 Rafína.
Tel: 22940 22780
Fax: 22940 23320.
Refurbished in 2003 and upgraded from Class C to Class A, the better of Rafína's two hotels is

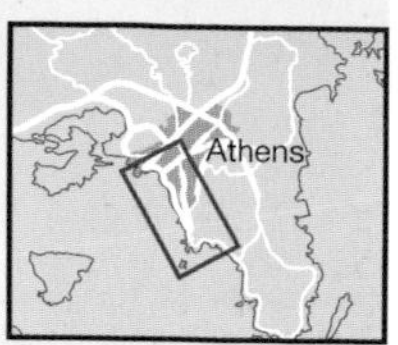

well placed near the port for a pre-ferry overnight, or a final stay after a return from the islands and an early-morning flight out from the nearby airport, 25 minutes away by regular bus. Moreover, the Avra has set its sights firmly on the business trade, with ample conference facilities and data ports. About two-thirds of the somewhat small, beige-and-tan décor rooms have direct or oblique sea views. Units are in three grades, including a superior "club floor" and junior suites. 96 rooms. Major credit cards. **€€**

Mistral
Alexándrou Papanastasíou 105, 185 33 Piraeus, Kastéla district.
Tel: 210 41 17 094
Fax: 210 41 22 096.
www.mistral.gr
A B-class, sea-view hotel in a quieter part of Piraeus, with blue-trimmed, vaguely nautical rooms and (necessary in this congested area) off-street parking. There's a restaurant, separate bar, pool and roof garden overlooking Mikrolímano. The Mistral would be ideal for a night before a ferry departure, but it's away from public transport and too far to walk to the port – you'll have to taxi there. 74 rooms. Major credit cards. 30 percent internet booking discount. **€€€**

KIFISIÁ

Kefalári Suites
Pendélis 1, corner Kolokotróni, 145 62 Kifisiá, Kefalári district.
Tel: 210 62 33 333
Fax: 210 62 33 330.
www.kefalarisuites.gr
This Tardis-like, pink-and-blue Art Deco mansion, a member of the Yes! chain, gives little away from the outside or the cramped reception area. Inside are six self-catering suites, individually theme-decorated (Africa, Aqaba, Jaipur for mock-safari, Arabian nights and the Raj respectively), or the more western "Boat House" and "Deck House". They all have kitchenettes, verandas, internet access, and CD/DVD players. There's also a small breakfast room, sun deck with teak furniture and a jacuzzi, as well as pleasant garden seating – but no dedicated parking, which surprisingly is a hassle even in leafy Kefalári. 6 units. €220 (junior) – €250 (superior). Major credit cards. **€€€€**

Pentelikon
Diligiánni 66, 145 62 Kifisiá, Kefalári district.
Tel 210 62 30 650
Fax: 210 80 10 314.
www.hotelpentelikon.gr
Built in 1929 but Belle Époque rather than Art Deco in style with its patterned wallpaper, ornate fireplaces and a hint of chintz, the rambling Pentelikon was the place to be seen around Athens during the 1930s. A 1980s refurbishment has restored the elegance to this suburban retreat, set in extensive landscaped gardens which help make it the quietest of the Kefalári lodgings. It's also the snootiest hotel around – riff-raff need not apply. You'd probably be snooty too if you had this history, and a Michelin-starred restaurant on the premises (read on). Each spacious room is individually decorated, and many have balconies overlooking the lovely rear lawn which edges up to the pool. There are extensive conference and banqueting facilities, including the Michelin-starred Vardis restaurant (closed Aug), which is a relative bargain at about €70 a head plus wine. Also

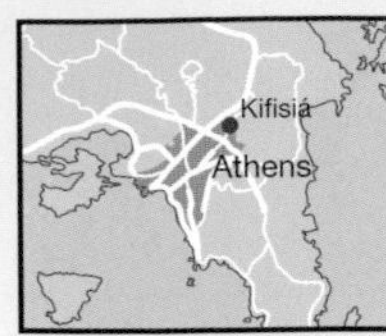

very popular among the walk-in trade is the much cheaper Sunday midday buffet at the adjacent La Terrasse restaurant. €250 (standard double) up to €2,000 (best suite). Major credit cards. **€€€€**

Semiramis
Hariláou Trikoúpi 48, corner Filadelféos, 145 62 Kifisiá, Kefalári district.
Tel: 210 62 84 400
Fax: 210 62 84 499.
www.semiramisathens.com
The green Kevlar balconies at the Semiramis (*below left*), as

BELOW: the stunning Semiramis pool, left, and penthouse, right.

much an art installation as a hotel, glow in the dark – a striking sight from afar. As avant-garde as the nearby Pentelikon is retro, the "ultimate design hotel", as it bills itself, flagship of the Yes! chain, won't be to everyone's taste. Each floor is colour-coded, and the colour scheme runs to chartreuse, dark lavender and hot pink as well as the aforementioned green. The front-facing rooms are a bit bigger, and most have balconies (extra large on the first floor), while all feature techno-widgets like remote button-controlled window shades, wi-fi access throughout and large flat-screen TVs. The improbably shaped chairs are more comfortable than they look. It's probably worth the splurge for either the penthouse units with superb views or one of the five bungalows by the pool. Other common areas include a fair-sized gym, a spa/*hamam*, a bar-restaurant at pool level and large dedicated parking (important for the business clientele which throng here). Major credit cards. **€€€€**

TwentyOne
21 Kolokotróni, corner Mykónou (where entrance actually is), 145 62 Kifisiá, Kefalári.
Tel: 210 62 33 521
Fax: 210 62 33 821.
www.twentyone.gr
More or less opposite its Yes! stablemate Kefalári Suites, the TwentyOne could hardly be more different. Industrial chic is extended to its limits in gunmetal-grey, white and wood hues with red accents and entertaining doodles as wall-art, though the result may still be a bit clinical for some, especially the bathrooms. It's worth the bit extra for superior-grade rooms and the five loft suites, which have especially high ceilings with skylights. Beds are a mix of twins and queen-size. Breakfast is delivered to the rooms, though there's an outdoor terrace restaurant (overhauled in 2006) for other meals, and free DVD player loan. Parking is limited to two dedicated spaces. 21 (surprise surprise) rooms. Major credit cards. **€€€**

ARGOLID PENINSULA

La Belle Hélène
Main road, Mykínes 212 00 (Mycenae)
Tel: 27510 76225
Fax: 27510 76179.
This 1862-built house is where a Heinrich Schliemann stayed during his 1870s archaeological excavations at Mycenae – his bed is still in use. The ambience remains almost Victorian, and conservation rules mean bathrooms are not en-suite, but the on-site restaurant and hospitality are excellent. The guestbook contains signatures of the famous (Agatha Christie, Virginia Woolf, among others) and infamous (assorted Nazi brass). 5 rooms. No credit cards. **€**

Candia House
211 00 Kándia Iríon
Tel: 27520 94060
Fax: 27520 94480.
www.candiahouse.gr
Candia House is a small personal luxury hotel owned by a delightful Athenian lady, an ex-publisher, who wanted to create a peaceful haven for her guests. Located 17km (11 miles) south-east of Návplio on a sandy beach, it is ideally placed for touring the Argolid. Each of 10 individually designed and furnished suites has living room, air-con, TV, phone, kitchen, balcony. Facilities include pool, bar, restaurant serving whole-foods, gym, sauna. Open May–Oct. 10 suites. Major credit cards. **€€€**

Marianna
Potamianoú 9, 211 00 Návplio
Tel: 27520 24265
Fax: 27520 99365.
www.pensionmarianna.gr
Restored and run by three hospitable brothers, this house-pension nestles against the rocky walls of Akronavplía fortress, its patios studded with Seville orange trees. Rooms, some with exposed masonry, are attractive and comfortable. Delicious home-made breakfasts are served on a raised terrace with fabulous views over the old town and the bay. 21 rooms. Major credit cards. **€€**

Byron
Plátonos 21, 211 00 Návplio
Tel: 27520 22351
Fax: 27520 26338.
www.byronhotel.gr
This elegant hotel with antique furnishings in the common areas occupies a tastefully restored mansion above Ágios Spyrídon church.

PRICE CATEGORIES

Unless otherwise stated, price guides are for a standard double room for one night without breakfast:
€ = under €70
€€ = €70–€120
€€€ = €120–€200
€€€€ = more than €200

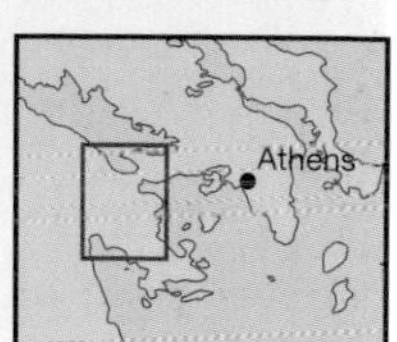

Rooms, some with balcony or at least a view over the town's tiled roofs, are more modestly decorated, with wooden floors and rugs, though bathrooms can be small. Breakfast may be taken on the open-air patio. 18 rooms. Major credit cards. **€€**

Kapodístrias
Kokínou 20, 211 00 Návplio
Tel: 27520 29366
Fax: 27520 29278.
www.hotelkapodistrias.gr
Uniquely antique-decorated rooms, with iron beds and canopies, in a 19th-century mansion just steps away from where President Kapodístrias was assassinated. 10 rooms. No credit cards. **€**

DELPHI AREA

Xenonas Generali
Eastern outskirts below clock-tower, 320 04 Aráhova.
Tel: 22670 31529
www.generalis-xenon.com
This restoration inn offers the best standard in town: nine unique, named rather than numbered rooms, most with fireplace. The decor in some can be a bit precious, but the welcome's warm and the breakfasts in the cozy bar-lounge are unusual. In the basement, an indoor pool, spa, *hamam* and sauna are all popular with the après-ski set, who drive prices into the highest category at winter weekends. 9 rooms. Major credit cards. **€€–€€€**

Paradosiakos
Xenonas Maria Village centre, just up a pedestrian lane from through road.
Tel: 22670 31803
Fax: 22670 31069.
One of Aráhova's two restoration inns, this occupies a pair of lovely old buildings with a range of rustic-decor doubles, triples and quads. €40 summer B&B, €75 winter; family quads €75–150 by season. **€–€€**

Pan
Pávlou ké Frederíkis 53, 330 54 Delfí.
Tel: 22650 82294
Fax: 22650 83244.
This adequate, comfortable small hotel enjoys fine views of the Gulf of Corinth. The best, newest rooms, sleeping four, are in the attic. Immediately opposite is their annexe, the Artemis, whose doubles equal the standard of the Pan's family quads (including tubs in the bathrooms), but on this side of the street are no views across the olive groves to the sea. 21 rooms jointly. Major credit cards. **€**

Sun View Pension
Apóllonos 84, far west end of upper commercial street, near Amalia Hotel, Delfí
Tel: 22650 82349.
Edkalentzis@internet.gr
Fair-sized rooms in pastel colours with original wall art; rear-facing ones are a bit dark. Pleasant, four-table breakfast area on the ground floor. Easy street parking adjacent. Breakfast included. No credit cards. **€**

Ganimede (Ganymidis)
Southwest market street, 330 52 Galaxídi.
Tel: 22650 41328
Fax: 22650 42160.
www.ganimede.gr
This historic little port some 28km (17 miles) south of Delphi makes a wonderfully relaxing base. The Ganimede/Ganymidis has been a restoration hotel since 1974, one of the first in Greece, founded by Bruno and Bill. Since 2004 energetic Kóstas and Khrysoúla Papaléxis have taken it on, thoroughly overhauling the rooms without compromising their old-fashioned charm. There are six doubles in the old ship-captain's mansion (best is No. 1) and a family suite with loft and fireplace across the courtyard-garden where a copious breakfast is served, still featuring Bruno's original exquisite recipes for patés and jams. 7 rooms. Open all year. Breakfast included. Major credit cards. **€€**

Galaxa
Eleftherias 8, 330 52 Galaxídi.
Tel: 22650 41620
Fax: 22650 42053.
Somewhat casually run if magnificently sited hillside hotel on the west shore of Hirólakas with limited private parking adjacent. Most of the rooms have some sort of water view, all have blue-and-white décor and somewhat small bathrooms. Manolis, your genial host, presides over the popular garden-bar. Breakfast included. Major credit cards. **€€**

SARONIC GULF ISLANDS

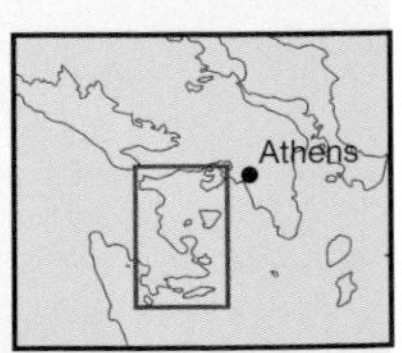

Égina

Eginitiko Arhontiko
corner Thomaïdou and Agíou Nikólaou, 180 10 Égina.
Tel: 22970 24156
Fax: 22970 26716.
www.aeginitikoarchontiko.gr
A late-18th-century ochre-and-orange neoclassical mansion, expanded after independence and now converted into a small hotel. Well-appointed rooms all have double beds, fridges and air-con. The *pièce de resistance* is the suite with painted ceilings. There's also a breakfast conservatory with coloured-glass windows. 12 rooms. No credit cards. **€**

Brown
southern waterfront, past Panagítsa church, 180 10 Égina
Tel: 22970 22271
Fax: 22970 25838;
www.hotelbrown.gr
Égina Town's top offering, this B-class/3-star hotel opposite the southerly town beach, occupying a former sponge factory dating from the 1880s, scores mostly for its vast common areas (terrace bar, buffet-breakfast salon). The best and calmest rooms are the garden bungalows at the rear; there are also galleried family suites sleeping four. 28 units. Breakfast included. Major credit cards. **€€**

Artemis
Kanári 20.
Tel: 22970 25195.
Very basic 1960s-vintage hotel, but the en-suite rooms (with fridge, balconies and heating/air-con) are adequate, and it's probably the quietest location in town, with views second to none over a pistachio orchard from the front units. No credit cards. €

Póros

Seven Brothers
180 20 Póros Town.
Tel: 22980 23412
Fax: 22980 23413.
www.7brothers.gr
Situated at the corner of a fairly quiet little square just off the seafront, this mock-neo classical, C-class hotel stands at the heart of pretty Póros Town. The rooms are simply furnished, but have balconies, internet connection, fridges, air-con and TVs. Open Apr–Oct (winter by arrangement). 16 rooms. Discounts for long stays and internet booking. Major credit cards. €

Pavlou
Megálo Neório,
180 20 Kalávria
Tel: 22980 22734
Fax: 22980 22735.
Epavlou@poros.gr
This 2004-renovated B-class hotel makes an ideal base for a family beach holiday. Half the rooms face the large pool out back, while the front rooms look to a beach where water-sports are offered. Respected taverna on site. 36 rooms. Major credit cards. €–€€ depending on season and room.

Ýdra

Bratsera
180 40 Ýdra.
Tel: 22980 53971
Fax: 22980 53626.
www.greekhotel.com/saronic/hydra/bratsera
Indisputably the top standard of accommodation on the island, this A-class/4-star hotel occupies a former sponge factory, and the extensive common areas (including a conference room and a medium-sized pool, the only one on Ýdra) serve as a *de facto* museum of the industry, with photos and artefacts. There are five grades of rooms, even the lowest having flagstone floors and proper shower stalls. Open mid-March to Oct. 14 rooms. Major credit cards. €€€

Miranda
180 40 Ýdra
Tel: 22980 52230
Fax: 22980 53510.
www.mirandahotel.gr
This 1810-vintage mansion has been sensitively converted into one of the most popular hotels in the town, with wood floors (except in the basement units) and fridges. Rooms (and rates) vary; best are Nos. 2 and 3, both with painted, coffered ceilings and large sea-view terraces. Large breakfasts are served out on the shaded courtyard during summer, but in the basement bar in winter. 14 rooms. Major credit cards. €€€

Piteoussa
Main lane out of town to southeast
Tel: 22980 52810
www.piteoussa.com
Named after the three giant pines out front, this upscale pension has just five ground-floor rooms refurbished to cutting-edge standards in 2004, with CD/DVD players and designer baths, with bathrobes, slippers and sundries provided. Quietest – though none are especially noisy – is No. 5 facing the garden. Open all year. Major credit cards. €–€€

Glaros
Lane inland from Alpha Bank, left after 50m
Tel: 22980 53679/52089.
Vast warren of a building with tiled-floor rooms on the first floor, all with newly tiled baths, fridges and TVs, most with balconies or terraces. The cheapest pension going on Ýdra, but the catch is the nearby belfry – which bongs you awake at weekends between 7am and 8am. No credit cards. €

Spétses

Nisia
Kounoupítsa district, 500m west of Dápia port, 180 50 Spétses Town, Spétses
Tel: 22980 75000
Fax: 22980 75012.
www.nissia.gr
Built on the grounds of an early-20th-century factory (of which only the Art Nouveau facade remains), this luxury facility embraces a large pool. Units range from 2-person studios at the back (€230) by way of 4-person maisonettes with 2 bedrooms, living room and kitchen (€450 for 4) to luxury 4-person units with sea-view salons (€570). Rates include breakfast, though kitchens are fully equipped. 29 units. Major credit cards. €€€€

Ikonomou (Economou) Mansion
400m from Dápia port, 180 50 Spétses Town
Tel: 22980 73400
Fax: 22980 74074
Spetses' premier restoration inn takes up part of an 1851-vintage property. The ground floor of the main house has six well-converted rooms (€175) retaining ample period features; a newer outbuilding hosts two luxury sea-view suites (€235). Breakfast is served by the fair-sized pool. No credit cards. €€

Villa Orizondes
500m inland from the Dápia, via Platía Orologíou
Tel: 22980 72509 or 6974469893
Spartan, variably sized rooms with fridge, air-con and TV in a quiet spot; more than half the rooms have double beds, and knockout sea-views over a bucolic orchard. No credit cards. €

PRICE CATEGORIES

Unless otherwise stated, price guides are for a standard double room for one night without breakfast:
€ = under €70
€€ = €70–€120
€€€ = €120–€200
€€€€ = more than €200

ACTIVITIES

THE ARTS, NIGHTLIFE, FESTIVALS, SHOPPING AND SPORTS

THE ARTS

Classical Concerts

Mégaro Musikís (Hall of Music) Vassilísis Sofías corner Kókalli; metro Mégaro Musikís; tel: 210 72 82 333; www.megaron.gr.The prime venue for classical music events, with three halls of varying sizes. The season generally runs from September to May.
Filologikís Sýllogos Parnassós (Parnassos Literary Society) Platía Agíou Georgíou Karýtsi 8; metro Panepistímio; tel: 210 32 23 917; www.lsparnas.gr. Chamber music concerts staged here two or three nights weekly, usually on either Monday, Wednesday, Friday or Saturday.
Benáki Museum, Pireós Annexe Pireós 138; tel: 210 34 53 111. Chamber music concerts at the on-site amphitheatre; consult www.classicalmusic.gr (Greek only, difficult to find your way around) for current information.

Opera

Ethnikí Lyrikí Skiní (Greek National Opera) at the Olympia Theatre Akadimías 59–61; metro Panepistímio; www.nationalopera.gr. The search continues for a permanent, acoustically satisfactory home for the national opera company – funding probably will have to be found to build one from scratch – but in the meantime operas are staged here from November to May. Before the season proper starts, the Olympia also hosts other concerts: Malian artists Amadou and Mariam were here October 2006.

Dance

Athens has a number of decent modern/contemporary dance companies, but curiously no permanent ballet troupe. Foreign guest ballet companies settle in at the Mégaro Musikís or the Olympia Theatre during the winter. Besides the venues here, check the ones listed under "Theatre".
Coronet Theatre Frýnis 11 corner Ymittoú, Pangráti; tel: 210 70 12 123; www.coronet.gr. Perennial, well-appointed venue for touring dance events as well as theatre; in late 2006 the Shaolin Kung Fu monks passed through.
Dora Stratou Theatre corner Arakýnthou and Mirtsiévsky, Filopáppou Hill; tel: 210 92 14 650; www.grdance.org. Established by folklorist Dora Stratou in 1953, this open-air theatre hosts stagings of traditional Greek song, dance and music from late May to late September (daily except Monday). It's undeniably touristy, but everyone should go at least once. The same foundation gives Greek dance classes during winter.
Shantom Tripóleos 35A, corner Évvias, Káto Halándri; tel: 210 67 17 529; www.shantala.gr. Small company and theatre dedicated to bharata natyam, created by Leda "Shantala", who spent years studying in India.

Theatre

If Athenians are somewhat indifferent to dance (unless it's something exotic and spectacular), they are positively mad about theatre. This can be anything from Shakespeare, Pirandello or Molière to the most avant-garde contemporary productions, via Beckett, Genet, Ibsen and Bergman. At the height of the winter season, the city supports well in excess of 100 theatres, large and small.

Town-centre ones are large and mostly comfortable, while "fringe" venues gravitate to Psyrrí, Gázi, Rouf and the area around the old Fix brewery. Productions are mostly in Greek, which may limit their appeal to foreigners. May sees various small experimental festivals before summer signals a break in most performances. But the summer Hellenic Festival does stage drama, mostly ancient Greek plays.

Amore Pringiponíson 10, Pédion Áreos; metro Viktória; tel: 210 64 68 009. Two halls here, the main and the "Exostí". Closed July/Aug.

Booze Cooperativa Kolokotróni 57; metro Monastiráki; tel: 210 32 40 944. A strange venue – from the street, it looks like a bar with distressed furnishings – which actually hosts anything from dance-theatre to plays.

Ethnikó Théatro/National Theatre Agíou Konstantínou 22–24; metro Omónia; tel: 210 52 23 242; www.n-t.gr. Sumptuous neo-classical building, designed by German architect Ernst Ziller. It houses two performance areas, including a highly regarded Piramitikí Skiní (Experimental Stage), and two other annexes within a few blocks.

Hytirio Ierá Odós 44, Rouf; tel: 210 34 12 313. A former converted foundry which has put on everything from Mark Twain's *King Leopold's Soliloquy* to modern dance.

Ilisia Denisi Vassilísis Sofías 54, Kolonáki; metro Mégaro Musikís; tel: 210 72 10 045 or 210 72 16 317. Large, plush, expensive theatre which tends to highlight foreign works, sometimes in the original language with Greek surtitles.

Roes Iákhou 16, Gázi; metro Thissío; tel: 210 34 74 312. Also serves as one of the venues for a regular springtime dance festival.

Theatro tis Imeras Gennimatá 20, Ambelókipi; metro Panórmou; tel: 210 69 29 090. Favours evergreen fare like Molière and Ibsen.

Theatro tou Neou Kosmou Antisthénous 7 corner Tharýpou; metro Syngroú-Fix; tel: 210 92 12 900. Three-level venue, mostly showing new Greek plays.

Thision Tournavíttou 7, Psyrrí; metro Thisío; tel: 210 32 55 444. One of the city's top experimental venues.

ABOVE: a shadow-puppet theatre in Pláka.

Treno sto Rouf Konstantinopóleos, just south of Pétro Rálli; tel: 210 52 98 922 or 6937 604988. Athens' most curious theatre – two former railway cars flanking a restaurant wagon (you may dine afterwards), all parked at a disused shunting station.

Cinema

We give numbers of all cinemas listed, but recordings of the (usually) two nightly screenings are likely to be in Greek only. Many cinemas close in summer unless they have air-conditioning or a roll-back roof. See also our list of reliable summer venues in the feature on page 67.

Alphaville Mavromiháli 168, Neápoli; tel: 210 64 60 521. Art-house cinema specialising in retrospectives of cult classics: film noir, Japanese, French New Wave. Summer operation with retractable roof.

Asty Koráï 4, centre; metro Panepistímio; tel: 210 32 21 925. First-run showing of foreign- and Greek-made arthouse fare. Closed summer.

Athineon Vassilíssis Sofías 124; metro Ambelókipi; tel: 210 77 892 122. Mostly action flicks, but worth an ogle simply for their lovingly hand-painted, almost Bollywood, promotional art (they refuse to hire the studio's posters).

Attikon Stadíou 19; metro Panepistímio; tel: 210 32 28 821. The city's oldest (1918) and most lavish Art Deco cinema; logical prime venue (along with the Apollon next door) for the September International film festival. Closed summer.

Danaos Kifissías 109, Ambelókipi; metro Ambelókipi; tel: 210 69 22 655. The typical

TICKET AGENCIES

Besides the Hellenic Festival box office (*see page 250*), there are few other agencies in Athens. Most Greeks avoid them because of the stiff commissions levied on credit-card purchases, and prefer to approach the box office of the venue itself, in person or by phone. One agency with a lower commission is **Tickethouse** at Panepistimíou 42 (tel: 210 36 08 366; www.tickethouse.gr), with long hours Mon–Fri and part Saturday, though the website for on-line purchase is mostly in Greek only, with a limited number of events available.

arthouse fare, both Greek and foreign, makes this a logical co-venue for the International Film Festival. Closed summer.

Embassy Patriárhou Ioakím 5, corner Irodótou, Kolonáki; metro Evangelismós; tel: 72 15 944. Quality environment for MOR and blockbuster playlist. Air conditioned for summer.

Filip Thásou 11, off Patisíon, Kypséli; tel: 210 86 47 444. The city's premier arthouse cinema, a bit the worse for wear but with frequent themed offerings (eg a week-long Karen Blixen festival in 2006).

Ideal Panepistimíou 46; metro Panepistímio; tel: 210 38 26 720. One of Athens' plushest movie palaces, restored after a fire in late 1990s with imported French seats and the first installation of Dolby sound (now almost universal).

P'ti Palais Filmcenter Vasiléos Georgíou tou Deftérou, corner Rizári, Pangráti; metro Evangelismós; tel: 210 72 91 800. Overhauled in 2000, shows a mix of first-run arthouse and Hollywood fare

Village Cinema Ymittoú 110, corner Hremonídou, Pangráti; tel: 210 75 72 440. The most convenient of suburban Athens' growing number of multiplexes (five screens here), with mall-type diversions to hand just outside; air-conditioned so it works in summer.

NIGHTLIFE AND CLUBS

From a fairly monochrome scene as recently as the early 1990s, Athens nightlife has now burst into a kaleidoscope of facets – Latin, jazz, rock, electronica – both live and DJ'd. Greek acoustic or minimally miked folk and *rebétika* are still there, of course; they've served their audiences too long to be abandoned completely. *Rebétika*, briefly defined (*see pages 64 5 for more*), was the music of the marginalised in early 20th-century Greece, given a huge boost by the influx of Asia Minor refugees. Comparisons are often made to American blues, but an analogy to Spanish flamenco is probably more illuminating. Since World War II it has been "domesticated" and served as godparent to *laïka* or Greek pop.

One thing to brace yourself for is the near-Scandanavian expense of a live-music night out in Athens. Hard drinks cost €6–11, wine is €35–40 a bottle, and there's typically a minimum consumption of €35 per person, on top of any basic admission charges (typically €8–12 per person). The time-honoured Exárhia youth strategy of nursing a single pricey drink all evening isn't possible at most of the options cited below. At the *rebétika* clubs cited, a bottle of whisky – lately the drink of choice for Greeks on a night out – will typically run to €70–100 per bottle, on the assumption that four people will share it. Most of the listed venues will do snacks or full meals of variable quality, and these are often priced more reasonably than the booze.

Rebétika, Nisiótika, Folk Revival

Alli Okhthi Artemónos 9, Goúva; metro Ágios Ioánnis; tel: 210 92 70 628. Smallish club that showcases more cutting-edge Greek groups like Mode Plagal.

To Baraki tou Vasili Didótou 3, Exárhia; metro Panepistímio; tel: 210 36 23 625; www.tobaraki.gr. Nightly acoustic, unamplified performances by young *rebétika* revivalists and singer-songwriters. After 1am, becomes an alternative "club". Closed summer.

Ennalax Mavromiháli 139, Neápoli; no nearby metro; tel: 210 64 37 416. Live folk music Thur–Sat. No cover but drinks moderately expensive. Reservations suggested.

Harama Párko Skopevtiríou, Kessarianí; tel: 210 76 64 869. Founded by *rebétika* great Vassilis Tsitsanis in the late 1940s, this well-worn *bouzoúki* continues to headline contemporary *rebétika* and *laïka* stars like Glykeria and Maryo. Intimate compared to the glitzy warehouse-clubs along Syngroú, but still expensive.

Perivoli t'Ouranou Lysikrátous 19, Pláka; metro Akrópoli; tel: 210 32 35 517. Going since the fall of the junta, this relatively restrained *bouzoúki* features, by turns, *rebétika* revivalists Giorgos Tziortzis and Babis Tsertos. Fairly expensive, but good value. Closed Mon, Tues and Jun–Sept.

To Pontiki Eptanísou 9, Kypséli; tel: 210 82 32 971; www.topontiki.com. Varying programme of *rebétika, laïka* and island music with minimal amplification. On the expensive side.

Rebetiki Istoria Ippokrátous 181, Neápoli. One of the less expensive *rebétika* clubs, lodged in a fine old house with acoustic sounds from the house band. Closed Wed and summer.

Stoa Athanaton Sofokléous 19, Varvákio Market hall; metro Monastiráki; tel: 210 32 14 362. Atmospheric first-floor room with retro decor that hosts one of the livelier surviving *rebétika* clubs. Unusually, there's an afternoon set as well as late-night (Mon–Sat at 3.30pm and 11pm), and it even tends to fill afternoons. Regular evening musicians include Takis Binis (who began his career with Tsitsanis in the 1950s), Haroula, and Dhimitris Tsaousakis (son of the great 1950s star Prodromos). Food reasonable, but drinks expensive.

Latin, "Ethnic" and Jazz

Alavastron Café Damáreos 78, Pangráti, no nearby metro; tel: 210 75 60 102. Primarily "ethnic" (Greek, African, Latin, Andean) and jazz playbill; past performers have included

Athens-based Armenian improviser Haig Yazdjian. Moderate ticket prices. Closed summer.
Half Note Trivonianoú 17, Méts; no nearby metro; tel: 210 92 13 310. Athens' longest established venue for quality jazz; all foreign touring big names stop in here. Closed Tues and most of summer.
Guru Bar "Jazz Upstairs" Platía Theátrou 10; metro Monastiráki; tel: 210 32 46 530. Jazz several nights weekly, by local and visiting bands, at this club-restaurant's upstairs bar.
Hilies Ke Dyo Nykhtes Karaïskáki 10, Psyrrí; metro Monastiráki; tel: 210 33 17 293. The name translates as "1002 Nights"; bands run the gamut from Middle Eastern, with belly-dancing at weekends, to Cretan or other Greek folk. Generic Middle East grub and hubble-bubbles on offer.
Parafono Asklipíou 130 corner Synesíou Kyrínis, Neápoli; tel: 210 64 46 512; www.parafono.gr. Small, cabaret-type club hosting jazz and blues by local musicians. May close Tues.
Palenque Farandáton 41, Ambelókipi; metro Ambelókipi; tel: 210 77 52 360; www.palenque.gr. Most durable and fun of the handful of Latin clubs, with a small dance floor, lessons 9–11pm nightly except Sat, then live acts and costumed shows (mostly Cuban or Brazilian).

Rock and Pop

An Club Solomoú 13–15, Exárhia; metro Omónia. Small basement club that's the heart of live rock action (mostly novice bands) for the district. Closed summer.
Gagarin 205 Liossíon 205, Thimarákia; metro Attikís; tel: 210 85 47 601; www.gagarin205.gr. One of the biggest (2,000 capacity) and best venues for rock and reggae, with summer premises in Fáliro.
Karaïskaki Stadium Néo Fáliro. Hosts mega rock/pop events, like Ricky Martin and Jennifer Lopez's appearances in 2006.
Mikró Musikó Théatro/Small Musical Theatre Veïkou 33, Makrygiánni; metro Syngroú-Fix; tel: 210 92 45 644; www.smallmusictheatre.gr. Started as an experimental venue but has broadened into mixed programming: rock, folk, jazz, improv, musical documentary screenings.
Stavros tou Notou Tharýpou 37corner Frantzí, Néos Kósmos; metro Syngroú-Fix; tel: 210 92 26 975. The main hall (Thur–Sat from 10.30pm onwards) and the "club" annexe (nightly) across Frantzí at No. 14A consistently books top, cutting-edge Greek musicians, such as Nikos Portokaloglou and Sokratis Malamas.

Unclassifiable venues

Bios Pireós 84, Gázi; tel: 210 34 53 35; www.biofighter.gr. One of the most versatile spaces around, a converted warehouse that puts on small drama and dance events as well as art and photo exhibits, electronica and other avant-garde music. Works as a café by day too; admission free or very low.
Diavlos Musiko Spiti Márkou Drákou 9, Koukáki; metro Syngroú-Fix; tel: 210 92 39 588. Cabaret-club hosting all genres, with name singers occasionally appearing. Closed May–Sep and Mon–Tues.
Mike's Irish Bar Sinópis 6, Ambelókipi; metro Ambelókipi; tel: 210 77 76 797; www.mikesirishbar.gr. Large basement venue with karaoke Monday nights, live, variable music at weekends. Cheapish admission and drinks.
Viviliopolio Ianos Stadíou 24; metro Panepistimíou; tel: 210 32 17 917. Very arty bookstore which also happens to host a grab-bag of events in its mezzanine café at time of writing an Epirot clarinet session by one of the illustrious Halkias family had just occurred.

FESTIVALS AND EVENTS

January

Ágios Vasílios-Protohroniá/New Year's Day, January 1. A public and family holiday.
Ta Ágia Theofánia (aka "Ta Fóta")/Epiphany, January 6. Blessing of the Waters – not just the church fonts, but the nearest body of natural water, which in Athens means the Attic coasts and Piraeus. In each major parish there, young men compete for the honour of retrieving a crucifix hurled out by the officiating priest or bishop.

February

Variable start date of the three **Carnival** weeks (Apókries). The Thursday of the second week is called **Tsiknopémpti**, after the smell of roasting meat (*tsíknisma*) which everyone is urged to consume on this day; it's impossible to get a taverna table on this evening without long advance booking.

March

Carnival observance climaxes in the run-up to the seventh weekend before Easter; there are plenty of fancy-dress parties with mummers in plastic masks – Venice it ain't – and plastic hammers are prominently sold with which young Athenians go about hitting each other over the head.

On **Kyriakí tis Tyrinís** (Cheese Sunday), family and restaurant meals are strong on dairy products, meat having already been dispensed with.

Lent truly begins the next day, **Katharí Deftéra** (Clean Monday), traditionally observed, weather permitting, with kite-flying outings and picnics on the numerous Athenian hills such as Filopáppou. After this date, no animal products or oil may be

SUMMER FESTIVALS

Athens' outdoor cultural events, staged at often stunning venues, rescue the city from summertime desolation, providing a reason for residents and visitors alike to linger a few extra days rather then heading straight out to the mountains or the islands.

Despite the a batch of new festival launched in the 1990s, the granddaddy of them all is still the **Hellenic Festival**, which runs from mid-May to late September, with a programme including choral concerts, dance and solo recitals. Performances are aimed at both visitors and Athenians, and tickets are affordably priced. Most events are staged at the atmospheric open-air Odeon of Herodes Atticus below the Acropolis, but the festival has grown so much since the late 1980s that a second venue, the Lykavitós Theatre, handles nearly as many events. To either venue, you're strongly advised to bring your own cushion and an extra layer of clothing, as performances end around midnight.

The **Epidaurus Festival** has stagings of ancient drama (in modern Greek) at both the main restored theatre, and the "little" theatre, at Epidaurus in the Peloponnesian Argolid. These events run from July through early August, every Friday and Saturday evening.

For information about both Hellenic and Epidaurus festival productions, contact the joint box office at Panepistimíou 39, in the arcade (tel: 210 32 21 459 or 210 92 82 900; www.hellenicfestival.gr) or the Herodes Atticus box office on the day of performances there from 6–9pm (tel: 210 32 32 771). Big-name events sell out quickly, so make this a priority upon arrival in Athens. The Lykavitós Theatre is contactable separately on tel: 210 72 27 233.

The best of the newer festivals include the June-to-July **Glyfada Festival**, with contemporary Greek musical performance in the Theatráki Exóni on Ýdras 11, adapted from an abandoned quarry at the foot of Mt Pendéli (info tel: 210 89 12 200), and the **Rematia Festival** at the same time in the Rematia Theatre in the northern suburb of Halándri (tel: 210 68 00 001), stronger on Balkan and Asian music. The **Vyronas Festival** runs for six weeks from July to September at the Théatro Vráhon "Melina Mercouri" in the suburb of Výronas, attracting a mix of jazz, rock, ethnic and Greek acts. For information tel: 210 76 55 748 or 210 76 62 066.

consumed by the devout (though shellfish, octopus and squid, being bloodless, are allowed); even fast-food outlets advertise *nistísma* (Lent-compliant dishes).

Evangelismós/Annunciation on March 25. Also the official start of the Greek independence uprising in 1821. Neat coincidence of the sacred and the patriotic, with military-ecclesiastical processions complemented by air-force fly-overs.

April

Páskha (Easter) usually falls in April – rarely in early May (the date usually, but not always, differs from Catholic/Protestant Easter). From Friday of Megáli Evdomáda (Holy Week) until the following Tuesday the city essentially shuts down, as families endeavour to return to their home villages to observe the holiday, although plenty of people – especially those of refugee ancestry with no other *patrída* or homeland in Greece – remain in Athens.

Megáli Pémpti/Maundy Thursday sees the baking of *tsourékia*, special twisted and glazed Easter breads, and the dying of red Easter eggs, some of these embedded in *tsourékia*. On **Megáli Paraskeví**/Good Friday there are numerous evening processions of an *Epitáfios* or symbolic bier of Christ, lavishly decorated with flowers by the women of the parish. The sacred chanting emanating from the churches is second to none, especially at the Russian Orthodox church of Agía Triáda on Filellínon Street.

The Saturday evening **Anástasi**/Resurrection service commences at around 10.30pm and climaxes at midnight when priests, announcing *Khristós anésti!* ("Christ is Risen!") emerge from the apsidal sanctuary of completely darkened churches bearing the light of eternal life on a candle. This is passed along to the candles clutched by every parishioner – including to the crowds outside the overflowing churches – as firecrackers and dynamite are detonated at a high-decibel level and prolongation more appropriate to an artillery barrage. Although the after-midnight chanting is in fact the most beautiful part of the service, most people go home at this point to break the Lenten fast with a meal of *mageritsa* (soup made from lamb tripe, rice, dill and lemon).

Later in the day there's an exodus of Athenians, either to in-town tavernas or *exohiká kéndra* (rural tavernas) across Attica, for the traditional Easter Sunday lunch of whole roast lamb on a spit.

Ágios Geórgios/St George April 23. This saint's day is celebrated most conspicuously at the eponymous chapel up on Lykavitós Hill. If St George falls before Easter, then it's observed on the Monday after Easter to avoid conflicting with Lenten austerities.

May

Protomagiá/Labour Day May 1. The big holiday of the Left, with parades and demonstrations; Zíto iy Ergatikí Protomagiá (Viva the Working Class First of May) is a common instructive graffito. Outings to the countryside am made by the politically less committed, where flowers are gathered to be fashioned into wreaths and hung on doors or balconies.

Summer cinemas (*theriná kinematografiká*) open on a date determined by the weather.

June

Acropolis Rally mid-month. A three-day auto marathon across the more rugged bits of the mainland; the start is at the base of the Acropolis, the finish at Kallimármaro stadium.

Ágios Ioánnis/St John's Eve June 23–24. In outlying suburbs, you may still see giant bonfires, on which May Day wreaths are burnt to expel the black magic of May. The young and fit traditionally jumped over the fire, similarly to purge themselves.

September/October

Athens International Film Festival (tel: 210 60 61 363; www.aiff.gr). For 10 days in mid-to-late September, the posher central cinemas play host to this event. By contrast the outdoor cinemas close, usually late September or the first week of October.

Tekhnopolis Festival lasts a week in mid-October. Live concerts, usually of an avant-garde/electronic nature, staged in the courtyard of this Gázi complex.

Óhi (No) Day October 28. The day Greece gave Il Duce two fingers up, and entered World War II on the Allied side; parades with a predictable military presence.

November

Athens Marathon On a Sunday early in the month; www.athens-marathon.com. The course follows the 2004 Olympics course from Marathon to the Kallimármaro stadium.

Anniversary of the Polytechnic Uprising November 17. Leftist groups organise a march on the US Embassy, which is typically pelted with refuse (less successfully now, given its daunting perimeter fortifications) in retaliation for its role in supporting the junta which suppressed the student protests with considerable loss of life.

December

Hristoúgenna/Christmas December 25. This is still not quite as commercial as in Anglo-Saxon countries, but getting there. Expect street illuminations, both public and private, thematically fitted storefronts and an alarming outbreak of inflatable Santas perched on balconies. During the Twelve Days of Christmas, a dwindling number of children shuffle about singing the traditional *kálanda* or carols to householders who are supposed to reward them with money or sustenance.

Paramoní Protohroniá/New Year's Eve December 31. Plenty of residential parties and private functions at restaurants, and usually street festivities at either Platía Kotziá or Sýntagma, but older people stay home and play cards for money. A special cake, the *vassilópita*, is baked, with a coin secreted in one slice; the person who gets it is supposed to be lucky for the next year.

SHOPPING

With the country's ever-greater integration into the pan-European economy, shopping in Greece is increasingly globalised – and predictable. Overseas chains like Virgin Megastore, Habitat, IKEA, Champion (owners of Marinopoulos supermarkets), Benetton, the Body Shop and Accessorize are familiar sights across central Athens, and need no particular introduction. However, suburban malls tend to be modest in size compared to those in Britain or the US, and even fast-food chains like McDonald's have had to tailor themselves to Greek tastes. For a more specifically Greek retail experience that can't be reproduced abroad, try one of the individual town-centre outlets listed below.

Art Gallery

Zoumboulakis Kriezótou 7 and Platía Kolonakioú 20; tel: 210 36 34 454 and 36 08 278; www.zoumboulakis.gr. The city's premier gallery, with painting and sculpture exhibitions by top Greek artists. The Kriezótou branch has a shop selling limited edition prints and silk-screens.

Department Stores

Attika Panepistimíou 9/Amerikís 4; tel: 211 18 02 600. 2004-founded, giant department store, occupying an entire city block in conscious imitation of London's Selfridge's. Seven floors of designer-label clothing, sporting goods, wardrobe accessories and household goods.

Notos Gallery Eólou 99 corner Lykoúrgou; metro Omónia; tel: 210 32 45 811. New incarnation of the old Lambropoulos Brothers department store, slightly more middle-of-the-road than rival Attika but just as large.

Designer Ware

Carouzos Kanári 12, Kolonáki; metro Sýntagma; tel: 210 36 27 123. Flagship store of a medium-sized fashion chain comprising eight outlets in Greater Athens, with the standard international labels for men and women.

Ice Cube Tsakálof 28, Kolonáki, no nearby metro; tel: 210 36 25 669. Cutting-edge designer bou-

tique with mostly foreign labels and a few household trophies.
Sole Sole Periklėous 37D; metro Monastiráki. Mislaid your sunglasses? Never fear, there's a reasonably priced name-brand replacement here.
Spiliopoulos Ermoú 63 (tel: 210 32 27 590) and Adrianoú 50 (tel: 32 10 018); metro Monastiráki. If you don't mind having last year's line of top name (women's) shoes, head for these bargain outlets.
La Strege son Tornate Háritos 9, Kolonáki; metro Evangelismós; tel: 210 72 12 581. Don't dare say "second-hand" about the stock here – it's "vintage" or "retro", and stock is priced accordingly.
YEShop Pindárou 38, Kolonáki; no nearby metro; tel: 210 36 15 278. Outlet for Greek designer Geórgios Eleftheriádes, but also a huge range of accessories – bags, hats, sunglasses – from across the world.

Greek Food and Drink

Ariston Voulís 10; metro Sýntagma; tel: 210 32 27 626. Bakery, going since 1910, renowned for its *tyrópites* (cheese pies) – though they also crank out *spanakópites* (spinach pies) and more exotic variants, usually only seen at sit-down tavernas, like *prassópites* (leek turnovers) and *kolokythópites* (courgette/zucchini pies).
Bahar Evripídou 31, central market; metro Panepistímio. Herbs and teas in bulk; one of several similar herbalists on this block, for example Elixir at No. 41.
Cake Irodótou 13, Kolonáki; metro Evangelismós; tel: 210 72 12 253. As the name says, but not sticky oriental cakes, rather western baked-on-site standards like carrot or cheesecake. Tiny seating area, but mostly to take away.
Ikologi Ellados Panepistimíou 57; metro Omónia. Athens' largest health-food shop, spread over two floors; upstairs is a small canteen doing excellent freshly-squeezed juices as well as snacks.
Loumidis Eólou 106, near Platía Kotziá; metro Omónia. The Loumidis family, of Asia Minor descent, run Athens' oldest (1923) coffee company. Their retail outet does western-style beans as well as Greek coffee, plus chocolates, teas and coffee-making paraphernalia.
Mesogeia Níkis 52; metro Sýntagma; tel: 210 32 29 146; also a branch on Sofokléous, corner Aristídou. As the name ("Mediterranean") suggests, specialty traditional foods from islands and mainland – *eleópasto* (tapinade) and other canned goods, liqueurs, cheeses, rusks and such.
Tsahnis Panepistimíou 49; metro Panepistímio; tel: 210 32 20 716. Tiny hole-in-the-wall specialising in nuts – especially pistachios from the Saronic Gulf island of Égina.
Vasilopoulos Stadíou 19; metro Panepistímio; tel: 210 32 22 405. Small deli spin-off of the national supermarket chain Alfa Vita Vasilopoulos, which like its parent does a good job of importing specialist gourmet and comfort food – at a price.
Vrettos Kydathnéon 41, Pláka; metro Akrópoli; tel: 210 32 32 110. Ancient bottle shop, with one wall stacked with strange, own-distilled liqueurs, the other with barrels. Functions as a bar by night.

BELOW: Zoumboulakis for art.

Bookshops

Compendium Navárhou Nikodímou corner Níkis; metro Sýntagma; tel: 210 32 21 248. Moved in 2005 to new, somewhat cramped premises; good for beach paperbacks and books about Greece. Very small used section; noticeboard for travellers and expats.
Eleftheroudakis Panepistimíou 17; metro Panepistímio; tel: 210 32 58 440; www.books.gr. Central branch of Athens' oldest "international" (ie foreign language) bookstore chain, with 14 other outlets across the city (including the airport). Very good in particular for books about Greece.
Iy Folia tou Vivliou (Book Nest) Panepistimíou 25–29, in the arcade; metro Panepistímio; tel: 210 32 31 703. Upstairs has a good selection of fiction and scholarly work on Greece; downstairs is a small travel section with maps and guides in English.
Reymondos Voukourestíou 18; metro Sýntagma; tel: 210 36 48 189. Noted for having the most complete stock of foreign-language magazines in town, a far greater range than sold at any kiosk.

Hiking/Travel Supplies

Anavasi Stoá Arsakíou 6a; metro Panepistímio. Retail outlet of this map publisher; also stocks GPS devices, Emvelia products and foreign-language guides in English.
Klaoudatos 28 Oktovríou 52, Pédion Áreos; metro Viktória. Large stock of hiking and climbing gear, including packs, stoves, water containers, sleeping bags and all related clothing.
Road Ippokrátous 39; metro Panepistímio; tel: 210 36 13 242. All their own maps, plus many English-language travel guides.

Music Recordings

Xylouris Panepistimiou 39, inside *stoá;* tel: 210 32 22 711. The widow and son of the late, great Cretan musician run this Aladdin's Cave of a shop, with just about every genre of Greek music crammed into a limited space.
Music Corner Panepistimíou 56, 106 78 Athens; tel: 33 04 000. Slightly pricey but very well selected and well displayed stock of folk, *rebétika* and new Greek trends on the ground floor.
Mr Vinylio Iféstou 24, inside *stoá;* tel: 210 33 12 813. For second-hand collectors, an excellent if pricey stock of old vinyl, as the name implies; also CDs.
Zaharias Iféstou 20, inside *stoá;* tel: 210 32 45 035. The best place for used CDs.

Crafts and Traditional Products

Centre of Hellenic Tradition Mitropóleos 59 or Pandróssou 36; metro Monastiráki; tel: 210 32 13 023. The arcade below the upstairs premises gives a good sampling of the pottery, lace, carved wood, embroidery and examples of just about every other surviving Greek craft to be had upstairs.
Kombologadiko Koumbári 6, Kolonáki; metro Evangelismós; tel: 210 36 24 267. The apotheosis of the *kombolói* (worry-bead rosary) – not your tourist knick-knack from olive wood or rhinestone, but precious objects in amber, black coral, cat's eye.
Lalounis Panepistimíou 6; metro Sýntagma; tel: 210 36 11 371. The central outlet of Greece's best-known family of jewellery designers emerged from a 2006 refit more dazzling than ever. The solid gold pieces are not exactly subtle.
Mastiha Shop Panepistimíou 6, corner Kriezótou; metro Sýntagma; tel: 210 36 32 750. Everything extracted and made from the mastic bush of Híos: soaps, shampoos, chewing gum, candles the lot. Not cheap, as mastic-resin-gathering is very labour-intensive. If you miss it, there's a branch at the airport on the departures concourse.
Pelikanos Adrianoú 115, Pláka; metro Akrópoli; tel: 210 32 19 846. Handmade copper- and brassware specialist, with a mix of antique and new-made pieces. Not cheap, but there are very few such outlets remaining.
Riza Voukourestíou 35, corner Skoufá. tel: 210 36 11 157. Like those embroidered curtains in that olde worlde taverna? Here's where to get them. They also have table place settings, furniture, embroidery.
Ioannis Samouilian Iféstou 36; metro Monastiráki. Oft-photographed musical-instrument maker in the heart of the flea market; the place to go for a *lýra* or a *bouzoúki*.
Vavas Iféstou 30; metro Monastiráki. Tiny stall specialising in nothing but wooden *távli* (backgammon) sets, from basic, unadorned models to inlaid ones (made in Syria, no matter what you may be told).
Eleni Votsi Xánthou 7, Kolonáki; metro Evangelismós; tel: 210 36 00 936. The woman who helped design the 2004 Olympic medals has an alluring line of gold jewellery set with (semi-)precious stones and even seashells.

BELOW: shoe shopping in Kolonáki

Antiques and Collectables

Theotokis Darousos Normanoú 7; metro Monastiráki; tel: 210 33 11 638. Posters, maps and old Greek advertisements, both originals and reproductions.
Ludwig Graffe Zoodohou Pigis 1; metro Panepistímio; tel: 210 38 43 055. Most complete and easy-to-navigate stock of the city's half-dozen or so rare-print merchants, but – like the others – pricey.
Kalarhaki Brothers Alipédou 40 corner Skylitsí 9, Piraeus; metro Piraeus. Most interestingly stocked of the permanent storefront dealers in the Piraeus flea-market. Not much portable except for some covetable red-and-white opaline lamps from the 1930s.

SPORTS

Spectator Sports

Despite its population being officially classified by the EU as the most obese and unfit in Europe, Greece is a sports-mad nation, all the more so since the Olympics garnered a respectable crop of medals for the home team. But with essentially no public pools, a paltry number of tennis courts and no cycling lanes – to name the most obvious deficiencies – athletics still means spectator sports, essentially basketball and football. The national basketball team finished second in the 2006 European Championships (beaten in the final by Spain), while the private clubs – Panathinaïkós, AEK and Olympiakós – have won European titles on a half-dozen occasions since 1968. The national footie squad stunned everyone by snatching the Euro 2004 title, though they have performed dismally every since, failing to qualify for the 2006 World Cup. This hasn't prevented a proliferation of papers devoted exclusively to football, and periodic outbreaks of hooliganism.

Children's Activities

In a society where children are inculcated very early into adult routines – including staying out late at tavernas – there was until recently very little in the way of specifically child-orientated activities, and there still isn't much.

Attica Zoological Park Gialoú district, Spáta; tel: 210 66 34 724. Opened in 2000 by Frenchman Jean-Jacques Lesueur, this is the closest thing the Athens area has to a zoo. Big cats, monkeys and even pygmy hippos, though it's most renowned as the third largest global collection of birds. Open daily year-round.

Mousio Ellenikís Pedikís Tékhnis/Museum of Greek Children's Art Kódrou 9, Pláka; tel: 210 33 12 621; www.childrensartmuseum.gr. (Tues–Sat 10am–2pm, Sun 11am–2pm; closed Aug; admission fee). As it says: the winning entries to an annual contest open to the under-14s.

Greek Children's Museum Kydathinéon 14, Pláka; metro Syndagma; tel: 210 33 12 995. (Tues–Fri 10am–2pm, Sat–Sun 10am–3pm; free admission, but some special programmes have a fee.) Aimed largely at Greek school groups, with labelling solely in Greek, but there are some interactive exhibitions.

Evgenidio Planetarium Pendélis 11, off Syngroú, Paleó Fáliro; tel: 210 94 69 600; www.evgenfound.edu.gr. (Open Wed–Sat.) Documentary films as well as the usual planetary projections.

ABOVE: fashion in Kolonáki.

Shops for Children

Jack in the Box Háritos 13, Kolonáki; metro Evangelismós; tel: 210 72 58 735. Old fashioned wooden and wind-up times, stuffed animals, puzzles.

Neverland Sólonos 18, Kolonáki; metro Sýntagma; tel: 210 36 00 996. Stuffed animals, board games and quality dolls-house furnishings are among the offerings here.

Football in Athens

Most Athenians root for one or other of the three permanent first-division teams which dominate both Athenian football and the Greek 16-team first division at large. (As noted above, the Big Three have also lent their name and funding to the main basketball teams.)

Panathinaïkós (aka PAO; www.pao.gr), in green-and-white livery, play temporarily – though in effect until further notice – at the Olympic stadium in Maroússi (metro Iríni or suburban buses along Leofóros Kifisías). Their green three-leaf clover graffiti – this *trfýlli* being synonymous with the team's cult – virtually carpets the city, signed off by ΘΥΡΑ 13, evoking the hallowed home-side gate at now-derelict Leofóros stadium in Ambelókipi.

Red-and-white Olympiakós (www.olympiacos.gr), lately the most successful side with nine championships since 1996, play at 2003-refurbished Karaïskáki Stadium in Néo Fáliro, comparatively easy to get to by a walkway from either the Fáliro metro or Fáliro tram stations. Traditionally the team of sailors and stevedores, supporters are nicknamed *gávri* or "anchovies" – as in the ubiquitous disparaging graffito *gávri flóri* ("anchovies" = wimps).

Athlitikós Ómilos Konstantinopóleos (AEK; www.aekfc.gr), who play in black and yellow, were founded by Asia Minor refugees, with the Byzantine double-headed eagle on their banner. They share Maroússi's Olympic stadium with Panathinaïkós for the time being, their old stadium in Néa Filadélfia now lying abandoned.

There are also lesser teams which often get into the first division, for example Paniónios (www.panionios.gr), the oldest team in the city, also with an Asia-Minor-descended fan base and antiquated grounds a few blocks off Syngroú in Néa Smýrni, Ionikós in Níkea and Egáleo in the eponymous western suburb. Matches, on Wednesday nights and Saturday afternoons as elsewhere in Europe, are not always well attended, so it can be easy to obtain tickets on the door the same day.

A–Z

An Alphabetical Summary of Practical Information

Admission

Within the Places section we have given typical opening hours based on recent patterns of operation, but these are subject to available funding for staff, and the only firm information is to be had at the site or musuem itself. Note that the last allowed entry is generally 15–20 minutes before the closing time stated in our descriptions. With few exceptions, all attractions have an admission charge. Always enquire as to whether there is an advantageously priced joint ticket with other nearby museums or sites. Admission is generally free on Sundays and holidays between November and March inclusive. Those aged 60 and over, as well as certified teachers and univesity instructors, tend to get one-third off admission prices, while bona fide students with proper documentation usually get about one-half off full price. These concessions do not necessarily apply to the handful of privately-run museums.

Budgeting for Your Trip

Athens is no longer the cheap destination people may remember from two or three decades ago – entry into the euro zone has had its effect. Keep the following ranges in mind when calculating a budget:

Accommodation: Average cost per person of a room with breakfast in a C-class–B-class/2-star–3-star hotel will be €40–65.

Admission charges: These vary from €2–4 for minor attractions to €12 for five-star sites like the Acropolis.

Local transport: Buses, trams and the metro are inexpensive by EU standards; if you plan to take more than four or five journeys in one day, a one-day, all-means travel pass at €3 is good value, the one-week pass at €10 is an even better deal. A taxi ride from, say, Ambelókipi back to the centre is unlikely to exceed €6 if you get an honest driver.

Meals: The sky's the limit here, with €80–100 possible at the capital's swankier eateries, but most meals at our recommended tavernas and restaurants won't exceed €15–20 per head, plus drink.

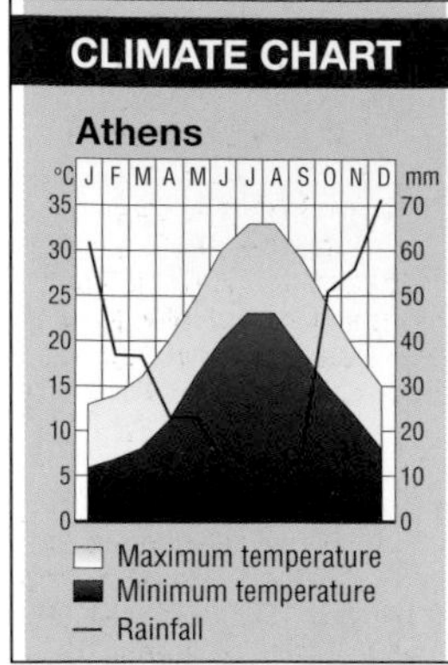

Climate and Clothing

Athens has a typical Mediterranean climate of long, dry summers, unpredictable autumns, relatively mild but often wet winters and short springs, although global climate change has made even these generalisations less useful than before.

Spring – construed as April through to early June – is very pleasant, with midday temperatures rarely in excess of 25°C/77°F, and brief showers likely only until early May. Night-time temperatures rarely drop below 15°C/60°F.

Summer temperatures regularly soar above 34°C/92°F, their effect made worse by air pollution and a complete absence of rain. Every few years there's a *kávsona* (scorching heat wave) that mows down numbers of elderly or ill people with compromised respiratory systems. Not for nothing does any Athenian who can manage it leave town for ancestral villages and/or second homes between the end of July and the beginning of September.

Autumn weather can be very unstable, with rainy periods from mid-October to mid-November alternating with the balmy weeks of *kalokeráki* or "Indian summer" – count on average midday temperatures of 21°C/69°F.

Winter can be grey and gloomy; the first really cold weather is said to first arrive with the *varvaroníkola*, the saint's days of Varvára and Nikólaos (Barbara and Nicholas) on December 4/6. But even here – especially during the *alkyonídes* or "halcyon days" of late January and early February – there are many clear, sunny days, though the period from mid-February to late March tends to be blustery and dank. Temperatures average about 12°C/54°F by day, but can dip to near-freezing after dark.

The rainy season lasts from mid-October to early April, with the wettest months being December, February and March. Downpours can be sudden and catastrophic, with a few inches in a few hours resulting in flooded streets and utility outages. Snow on the ground is rare – usually once every two or three years – but even a few centimetres can be cataclysmic, as the city is habitually unequipped and must secure snowploughs from elsewhere.

Clothing

The local dress code can best be summarised as "smart casual". Except in Exárhia, grunge attire is out – for most Greeks, poverty is an uncomfortably close memory, and it will be assumed that you are either making light of hard times, or have no self-respect, or both. Similarly, beachwear or bare chests once off the beach – even in casual Glyfáda – is a no-no. Really formal wear, however, is only necessary for the rarified confines of the poshest restaurants, eg the roof garden at the Grande Bretagne or the Vardis at Kifisiá's Hotel Pentelikon.

From April to October, bring lightweight, breathing, cotton clothing. During those two months, a light jacket or cardigan will be useful at supper time, as tavernas have no way of heating outdoor seating other than transparent wind-barriers. From November to March, warm trousers for men, long dresses for women and long sleeves for both sexes come in handy. An actual overcoat is usually needed from December onwards. A small collapsible umbrella in your luggage is useful during winter; if you forget and are caught in a storm, street vendors (usually Bengalis or Kurds) at the tops of the metro escalators will oblige you with a range of models for sale.

When visiting any monastery or church, men should wear long trousers and women should wear skirts or dresses, not trousers, and additionally cover their shoulders.

Crime and Safety

Athens has a deserved reputation for being one of Europe's safer capitals. There are few "no-go" areas – though Omónia, Platía Váthis and Platía Viktórias are not terribly salubrious after dark – and the presence of ordinary people, and attended kiosks, on the street until very late contributes to this air of security. Use common sense – not carrying unnecessarily large amounts of cash or leaving hire cars unlocked – and nothing untoward should happen. There are only two areas where there is an established pattern of car break-ins – Psyrrí and Exárhia – so it may be wise to use covered, secure car-parks there. The new metro (Lines 2 and 3) is heavily policed and pretty crime-free, though pick-pocketing and bag-slashing have been reported on the old ISAP (Line 1).

If you're unlucky enough to become a victim, dial 100 (or call 12 from a mobile) for serious crimes against persons (assault etc), but dial 171 for the Tourist Police which deals with thefts. The main police headquarters are at Leofóros Alexándras 173, Ambelókipi (tel: 210 647 6000). The Tourist Police have walk-in premises on Veïkou in Koukáki district.

Customs

Arrivals from EU countries are no longer subject to customs controls. Those coming from non-EU states have a duty-free allowance of 200 cigarettes (or 50 cigars or 250 grammes of tobacco), 1 litre of spirits or 2 litres of wine, and one 50ml bottle of cologne. Spirits and cigars in particular are reasonably priced in Greece, as are local (and some foreign) wines, so there's no real need to bring these in anyway. Pets can be freely imported as long as they have health certificates showing current vaccinations. Consumer electronic items such as laptops and video cameras no longer attract any undue attention, as long as it's just one per customer.

Disabled Travellers

Public transport at least is increasingly adapted to disabled travellers' needs. Most metro stations have elevators down from street level, and "kneeling" buses are increasingly common. Some – by no means all – museums have wheelchair ramps, the Acropolis is now wheelchair-accessible, and many of the better hotels class B and above (such as the Herodion in Makrygiánni) have rooms with wheelchair-adapted bathrooms.

Electricity

Athens mains voltage is 220–240 volts, 50 hertz, out of double round-pin sockets. UK visitors will need a 3-to-2-pin adaptor, which should be purchased at the departure airport if not sooner; they are impossible to find in Greece. By contrast, rectangular-to-round-pin adaptors for use by North Americans are easy to find, but be sure your shaver or hair-dryer is dual voltage. Transformers are so expensive and bulky that it's not worth buying one to cater to an imported mono-voltage appliance – just buy another hair dryer locally.

Embasssies

Australia Dimitríou Soútsou 37, Ambelókipi; tel: 210 87 04 000; www.ausemb.gr
Canada Ioánnou Gennadíou 4, Kolonáki; tel: 210 72 73 480; www.athens.gc.ca
Ireland Vasiléos Konstandínouu 7, Pangráti; tel: 210 72 32 771
South Africa Kifisías 60, Maroússi; tel: 210 61 06 645; www.southafrica.gr
UK Ploutárhou 1, Kolonáki; tel: 210 210 72 72 600; www.british-embassy.gr
US Vasilísis Sofías 91; tel: 72 12 951; www.usembassy.gr

Emergencies

Dial 166 to summon an ambulance, or 1434 for the closest hospital. The designated casualty hospital for Greater Athens is **KAT**, out in Kifisiá with its own ISAP stop ("KAT"), but their performance is variable to say the least. You might prefer the more central emergency wards of the **Evangelismós Hospital**, Ypsilándou 45–47, Kolonáki (tel: 210 720 1000), or the **Alexándra Hospital** at Vasilísis Sofías 80 (tel: 210 33 81 100, opposite the Mégaro Musikís. If your travel insurance covers this, you might want to go to a private clinic; the US Embassy website has lists of specialists and hospital addresses.

Entry Regulations

Visitors from the EU and the EEA can stay indefinitely on production of a passport or valid identity card; either must be valid for at least three months after your arrival date. Citizens of the US, Australia, New Zealand, Canada and South Africa receive mandatory entry and exit stamps in their passports and can stay, as tourists, for 90 days (cumulative) in any 180-day period.

Extended Stays

Unless of Greek descent, or married to an EU/EEA national, visitors from non-EU/EEA countries are currently not being given extensions to the basic three-month tourist visa. You must leave not just Greece but the entire Schengen Zone – which comprises the EU as it was before May 2004, minus Britain and Ireland, plus Norway and Iceland – and stay out until the 90-days-in-180 rule as described above has been satisfied. If you overstay your allowed time and then leave voluntarily, you'll be hit with a huge fine upon departure – anywhere from €587 to €1,174 – and possibly be barred from re-entering for some time. No excuses will be entertained except a medical certificate stating you were immobilised in hospital.

Gay Athens

Despite having given the term "Greek love" to the world, Greece remains deeply ambivalent about homosexuality – conceded as "to be expected" in the arts, theatre and music scenes (there are a disproportionate number of lesbian vocal stars) but apt to be deep in the closet elsewhere. The rampant 2004–05 gay sex scandals amongst the nominally celibate senior Orthodox clergy

BELOW: University pillar.

did at least blow the lid off the prevailing hypocrisy on the subject. All that said, Athens has an increasingly thriving gay scene, even if many club premises – like their attendees – are still "closeted" as unsigned, anonymous bunkers.

There are four acknowledged nuclei of activity: the intersection of Syngroú and Lembési, the latter street with three of the most long-lived exclusively gay clubs in the city (The Guys at No. 8, Granazi at No. 20 and Lamda at No. 15); two unmarked transvetite/drag-queen bars around the junction of Androútsou and Zan Moreás in nearby Koukáki; plus mixed but gay-friendly premises in Exárhia (where Fairytale at Kolléti 25 is the city's premier lesbian venue) and Gázi, in the latter district along Persefónis, Triptolémou and busy Konstantinopóleos streets. Gay Greeks are as nocturnally sociable as any other citizen and there's little point showing up much before 11pm. For further information, consult the nationwide gay website www.deon.gr.

Health Care

No inoculations are required for entering Greece. Athens tap water is safe to drink, but some people complain of its hardness; bottled water is ubiquitous. You shouldn't have gastrointestinal problems from eating at any of our recommended restaurants, but all the same it's probably best, in summer, to eat *magireftá* (cooked casserole dishes) at lunchtime rather than at supper after they've sat in the heat all day. Avoid meat or seafood in chiller cases that looks long in the tooth – it very likely is, especially on Sunday. In summer, use a sunhat if necessary and sunscreen lotion. Hats sold locally change every season and may not be to your taste. Sunscreen of up to SPF 30 is readily available in pharmacies, at prices comparable to overseas.

Chemists/Pharmacies

These (*farmakía* in Greek) are indicated by a sign with a green cross. All are open from Monday to Friday 9am–2pm, plus 5.30–8.30pm Tuesday, Thursday and Friday; outside these hours the rota/duty pharmacy is listed on a bilingual sheet posted on the door.

The price of medications is controlled in Greece, and many formulas are available inexpensively which would be on prescription only overseas. If you need to replace something brought from overseas, show the label and/or product literature to the pharmacist and they will find the equivalent local formula, often generic.

Insurance

EU nationals can receive free medical attention in Greek state-run hospitals on the same basis as residents. You'll need a European Health Insurance Card as proof of eligibility. (In the UK you can order one through a post office or on-line at www.dh.gov.uk/travellers.)

However Greek state hospital in-patient care often leaves much to be desired – relatives bringing in bedding and extra food for relatives, bribes to doctors and nurses to jump queues or provide "extra" services – so all non-EU citizens, as well as EU nationals, might care to investigate travel insurance policies that cover private medical care and (if necessary) emergency repatriation.

Internet Cafés

There are a number of these across central Athens, though some tend to be rather smoky. Rates vary from €1.50–4 per hour, with cheaper rates at night. Some to try include:

Bits & Bytes Kapnikaréas 19, Monastiráki
QuickNet Gládstonos 4, Omónia
Café 4U Ippokrátous 44, Exárhia
EasyInternet Platía Syntágmatos, west side.

Kiosks (*Períptera*)

These quintessentially Greek institutions are strategically placed on street corners and *platíes*; just occasionally they occupy hole-in-the-wall shopfronts. The larger ones are almost small shops, stocking bus tickets, phone-cards, sweets and nuts, cold drinks, contraceptives, magazines, newspapers, cigarettes, blank CDs, pens and pencils. If you're lost, the proprietors usually know the area well.

Lost Property

The Metro operates its own lost property office; enquire at the ticket window at any station. Otherwise, there is general lost property division at the main police headquarters at Leofóros Alexándras 173.

Maps

The maps in this guide will do fine for a short visit, but if you end up spending longer in Athens you'll want a proper, exhaustive atlas. The most widely sold and renowned is the *Athína-Pireás Proástia Hártis-Odigós* (*Athens-Piraeus-Suburbs Map Guide*) published by Nikolaos Fotis (€20); there's also a second volume at the same price for rural Attica. Both are in Greek only but show absolutely everything, including cinemas, major concert venues and hotels.

Emvelia Publications publishes a smaller version in Roman alphabet (€12). Either Emvelia or its competitors Road Editions and Anavasi do maps for the Saronic Gulf Islands, while both Road and Anavasi have topographic hiking maps available for Mount Párnitha. For dedicated map retailers, see our bookstore listings on page 252 under "Activities".

Media

Newspapers and magazines

British newspapers are readily available in central Athens, by noon of the same day of publication. The *International Herald Tribune* (daily except Mon) includes as a free bonus an abridged English version of the respected Greek daily *Kathimerini* (also at wwww.ekathimerini.com). *Time* and *Newsweek* are also widely sold.

There are few surviving English-language publications other than the *Athens News*, something of a cross between newspaper and magazine, issued every Friday (also on www.athensnews.gr but copy is a week behind), and *Odyssey*, a glossy bi-monthly magazine with its eye firmly on the diaspora Greek market. *Athens News* has fragmentary events listings; for a more complete summary, you'll have to master enough Greek (alphabet) to interpret *Athinorama* (every Thursday) and *Exodos* (also Thurs), the two main listings magazines, as well as the free *Lifo* and *Athens Voice*. The latter contains a Shortlist in English.

Radio and Television

The two state-run radio channels are ER1 (a mix of news, talk and popular music) and ER2 (strictly popular music), but these are dwarfed by literally dozens of private stations in and around Athens – even the tiny islands of the Saronic Gulf all have at least one local station apiece.

Greece's state-funded TV stations, ET1, NET and (from Thessaloníki) ET3, likewise lag behind private channels – Antenna, Star, Alpha, Alter and Makedonia TV – in the ratings, though not necessarily in quality of offerings. Programming comprises a mix of soaps and sitcoms (both local and imported Latin American), game shows, movies and sports, with lately a leavening of wildlife documentaries, costume dramas, reality TV and today-in-history features. All foreign films are broadcast in their original language, with Greek subtitles. Most private channels operate around the clock; public stations broadcast from around 5.30am until 3am.

ABOVE: Roman paving.

The better hotels provide (often for a fee) various cable and satellite channels, including CNN, MTV, Filmnet, BBC World, French TV5 and Italian Rai Due.

Money Matters

The currency of Greece is the euro (*evró*), divided into one hundred cents (*leptá*). It comes as coins of 1, 2, 5, 10, 20 and 50 cents, as well as 1 and 2 euros. Notes come in denominations of 5, 10, 20, 50, 100, 200 and 500 euros. You are unlikely to see the larger-denomination notes, and indeed Greeks view them with suspicion as they have often been counterfeited.

The easiest way to obtain money while visiting Athens is by using one of the bank ATMs (autoteller machines) that are literally on every street corner in the centre. Using a debit card is marginally cheaper than using a credit card. Exchange of traveller's cheques in Greece has just about ceased, and you face a long wait inside the bank branch and assorted paperwork if you insist on this.

Banking hours are Mon–Thur 8.30am–2.30pm and Fri 8.30am–2.30pm. It is also possible to change sterling or US dollar notes outside these hours at a number of exchange bureaux which have sprung up in central Athens, but proclamations of "no commission charged" should be treated sceptically – the rate of exchange will likely be disadvantageous. The official rate for any outside currency against the euro is posted in bank windows, or viewable at www.oanda.com.

Credit cards are not widely accepted in the more modest tav ernas or in hotels below C-class. They are, however, almost mandatory for car rental, and very useful for buying air tickets. A few merchants or travel agents may levy a 3-percent commission for use of credit cards for certain tickets. Visa and Mastercard are more widely recognised than Diner's or American Express.

Tipping

Service is nominally included in hotel rates and restaurant/taverna prices, but a few euros at the end of your stay for the chambermaid is appreciated, and you should leave the spare change on the table for the serving staff at tavernas – large parties should leave somewhere between five and ten percent of the bill extra. For taxi drivers, if they've charged you correctly, you should "round up" to the next euro.

Opening Hours

It's risky to generalise about this, as there are so many variations owing to professional idiosyncracies that it's best to count on getting things done only from Monday to Friday, 9.30am to 1pm. For example, delis and butchers are not allowed to sell fresh meat during summer afternoons; similarly fishmongers are only open in the morning until they sell out (usually by noon or 1pm). Major travel agencies are open continuously from about 8.30am to 8pm Monday to Saturday. Supermarkets much the same, open from 8.30am to 9pm Monday to Friday, until 6pm or 7pm on Saturday.

For other kinds of shops, working hours are Monday, Wednesday and Saturday from approximately 9am–2.30pm, and Tuesday, Thursday and Friday 8.30am–2pm and again from 6 to 9pm. During the cooler, shorter-day months the morning schedule shifts slightly forward, the evening session a half-hour or even a full hour back. In Athens many enterprises have taken to keeping a continuous schedule (*synehés orário*) during the winter, but there is considerable resistance to this among their peers, even with pressure being brought to bear by the EU, and the periodic threat of its legal enforcement. Professional practices offering a service frequently operate a straight 9am-to-5/6pm schedule.

Postal Services

Post offices, recognisable from their signs with a stylised Hermes' head on a blue background, are generally open Monday to Friday 7.30am–2pm, though the Sýntagma branch (corner Mitropóleos) keeps longer hours (Mon–Fri 7.30am–8pm, Sat 7.30am–2pm, Sun 9am–1pm). Large parcels are handled at the branch at Mitropóleos 60 (Mon–Fri 7.30am–8pm). Parcels to be sent outside of the EU are best presented unsealed, as they will be inspected; major post offices sell various box packs, but they don't provide tape, twine or scissors – come prepared. *Poste restante* is collected only at the Eólou 100 branch, near Omónia. Post offices are also designated disbursal branches for Western Union money wires (you can also send money overseas from postal counters).

Airmail letters take three to seven days to reach the rest of Europe, five to 12 days to get to North America, and a bit longer for Australia and New Zealand. For a modest fee (about €3) you can shave a couple of days off delivery time to any destination by using the express service (*katepígon*). Registered (*systiméno*) delivery is also available for a similar amount, but works out quite slow unless it's coupled with express service. Experience has shown that outgoing express post to overseas destinations is just as fast as private courier services such as DHL, ACS, Speedex and FedEx, which all have multiple branches in Athens.

Ordinary post boxes are bright yellow, express boxes dark red, but it's prudent to use only those right next to a post office, since days may pass between collections at street-corner boxes. If you are confronted by two slots, "ESOTERIKÓ" is for domestic mail, "EXOTERIKÓ" for overseas. Often there are more: one box or slot for mail into Athens and suburbs, one for other parts of Greece, and one for overseas; if in doubt, ask someone.

If you just want a stamp (*grammatósimo*) for a simple letter or postcard, these can be purchased at an authorised postal agency (usually a stationery store). Rates for up to 20g are currently a uniform 65c to all overseas destinations.

Public Holidays

On the following public holidays, absolutely everything will be shut except tourist and travel services:

1 January *Protohroniá* (New Year's Day)
6 January *Theofánia* (Epiphany)
25 March *Evangelismós* (Annunciation) First Monday of Lent (variable, 48 days before Easter)
Good Friday (variable April/May)
Easter Sunday (variable April/May)
May 1 *Protomagiá* (Labour Day)
Pentecost or Whit Monday (50 days after Easter)
15 August *Kímisis tis Theotókou* (Assumption of the Virgin)
October 28 "*Óhi*" (No) day
25 December *Hristoúgenna* (Christmas)
26 December *Sýnaxis tis Panagías* (Gathering of the Virgin's Entourage)

Strikes

Strikes are a fact of Athenian (and Greek) life, affecting all sectors from rubbish collection to museum staff to public transport. The ones most likely to change travel plans are those of bus drivers, taxi drivers, the metro, ferry crews, air traffic controllers and Olympic Airways – fortunately, never all striking simultaneously. They usually last

GREEK PHONE NUMBERS

During 2002–03, all Greek phone numbers changed over to a ten-digit system similar in principal to France's. There are no more area codes per se; the old code, suitably modified (in Athens, 210), has become the prefix of the number, all digits of which must be dialled, even within the same region. All land lines start with 2, all mobiles start with 6. 0800 denotes a toll-free/freefone number, while 0801 denotes a lo-call/urban rate number.

only one or two days, and you will usually have at least as much advance notice to make alternative arrangements – eg returning from an island side-trip by ferry instead of by plane, or vice versa.

If you miss a return flight home owing to industrial action, travel insurers show different degrees of sympathy concerning reimbursal for new or upgraded tickets – read the exclusions and conditions carefully beforehand (pedantic insurers may construe strikes as "insurrection, commotion or civil disorder" and thus not pay out).

Telecommunications

Call boxes installed by OTE, the national telecoms entity – poorly maintained and invariably sited at the noisiest street corners – work only with phonecards (*tilekártes*). These come in various denominations and are available from kiosks and post offices. Despite mysterious numbers scribbled on the appropriate tabs, call boxes cannot be rung back. However, green, countertop cardphones kept by many hotels can be rung. Other options for local calls include counter coin-op phones in bars, *kafenía* and hotel lobbies. These take small euro coins and also can be rung back as a rule.

Local and Greek intercity calls to land lines are affordable on OTE *tilekártes*, but their overseas rates are exorbitant. Accordingly lots of competition has sprung up, either piggyback programmes for land-lines or pre-paid calling cards, which is what most savvy visitors use. These cards can be used with any call box or subscriber land line (including a hotel-room extension), but not mobiles. They all involve calling a free access number beginning with 807 and then entering a 12-digit code, followed by the number you want. Sound quality can vary but rates are as much as two-thirds less than OTE 's. We've had good luck with Altec's Talk

USEFUL NUMBERS

Directory enquiries within Greece 11888
International operator/ enquiries 139
Speaking clock 141

International calls
Dial 00 followed by country code:
Australia 61
Eire 352
New Zealand 64
UK 44
US 1
South Africa 27

Talk, which can provide over 90 minutes of chat to the UK and many other European countries for €5 – ie 3.7 cents per minute, VAT inclusive.

Avoid making anything other than brief local calls from hotel rooms, as rates – at 20 to 30 cents per unit – are typically double or triple the basic OTE tariffs. An exception is dialling up internet access numbers from your laptop; these are low-cost calls and even multiplied by three will still work out much cheaper than using an internet café.

Mobiles

You may form the impression that Greeks are a sub-species, evolved to come into the world joined at the hip with a *kinitó*, as mobiles/cellphones are called here. In a population of roughly 11 million, there are claimed to be over 7 million mobile handsets in use. Four networks operate at locally at present, and coverage in Athens is comprehensive, extending even into the metro tunnels. Contract-free plans are heavily promoted in Greece, and if you're here for more than a week or so, buying a Greek pay-as-you-go SIM card (for €15–20) from any of the numerous mobile phone outlets – Germanos is relatively impartial, selling most plans – will pay for itself very quickly compared to attempting to roam with your home number. You can re-use the same number on your next visit as long as you recharge at least once yearly. Attempting to roam with your home provider will land you with outrageous charges of over 75c equivalent per minute minimum (for UK providers, and even more for North American ones), no matter where you're calling, plus almost as much to have incoming calls forwarded to you.

Text messaging is a far cheaper alternative if you choose not to get a Greek SIM. Top-up cards – starting from €9–10 depending on the network – are available at all post offices and *períptera* (street-corner kiosks). If your UK provider refuses to furnish you with an unblock code for your handset, most mobile shops in Athens are able to unblock phones for a small charge with a simple computer procedure. North American users will only be able to use tri-band phones in Greece.

Time Zone

Greece is two hours ahead of Greenwich Mean Time, and observes Daylight Savings in line with the rest of Europe: clocks one hour ahead at 3am on the last Sunday of March, one hour back at 3am on the last Sunday of October. For North America, the difference is 7 hours for Eastern Time (New York), 10 hours for Pacific Time (Los Angeles), except for those few weeks in April when Greece is already on Daylight Savings but America isn't yet.

Toilets

Public toilets are rare, usually a subterranean premises in the centre of a park or *platía* where you should leave 20–30c for the attendant. If you use the facilities in one of the numerous bars or cafés, it's polite to buy a drink. Signs constantly warn you to throw used paper into the basket of foul paper adjacent, rather than down the pan, but this must rank as one of the greatest urban myths in Greece. As long as you don't wad half a roll at a time into the bowl, followed by toothpicks, sanitary napkins etc, you shouldn't cause problems in any but the very oldest, almost-vanished models hooked up to narrow, S-bend plumbing.

Tourist Information

The Greek National Tourist Office (EOT in Greek) has a booth in the arrivals concourse at Elefthérios Venizélos Airport, and also in midtown Athens at Amalías 26, just off Sýntagma between the Russian Orthodox and Anglican churches (open summer Mon–Fri 9am–7pm, Sat–Sun 10am–4pm; winter Mon–Fri 9am–2pm; tel: 210 33 10 392; www.gnto.gr). They keep useful information sheets on current museum and archeological site opening hours, and also specimen ferry/catamaran schedules (more for the Aegean islands than the Saronic Gulf islands, it must be said). They also dispense a free folding map of Athens, adequate for a stay of a few days.

EOT Offices Abroad

Australia 51 Pitt St, Sydney, NSW 2000; tel: 02/9241 1663; email hto@tpg.com.au.
Canada 91 Scollard St, 2nd Floor, Toronto, ON M5R 1GR; tel: (416) 968-2220; email grnto.tor@sympatico.ca
UK 4 Conduit St, London W1R 0DJ; tel: 020/7495 4300; email EOT-greektouristoffice@btinternet.com
USA 645 5th Ave, New York, NY 10022; tel: (212) 421-5777, plus several other branches across the country.

Value Added Tax (VAT)

VAT – sales tax to Americans, abbreviated *Fi-Pi-Ah* in Greek – is levied at a somewhat confusing plethora of rates in Greece, ranging from 6 to 19 percent. However this need not concern the visitor as it is always included in the price charged for the goods or services – with the exception of quotes for car hire.

As in other EU countries, there is a VAT refund scheme for purchasers domiciled outside of the EU, but you need to spend over €100 on a single item – a limit you're only likely to broach if you buy gold jewellery, a fur coat or a designer frock. Ask at the time of purchase if the shop participates in the scheme; you have to fill in a triplicate form and then hand this in to customs for validation upon leaving the country. Eventually you might get a refund cheque.

Websites

Websites for hotels, museums, publications, attractions etc have been included in other sections of this guide. However, the following general websites are of interest, especially before arrival:
www.athensguide.com
www.accessathens.com
www.culture.gr
www.gtp.gr

Weights and Measures

Greece follows the metric system, though it also uses one additional unusual measure of area, the *strémma*, equal to 1,000 sq. metres or roughly a ¼ acre. To convert kilometres into miles divide by 1.6093; to convert metres into feet divide by 0.3048; to convert kilogrammes into pounds divide by 0.4536.
1km = 0.6214 mile
1cm = 0.394 inch
1 kg = 2.2lb.
To convert Celsius temperatures to Fahrenheit, multiply by 9, divide the result by 5, then add 32.

Women Travellers

Lone female visitors may still be targeted for attention by predatory Greek males, especially around beach bars and after-hours discos, but in general machismo is no longer more of a problem than anywhere else in southern Europe. Inexorable changes in Greek culture mean that Greek women have much more sexual freedom than previously, especially in the cities. There is now little controversy in their spending time with their male counterparts, including cohabiting before (or instead of) marriage.

BELOW: young Greeks are more relaxed about relationships.

LANGUAGE

UNDERSTANDING GREEK

The Origins of Greek

Modern Greek is an Indo-European language, but unlike Romance languages such as French or Italian it has no close living relatives, and has no familial connection with the Turkish and Albanian spoken in neighbouring countries (though is distantly related to Slavic languages). It has evolved gradually from the Greek of ancient Athens, via the *Koine* Greek of the New Testament. Despite this pedigree, and a large number of words and expressions taken directly from ancient Attic, the grammar and pronunciation are so different that scholars of ancient Greek who tried to speak it in contemporary Athens would be understood as well as someone uttering Chaucerian English in today's London.

The large vocabulary little changed from ancient Greek is due in part to the attempted imposition of an artificial form of *katharévousa* ("cleansed") Greek, in the years following independence in 1830. The national elite determined that, as part of a drive to restore bygone glories, the language of the peasantry's daily life – *dimotikí* – was to be purged of the Venetian, Italian, Slavic and (most of all) Turkish accretions acquired in the preceding centuries. Also, long-dead verbs and grammatical constructions were to be dusted off and put back into circulation. Like most top-down mandates of the kind, this was doomed to eventual failure, but not before a century and a half of see-saw battles ensued – some literally, in that heads were broken during street battles on the subject. Support of *katharévousa* was linked to the power structure and political conservatism (except, curiously, for the Metaxás dictatorship), while *dimotikí* was associated with the Left, both Communist and Republican, as well as most literary production. After a last gasp of *katharévousa* under the colonels' junta, this *diglossiá* or linguistically schizoid state finally came to an end with the official enthronement of *dimotikí* in 1976 during the first post-junta civilian government.

Except for the legal professions, whose documents tend toward *katharévousa*, and one retrograde newspaper, the old "official" dialect has withered away except for slightly ironic use in speech – and the names of a surprising number of bars, shops and restaurants (eg, En Plo, Enallax, En Levko etc) tending even towards ancient Greek.

Basic Rules

Greek is a phonetic language, although diphthongs (detailed on page 264) produce some unexpected results. It is also inflected, preserving all but one of the case endings inherited from ancient Greek, and retains three genders (masculine, feminine, neuter). Adjectives must agree in number, case and gender with their subject. For simplicity's sake, we cite adjectives and nouns as neuter in the vocabulary tables (except for some numbers).

Verb structure is unremittingly complex, with two basic conjugation paradigms but constructions in both active and passive voices – with passive verbs often having a transitive sense. Greek makes the distinction between the informal (*essý*) and formal (*essís*) second person, as French does with *tu* and *vous*. Young people and much older people often use *essý* even with total strangers, though if you greet someone familiarly and they respond formally, it's best to adopt their usage as the conversation continues, to avoid offence.

All this considered, the alphabet, seemingly so daunting at first, is the least of your worries. Most people learn to decipher it within a week or so.

Pronunciation and Transliteration

Greek	Transliteration	Pronunciation
Αα	*a*	a as in father
Ββ	*v*	v as in vet
Γγ	*g*	y as in yes except before consonants or a, o or ou when it's a breathy g
Δδ	*d*	th as in then
Εε	*e*	e as in get
Ζζ	*z*	z sound
Ηη	*i*	i as in ski
Θθ	*th*	th as in theme
Ιι	*i*	i as in ski
Κκ	*k*	k sound
Λλ	*l*	l sound
Μμ	*m*	m sound
Νν	*n*	n sound
Ξξ	*x*	x sound, never z
Οο	*o*	o as in toad
Ππ	*p*	p sound
Ρρ	*r*	r sound
Σσ	*s*	s sound, except z before m or g; single and double sigma are the same
Ττ	*t*	t sound
Υυ	*y*	y as in barely
Φφ	*f*	f sound
Χχ	*h*	ch before vowels, harsh h sound, like ch in loch, kh before consonants
Ψψ	*ps*	ps as in lips
Ωω	*o*	o as in toad, indistinguishable from omicron above

Combinations and diphthongs

Greek	Transliteration	Pronunciation
AI, αι	*e*	e as in hey∞
AY, αυ	*av/af*	av or af depending on following consonant
EI, ει	*i*	long i, exactly like i or h
EY, ευ	*ev/ef*	ev or ef, depending on following consonant
OI, οι	*long i*	exactly like i or h
OY, ου	*ou*	ou as in tourist
ΓΓ, γγ	*ng*	as in angle; always medial
ΝΓ, νγ	*g/ng*	g as in goat at the beginning of a word, ng in the middle
ΝΞ, νξ	*nx*	nx; only medial or final
ΜΒ, μβ	*b/mb*	b at the beginning of a word, mb in the middle
ΝΤ, ντ	*d/nd*	d at the beginning of a word, nd in the middle
ΤΣ, τσ	*ts*	ts as in hits
ΤΖ, τζ	*tz*	dg as in judge, j as in jam

Basic Expressions

Yes *Né*
Certainly *Málista*
OK, agreed *Endáxi*
No *Óhi*
Please *Parakaló*
Thank you (very much) *Efharistó (polý)*
I (don't) understand *(Dén) Katalavéno*
Speak slower, please *Parakaló, na milísate pió sigá*
How do you say it in Greek? *Pós légete avtó sta Elliniká?*
I don't know *Dén xéro*
Do you speak English? *Miláte angliká?*
Sorry/excuse me *Signómi*
Today *Símera*
Tomorrow *Ávrio*
Yesterday *Khthés*
Now *Tóra*
Later *Argótera*
In the morning *Tó proï*
In the afternoon *Tó apógevma*
In the evening *Tó vrádi*
Here *Edó*
There *Ekí*
Good *Kaló*
Bad *Kakó*
Quickly *Grígora*
Slowly *Sigá*

Greetings and Partings

Hello/goodbye (literally, "your health") *Gía sou/giá sas*
Hello *Hérete*
Good morning *Kalí méra*
Good evening *Kalí spéra*
Good night *Kalí nýkhta*
Goodbye *Adío*
How are you? *Tí kánis/Tí kánete?*
I'm fine *Kalá íme*
And you? *Ké essýs?*
What's your name? *Pós se léne?*
My name is... *Mé léne...*
Mr/Mrs *Kýrios/Kyría*
Miss *Despinís*
See you tomorrow *Thá sé dó ávrio*
See you soon *Kalí andámosi*
Let's go *Páme*
Bon voyage *Kaló taxídi*

At the Hotel

Hotel *Xenodohío*
Rented rooms *Enikiazínena domátia*
This is the address *Na tin diéfthynsi*
I'd like a room... *Tha íthela ena domátio...*
  for one/two/three people *giá éna/dýo/tría átoma*
  for one/two/three nights *giá mía/dýo/trís vradiés*
  with a double bed *me dipló kreváti*
  with a shower *me doús*
  with a view *me théa*
Can I see it? *Boró ná tó dó?*
hot water *zestó neró*
cold water *krýo neró*
air-conditioning *klimatismós*
fan *anamistíra*

Emergencies

Please help me *Parakaló, ná mé voithíste*
I'm ill *Íme árostos/árosti*
I've lost my passport/wallet *Éhasa to diavatiriómou/portofóli mou*
Call an ambulance *Fonáxte éna asthenofóro*
police *astynomía*
doctor *giatrós*
hospital (with casualty ward) *nosokomío (gia epígon peristatiá)*

Shopping

bakery *foúrnos*
food shop *bakáliko*
street market *laïkí agorá*

fresh *frésko, nopó*
organic *viologikó*
pharmacy, chemist *farmakío*
post office *tahydromío*
post card *kartpostál*
stamps *grammatósima*
bookshop *vivliopolío*
stationer's *hartopolío*
petrol/gas station *venzinádiko*
bank *trápeza*
money *leftá/khrímata*
Have you got...? *Éhete...?*
I'll take it *Tha ton páro*
a bag *mía sakoúla*
wrapped *tyligméno*
Do you accept credit cards? *Déheste pistotikés kártes?*
receipt *apódixi*
this one *aftó*
that one *ekíno*
size *mégethos*
big *megálo*
small *mikro*
a little *lígo*
a lot *polý*
too much *pará polý*
together (with) *mazí (mé)*
without *horís*
cheap *ftinó*
expensive *akrivó*
more *perisótero*
less *ligótero*

Moving About and Sightseeing

bus, coach *leoforío, púlman*
bus station *praktorío leoforíon, ktel*
bus stop *stássi*
route start-point *afitírio*
car *aftokínito, amáxi*
I'd like to hire a car (tomorrow)... *Tha íthela na nikiáso éna avtokínito (ávrio)...*
...for three days/a week *...giá tris méres/mía evdomáda*
motorbike, scooter *mihanáki, papáki*
taxi *taxí*
Set the meter to zero, please *Mideníste to rolói, parakaló*
ship *plío/karávi*
high-speed boat, catamaran *tahyplóö, katamarán*
hydrofoil *delfíni*
harbour *limáni*
train *tréno*
suburban train *proastyiakós*
train station *sidirodromikós stathmós*
on foot *mé tá pódia*
trail *monopáti*
A single ticket to... *Éna apló isitírio yiá...*
A return ticket *Éna isitírio mé epistrofí*
What time does it leave? *Ti óra févgi?*
What time does it arrive? *Ti óra ftháni?*
How many kilometres? *Póssa hiliómetra?*
How many hours? *Pósses óres?*
Where are you going? *Poú páte?*
I'm going to... *Páo stó...*
I want to get off at... *Thélo ná katévo stó...*
The road to... *O drómos giá...*
near *kondá*
far *makriá*
left *aristerá*
right *dexiá*
straight ahead *katefthia, ísia*
beach *paralía, ammoudiá*

Idiomatic Expressions

Like all other languages, Greek has numerous idiomatic expressions which you hear constantly. These are a few of the most common.
Éla! Come (literally), but also Speak to me! You don't say!
Oríste! Literally, Indicate!; in effect, What can I do for you?
Embrós!/Légete! Standard phone responses
Tí néa? What's new?
Tí gínete? What's going on (here)?
Étsi k'étsi So-so
Ópa! Whoops! Watch it!
Po-po-po! Expression of dismay or concern, like the French "O là là!"
Pedí moú My boy/girl, sonny, friend, etc.
Maláka(s) Literally "wanker/jerk", but often used (don't try it!) as an informal term of address.
Sigá sigá Take your time, slow down

sea *thálassa*
cave *spiliá*
church *ekklisía*
monastery *monastíri*
museum *mousío*
archeological site *arheologikós hóros*
open *anikhtó*
closed *klistó*
free entrance *ísodos eléftheros*
village *horió*

Numbers

1 *énas/éna/mía*
2 *dýo*
3 *trís/tría*
4 *tésseres/téssera*
5 *pénde*
6 *éxi*
7 *eftá*
8 *okhtó*
9 *ennéa* (or more slangy, *enyá*)
10 *déka*
11 *éndeka*
12 *dódeka*
13 *dekatrís*
14 *dekatésseres* (and so on up to 19)
20 *íkossi*
21 *íkossi éna* (all compounds written separately thus)
30 *triánda*
40 *saránda*
50 *penínda*
60 *exínda*
70 *evdomínda*
80 *ogdónda*
90 *enenínda*
100 *ekató*
150 *ekatón penínda*
200 *diakóssies/diakósia*
500 *pendakóssies/pendakósia*
1,000 *hílies/hília*
2,000 *dýo hiliádes*
1,000,000 *éna ekatomírio*
first *próto*
second *déftero*
third *tríto*

Days of the Week and the Time

Sunday *Kyriakí*
Monday *Deftéra*
Tuesday *Tríti*
Wednesday *Tetárti*
Thursday *Pémpti*

Friday *Paraskeví*
Saturday *Sávato*
What time is it? *Tí óra íne?*
One/two/three o'clock *Mía íy óra/d ýo iy óra/trís íy óra*
Twenty minutes to four *Tésseres pará íkossi*
Five minutes past seven *Eftá ké pénde*
Half past eleven *Éndeka ké misí*
In half an hour *Sé misí óra*
In a quarter-hour *S'éna tétarto*
In two hours *Sé d ýo óres*

Dining Out

Liquid refreshment

b ýra **beer**
frappé **whipped iced instant coffee**
fredduccíno **whipped iced cappuccino**
gála **milk**
kafés fíltro **french-style filtered coffee**
kafés ellinikós... **greek coffee...**
skéto **unsweetened**
métrio **medium sweet**
glykós **cloyingly sweet**
krasí **wine**
áspro **white**
kokkinéli/rozé **rosé**
kókkino/mávro **red**
éna tétarto... **quarter-kilo (250ml)...**
misó kiló... **half kilo (500ml)...**
éna kílo... **a kilo (1 litre)...**
h ýma **bulk (wine)**
limonáda **lemonade**
metalikó/emfialoméno neró **mineral/bottled water**
neskafé **instant coffee**
oúzo **anise-flavoured grape distillate**
portokaláda **orangeade**
rakí **cretan distilled spirit, unflavoured**
tsáï **tea (english)**
tsáï vounoú **"mountain" (sage) tea**
tsípouro **distilled mainland spirit, usually unflavoured**

Basics

aláti **salt**
avgá **eggs**
boukáli **bottle**
dípno **supper**
katálogos, menoú **menu**
o logariasmós **the bill**
mahéri/piroúni/koutáli **knife/fork/spoon**
maheropírouna **cutlery**
mesimerianó **lunch**
méli **honey**
neró **water**
piáto **plate**
potíri **glass**
proïnó **breakfast**
psomí... **bread...**
olikís **wholemeal**
sikalísio **rye**
servítsio **basket with bread, salt, pepper, cutlery**
ládi **oil**
x ýdi **vinegar**
záhari **sugar**

Menu Decoder

Cooking terms

akhnistó **steamed**
frikasé **stew, either lamb, goat or pork, made with celery**
giakhní **stewed in oil and tomato sauce**
gemistá **stuffed (squid, vegetables, etc)**
iliókafto **sun-dried**
kimá **minced (meat)**
kokkinistó **stewed in tomato sauce**
kondosoúvli **any spit-roasted beast, whole or in chunks**
kourkoúti **egg-and-flour batter**
makaronáda **any spaghetti/pasta-based dish**
pastó **marinated in salt**
psitó **roasted**
saganáki **cheese-based red sauce; also any fried cheese**
skáras, sti skára **grilled**
sti soúvla **spit-roasted**
stifádo **any meat stew with tomato and boiling onions**
stó foúrno **baked**
tiganitó **pan-fried**
tis óras **grilled/fried to order**

Soups and starters (Soúpes ke orektiká)

avgolémono **egg and lemon soup**
bekrí mezé **pork chunks in red sauce**
bouréki, bourekákia **courgette/zucchini, potato and cheese pie**
dolmádes, giaprákia **vine leaves stuffed with rice**
fasoláda **bean soup**
fáva **purée of yellow peas, served with onion and lemon**
féta psití **baked feta cheese slabs with chili**
galot ýri **curdled creamy dip**
hortópita **turnover or pie stuffed with wild greens**
kápari **pickled caper leaves**
kopanistí, khtypití **pungent fermented cheese purée**
lahanodolmádes **stuffed cabbage leaves**
mavromátika **black-eyed peas**
melitzanosaláta **aubergine/ egg-plant dip**
piperiá florínes **marinated red sweet macedonian peppers**
plevrótous **oyster mushrooms**
rengosaláta **herring salad**
revythokeftédes **chickpea (garbanzo) patties**
salingária **garden snails**
skordaliá **garlic dip**
spanakópita **spinach pie**
taramosaláta **cod roe paté**
tyrokafterí **cheese dip with chilli** (different from *kopanistí*)
tyrópita **cheese pie**
tzatzíki **yoghurt and cucumber dip**
tzirosaláta **cured mackerel dip**

Cheese (Tyrí)

ageladinó **cow's-milk cheese**
féta **salty-creamy white cheese**
graviéra **gruyère-type hard cheese**
katsikísio **goat cheese**
kasséri **medium-sharp cheese**
myzíthra **sweet cream cheese**
próvio **sheep cheese**

Vegetables and salads (Lahaniká ke salátes)

ambelofásola **crimp-pod runner beans**
angináres **artichokes**
angoúri **cucumber**
ánitho **dill**
bámies **okra, ladies' fingers**
briám, tourloú **ratatouille of zucchini, potatoes, onions, tomato**

domátes tomatoes
fakés lentils
fasolákia french (green) beans
fasóles small white beans
gígantes white haricot beans, usually in tomato sauce
horiátiki (saláta) greek salad (with olives, feta etc)
hórta greens (usually wild), steamed
kolokythákia small courgette/zucchini
koukiá broad fava beans
maroúli lettuce
melitzánes imám aubergine/eggplant slices baked with onion, garlic and copious olive oil
patátes potatoes
piperiés peppers
radíkia wild chicory – a common *hórta*
rókka rocket, arrugula
rýzi/piláfi rice (usually with *sáltsa* – sauce)
spanáki spinach
vlíta notchweed – another common *hórta*

Fish, shellfish and seafood (Psári ke thalassiná)

ahiní sea urchin (roe)
astakós aegean lobster
atherína sand smelt
bakaliáros cod or hake, usually the latter
barbóuni red mullet
fangrí common bream
galéos dogfish, hound shark, tope
garídes shrimp, prawns
gávros mild anchovy
gialisterés smooth venus (type of clam)
glóssa sole
gópa bogue
kalamarákia baby squid
kalamária squid
karavídes crayfish
kefalás axillary bream
koliós chub mackerel
koutsomoúra goatfish (small red mullet)
khténia scallops
kydónia warty venus (type of clam)
lakérda light-fleshed bonito, marinated
marídes picarel
melanoúri saddled bream

TABLE TALK

Can we see the menu? *Boroúme na doúme ton katálogo?*
May we order? *Bouroúme na parangelísoume?*
What's today's special? *Pió íne to piáto iméras?*
I'm a vegetarian (m/f) *Íme hortofágos/hortofági*
Do you have wine by the carafe? *Éhete krasí hýma?*
Cheers! *Stingiássas!*
The bill (check), please *To logariásmo, parakaló*

ménoula sprat
mýdia mussels
okhtapódi octopus
pandélis corvina; also called *sykiós*
petalídes limpets
peskandrítsa monkfish
platý skate, ray
sardéles sardines
sargós white bream
seláhi skate, ray
skáros parrotfish
skathári black bream
skoumbrí atlantic mackerel
soupiá cuttlefish
synagrída dentex
thrápsalo large, deep-water squid
tsipoúra gilt-head bream
xifías swordfish

Meat and main courses (Kréas ke kyria piáta)

arní lamb
biftéki hamburger
brizóla pork or beef chop
giouvétsi baked clay casserole of meat and *kritharáki* (short pasta)
hirinó pork
keftédes meatballs
kokorétsi liver/offal roulade, spit-roasted
kotópoulo chicken
kounéli rabbit
loukánika spicy course-ground sausages
moskhári veal
moussakás aubergine, potato and lamb-mince casserole with béchamel topping
païdákia rib chops, lamb or goat
papoutsákia stuffed aubergine/eggplant "shoes", like *moussakás* without béchamel
pastítsio macaroni "pie" baked with minced meat
patsás tripe soup
psaronéfri pork tenderloin medallions
soutzoukákia minced meat rissoles/beef patties
spetzofáï sausage and pepper red-sauce stew
sykóti liver
tiganiá pork chunks fried with onions

Sweets and desserts (Glyká ke epidórpia)

baklavás honey and nut pastry
bougátsa salt or sweet cream pie served warm with sugar and cinammon
galaktobóuriko custard pie
giaoúrti yogurt
halvás sweetmeat of sesame
karydópita walnut cake
kréma custard
loukoumádes dough fritters in honey syrup and sesame seeds
pagotó ice cream
pastélli sesame and honey bar
ravaní spongecake, lightly syruped
ryzógalo rice pudding
simigdalísios halvás semolina halva

Fruit (Froúta)

ahládia big pears
aktinídia kiwis
fistíkia pistachio nuts
fráoules strawberries
giarmádes autumn peaches
gréypfrout grapefruit, yellow
himoniátiko autumn melon (cassava in USA)
karpoúzi watermelon
kerásia cherries
krystália miniature green pears
kydóni quince
lemónia lemons
míla apples
pepóni persian/galia-type melon
portokália oranges
rodákina summer peaches
sýka figs
stafýia grapes
vaniliés dark plums

FURTHER READING

Following is a bibliography of titles related directly to Athens in all eras. As imprints and availability change constantly, we do not give publishers or editions; any book which is currently out of print can likely be found easily, at a competitive price, on used bookseller websites such as www.abe.com/www.abe.co.uk and www.bookfinder.com.

The Classics, Ancient Religion and Society

Mary Beard ***The Parthenon***. A fresh look at the building, its relief art and actual religious purpose, in the light of recent scholarship.

Walter Burkert ***Greek Religion: Archaic and Classical***. Thorough coverage of the deities and their antecedents in the Middle East, rites and the major festivals.

James Davidson ***Courtesans and Fishcakes***. How consumption and consummation – of/with wine, women, boys and seafood – affected society and politics in ancient Athens, and tailed over into modern attitudes.

R. Gordon Wasson, Carl Ruck and Albert Hoffman ***The Road to Eleusis: Unveiling the Secret of the Mysteries***. Who better qualified than the magic-mushroom man and the discoverer of LSD to argue that the Eleusinian mysteries were at least partly a psychedelic trip, courtesy of grain-ergot fungus?

Thucydides ***History of the Peloponnesian War***. The standard chronicle of the campaigns, by a cashiered Athenian officer.

Xenophon ***The History of My Times***. Thucydides' account stops in 411 BC; this follows events onward to 362 BC.

Plato ***The Republic*** and ***The Symposium***. The standard undergraduate philosophy texts, perhaps even more meaningful if read in the city where they were written.

Greece: General History and Society

Richard Clogg ***A Concise History of Greece***. Far and away the best one-stop summary of the subject, from the end of Byzantium to the millennium; copious maps and literate captions to artwork are further pluses.

Michael Llewellyn Smith ***Ionian Vision: Greece in Asia Minor 1919–22***. Benchmark work by a former long-serving UK ambassador to Greece, on the disastrous campaign that ultimately landed over a million refugees in the country, nearly half of them in and around Athens.

James Pettifer ***The Greeks***. A useful, if spottily edited, introduction to all aspects of contemporary Greece, up to the millennium.

Medieval Athens to Independence

Molly Mackenzie ***Turkish Athens***. Personalities and events from the collapse of the Florentine duchy to the early years of the modern state.

Terence Spencer ***Fair Greece Sad Relic: Literary Philhellenism from Shakespeare to Byron***. How the scribblings of poets and Grand Tourists in Ottoman Greece spurred European support for the 1821 uprising. The Zorba stereotype is centuries old – the feckless, "merrie Greeke" was already described in the 1500s.

William St Clair ***Lord Elgin and the Marbles***. The 1998 update of St Clair's landmark 1967 study, tracing the misadventures of the hotly disputed Parthenon friezes.

Refugee Studies

Bruce Clark ***Twice a Stranger: How Mass Expulsion Forged Modern Greece and Turkey***. Superbly written study, slightly biased towards the Greek side of things, which looks beyond the Lausanne Treaty to the lives of the people affected, and how both countries are only finally digesting the whole experience nearly a century on.

Renée Hirschon ***Heirs of the Greek Catastrophe: The Social Life of Asia Minor Refugees in Piraeus***. During the junta years Hirschon did fieldwork in Kokkiniá, where her hosts clung tenaciously to a separate identity three generations after the population exchanges.

Gail Holst-Warhaft ***Road to Rebetika: Songs of Love, Sorrow and Hashish***. The refugee influx provided a huge boost to this already-existing genre of urban lowlife music, of which Holst-Warhaft is one of the pre-eminent foreign scholars. Song lyrics and updated discography as a bonus.

World War II and the Civil War

Iakovos Kambanelis ***Mauthausen***. Resistance member Kambanelis was sent to the eponymous concentration camp, described in gruesome detail, but the bulk of the action is post-liberation, when the more idealistic inmates come to realise that the post-war world will be

scarcely different from the wartime one. The basis of the ***Mauthausen Trilogy*** song cycle by Mikis Theodorakis.
Mark Mazower ***Inside Hitler's Greece: The Experience of Occupation, 1941–44***. Shows how the complete demoralisation of Greece after its invasion and the incompetence of conventional politicans led to the rise of ELAS and EDES, savage German reprisals and the subsequent civil war. The photos alone are worth the price.
C. M. Woodhouse ***The Struggle for Greece, 1941–49***. Despite the recent opening of Soviet archives, this is a never-superseded study of the so-called "three rounds" of resistance and rebellion; remarkably objective considering Woodhouse's Tory politics and his role in the British mission to resistance forces.

The Junta Years

Oriana Fallaci ***A Man***. Roman à clef for the author's involvement with Alekos Panagoulis, the army officer who attempted to assassinate Colonel Papadopoulos in 1968, then survived prison and torture. An unbelievably tough and prickly character, Panagoulis was himself killed in unsolved circumstances in 1975.
Peter Murtagh ***The Rape of Greece***. A breezy, easy-reading overview of the seedy background to the colonels' coup – specifically the links between royal palace, US Embassy and Greek CIA – and the brave but ultimately futile "Democratic Defence" resistance organised by foreigners and Greeks.
Eleni Vlachos ***House Arrest***. Vlachos (or Vlachou) was the editor-proprietor of respected daily *Kathimerini* in the 1960s and '70s. Rather than printing censored pages mandated by the junta, she published a blank cover in protest – and got placed under house arrest for her defiance. This is the story.

Foreigners' Views of Athens

Michael Llewellyn Smith ***Athens: A Cultural and Literary History***. Thematically divided into "The City of Visitors" – mostly illustrious, from Chateaubriand to Churchill – "The City of Olympians", the revival of the Olympic ideal in 1896, and the eve of the 2004 Games; and "The City of Athenians", how its inhabitants have experienced it through the ages. The best omnibus volume.
Kevin Andrews ***Athens***. The city as seen in the mid-1960s, at the dawn of modernisation and "touristification", by a gifted essayist and long-resident philhellene.
Patricia Storace ***Dinner with Persephone***. The New York poet, resident a year in Athens (with regular forays to the provinces), shows how permeated – and imprisoned – Greece is by its imagined past.
Catherine Temma Davidson ***The Priest Fainted***. Fictionalised autobiography in which a Jewish-Greek-American sets out to discover what made her mother flee the country three decades previously; generous slices of 1980s Athens, especially south of the Acropolis.
Sofka Zinovieff ***Eurydice Street***. Zinovieff first came to Greece as an anthropology student in the early 1980s, then returned in 2001 with her family to live in Athens. In this case love is not blind, with sharp observations on nationalism, leisure, party affiliation and the victims of November 17, among other matters.

Greek and Foreign Fiction set in Athens

Kostas Mourselas ***Red Dyed Hair***. Politically incorrect anti-hero Emmanuil Retsinas is the eye of the storm in this lowlife epic set in and around Piraeus. Basis of a long-running TV series.
Maro Douka ***Fool's Gold***. A young woman from a good family has her idealism and illusions purged by involvement with sexist pigs in the clandestine resistance to the junta.
Andreas Franghias ***The Courtyard***. A well-observed if bleak chronicle of the struggling inhabitants of an Athenian shanty-town, circa 1952.
Olivia Manning ***The Balkan Trilogy, vol 3: Friends and Heroes***. Guy and Harriet Pringle escape Bucharest for Athens in the last months before the invasion of spring 1941.

FEEDBACK

We do our best to ensure the information in our books is as accurate and up-to-date as possible. The books are updated on a regular basis, using local contacts, who painstakingly add, amend and correct as required. However, some mistakes and omissions are inevitable and we are ultimately reliant on our readers to put us in the picture.

We would welcome your feedback on any details related to your experiences using the book "on the road". Maybe we recommended a hotel or restaurant that you liked (or another that you didn't), or perhaps you have discovered interesting new attractions, or facts and figures the country itself. The more details you can give us (particularly with regard to addresses, emails and telephone numbers), the better.

We will acknowledge all contributions, and we'll offer an Insight Guide to the best letters received.

Please write to us at:
Insight Guides
PO Box 7910
London SE1 1WE
United Kingdom
Or send email to:
insight@apaguide.co.uk

Art & Photo Credits

AFP/Getty Images 47
akg-images 20, 42, 45, 124TR, 124B, 125T, 181B
akg-images/Binder 62
akg-images/John Hios 64
akg-images/Erich Lessing inside back flap
Alamy 129B, 190B, 193B
Pete Bennett/Apa 165, 168, 196T
Bettman/Corbis 66
Bridgeman Art Library 123, 124TL
Henri Bureau/Sygma/Corbis 46
Corbis 67
Dimitrios Doumas 41, 152
Courtesy of Fresh Hotel Athens 237T&B, 238
Glyn Genin/Apa back cover CR, 2/3, 7TR, 7BR, 8BL, 14, 16, 28, 35, 36, 37, 39, 50, 52, 56, 57, 61, 68, 83, 86T, 104, 105T, 106T, 107, 110, 111, 126, 127, 128, 129T, 136, 137, 139T, 139B, 140, 141T, 141B, 142T, 142B, 143, 147T, 148, 150, 151T, 153T, 153B, 154, 155B, 159, 169T, 169B, 170T, 171, 172, 173, 175TL, 175B, 176, 177T, 177B, 178TR, 178C, 178BC, 178BR, 179, 180, 181T, 183T, 183B, 184T, 184B, 185B, 185T, 186T, 186B, 188, 189, 191T, 194T, 194B, 195T, 195B, 196B, 202T, 202B, 204T, 204B, 205T, 205B, 206T, 207T, 207B
Gennadios Library 40
Getty Images 38, 55
Courtesy of the National Archive of Greece 65
Hemis/Alamy 60
Mary Evans Picture Library 17, 29
Nowitz Photography back cover CL, 1, 3BR, 4T, 4C, 5BR, 6T, 6B, 7C, 8T, 8BR, 9T, 9B, 10/11, 12/13, 18, 19, 21, 22, 23, 24, 25, 26, 27, 30, 31, 32, 33, 34, 48, 49, 51, 53, 54, 70, 72, 76, 77, 78, 81, 82, 84T, 84B, 85, 86B, 87, 88T, 88B, 89B, 89T, 90, 91, 92, 93, 94T, 95, 96, 97T, 97B, 98T, 98B, 100, 101, 102, 103, 105, 106, 108, 109T, 109B, 112, 113, 115, 116, 116T, 117, 118, 119, 121, 144, 145, 146, 147B, 151B, 155T, 156, 164, 167T, 167B, 170B, 191B, 192T, 193T, 208, 210, 211, 212B, 212T, 213T, 213B, 214T, 214B, 215, 216, 217T, 217B, 218T, 218B, 220, 221, 222T, 223, 232, 247, 252, 253, 257, 259, 262
Panopix 226, 231
Photolibrary 219, 225
Redferns 63
Coutesey of Saint George Lycabettus Hotel 234, 239, 240
Zabert Sandmann/Photolibrary 59
Courtesy of Semiramis Hotel 242L, 242R
TopFoto 43, 44
Frank Wieder/Photolibrary 58
Gregory Wrona/Apa 120, 190T, 198, 200, 201, 203, 206B, 209, 221, 224

Picture Spreads

122/125: All pictures courtesy The Benaki Musuem

132/135: Glyn Genin/Apa 132/133TC, 132BL, 132BR, 134TL, 134BL, 134/135; **Nowitz Photography** 132TL, 134CR, 135CL, 135TR, 135BC

160/163: Glyn Genin/Apa 160BL, 160CR, 161BR, 162TL, 162/163TR, 163BL; **Nowitz Photography** 160TL, 160/161TC, 161BL, 162BL, 162BR, 163BR

178/179: All images **Glyn Genin**

Map Production: Neal Jordan-Caws, Dave Priestley and **Stephen Ramsay**

Production: Linton Donaldson

Athens Street Atlas

The key map shows the area of Athens covered by the atlas section. An index of street names and places of interest shown on the maps can be found on the following pages. For each entry there is a page number and grid reference.

Map Legend

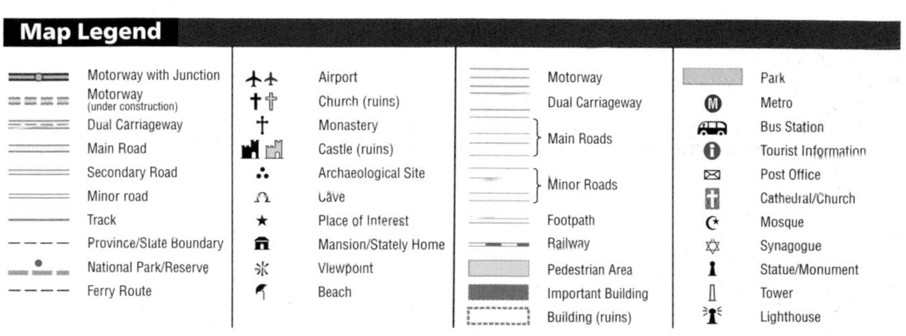

page 272
page 275
page 276
page 279
AREOS PARK
IOANNINON
LENORMAN
AHARNON
LIOSION
LEOFOROS ALEXANDRAS
PANORMOU
National Archaeological Museum
PALAMIDIOU
H. TRIKOUPI
IPPOKRATOUS
D. SOUTSOU
LYKAVITÓS HILL
Theatre of Lykavitós
AG. KONSTANTINOU
ACHILLEOS
L. KONSTANDINOUPOLEOS
AKADIMIAS
PANEPISTIMIOU (EL. VENIZELOU)
STADIOU
P. TSALDARI (PIREOS)
ATHINAS
PAPADIAMANTOPOULOU
LEOF. EL. VENIZELOU
YMITTOU
ERMOU
MITROPOLEOS
LEOF. EL. VENIZELOU
POULOPOULOU
PIREOS
SYNGROU PARK
Ancient Agora of Athens
APOST. PAVLOU
Acropolis
THESSALONIKIS
NATIONAL GARDENS
LEOF. V. KONSTANDINOU
LEOF. AMALIAS
DION. AREOPAGITOU
SPIROU
MERKOURI
YMITTOU
LEOF. ETHNIKIS ANTISTASEOS
FILOLAOU
FILOPAPPOU HILL
Stadium
LEOF. SYNGROU
YMITTOU
FILOLAOU
FORMIONOS

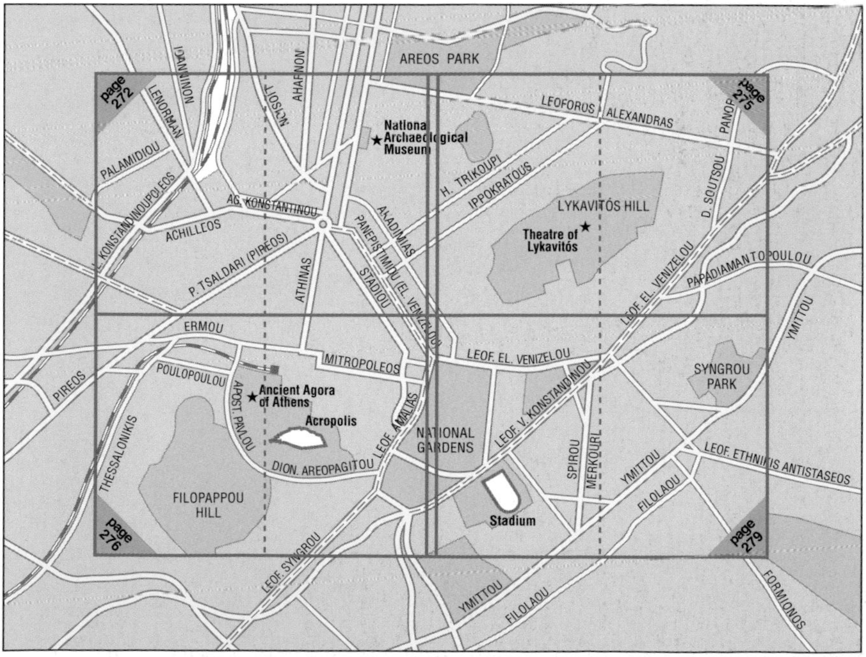

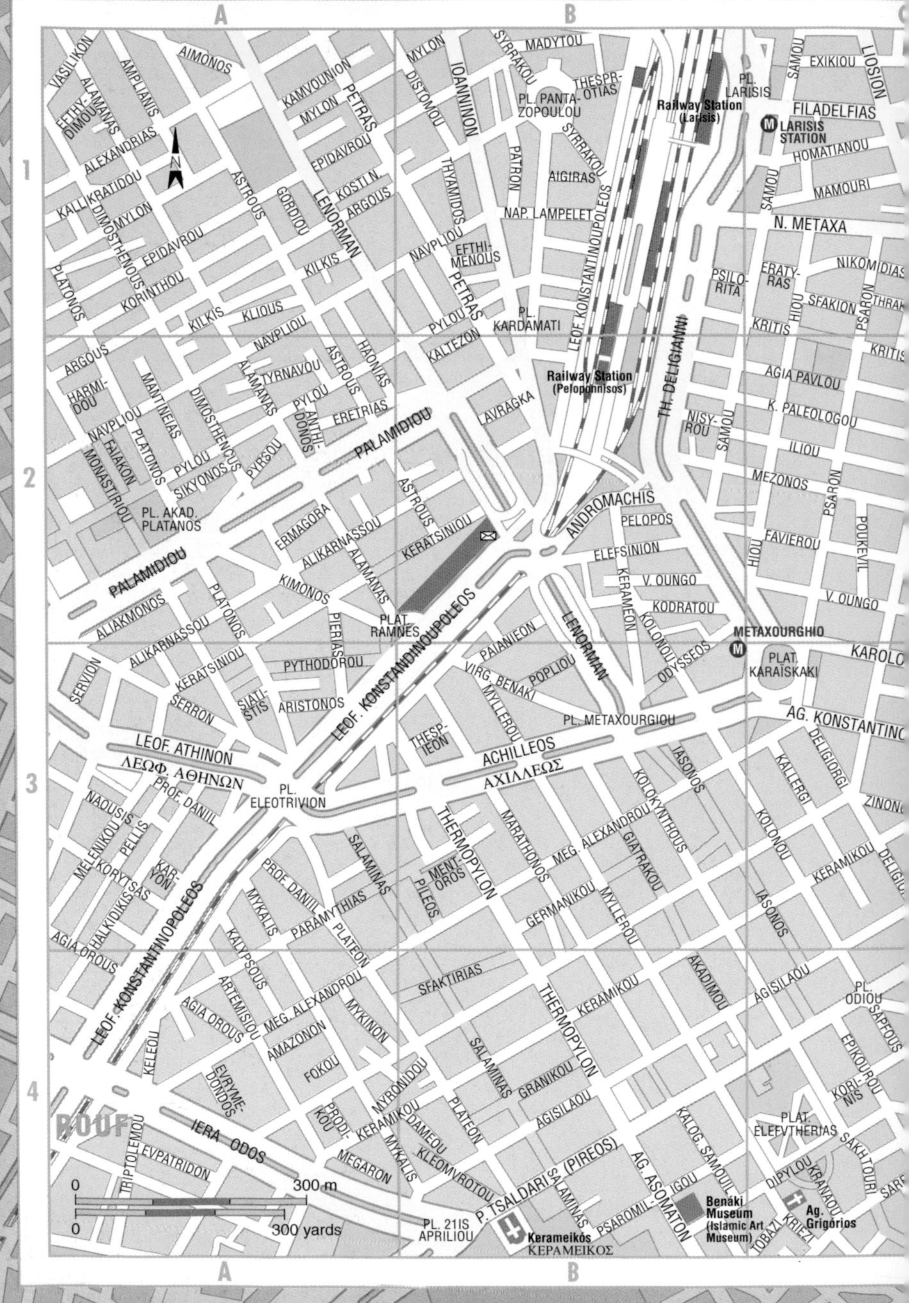
A
B
1
2
3
4
Railway Station
(Larisis)
LARISIS STATION
Railway Station
(Peloponnisos)
METAXOURGHIO
PL. PANTA-ZOPOULOU
PL. LARISIS
PL. KARDAMATI
PL. AKAD. PLATANOS
PLAT RAMNES
PL. ELEOTRIVION
PL. METAXOURGIOU
PLAT. KARAÏSKAKI
PL. ODIOU
PLAT. ELEFVTHERIAS
PL. 21IS APRILIOU
ROUF
LEOF. KONSTANTINOUPOLEOS
LEOF. ATHINON
ΛΕΩΦ. ΑΘΗΝΩΝ
ACHILLEOS
ΑΧΙΛΛΕΩΣ
PALAMIDIOU
IERA ODOS
P. TSALDARI (PIREOS)
TH. DELIGIANNI
LENORMAN
N. METAXA
AG. KONSTANTINOU
Benáki Museum
(Islamic Art Museum)
Keramei̇kós
ΚΕΡΑΜΕΙΚΟΣ
Ag. Grigórios
300 m
300 yards

D
E
1
2
3
4
PLAT. VIKTORIAS (KYRIAKOU)
VIKTORIA
GKYÍLFORDOU
AREOS PARK
MAVROMATEON
FERRON
ELLIS
MIHAIL VODA
ALKIVIADOU
DIDYMOU
IOULIANOU
FYLIS
ARISTOTELOUS
ENIANOS
ΠΑΤΗΣΙΩΝ (28ης ΟΚΤΩΒΡΙΟΥ)
PLATIA EGYPTOU
LEOF. ALEXANDRAS
ΛΕΩΦ. ΑΛΕΞΑΝΔΡΑΣ
SMYRNIS
HARISSIS
AKAKIOU
AHARNON
3RD SEPTEMVRIOU
IPIROU
METSOVOU
Ag. Vasilios
KYVELIS
SARIPOLOU
BOUBOULINAS
ZEMI
NOTARA
SP. TRIKOUPI
PLAPOUTA
FAISTOU
MAKEDONIAS
LIOSION
VASIL. IRAKLIOU
National Archaeological Museum
ΑΡΧΑΙΟΛΟΓΙΚΟ ΜΟΥΣΙΟ
EXARHIA
KALLIDROMIOU
SOURMELI
PL. MAVROKORDATOU
KARNOKOPTIRIOU
SACHINI
TRAÏMPER
K. PALEOLOGOU
MAGER
MARNI
POLYTEKHNIOU
PATISION (28TH OKTOVRIOU)
School of Fine Arts
Polytechnic School
KOUNDOURIOTOU
TOSITSA
METHONIS
STOURNARI
TARELLA
SONIEROU
MEZONOS
PL. ANEXARTISIAS
SOLOMOU
KAPODISTRIOU
KANINGOS
TZORTZ
BOTASI
TSAMADOU
IFONOMOU
ERESOU
FAVIEROU
HALKOKONDYLI
3RD SEPTEBRIOU
ΑΙΟΛΟΥ
PLATIA EXARHION
DERVENION
VERANZEROU
MENANDROU
PLAT. LAVRIOU
PLAT. KANINGOS
PATOUSA
KOLETTI
THEMISTOKLEOUS
VALTETSIOU
A. METAXA
ARAKOVIS
XOUTHOU
SOKRATOUS
SATOVRIANDOU
ΠΑΤΗΣΙΩΝ
Police Station
KLISOVIS
GRAVIAS
EMM. BENAKI
TZAVELLA
MANIS
NIKIFOROU
KOUMOUNDOUROU
National Theatre
ΘΕΑΤΡΟΝ ΕΘΝΙΚΟΝ
KOTOPOULI
DOROU
GLADSTONOS
ΑΓ. ΚΩΝΣΤΑΝΤΙΝΟΥ
PLATIA OMONIAS
OMONIA
(OMONIA SQUARE)
PATISION
EOLOU
NIKITARA
GAMVETA
AKADIMIAS
SOLONOS
ZALONGOU
KIAFAS
700D. PIGIS
H. TRIKOUPI
GIDOTOU
VILARA
GERANIOU
ZINONOS
Polykliniki
ATHINAS
PANEPISTIMIOU (ELEFTHERIOU VENIZELOU)
FIDIOU
NAVARINOU
MAVROMIHALI
IPPOKRATOUS
ΠΑΝΑΓΗ ΤΣΑΛΔΑΡΗ
LYKOURGOU
KLEISTHENOUS
ANAXAGORA
EVPOLIDOS
STADIOU
SANTAROZA
PL. KOTZIA
G. STAVROU
ARSAKI
State Opera House
ASKLIPIOU
Cultural Centre of Athens
SOFOKLEOUS
Dimarhío (Town Hall)
KRATINOU
National Library
R. FERAIOU
University
MASSALIAS
ARMODIOU
PESMAZOGLOU
ΣΤΑΔΙΟΥ
P(I)CHOU GRIGORIOU V.
SINA
DIPLARI
EVRIPIDOU
Varvákio (Central Market)
FILOPOIMENOS
ARISTIDOU
Academy
KORAI
PANEPISTIMIO
ΠΑΝΕΠΙΣΤΗΜΙΟΥ
PSYRRI
ARISTOFANOUS
ESKHYLOU
AGIO DIMITRIOU
KALAMIDA
PL. IEROU LOHOU
Ag. Theodóri
DRAGATSANIOU
PL. KLAVTHMONOS
Ag. Dionýsios
VISSARIONOS
Ag. Iríni
Golden Virgin of the Cave
PRAXITELOUS
ED. LO
City of Athens Museum
OMIROU
Ag. Dimitrios

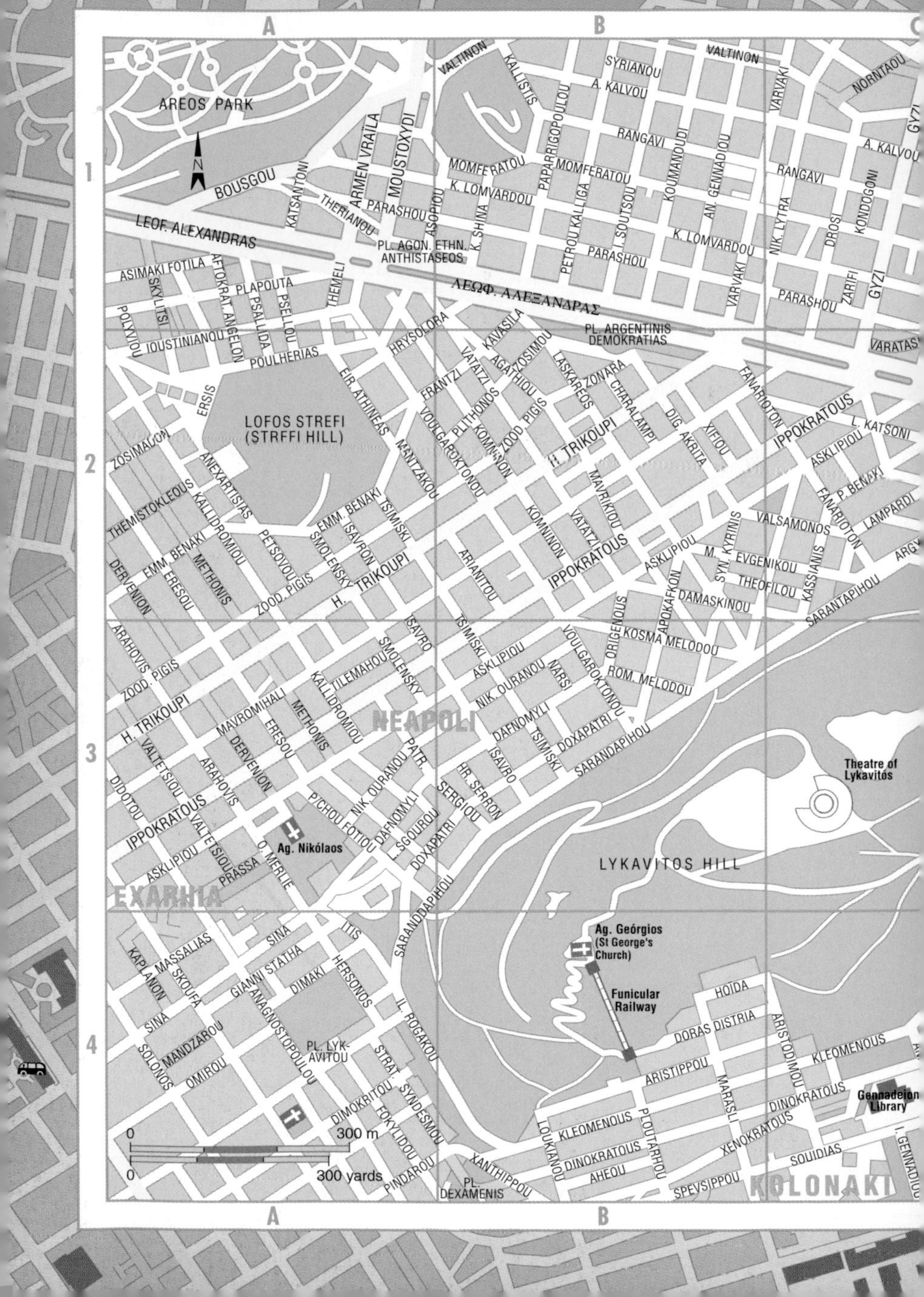
A
B
C
1
2
3
4
AREOS PARK
N
BOUSGOU
LEOF. ALEXANDRAS
ΛΕΩΦ. ΑΛΕΞΑΝΔΡΑΣ
VALTINON
KALLISTIS
SYRIANOU
A. KALVOU
RANGAVI
MOMFERATOU
K. LOMVARDOU
PARASHOU
PAPARRIGOPOULOU
PETROU KALLIGA
I. SOUTSOU
KOUMANOUDI
AN. GENNADIOU
VARVAKI
NIK. LYTRA
DROSI
KONDOGONI
ZARIFI
GYZI
NORNTAOU
ARMEN VRAÏLA
MOUSTOXYDI
KATSANTONI
THERIANOU
ASOPIOU
K. SHINA
PL. AGON. ETHN. ANTHISTASEOS
ASIMAKI FOTILA
AFTOKRAT. ANGELON
SKYLITSI
PLAPOUTA
PSALLIDA
PSELLOU
THEMELI
POLYVIOU
IOUSTINIANOU
POULHERIAS
PL. ARGENTINIS DEMOKRATIAS
VARATASY
HRYSOLORA
KAVASILA
VATATZI
AGATHIOU
ZOSIMOU
LASKAREOS
ZONARA
CHARALAMPI
FANARIOTON
IPPOKRATOUS
L. KATSONI
ERSIS
LOFOS STREFI (STREFI HILL)
EIR. ATHINEAS
FRANTZI
PLITHONOS
VOULGAROKTONOU
KOMNINON
ZOOD. PIGIS
H. TRIKOUPI
DIG. AKRITA
XIFIOU
ASKLIPIOU
P. BENAKI
LAMPARDI
ZOSIMADON
ANEXARTISIAS
MANTZAKOU
THEMISTOKLEOUS
KALLIDROMIOU
EMM. BENAKI
TSIMISKI
ISAVRON
SMOLENSKY
PETSOVOU
METHONIS
ERESOU
DERVENION
MAVRIKIOU
VATATZI
ARIANITOU
VALSAMONOS
M. KYRINIS
SYN.
EVGENIKOU
KASSIANIS
THEOFILOU
DAMASKINOU
APOKAFKON
ORIGENOUS
SARANTAPIHOU
ARGY
ARAHOVIS
ISAVRO
TILEMAHOU
KOSMA MELODOU
ROM. MELODOU
NIK. OURANOU
NARSI
DAFNOMYLI
DOXAPATRI
SARANDAPIHOU
NEAPOLI
MAVROMIHALI
VALTETSIOU
DIDOTOU
PATR.
HR. SERRON
SERGIOU
P/CHOU FOTIOU
L. SGOUROU
Ag. Nikólaos
PRASSA
O. MERLIE
EXARHIA
Theatre of Lykavitós
LYKAVITOS HILL
Ag. Geórgios (St George's Church)
Funicular Railway
SARANDAPIHOU
ITIS
SINA
MASSALIAS
KAPLANON
SKOUFA
GIANNI STATHA
ANAGNOSTOPOULOU
DIMAKI
HERSONOS
IL. ROGAKOU
MANDZAROU
SOLONOS
OMIROU
PL. LYK-AVITOU
STRAT. SYNDESMOU
DIMOKRITOU
FOKYLIDOU
PINDAROU
PL. DEXAMENIS
XANTHIPPOU
HOÏDA
DORAS DISTRIA
ARISTODIMOU
KLEOMENOUS
ARISTIPPOU
MARASLI
DINOKRATOUS
Gennadeion Library
LOUKIANOU
PLOUTARHOU
AHEOU
XENOKRATOUS
SOUIDIAS
I. GENNADIOU
SPEVSIPPOU
KOLONAKI
0
300 m
0
300 yards

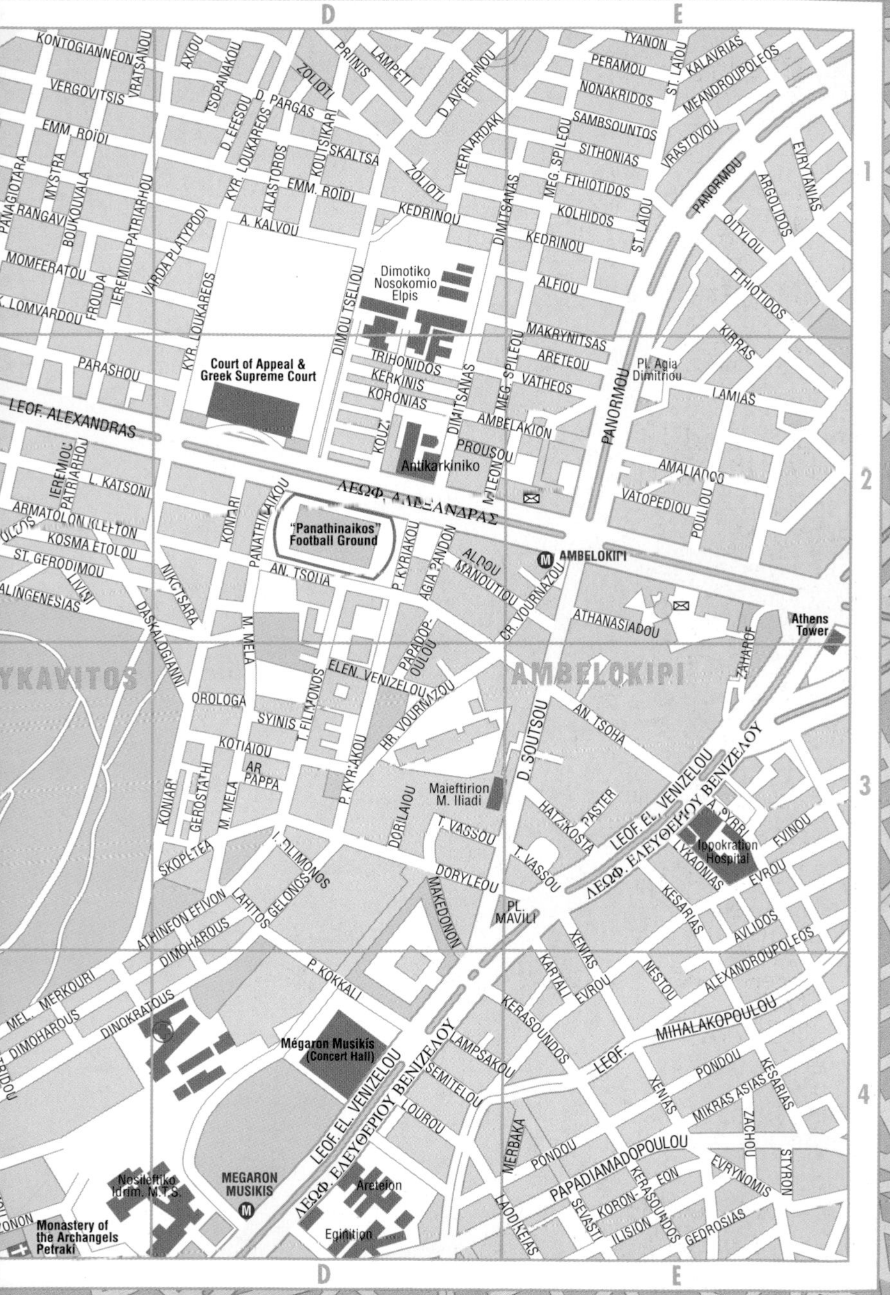
D
E
1
2
3
4
KONTOGIANNEON
VRATSANOU
AXIOU
VERGOVITSIS
TSOPANAKOU
D. PARGAS
ZOLIOTI
PRINIS
LAMPETI
D. AVGERINOU
EMM. ROÏDI
D. EFESOU
KYR. LOUKAREOS
SKALTSA
KOUTSIKARI
ALASTOROS
PANAGIOTARA
MYSTRA
BOUKOUVALA
RANGAVI
IEREMIOU PATRIARHOU
VARDA PLATYPODI
A. KALVOU
KEDRINOU
VERNARDAKI
MOMFERATOU
FROUDA
K. LOMVARDOU
Dimotiko Nosokomio Elpis
DIMOU TSELIOU
TRIHONIDOS
KERKINIS
KORONIAS
PARASHOU
Court of Appeal & Greek Supreme Court
LEOF. ALEXANDRAS
ΛΕΩΦ. ΑΛΕΞΑΝΔΡΑΣ
Antikarkiniko
KOUZ.
DIMITSANAS
PROUSOU
AMBELAKION
L. KATSONI
IEREMIOU PATRIARHOU
ARMATOLON KLEFTON
KOSMA ETOLOU
ST. GERODIMOU
PALINGENESIAS
LIVINI
KONIARI
PANATHINAIKOU
"Panathinaikos" Football Ground
P. KYRIAKOU
AGIA PANDON
ALDOU MANOUTIOU
AN. TSOHA
DASKALOGIANNI
NIKITSARA
M. MELA
CR. VOURNAZOU
AMBELOKIPI
ATHANASIADOU
PAPADOPOULOU
ELEN. VENIZELOU
T. FILIMONOS
HR. VOURNAZOU
OROLOGA
SYINIS
KOTIAIOU
AR PAPPA
GEROSTATHI
KONIARI
P. KYRIAKOU
DORILAIOU
Maieftirion M. Iliadi
T. VASSOU
SKOPETEA
I. FILIMONOS
DORYLEOU
MAKEDONON
PL. MAVILI
ATHINEON EFIVON
LAHITOS
GELONOS
DIMOHAROUS
P. KOKKALI
MEL. MERKOURI
DIMOHAROUS
DINOKRATOUS
Mégaron Musikís (Concert Hall)
LEOF. EL. VENIZELOU
ΛΕΩΦ. ΕΛΕΥΘΕΡΙΟΥ ΒΕΝΙΖΕΛΟΥ
LAMPSAKOU
SEMITELOU
LOUROU
Nosileftiko Idrim. M.T.S.
MEGARON MUSIKIS
Areteion
Eginition
Monastery of the Archangels Petraki
ZONON
TYANON
PERAMOU
ST. LAÏOU
KALAVRIAS
MEANDROUPOLEOS
NONAKRIDOS
SAMBSOUNTOS
SITHONIAS
VRASTOVOU
MEG. SPILEOU
FTHIOTIDOS
KOLHIDOS
KEDRINOU
PANORMOU
ARGOLIDOS
EVRYTANIAS
OITYLOU
FTHIOTIDOS
ALFIOU
MAKRYNITSAS
ARETEOU
VATHEOS
KIRRAS
Pl. Agia Dimitriou
LAMIAS
AMALIADOS
VATOPEDIOU
POULIOU
M. LEONT.
AMBELOKIPI
Athens Tower
ZAHAROF
AN. TSOHA
D. SOUTSOU
PASTER
HATZIKOSTA
T. VASSOU
LEOF. EL. VENIZELOU
ΛΕΩΦ. ΕΛΕΥΘΕΡΙΟΥ ΒΕΝΙΖΕΛΟΥ
Ippokration Hospital
LYKAONIAS
EVINOU
EVROU
KESARIAS
AVLIDOS
ALEXANDROUPOLEOS
XENIAS
KARTALI
EVROU
NESTOU
KERASOUNDOS
LEOF. MIHALAKOPOULOU
PONDOU
XENIAS
KESARIAS
MIKRAS ASIAS
ZACHOU
MERBAKA
PONDOU
PAPADIAMADOPOULOU
STYRON
EVRYNOMIS
KERASOUNDOS
EON
KORON-
SEVASTI
ILISION
GEDROSIAS
LAODIKEIAS

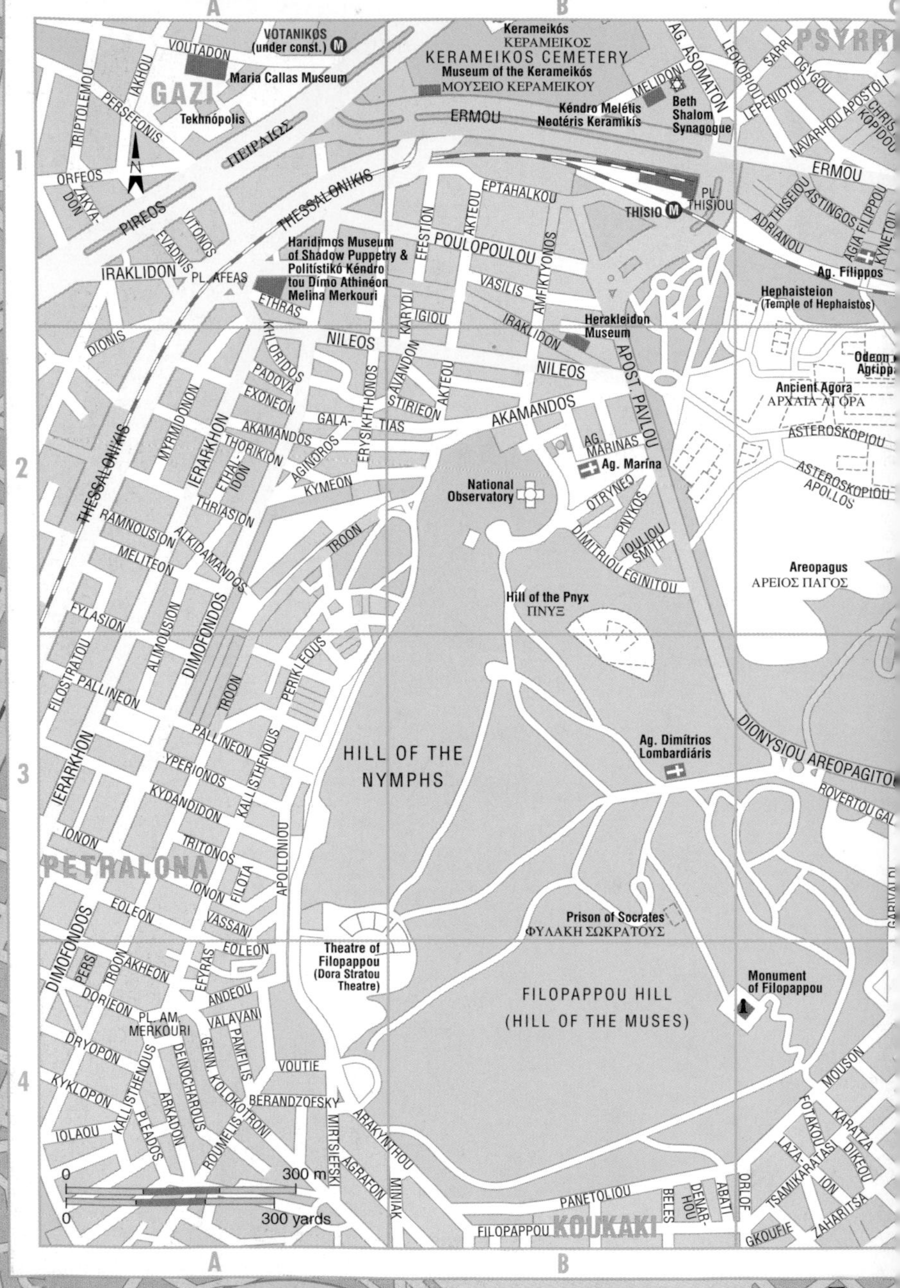
A
B
1
2
3
4
VOTANIKOS (under const.)
Keramеikós
ΚΕΡΑΜΕΙΚΟΣ
KERAMEIKOS CEMETERY
Museum of the Kerameikós
ΜΟΥΣΕΙΟ ΚΕΡΑΜΕΙΚΟΥ
Maria Callas Museum
GAZI
Tekhnópolis
ΠΕΙΡΑΙΩΣ
ERMOU
Kéndro Melétis Neotéris Keramikís
Beth Shalom Synagogue
PSYRRI
THISIO
PL. THISIOU
Haridimos Museum of Shadow Puppetry & Polítistikó Kéndro tou Dímo Athinéon Melina Merkouri
PL. AFEAS
Ag. Fílippos
Hephaisteion (Temple of Hephaistos)
Herakleidon Museum
Odeon of Agrippa
Ancient Agora
ΑΡΧΑΙΑ ΑΓΟΡΑ
Ag. Marína
National Observatory
Areopagus
ΑΡΕΙΟΣ ΠΑΓΟΣ
Hill of the Pnyx
ΠΝΥΞ
HILL OF THE NYMPHS
Ag. Dimítrios Lombardiáris
PETRALONA
Prison of Socrates
ΦΥΛΑΚΗ ΣΩΚΡΑΤΟΥΣ
Theatre of Filopappou (Dora Stratou Theatre)
FILOPAPPOU HILL (HILL OF THE MUSES)
Monument of Filopappou
PL. AM MERKOURI
KOUKAKI
0
300 m
0
300 yards

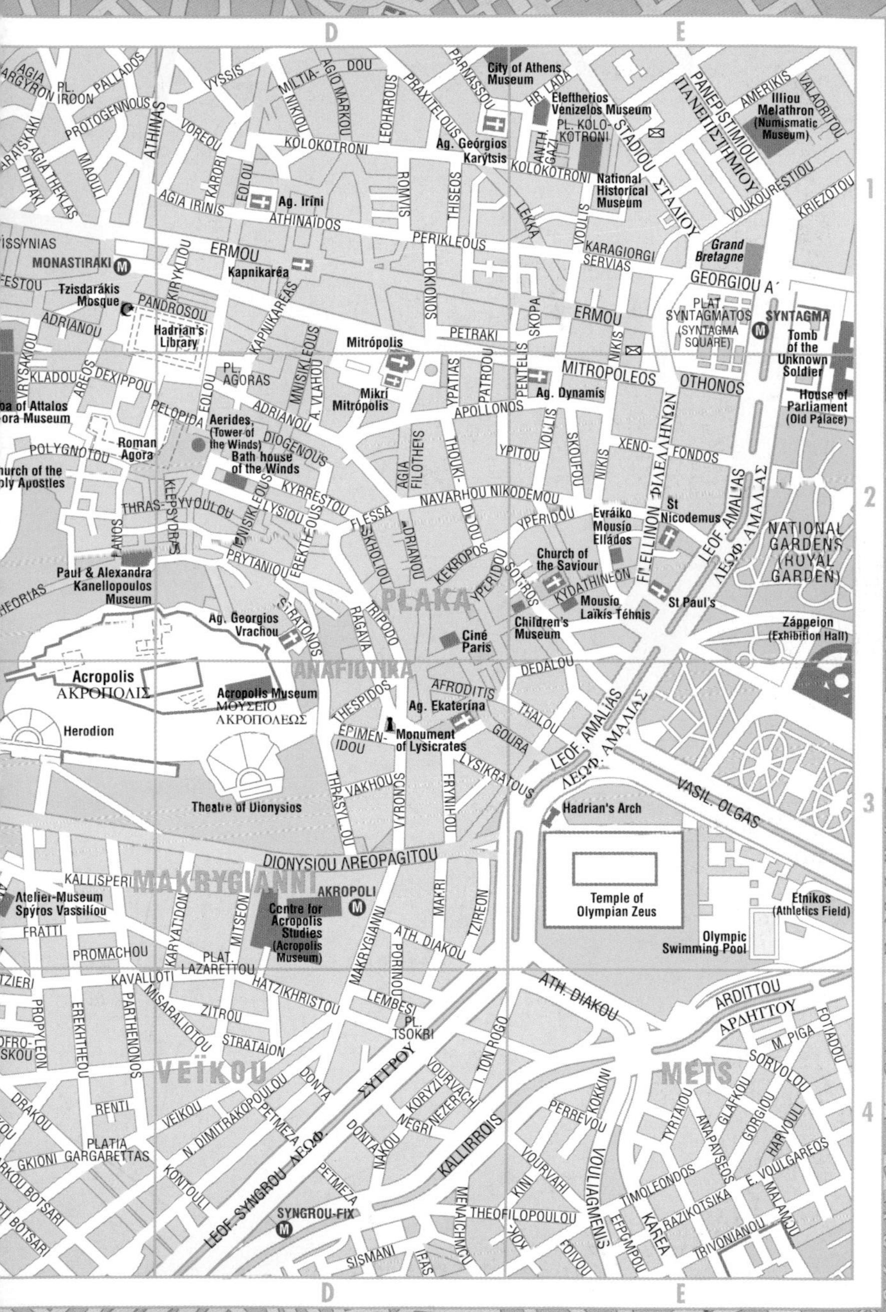
D
E
City of Athens Museum
Eleftherios Venizelos Museum
Illiou Melathron (Numismatic Museum)
Ag. Geórgios Karýtsis
Ag. Iríni
National Historical Museum
MONASTIRAKI
Kapnikaréa
Grand Bretagne
Tzisdarákis Mosque
Hadrian's Library
PLAT SYNTAGMATOS (SYNTAGMA SQUARE)
SYNTAGMA
Tomb of the Unknown Soldier
Mitrópolis
Mikrí Mitrópolis
Ag. Dynamís
House of Parliament (Old Palace)
Stoa of Attalos
Agora Museum
Roman Agora
Aerides, (Tower of the Winds)
Bath house of the Winds
Church of the Holy Apostles
Evráiko Mousío Elládos
St Nicodemus
NATIONAL GARDENS (ROYAL GARDEN)
Church of the Saviour
Paul & Alexandra Kanellopoulos Museum
PLAKA
Mousío Laïkís Téhnis
St Paul's
Ag. Georgios Vrachou
Children's Museum
Ciné Paris
Záppeion (Exhibition Hall)
ANAFIOTIKA
Acropolis
ΑΚΡΟΠΟΛΙΣ
Acropolis Museum
ΜΟΥΣΕΙΟ ΑΚΡΟΠΟΛΕΩΣ
Ag. Ekaterína
Herodion
Monument of Lysicrates
Theatre of Dionysios
Hadrian's Arch
MAKRYGIANNI
AKROPOLI
Atelier-Museum Spýros Vassilíou
Centre for Acropolis Studies (Acropolis Museum)
Temple of Olympian Zeus
Etnikos (Athletics Field)
Olympic Swimming Pool
VEÏKOU
METS
PLATIA GARGARETTAS
SYNGROU-FIX
1
2
3
4

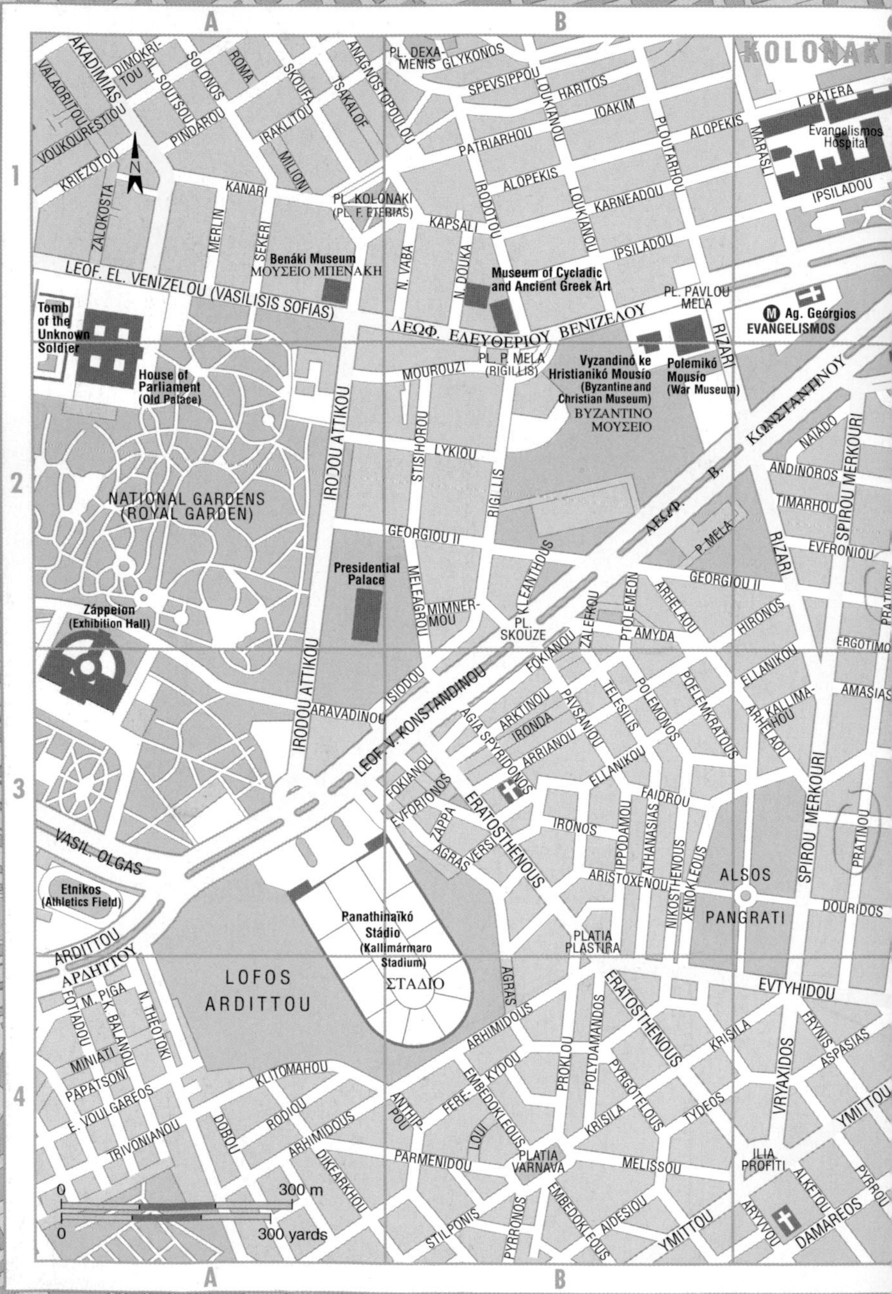
KOLONAKI
Evangelismos Hospital
Benáki Museum
ΜΟΥΣΕΙΟ ΜΠΕΝΑΚΗ
Museum of Cycladic and Ancient Greek Art
Tomb of the Unknown Soldier
House of Parliament (Old Palace)
Ag. Geórgios
EVANGELISMOS
Vyzandinó ke Hristianikó Mousío (Byzantine and Christian Museum)
ΒΥΖΑΝΤΙΝΟ ΜΟΥΣΕΙΟ
Polemikó Mousío (War Museum)
NATIONAL GARDENS (ROYAL GARDEN)
Presidential Palace
Záppeion (Exhibition Hall)
Etnikos (Athletics Field)
Panathinaïkó Stádio (Kallimármaro Stadium)
ΣΤΑΔΙΟ
LOFOS ARDITTOU
ALSOS
PANGRATI
PLATIA PLASTIRA
PLATIA VARNAVA
LEOF. EL. VENIZELOU (VASILISIS SOFIAS)
ΛΕΩΦ. ΕΛΕΥΘΕΡΙΟΥ ΒΕΝΙΖΕΛΟΥ
LEOF. V. KONSTANDINOU
ΛΕΩΦ. Β. ΚΩΝΣΤΑΝΤΙΝΟΥ
VASIL. OLGAS
ARDITTOU
ΑΡΔΗΤΤΟΥ
0
300 m
0
300 yards

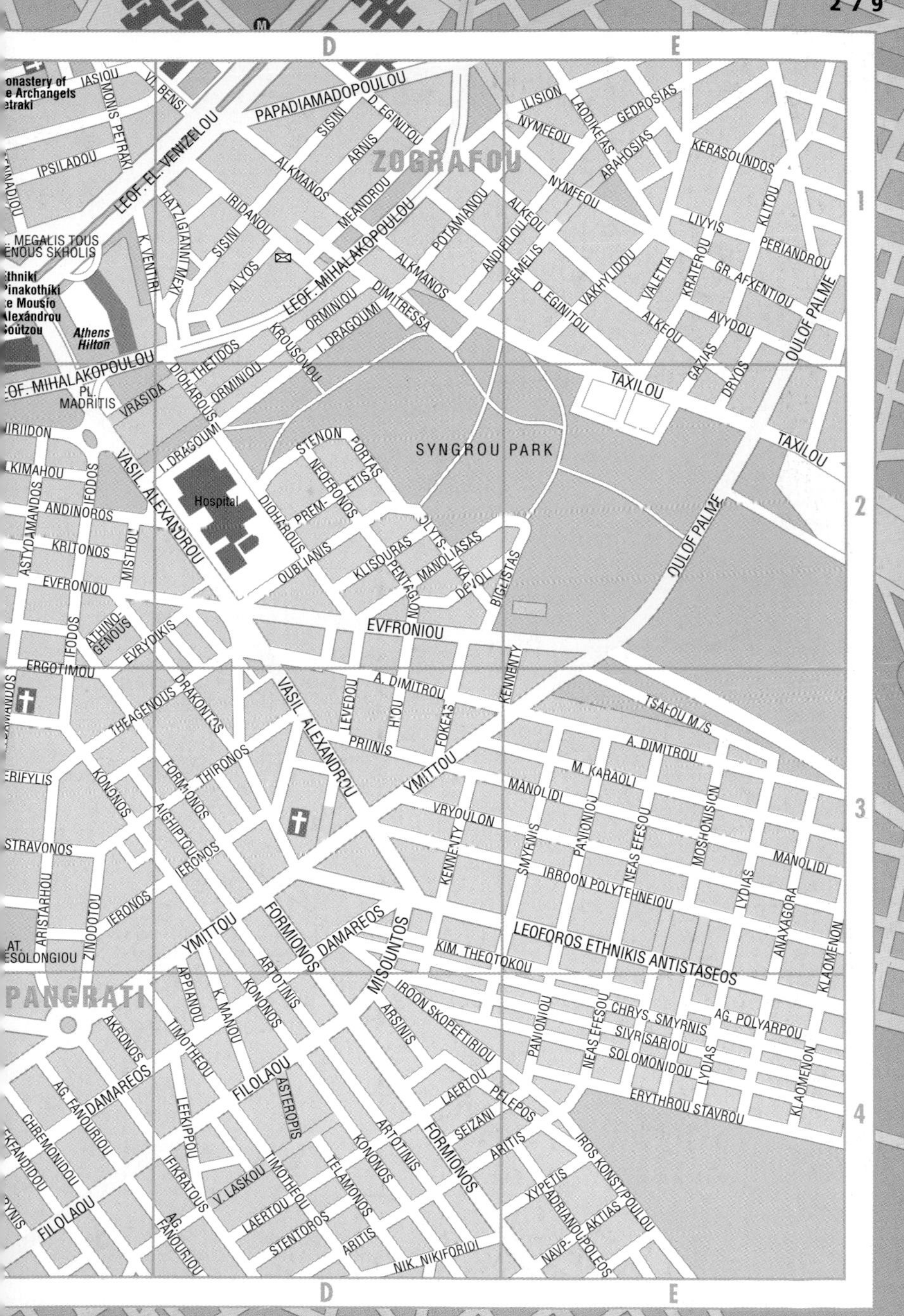
D
E
1
2
3
4
ZOGRAFOU
PANGRATI
SYNGROU PARK
Hospital
Athens Hilton
IASIOU
MONIS PETRAKI
VI. BENSI
PAPADIAMADOPOULOU
D. EGINITOU
SISINI
ARNIS
ILISION
LAODIKEIAS
GEDROSIAS
NYMFEOU
ARAHOSIAS
KERASOUNDOS
IPSILADOU
LEOF. EL. VENIZELOU
HATZIGIANNI MEXI
IRIDANOU
ALKMANOS
MEANDROU
LEOF. MIHALAKOPOULOU
POTAMIANOU
ALKEOU
ANDIFILOU
SEMELIS
LIVYIS
KLITOU
PERIANDROU
VALETTA
KRATEROU
GR. AFXENTIOU
VAKHYLIDOU
D. EGINITOU
AVYDOU
OULOF PALME
K. VENTIRI
SISINI
ALYOS
ORMINIOU
DIMITRESSA
I. DRAGOUMI
KROUSOVOU
THETIDOS
DIOHAROUS
VRASIDA
PL. MADRITIS
TAXILOU
GAZIAS
DRYOS
STENON
PORTAS
NEOFRONOS
ETIS
PREM-
I. DRAGOUMI
VASIL. ALEXANDROU
KIMAHOU
IFODOS
ASTYDAMANDOS
ANDINOROS
KRITONOS
MISTHOU
EVFRONIOU
DIOHAROUS
OUBLIANIS
KLISOURAS
PENTAGON
MANOLIASAS
DEVOLI
BIGLISTAS
EVFRONIOU
ATHINO-GENOUS
EVRYDIKIS
ERGOTIMOU
KENNENTY
A. DIMITROU
LEVEDOU
HIOU
FOKEAS
PRIINIS
THEAGENOUS
DRAKONTOS
TSAFOU M/S.
A. DIMITROU
M. KARAOLI
MANOLIDI
KONONOS
FORMIONOS
THIRONOS
YMITTOU
VRYOULON
KENNENTY
SMYENIS
PANIONIOU
NEAS EFESOU
MOSHONISION
MANOLIDI
LYDIAS
IRROON POLYTEHNEIOU
STRAVONOS
AIGHIPTOU
IERONOS
ARISTARHOU
ZINODOTOU
IERONOS
YMITTOU
FORMIONOS
DAMAREOS
MISOUNTOS
ANAXAGORA
KLAOMENON
LEOFOROS ETHNIKIS ANTISTASEOS
KIM. THEOTOKOU
APPIANOU
K. MANOU
ARTOTINIS
KONONOS
IROON SKOPEFTIRIOU
ARSINIS
PANIONIOU
NEAS EFESOU
CHRYS. SMYRNIS
AG. POLYARPOU
SIVRISARIOU
SOLOMONIDOU
LYDIAS
KLAOMENON
ERYTHROU STAVROU
AKRONOS
TIMOTHEOU
FILOLAOU
ASTEROPIS
LAERTOU
PELEPOS
DAMAREOS
AG. FANOURIOU
CHREMONIDOU
LEFKIPPOU
IFIKRATOUS
V. LASKOU
TIMOTHEOU
TELAMONOS
KONONOS
ARTOTINIS
FORMIONOS
SEIZANI
ARITIS
IROS KONST/POULOU
XYPETIS
ADRIANOUPOLEOS
AKTIAS
NAVP-
FILOLAOU
AG. FANOURIOU
LAERTOU
STENTOROS
ARITIS
NIK. NIKIFORIDI

STREET INDEX

G

H

I

J–K

L

M

PLACES OF INTEREST

General Index